WRITING
WITH
PICTURES

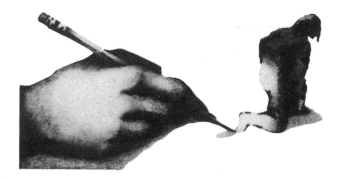

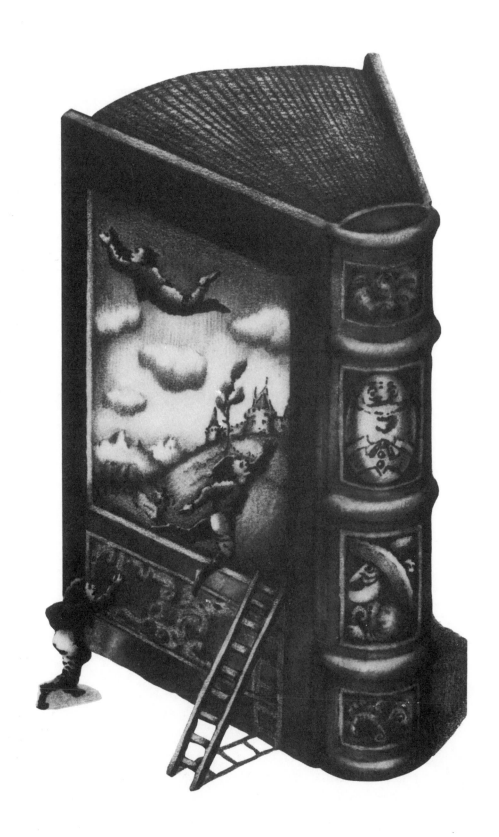

URI SHULEVITZ

WRITING WITH PICTURES

HOW TO WRITE AND ILLUSTRATE CHILDREN'S BOOKS

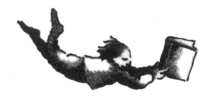

WATSON-GUPTILL PUBLICATIONS/NEW YORK

First Published in 1985 by Watson-Guptill Publications, an imprint of the
Crown Publishing Group, a division of Random House, Inc., New York

www.crownpublishing.com
www.watsonguptill.com

**Library of Congress
Cataloging-in-Publication Data**
Schulevitz, Uri, 1935-
    Writing with pictures. Pbk. ed.

    Bibliography: p.
    Includes index.
    1. Picture-books for children—Authorship.
1. Title.
PN147.5.S58   1985   808.06'8   85-15604
ISBN 0-8230-5935-9

Manufactured in China

Paperback edition, first printing 1997

        10 11 12 13 14 / 14 13 12

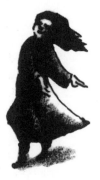

Acknowledgments

This book is dedicated to all who have ever taught me.

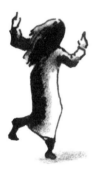

Looking back at the more than ten years I have worked on this book, it seems that no author has owed so much to so many. I wish to express my gratitude to all who have helped me directly or indirectly.

To Dr. Isabel Wright, for her editorial criticism of Part One of the manuscript. To John Fox and Donna Brooks, for helping me to rewrite Chapters 3 and 12 respectively and for their additional comments. To Peter Hopkins, for contributing quotes and for always being available to discuss artistic issues. To my colleagues Ann Schweninger, Pat Roche, Kristen Lawson, and Jane Freeman, for commenting on the manuscript, contributing information, and giving much-needed encouragement. To Lois Krieger, for her dedication and skill in the preliminary editing.

To all those who contributed to Part Four of this book. To Atha Tehon, for her caring review of this section and valuable suggestions. To Dorris Janowitz and Nanette Stevenson, for their comments. To Monica Brown, Dorothy Hagen, Barbara Hennessy, and Ava Weiss, for information on book production. To William Joslin, Philip Poggio, and Russell Schou at Eastern Press, for information on printing and how best to prepare art for reproduction. To Jean Bourges of Bourges Color Corporation, for her suggestions. To Martha Alexander and Ariane Dewey, for information on color preseparation. To Jennifer Anderson, for help in editing.

To all my friends and the many others who gave me information and encouragement. To Barbara Lucas, for her early support when other editors turned down the book. To Alan Benjamin, Donna Brooks, Lee Deadrick, Jane Feder, Liz Gordon, Susan Hirschman, and Margaret McElderry, for discussing how to find a publisher. To Michael Eisenberg, for his generous promotional suggestions. And to all my former students—those who commented on the manuscript and those whose work was a basis for my examples.

To all my colleagues who have so generously given permission to use their work free of charge: Martha Alexander, Jose Aruego, Bonnie Bishop, Crosby Bonsall, Gary Bowen, Chris Conover, Ariane Dewey, Donna Diamond, Richard Egielski, Antonio Frasconi, Domenico Gnoli, M. B. Goffstein, Geoffrey Hayes, Tana Hoban, Nonny Hogrogian, Ruth Krauss, Cynthia Krupat, Arnold Lobel, Joseph Low, Randy Miller, David Palladini, Jacob Pins, Maurice Sendak, Marc Simont, William Steig, and Margot Zemach. To Ann Durrell, Phyllis Fogelman, Phyllis Larkin, Stephen Roxburgh, and Ada Shearon, for helping to secure permission. And to all the publishers, for granting permission.

To James Craig, for referring me to Watson-Guptill Publications, for his criticism and encouragement when it was much needed—not to mention his invaluable contribution in designing this book. To everyone at Watson-Guptill who has been involved with this book. To Don Holden, who believed in the project, made suggestions, and acquired the book. To David Lewis, for his support and suggestions. To Betty Vera, for her generous editorial help. To Mary Suffudy, for her contributions in the overall planning of the book. To Sue Heinemann, who patiently and generously edited, organized, wrote, and rewrote when needed, shaping the book as a whole as well as supervising every detail—I can't think of anyone who would have done as much or as well as she. To Carole Forman, for securing permissions and indexing. To Ellen Greene, for supervising production. And to everyone else at Watson-Guptill who has expressed enthusiasm and given support—Nancy Baussan, Virginia Croft, Glorya Hale, Jules Perel, and others.

Contents

Acknowledgments   5

Introduction   9

Part One
Telling the Story

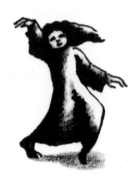

  1. Picture Book or Story Book?   15
  2. Picture Sequence   18
  3. The Story: A Complete Action   30
  4. Story Content   47
  5. Picture Book Characteristics   51

Part Two
Planning the Book

  6. Storyboard and Book Dummy   67
  7. Size, Scale, and Shape   89
  8. The Structure of a Printed Book   113

Part Three
Creating the Pictures

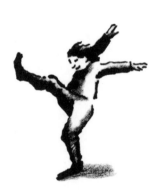

  9. The Purpose of Illustration   120
10. Drawing Figures and Objects   136
11. Visual References   152
12. Picture Space and Composition   167
13. Principles of Technique   186
14. Style   198

Part Four
Preparing for Reproduction

15. Printing Basics   208
16. Color Preseparation   214
17. Techniques for Reproduction   242

Envoi   255

Appendices

Finding a Publisher   258
Bibliography   264
Credits   265
Index   268

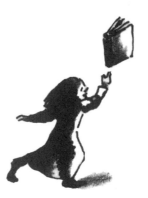

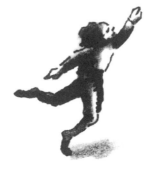

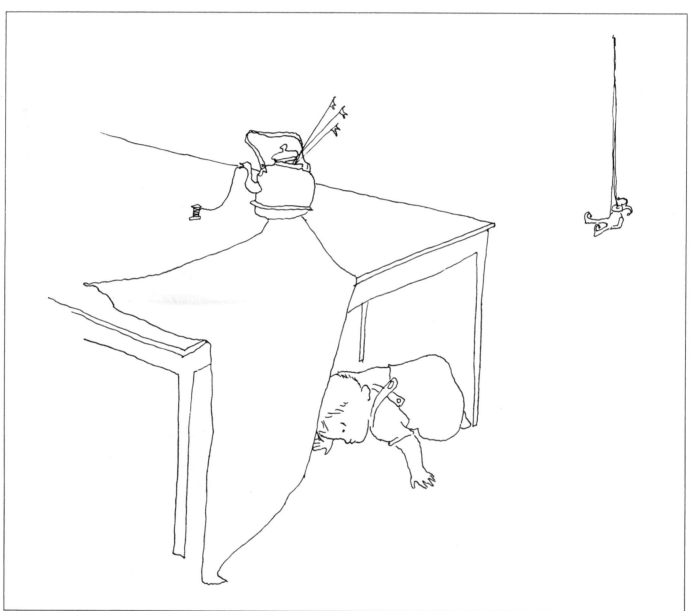

From *The Moon in My Room*

Introduction

I have never exactly "made" a story. With me the process is much more like bird watching than like either talking or building. I see pictures. . . . Keep quiet and watch and they will begin joining themselves up. . . . I have no idea whether this is the usual way of writing stories, still less whether it is the best. It is the only one I know: Images always come first.

C. S. Lewis

It was my good luck, when I began toting my portfolio around to publishers in 1962, that Susan Hirschman (then at Harper and Row) was the first editor I saw. I had come with the hope that she might give me a book to illustrate. She looked at my portfolio and liked my work, but she had no manuscript for me to illustrate. She suggested I try writing my own picture book. I was horrified.

Write my own story? Impossible. I was an artist, not a writer, I thought. I could imagine myself in various activities, but never in my wildest dreams had I imagined myself a writer. Writing seemed a mysterious activity, suited to those who had magical ways with words. To me, using words was like taming wild tigers.

"I don't know how to write," I said.

"Why don't you try?" she asked.

"But," I said—and here, I thought, was an insurmountable obstacle—"I have been speaking English for less than four years."

"Don't worry," she reassured me, "we'll fix your English."

There was nothing to do but try. And try I did, many times. I went back to Susan Hirschman's office for months, bringing my awkward writing efforts. Her criticisms and suggestions served as my apprenticeship. After many unsuccessful attempts, I finally came up with a picture book. With minor changes, it became *The Moon in My Room*, my first book. If not for those many unsuccessful attempts, I don't think I could have written it.

I eventually understood that my initial fear that I could not write was based on a preconception that writing was strictly related to words and to spoken language. I had assumed that using many words skillfully was central to writing. I was overlooking what was of primary importance—*what* I had to say. And I was overwhelmed by what was of secondary importance—*how* to say it.

Once I understood that *what* I had to say was of primary importance, I began to concentrate on what would happen in my story. First I visualized the action, and then I thought of how to say it in words. I realized that all I had to do was communicate the action as simply as possible. The few words necessary to communicate the story fell into place on their own. It was all so simple and natural.

It also dawned on me that I could channel my natural inclination to visualize into my writing. Assuming that each of us has a preference for one of the sense perceptions, we can capitalize on that preference in our writing. If you like to talk and you feel at ease with the spoken word, you can take a conversational approach to writing. But if you are inclined to see pictures, as I am, a visual approach makes more sense. That is how I wrote *The Moon in My Room;* the story unfolded in my head like a movie. I was the camera seeing the action conveyed by pictures.

Furthermore, the use of this visual approach, with which I have always felt at ease, released a flow of images I hadn't experienced before. There was no doubt, *writing with pictures* was my way. Years later, I learned that when writing, C. S. Lewis saw pictures, too; that with him, "images always come first." A visual approach is used by scientists as well. The

Dutch physicist Kekulé described his discovery of the structural theory of the atom in this way:

> One beautiful summer evening I was riding on the last omnibus through the deserted streets. . . . I fell into a reverie. Atoms flitted before my eyes. . . . I saw that frequently two smaller atoms were coupled together, that larger ones seized the two smaller ones, that still larger ones held fast three and even four of the smaller ones and that all were whirled around in a bewildering dance. . . . I spent part of the night writing down sketches of these dream pictures.*

Writing with pictures proved valuable not only in my own work, but also in teaching others how to write. The visual thinking essential to picture-book making can be extended to writing for people in the visual arts and can increase the ability to visualize in writers without an art background. Visual thinking can also help a writer to avoid excessive wordiness.

It is this visual approach—an approach based on my writing and teaching experience—that I would like to introduce in this book.

The approach I used for the illustrations for *The Moon in My Room* was derived from drawings I did one day while talking on the telephone. As I talked I doodled, and I noticed they had a fresh look; the lines appeared to be moving across the page. Looking back, I am amazed that this happened so unexpectedly, for in addition to my preconception about writing, I also had a preconceived idea of how an illustration evolves. I had assumed it would require much effort. But instead, while my mind was busy with the phone conversation, I let the lines flow effortlessly through my hand onto the paper; they seemed to have a life and an intelligence of their own. The lines led my hand, and my hand followed without imposing my

*William J. J. Gordon, *Synectics* (New York: Macmillan, 1961).

desires on those lines. True, it subsequently took considerable work and effort to develop the doodles into appropriate illustrations, but that was at a later stage.

In teaching, I have seen that students often excuse a poor illustration by claiming they can't draw or they lack artistic talent. But the real problem lies in unclear thinking. Many students without much art experience imagine they have to produce works of art—when all they need do is record, in the best way they can, what they are seeing around them or in their minds. A similar mistake is sometimes made by some students with an extensive art background; they spend all their energy creating "beautiful" drawings while neglecting the vital aspects of illustration—readability, coherence, and how it relates to the text.

I used to believe that learning means accumulating knowledge. But I have found that this can also be a way to cover up ignorance. Unlearning, giving up preconceptions and dropping pretense, can be the more practical way. Only in the second stage—developing and organizing material—is previous knowledge or art experience helpful.

When asked why they want to write children's books, many people reply, "I love children." Sentimentality, unfortunately, is no help; in fact it is a hindrance. Sentimentality does not replace the craft that is essential in making good children's books. Your first obligation is to the book, not to the audience. Only by understanding the book's structure—including its mechanical structure—and how it functions can you make a good book.

When working on your first book, you may ask: Am I happy with the book? Am I happy with the illustrations? These seemingly innocent questions actually shift the importance from the book and the illustrations to yourself. A happy book will inevitably make a happy author. Therefore ask: Is the book happy? Are the illustrations happy?

In other words, is the story told with clarity? Are the characters unique? Is the setting specific? Is the ending consistent with the beginning? Does the story adhere to a unified code? Does the text division follow the natural units of the story? Has the book achieved the right blend of spontaneity and planning? Is the book's form an organic outgrowth of its content? Are the size, scale, and shape of the book most suited to its content and mood? Are the pictures accurate and readable, and do they capture the content and the mood? How do they relate to each other? Are all the parts of a picture unified, and do they help one another to achieve the picture's goal? Are all the parts of the book coordinated into a coherent whole?

When such questions are considered, you can better understand the needs of the book and tell whether it is truly happy. Ultimately, beyond showing you how to cope with the mechanical problems of making a book, the aim of this book is to teach you how to ask these questions and to find the answers to them yourself.

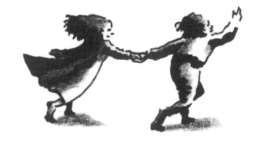

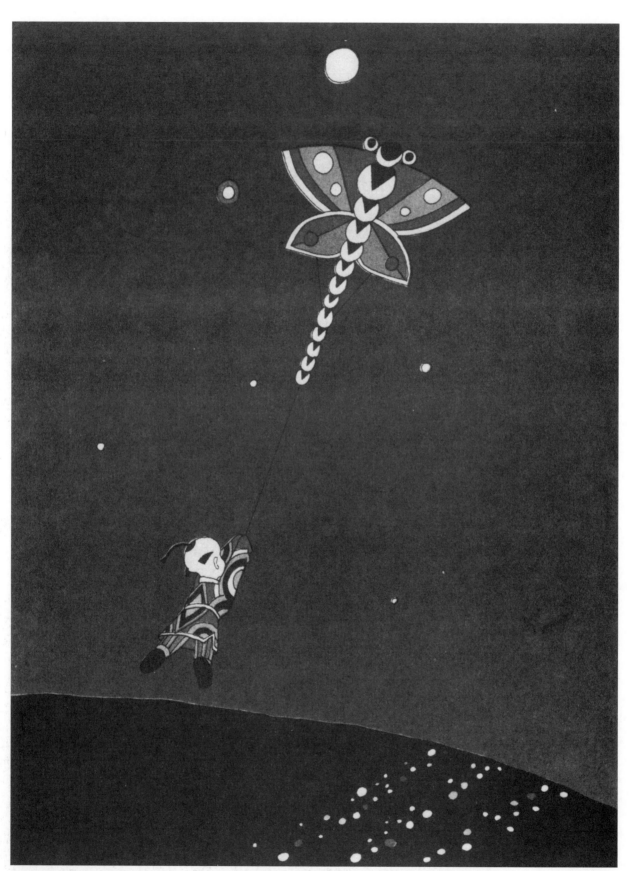

From *The Wonderful Kite*

Part One   Telling the Story

Originality does not consist in saying what no one has ever said before, but in saying exactly what you think yourself.

James Fitz-James Stephen

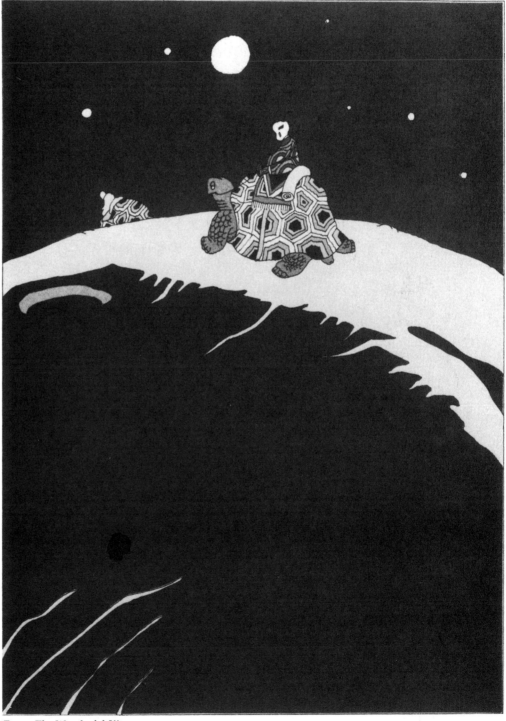

From *The Wonderful Kite*

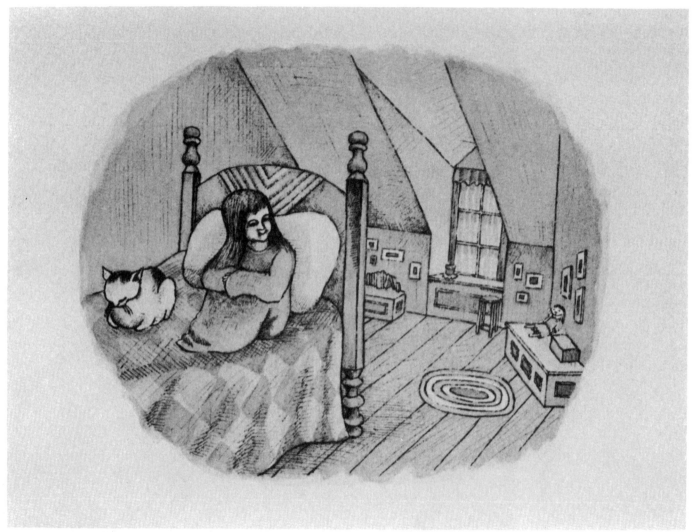

From *Rain Rain Rivers*

1. Picture Book or Story Book?

*Not the whole forest—
just one leaf.*

P. L. Travers

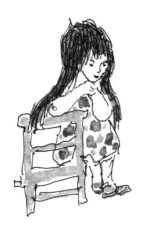

To create a good picture book or story book, you must understand how the two differ in concept. A *story book* tells a story with words. Although the pictures amplify it, the story can be understood without them. The pictures have an auxiliary role, because the words themselves contain images.

In contrast, a true *picture book* tells a story mainly or entirely with pictures. When words are used, they have an auxiliary role. A picture book says in words only what pictures cannot show (except in some rare cases, which will be explained later in Chapter 5). It could not, for example, be read over the radio and be understood fully. In a picture book, the pictures extend, clarify, complement, or take the place of words. Both the words and the pictures are "read." Naturally, such an approach leads to using fewer words—or sometimes none at all.

The difference between a story book and a picture book, however, is far more than a matter of degree, of the amount of words or pictures—it is a difference in concept.

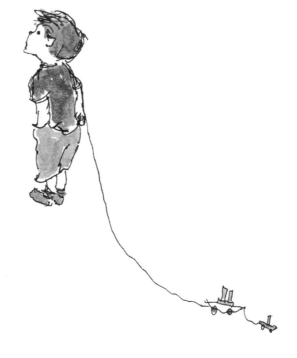

The Story Book Concept

Typical storytelling consists mostly of narrating what is seen and heard:

> "Ah!" said the old man, turning to me with a sigh, as if I had spoken to him but that moment, "you don't know what you say when you tell me that I don't consider her."

In this example from Charles Dickens's "Master Humphrey's Clock," what is seen ("turning to me") and what is heard ("Ah! . . . you don't know . . .") are both expressed in words.

A story book takes the same approach. Take, for example, Beatrix Potter's *The Tale of Peter Rabbit*:

> Mr. McGregor was on his hands and knees planting out young cabbages, but he jumped up and ran after Peter, waving a rake and calling out, "Stop thief!"

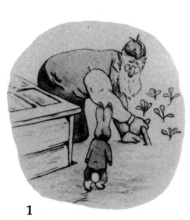

1

These words are accompanied by an illustration of Mr. McGregor planting cabbages (**Figure 1**). Although Beatrix Potter's pictures add a visual dimension to the story, *The Tale of Peter Rabbit* can be fully understood without them. In addition to telling the story, the words themselves contain images. The picture simply underlines the description: "Mr. McGregor was on his hands and knees."

Although Potter's story differs from Dickens's in format, length, and degree of complexity, *The Tale of Peter Rabbit* and "Master Humphrey's Clock" tell a story in the same way. *The Tale of Peter Rabbit* is a story book.

The Picture Book Concept

Picture books are "written" with pictures as much as they are written with words. A picture book is read to the very young child who doesn't know how to read yet; consequently, the child sees the pictures and hears the words directly, without having to deal with the intermediate step of reading the printed word. By telling a story visually, instead of through verbal description, a picture book becomes a dramatic experience: immediate, vivid, moving. A picture book is closer to theater and film, silent films in particular, than to other kinds of books. It is a unique type of book.

Without the pictures (**Figure 2**), the words in Randolph Caldecott's *Hey, Diddle, Diddle* would be meaningless. The nonsense words "Hey, diddle, diddle" are a kind of soundtrack; it is the pictures that tell the story. Caldecott's picture books, created between 1878 and his death in 1886, are probably the first fully developed examples of the true picture book.

In **Figure 3**, a picture from Maurice Sendak's *Where the Wild Things Are*, the words say only that the mischief is "of one kind." The picture completes the information. The "wild rumpus," in a later sequence of the book, is wholly conveyed through pictures. No words are used at all.

With **Figure 4**, the accompanying words read: "One Monday morning" (in my book by the same title). If you listened only to the words, you might imagine a sunny day in the country. The picture tells us that, in fact, it is a rainy day and the setting of the story is a street of dreary tenement houses in a large city. This "description" would have been represented by words in a story book. Here it is contained in a picture. "One Monday morning" is a general statement, extended by the specific details that the picture provides. It is the picture that completes the information.

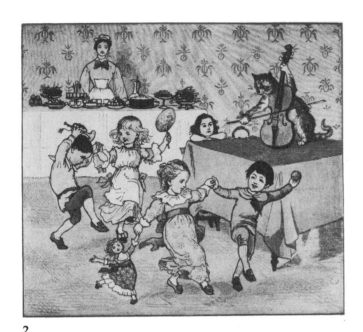

2

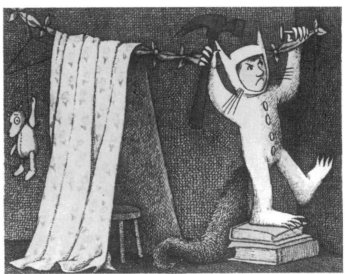

3

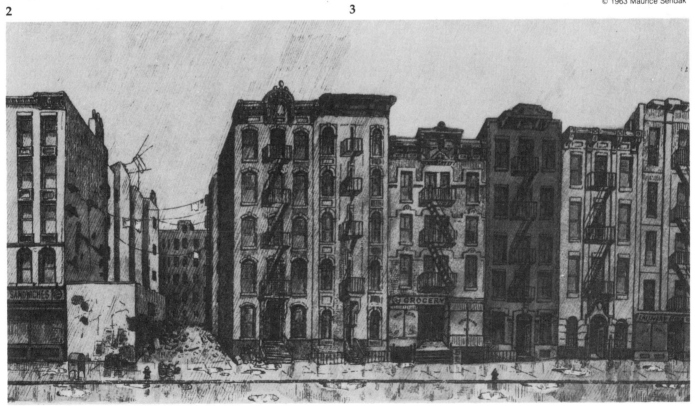

4

2. Picture Sequence

Picture books communicate through pictures and words, or sometimes through pictures alone. For picture books to be understood by children, you must know how to communicate clearly. And to do this, you must understand the rules governing the use of pictures in picture books.

The best way to begin is by using a series of pictures without words—ones that show a simple action, such as the sun rising. Whatever the beginning or ending, the picture sequence must have continuity and make sense.

A picture sequence is like a pantomime; it presents an action, such as a figure dancing or a face smiling, which can be seen readily and understood immediately. When you show an action—*what* is happening—you avoid the difficulties that may arise in trying to show general ideas, such as "progress," "peace," or "patience." In developing an action picture sequence, you try to achieve clarity *so total* that it can be grasped as instantly as a road sign. Clarity of communication is also important because the reader's enjoyment depends on it.

Actor and Stage

A picture sequence has two elements: one active, the other stationary—an "actor" and a "stage." Without an actor, there would be no action— nothing would happen. But the stage is also necessary. Without the stage, we can't tell if the actor is moving.

Figure 1. The empty frame sets the stage. We expect something to happen—anything can happen.

Figure 2. A line is introduced. But it could mean any number of things.

Figure 3. When followed by a frame with a boat, the line "reads" as water.

Figure 4. Here, followed by a walking figure, the line reads as ground.

Figure 5. And now the same line reads as a tightrope in midair. Clearly, in Figures 3, 4, and 5, the second frame determines the meaning of the first.

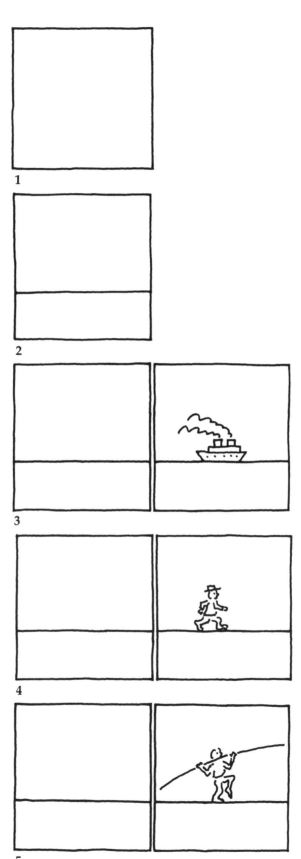

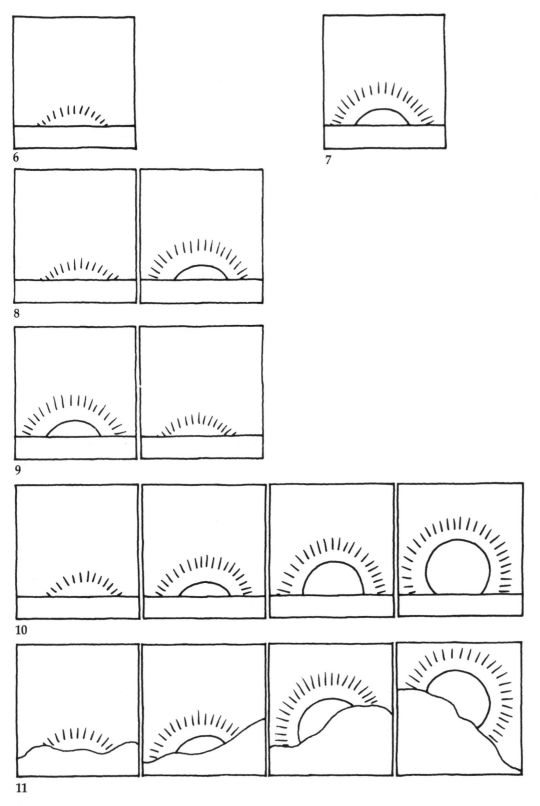

6

7

8

9

10

11

Figures 6–9. Viewed alone, Figure 6 might be a sun rising, and Figure 7 a sun setting. When we combine the two frames using the order in Figure 8, we get a sun rising. If, however, we reverse the order of the pictures, as in Figure 9, we get a sun setting. Of course, in Figures 8 and 9, our familiarity with the scene helps us recognize what is happening.

Figure 10. But familiarity alone isn't enough. For a picture sequence to be readable, actor and stage must relate clearly to each other. This sun sequence is clear not only because of its familiarity, but also because the actor (the sun) is moving clearly in relation to the stage (the horizon).

Figure 11. Here you can see what happens when actor and stage do not relate clearly. We are confused about who the actor is and what the stage is since both the horizon and the sun seem to be moving. In fact, we are no longer sure what is happening. Is the earth swelling? Is it an earthquake? Is it a tidal wave? This sequence seems to be a series of erratic frames lacking clear progression and making little sense. It loses readability.

Readability

Readability means that we can easily follow the action from one frame to the next, that we can understand what is happening. The readability of a picture sequence depends on a clear actor-stage relationship. The actor-stage relationship may change, but it must always be clear.

Figure 12. This sequence has neither frames nor stage; we cannot tell whether the car is moving at all.

Figure 13. Now the car is moving because we have added the frames. The frames are the stage for the actor—the car. We have shown movement by making the changes between actor and stage clear. We depend on the actor-stage relationship to show movement in a picture sequence.

Figure 14. Adding a specific setting gives the sequence a sense of place and makes it more interesting. Now it is also easier to tell where the car is going.

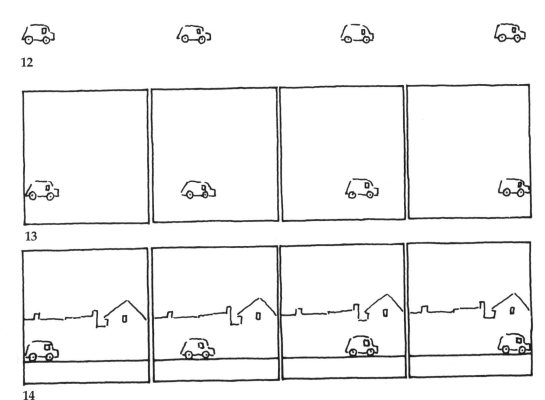

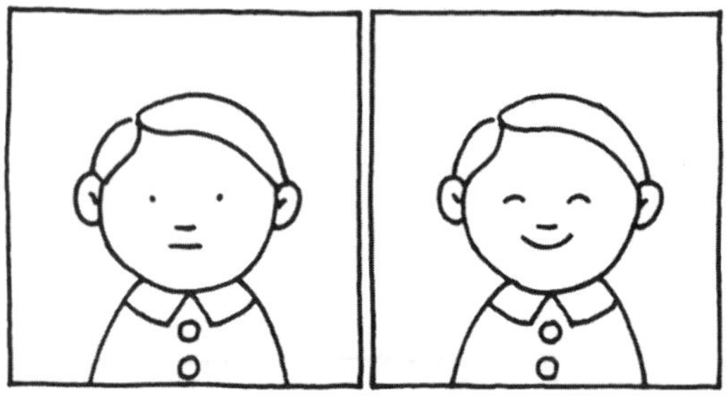

15

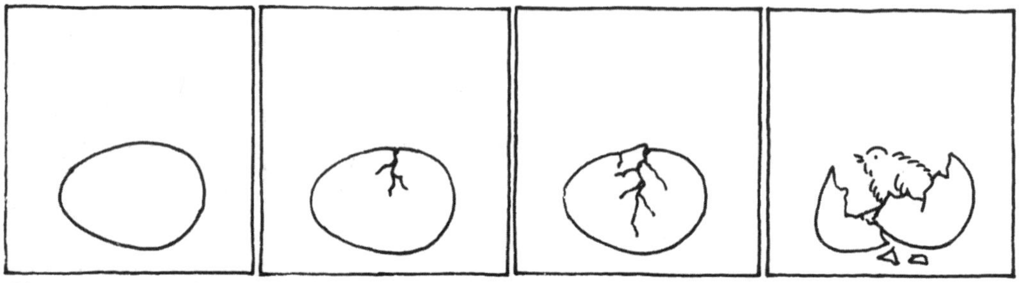

16

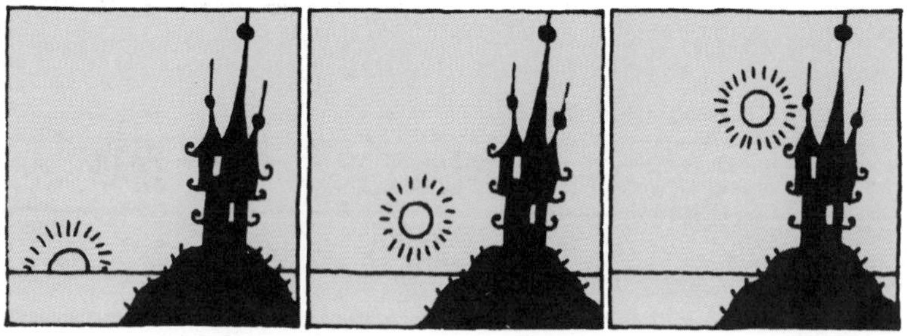

17

Figure 15. In Figures 6–14 the stage and actor were distinctly separate elements. Sometimes, however, they may be one and the same, as in this boy's head. The boy's mouth and eyes move and become the actor on his stationary face, which is the stage. When subtle action is shown in a small space, it requires precise detail and a closeup focus to be noticed.

Figure 16. The egg in this sequence is in the process of changing. Initially, it is both stage and actor, but by the fourth frame the relationship has changed: the newly hatched bird has become the actor and the broken egg has become the stage. This sequence shows one of the ways the actor-stage relationship can change.

Figure 17. We have seen how in a picture sequence the actor moves and the stage provides a motionless background. In this figure, however, it is not the familiar rising sun that draws our attention but the mysterious, motionless castle. We expect something to happen with the castle, which is the real actor in this sequence, not the moving sun. The usual actor-stage roles have been reversed.

Consistency

A picture sequence is a phrase written with visual symbols instead of words. Normally, before one can read, one must learn the alphabet. But a picture sequence can be read without learning the alphabet. The first few frames suggest a set of rules, or a *picture code*, which tells us how to read the sequence. The code promises us how the sequence will be drawn and how it will progress. When that promise is breached, we have difficulty reading the sequence.

Figure 18. Here the first two frames promise how the sequence will be drawn. The third frame breaches that promise by switching to a different way of drawing, inconsistent with the preceding frames. As a result, the reader is confused: Why has the style of drawing suddenly changed? The change distracts our attention.

Figure 19. The last frame in this sequence breaks the continuity by suddenly switching from the setting of the preceding three frames. In the fourth frame the disappearance of the horizon line is disorienting. Moreover, the kind of lines used to portray the roadway are suddenly used to portray the energy of a crash. It is confusing when visible objects are depicted with the same kind of lines as energy, which cannot be seen.

Figure 20. If, however, we use this frame as the fourth one in the sequence, it is more consistent with the preceding frames.

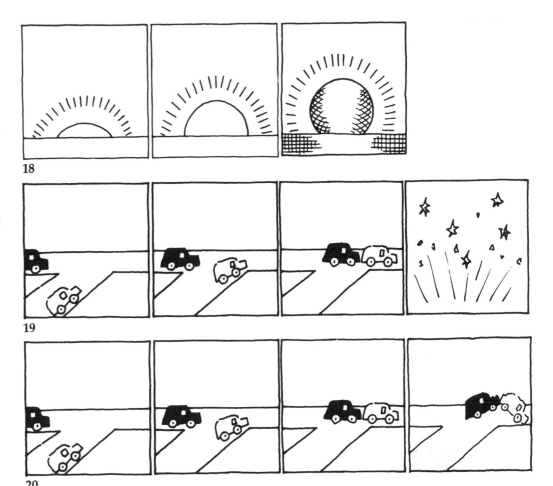

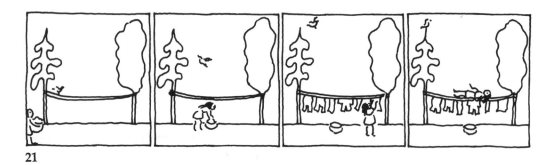

21

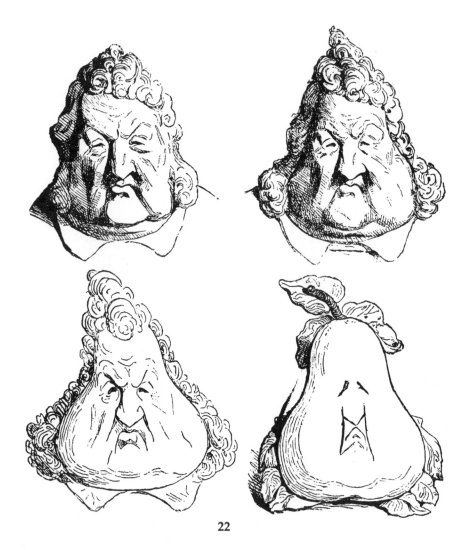

22

Figure 21. This sequence begins with a girl hanging laundry and ends with an incredible feat, inconsistent with the previous frames: she is sleeping on the laundry line. The first three frames promise an everyday activity, but frame 4 switches to fantasy. A fourth frame consistent with the preceding frames might have shown her sleeping under the tree, or reading a book, or sitting and watching the bird, or walking home, or any number of other possibilities.

Figure 22. In *Louis Philippe and the Pear*, Charles Philipon transforms the king into a pear. But the progression is gradual and consistent. No code has been breached, for the surprise ending is implied at the beginning: the face of frame 1 contains the pear of frame 4.

Pace

The pacing, or rate of progress, of a picture sequence should be treated in the same way as the picture or drawing code: it should be appropriate to and consistent with the content, and it should enhance communication. There is no picture sequence without movement or change, but it is difficult to understand a sequence when it moves too fast or too slow. The pacing should reflect the movement of the actor and the mood.

Figure 23. Here the sudden acceleration in frame 4 breaches the pace established in frames 1 through 3. We expect plants to grow at an even pace. In this sequence the pace is not only inconsistent, but also inappropriate to the subject. In a picture sequence everything must be appropriate to its subject.

Figure 24. We feel more at ease with this sequence because the gradual increase in size shows a consistent pace, more in keeping with its subject.

Figure 25. If we take these two illustrations from *Puss in Boots* out of context and view them as a picture sequence, they are confusing. We don't know what happened in between frames 1 and 2. Too much has changed at once.

Figure 26. This sequence shows the opposite. It is hard to understand because it moves too slowly and the differences in the position of the feet are too subtle. When movement is too slow, the reader may miss it entirely or get confused, or bored. You have to know when to quicken the pace in a picture sequence in order to hold the reader's attention.

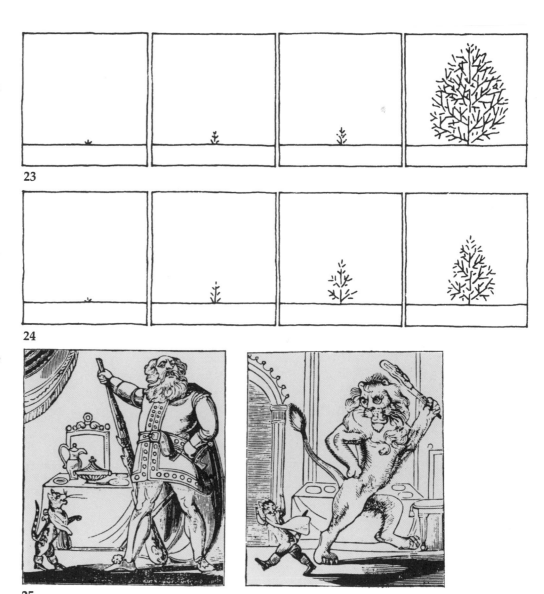

23

24

25

26

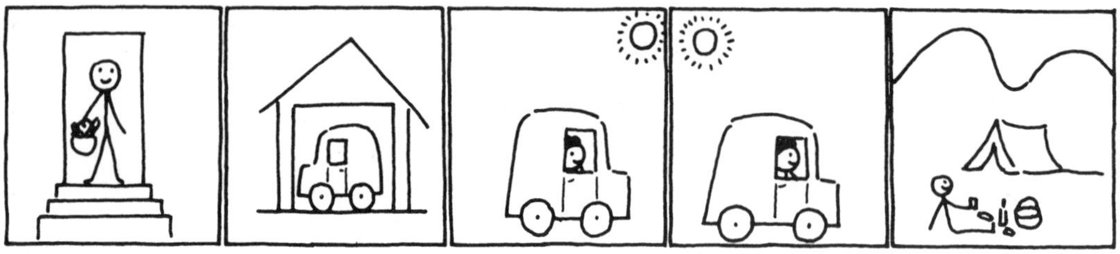

27

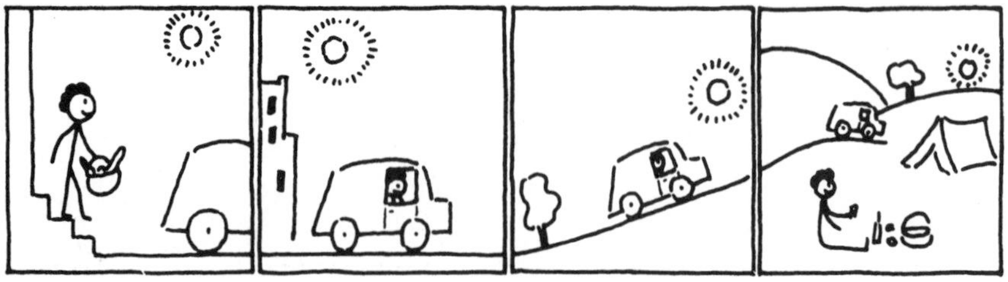

28

Clear Progression

In addition to the pacing, we need a clear progression. One frame should follow the next logically and add to the story, compelling the reader forward.

Figure 27. This sequence makes little sense. It could be read as someone driving to the mountains to go camping. But the figure is not depicted consistently so we cannot be certain that the bald man in frames 1 and 5 is the same person shown with hair in frames 3 and 4. Furthermore, the progression isn't smooth: steps are missing between frames 1–2, 2–3, and 4–5, whereas frames 3 and 4 are repetitious. The sequence doesn't move smoothly in one direction.

Figure 28. The transitions are smoother in this revised sequence. Frame 1 efficiently combines the action of frames 1 and 2 of Figure 27. In frames 2 and 3, repetition has been avoided by showing the progression from city to country. The sun moves throughout the day, indicating the passage of time. The figure's appearance is consistent. These improvements didn't require more sophisticated drawing; rather, they called for thinking about the content and the details with greater care.

Figure 29. This sequence is hard to read. It has no clear progression and makes no sense. When, expecting a picture sequence, we find a puzzle instead, we may become disappointed, frustrated, or bored. And then we are unlikely to continue reading. This is especially true of children's books, where enjoyment and interest are essential.

Figure 30. The changes in this man's appearance are very accelerated, and many years of his life are condensed into five frames. A child may not see him as the same person. For a progression to be clear, it must be within the reader's comprehension. This sequence violates the code because it is removed from a child's own life experience. Such an idea, familiar and possibly enjoyable to grown-ups, is too intellectual and abstract for very young children. Concrete, simple life situations make better children's stories.

Figure 31. We can easily read this simple action. We can follow the little girl getting up and starting a new day. The lively progression is in accord with the content.

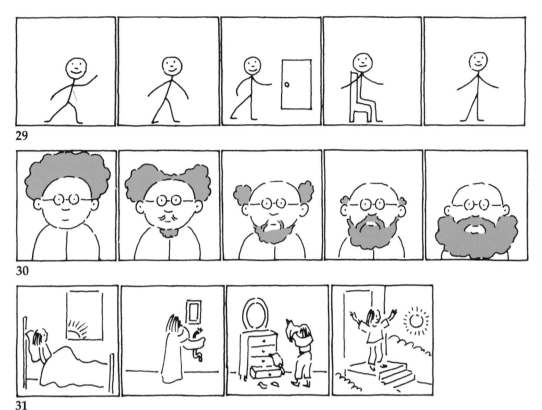

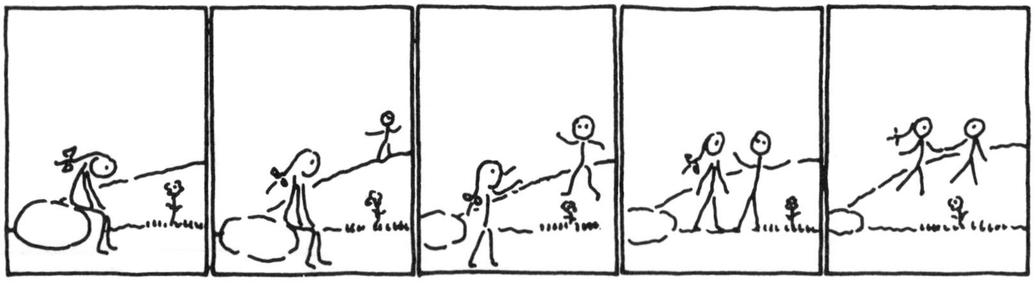

32

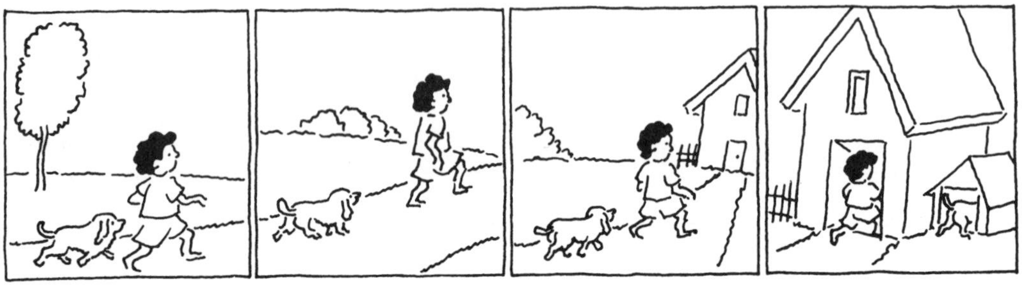

33

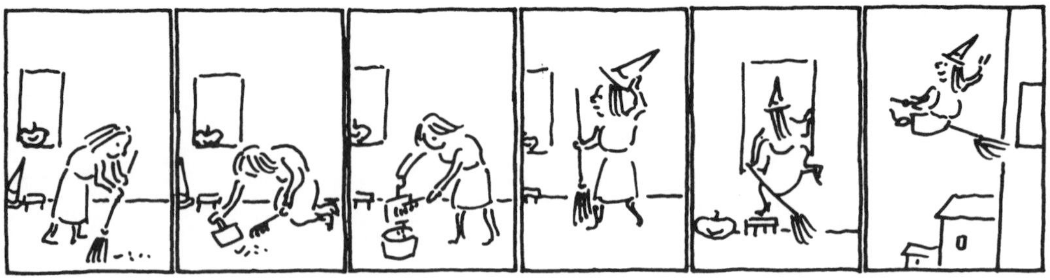

34

The Familiar and the Unexpected

It is easier to communicate with a picture sequence if the context is familiar. But relying on familiarity alone may limit your subject matter. Once you know how to communicate through a picture sequence, you can present unfamiliar situations and still be clear. And it is often the unfamiliar or the unexpected in a sequence that most arouses interest.

Figure 32. The girl here seems sad until the boy shows up. But what follows is a predictable action with stereotypical actors. Even though the story is clear, the result is a dull sequence.

Figure 33. At first glance this sequence may seem predictable. Though the dog is not on a leash, he seems to follow the boy. We expect him to follow the boy all the way to the boy's house. But when the walk is completed, they go into their respective houses. We discover that they were two friends going for a walk and not merely a dog following his master.

Figure 34. This actor is no stereotype, and her seemingly familiar routine leads to an unpredictable outcome. The code, however, has not been breached. The sequence simply uses what has been there all along: the Halloween pumpkin on the windowsill, the witch's hat on the floor, and of course, the broom in the woman's hand. We did not initially make the connection between the woman, the hat, and the broom. She knew something all along that we didn't.

Figure 35. When we see the familiar egg, we may expect a small bird or a chicken. When an ostrich hatches, it is an unexpected and pleasant surprise.

Figure 36. By reversing the commonplace, this sequence has taken an unexpected turn. We are not supposed to enjoy a rainy day; sunny days are supposed to be more fun. But this boy loves rain. He is an individual.

To summarize: When the actor-stage relationship is clear, when the picture code is consistent, when the progression is appropriate to the action, the picture sequence will "speak" to the reader. The more clearly the picture sequence speaks, the more enjoyment the reader will be able to get from it. And giving a feeling of satisfaction is essential in children's books.

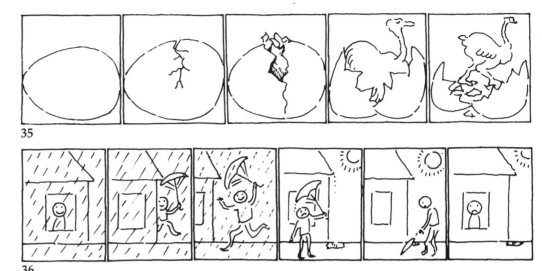

35

36

3. The Story: A Complete Action

We have seen what a picture sequence is. But a picture sequence is like an incomplete sentence; it is not a story. A story consists of many sequences; it presents a progression of events from beginning to end. That progression of events is the action of the story. At the beginning, an objective is stated or suggested, or a problem is introduced. The action of the story is complete when the objective is attained or the problem resolved. A satisfying children's story always presents a *complete action*. When we read:

> Hey, diddle, diddle,
> The cat and the

it is incomplete and we are disappointed not to be given the complete rhyming couplet:

> Hey, diddle, diddle,
> The cat and the fiddle.

Similarly, when any part of the action is missing, the action is incomplete.

In its most rudimentary form, a complete action can be schematized as a series of square dots. If we "read" the three frames in **Figure 1**, a pattern emerges. When we reach the third frame, however, we feel unsettled: it lacks balance and feels incomplete. We feel as if a promise had been made but not kept. By adding a fourth frame, as in **Figure 2**, balance is regained: the pattern has been completed. We feel more at ease.

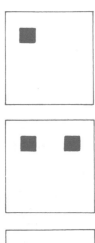

1

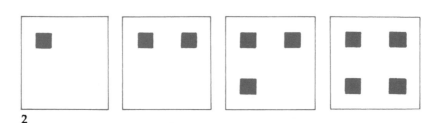

2

Achieving an Objective

In most general terms, any action already contains its objective, whether stated or suggested, and this objective must be achieved for the action to be complete.

When we look at **Figure 3**, we assume that the actor's objective is to have fun playing on the slide. The sequence, however, ends with him frustrated and possibly injured. Obviously, this action is incomplete—the objective has not been reached.

In contrast, taken by itself, **Figure 4** presents a complete action because the actor successfully accomplishes what he has set out to do. Viewed as a continuation of Figure 3, it also provides a successful ending to the action of that sequence.

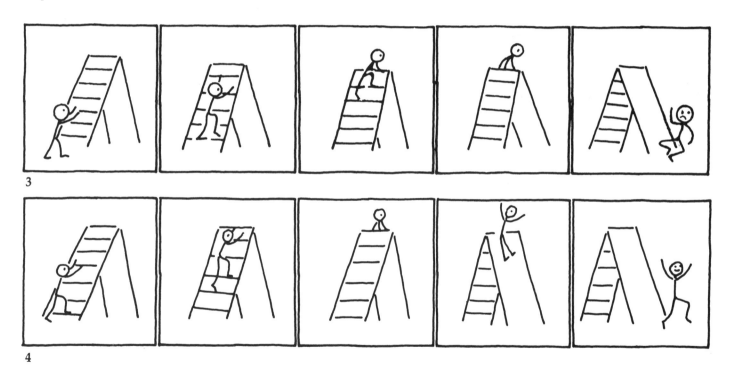

3

4

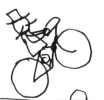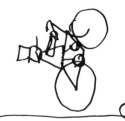

5

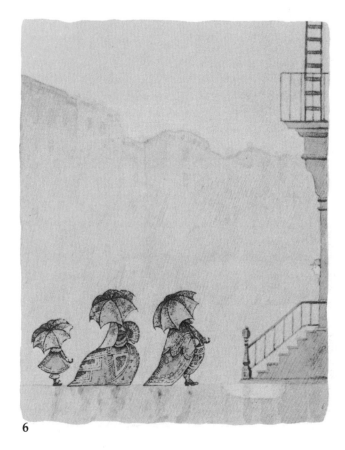

6

The Vicious Cycle by Bonnie Bishop (**Figure 5**) never comes to an end. The cyclist is caught in endless motion, never reaching his destination. An action without an ending is a series of movements going nowhere and thus remaining incomplete. Although charming, *The Vicious Cycle* reminds us of the myth of Sisyphus, who endlessly rolls his heavy rock up a hill, only to watch it roll back again. The cyclist, however, seems to have more fun than Sisyphus had.

Children's books need a definite ending. The French song that gave me the idea for my book *One Monday Morning* also involved endless repetition. One could sing it indefinitely: a king, a queen, and a little prince come back day after day—Monday, Tuesday, Wednesday, and so on—to visit a little boy, but they never find him at home (**Figure 6**). It may be enjoyable to sing this song for a while, but it would be boring and ultimately frustrating to read it as a story. In the book a new character joins the procession every day. And the action is completed when, on Sunday, the king, the queen, and the little prince finally find the boy at home. Ending the action this way rewards the king, the queen, the little prince, and the reader—and justifies their repeated visits.

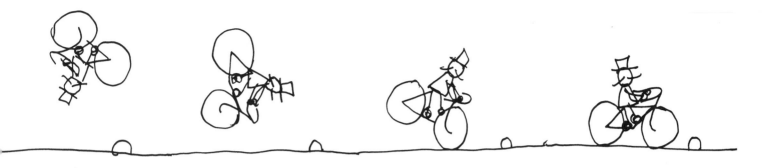

From Complete Action to Story

A satisfying children's story must present a complete action, but it must also do more than that. **Figure 7**—*The Meal*—is a complete action. Here the actor is driving to eat at a restaurant in town. After a short journey, he reaches his destination and enjoys his meal. He has achieved what he set out to do. Yet although the action is complete, the story is not quite satisfying.

Man, *house*, *car*, and *meal* are words, abstractions. But particular men, houses, cars, and meals are real. Only a unique "somebody" can trigger an emotional response in the reader. John D. MacDonald says, "Story is something happening to someone you have been led to care about." But you cannot care for a nonentity. Similarly, a story has to be about a specific incident; otherwise there is not enough significant information to interest the reader.

With **Figure 8**—*Picnic*—at last we have a complete action that is also a simple story (see next page). But why is *Picnic* a story and *The Meal* not? *The Meal* reads essentially like an outline of a journey, or an idea for a story. In contrast, *Picnic* is specific, concrete. It has details: the actor's appearance, his dress, the picnic basket,

the sailboat with wheels, the landscape along the way, and so on. Even some of the actor's inner nature comes out: his determination, his hard work. There are also details of the action itself: the steep climb, pushing the boat, the man wiping his forehead, the boat running away, the man hanging on. Through these details, a world is created that is rich enough for the reader to vividly imagine. Detail is necessary to good storytelling because it is the substance of what is unique and real.

The action of *Picnic*, although essentially simple, contains elements of the unexpected, as in real life. The actor emerges as an individual with whom the reader can sympathize, so when he attains his objective it matters to the reader. Only when the reader cares and likes the actor does the story's ending matter to the reader. Otherwise, not only would the ending not matter, but the action of the story would seem superfluous, or even irritating.

In *Picnic* the action is complete not merely because the actor arrives at the picnic, but because his *desire* has been fulfilled. The reader experiences the completion of this action only when the actor fulfills his desire at the end of the story.

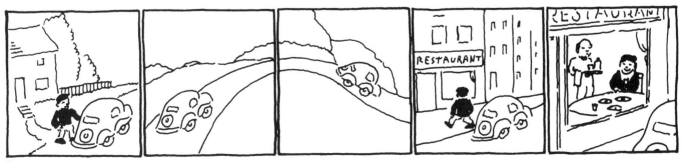

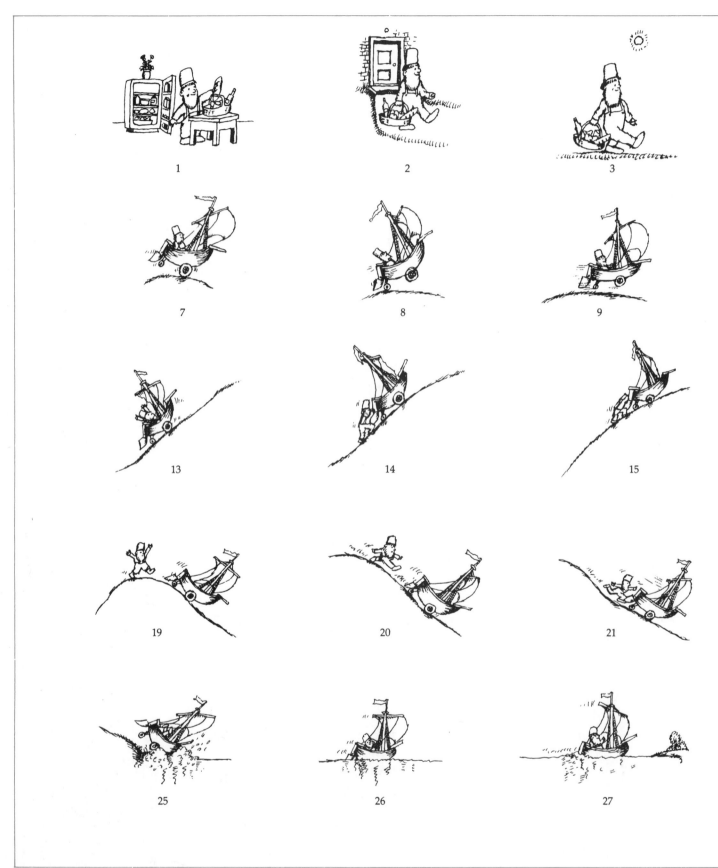

8. The Picnic

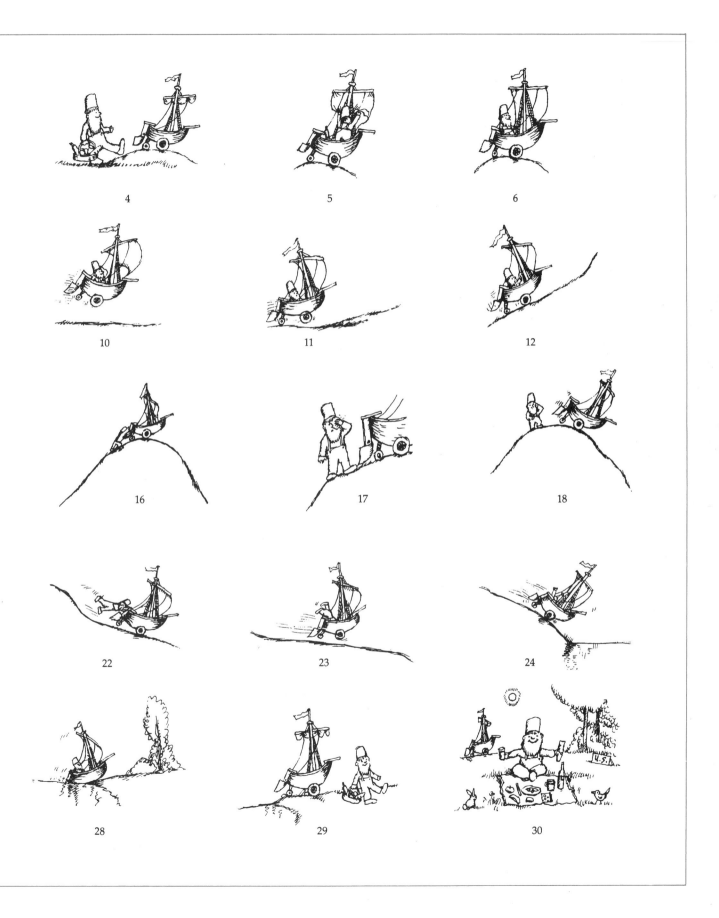

Sometimes a complete action consists of solving a problem. In **Figure 9**—*The Flea* by Wilhelm Busch—the actor's sleep is disturbed by a flea. Once the problem is solved, he can return to sleep. *The Flea* has the details necessary to make the action real and the actor an individual. Because we can sympathize with his problem—the need for a peaceful night's sleep—its solution feels like a complete action.

The action of a story need not be a simple physical action, although it usually involves physical action. The true action of *The Flea* lies in the goal of the actor and his achieving it. Later in this chapter we shall see some more complex forms that the action of a story may take, but for now it is enough to understand the principle of complete action.

The beginning of a complete action either asks directly or suggests: What is going to happen? Will the goal be reached or the problem solved? These questions must be answered fully by the end. The answers at the end must not frustrate the questions at the beginning. The end must be the direct outcome of the beginning; no substitute answers will do.

Imagine a story that begins with a boy who wants to fix his broken toy. He starts to work on it, but must stop because it is time for bed. He dreams of fixing a similarly broken toy and then playing with it. The dream ends with his getting sleepy and going to bed, and that is the end of the story as well. No more is said about the real broken toy that triggered the boy's dream. But fixing the toy in a dream is no substitute for fixing a real toy. Such an ending does not solve the problem introduced in the beginning. It ignores the boy's desire. If, for instance, his dream had shown him how to fix his real toy, which he then proceeded to do upon awakening, the story would have been completed and enriched.

Some authors would be surprised to learn that their stories may not be complete actions. Today, so many stories in books and films are merely a series of sequences, or extended sequences pretending to be complete actions, that writers may not be fully aware of the

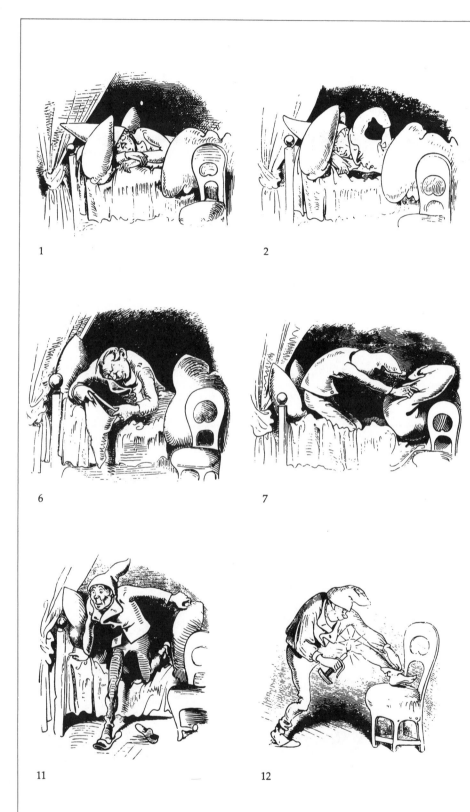

1

2

6

7

11

12

9. The Flea

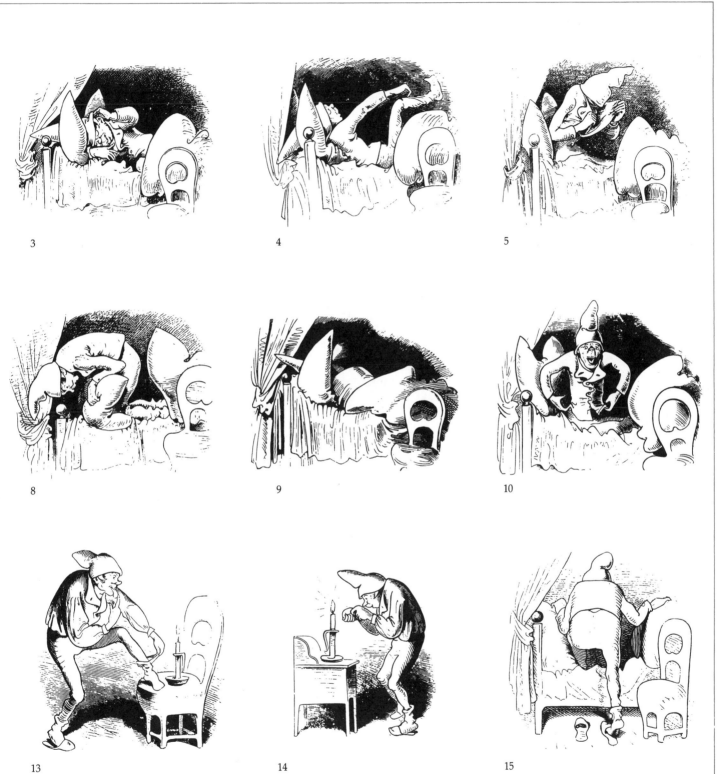

3

4

5

8

9

10

13

14

15

difference. But, although a story for adults can have an ending that merely suggests the completion of its action, a successful children's story must fully and clearly complete its action. Adults can resolve an action in their own minds after a story has ended, but young children cannot. The author must complete the action for them, because young children usually accept a story wholeheartedly and wouldn't conceive of questioning or changing it.

Incomplete action is a disturbing state, as if the world were out of balance; it can only regain its balance when the action is completed, after which life can resume peacefully. When the objectives introduced in stories aren't fully accomplished, when questions raised aren't fully answered, or when problems aren't resolved explicitly, the action remains incomplete for young readers and they are left hanging, frustrated, or unfulfilled. The suspense a story creates must be fully released at the end.

Unfolding the Story

A complete action introduces an objective and *unfolds* until the objective is reached. Details are revealed and events occur. The unfolding process is as important to a story as the objective; in fact, storytelling is that process of unfolding.

In **Figure 10**—*The Magic Trick*—you can see how the story unfolds from frame to frame. Each frame, however clear, reveals only partial information until the last frame explains the "story" by showing the entire picture. It is like a picture scroll that is slowly unrolled. It unfolds a picture until its parts build up to one complete unit. If the last frame had been presented without the steps leading up to it, the reader would not have felt any curiosity or suspense.

The Magic Trick unfolds, but it is not a story. Storytelling is a process that takes place over time. The time element in *The Magic Trick* is in the reader's mind, not in the action itself. The picture is static. Even so, it is worth noting how a static picture, unfolded properly, can hold our attention.

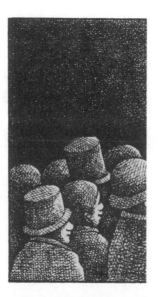

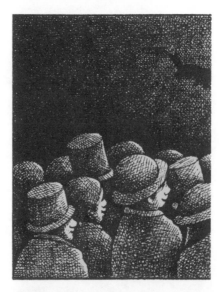

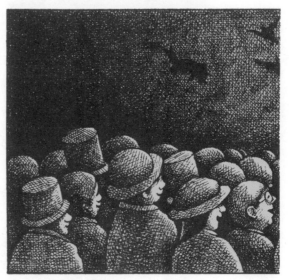

10. The Magic Trick

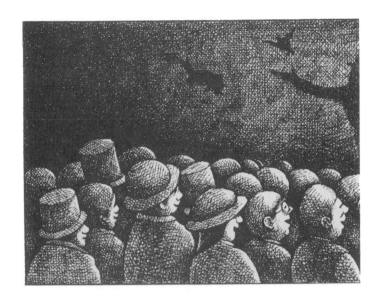

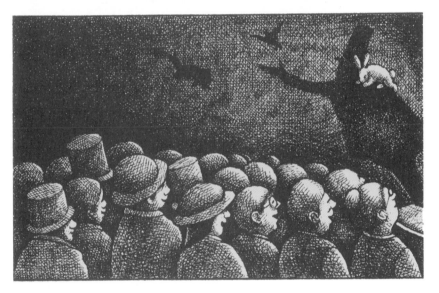

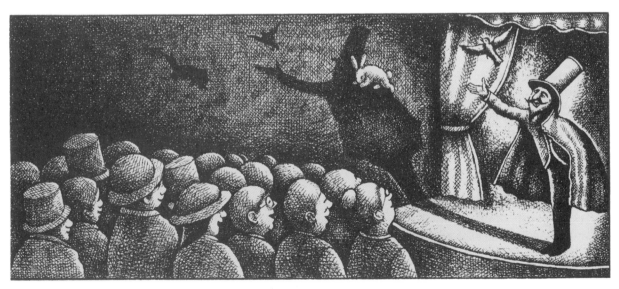

Sophie's Picnic
by M. B. Goffstein

Before the sun came up
Sophie cut a thick wedge of cheese,
a large slice of sausage,
broke off half a loaf of bread,
picked a hard green pear,
and pushed them all into a hole
in the hem of her long full skirt.

She filled a jar with water
and put a lettuce leaf inside it.
She wrapped the jar in one kerchief,
put another on her head,
stepped into her wooden sabots
and walked, clap, clap, clap,
until the sun was high above her
and she came to a sweet field of grass.
Then Sophie felt around the bottom of her skirt
and worked her lunch through the hole in the hem.
She sat down and laid it all out in her lap.
Then she began:

She took a little bite of sausage
then a big bite of bread,
a little bite of sausage
and a big bite of bread,
until she had finished them up.

Then Sophie unwrapped the jar of water,
unscrewed the top
and took a nice long drink.
She fished out the lettuce leaf
and ate it to clean out her mouth.

She had a bite of pear
with a bite of cheese,
a bite of pear
with a bite of cheese,
and when they were gone
Sophie took another long swallow of water,
then lay down, smiling at the sun.

After a while she sat up
and got a small square of chocolate
out of her jacket pocket.
She took tiny bites
and drank some water.

When every speck was gone
Sophie wrapped the jar up
and walked home, clap, clap, clap,
before the sun went down.

Some stories rely so heavily on the unfolding process that they contain only the simplest of actions. Yet they are still satisfying stories. *Sophie's Picnic* by M. B. Goffstein is a good example.

Although *Sophie's Picnic* contains no pressing problem to be solved or question to be answered, it has the minimal amount of suspense necessary for the reader to keep reading. This is achieved mainly through the gradual unfolding from a beginning to an end. It is a satisfying, complete action, which conveys Sophie's pleasure at her picnic.

Whereas *The Magic Trick* is a story idea, *Sophie's Picnic* is a story with detail. The difference is not that *Sophie's Picnic* uses words—a similar story could be told in pictures. The difference is in the complexity of the unfolding process. Sophie's character, her careful and highly personal way, is shown through the carefully chosen details of what she does and how she does it. We find *Sophie's Picnic* interesting because as the meticulous preparation and the picnic itself unfold, so does Sophie's character. The author doesn't say a word about her personality, but it comes out through her actions.

Unlike *The Magic Trick*, which is a static picture limited in how it can unfold, *Sophie's Picnic* could move in a variety of directions. The time element in *Sophie's Picnic* is independent of what the reader brings to it. The action that takes place is generated by the actor, not by the reader, and takes place in time. Because it is a single picture, and not a sequence in the sense we used earlier, *The Magic Trick* is predetermined; it doesn't move, but depends on the reader's movement in viewing it. Whereas Sophie is alive and does the unexpected, the frames of *The Magic Trick* are not by themselves very interesting; our pleasure lies in discovering the complete picture at the end. On the other hand, the climax of *Sophie's Picnic*, the picnic itself, is no more enjoyable than every step along the way.

Establishing a Unifying Link

Whenever there is unfolding, there is a unifying link. *The Magic Trick*'s unifying link is the single picture it unfolds. In *Sophie's Picnic* the unifying link is Sophie; she is the actor whom the reader follows through every step of the unfolding. How does the unifying link work in an action that has many pictures or a story that has many events?

An action or theme that develops from beginning to end holds our interest, whereas a listing of unrelated events or objects without a unifying element does not. The unifying link is the string that makes the beads into a necklace, to use an analogy by Ortega y Gasset.

This effect can be seen in *The Tragical Death of an Apple Pie* (**Figure 11**). Here the letter A—an apple pie—is treated in various ways by all the subsequent letters of the alphabet ("B Bit it, C Cut it, D Dealt it"). A similar presentation of the alphabet is given in Marilee Robin Burton's *Aaron Awoke* ("Aaron awoke, Bathed in bubbles, Combed his curls, Dressed for the day"). In both cases, there is a unifying link—the apple pie or the boy Aaron—from which the action stems, connecting the separate elements and generating interest. Alphabet books with arbitrary words and no inner link (A for Apple, B for Bear, C for Carpet, D for Door) do not generate such interest.

A unifying link is also important in such cumulative stories as *The Five Chinese Brothers* (a folk tale that tells what happens to the five brothers) and *One Monday Morning* (with the repeated visits of the king, the queen, and the little prince). It is one of the reasons that they make more enjoyable reading than a telephone book or a warehouse inventory. These stories have continuity; they tell what happened to the same object or characters.

The unifying link in *The Very Hungry Caterpillar* by Eric Carle is a tiny caterpillar who looks for food and keeps eating his way through it. On Monday he eats one apple, on Tuesday two pears, on Wednesday three plums, on Thursday four strawberries, and so on. By eating holes in the various fruits, the caterpillar is literally the string that ties those beads into a necklace. Without the unifying link, this cumulative story would have been a boring counting book. The caterpillar's action—hungrily eating everything in sight—unifies and ties many events into an engaging story.

Holding the Reader's Interest

For a story to succeed, the reader must be engrossed in each successive moment of the story and must care about what happens next, or at least be curious enough to want to know. When the reader is absorbed in every step, the next step is fresh, a new experience. One of the tests of a good story is its ability to hold the reader in the present at every moment of its unfolding. How can this be achieved? In its simplest form, as in *The Magic Trick*, it has to do with the reader wanting to discover what is unknown, to see the entire picture, or the complete action, after having seen its beginning. But you can't count on the unknown alone to impel someone to keep reading. The reader must also care enough about the beginning to want to know the rest of the story.

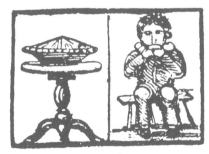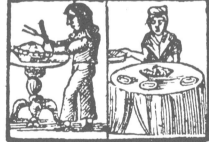

A apple pie.   B bit it.   C cut it.   D dealt it.

11

12

13

14

15

One way to hold the reader's interest is by introducing uncertainty or suspense. The nature of each picture or sequence in the unfolding of an action can contribute to the suspense. We might envision a possible continuation of the action in *The Meal*, which was depicted in Figure 7 (p. 33). The first frame in our continuation shows the actor leaving the restaurant and going to his car (**Figure 12**).

In the next frame—**Figure 13**—we see the car moving along a road. The stretch of road that the actor can see at a given time sets our expectations. Here, where the road is flat and the actor can see for a great distance, the journey seems predictable. We can imagine him continuing in this way for a while.

With **Figure 14**, the scene changes. It is night and the actor can see only that small portion of road lit by the car's lights. The "time frame" of this picture is shorter. Like the actor, we cannot see very far ahead and thus the journey seems less predictable.

Then, in **Figure 15**, we encounter a shift in the scenery and a sense of possible danger. When the actor drives at night on a road with unexpected turns, the stretch of road he can see at one time becomes shorter. The actor has to watch the road very carefully, and our suspense increases. The sequence is no longer predictable. We become concerned about the actor's safety and wonder what will happen next.

In **Figure 16** we can see how these separate pictures could work together in an actual story. In this story—*After the Meal*—the actor leaves the restaurant and

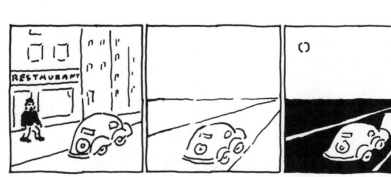

16

begins to drive home. On his way he has to drive up a winding mountain road. The sky darkens. A heavy rain begins to fall. After a treacherous trip, he finally arrives safely home, where he can read his favorite picture book.

The reader's desire to know what happens next depends to a great extent on *how* the story unfolds. In *After the Meal* the reader identifies with the actor and experiences, with him, the drive from the restaurant to his safe return home. Not all stories, however, have this kind of suspense. In *Sophie's Picnic*, for instance, there is no "uncertainty" to speak of. Through the process of unfolding, the reader participates in and enjoys the concrete details that gradually add up to a complete action.

Completing the Action

A good ending should add focus and significance to the unfolding that has preceded it. Unfolding by itself can be satisfying, but add a satisfying ending and you get a more fulfilling story.

The foremost requirement of an ending is that it complete the action of the story in a logical manner. This is a common weakness of beginning writers. The following example is modeled on a story written by a student and is typical of this problem:

> The townspeople were unhappy because they had to work hard. One day a miracle man appeared. Seeing how unhappy the people were, he introduced bright colors into their surroundings. They became happy.

This ending, happy as it is, doesn't explain how the introduction of color solved the townspeople's problem or their attitude toward hard work. It does not relate to the problem introduced in the beginning of the story. Even though intended as a fantasy, the story is unconvincing because it does not observe the logic of cause and effect.

The logic of cause and effect explains how and why one event follows another. In a story like *Sophie's Picnic* one event follows another in a natural time sequence; this flow of events conforms to our life experience. Such a story tells us with consistency and without digression what happened just as a chronological report would. But in other kinds of stories, not conforming to our life experience—fantasies, for example—we need the rigorous logic of cause and effect to accept their credibility. Otherwise, they may seem accidental or improbable and we won't care about them.

This kind of cause-and-effect logic is evident in Kafka's *Metamorphosis*. In *Metamorphosis* (not a story for children), the hero awakens in the beginning of the story to discover that he has become an insect. Everything that follows this extraordinary event, however, is an absolutely plausible, logical outcome of it. The unexplained beginning triggers a chain of cause-and-effect events that make up the rest of the story. As incredible as Kafka's *Metamorphosis* is, its rigorous logic makes it believable as a story. Any divergence from convention or from a familiar situation must be handled carefully lest it distract, confuse, or weaken a story.

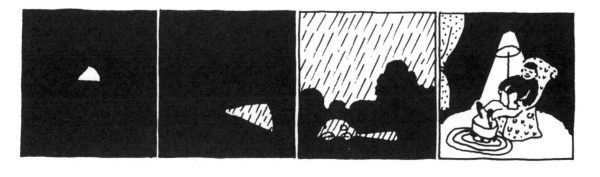

Another point to remember is that an ending will not succeed if someone or something has been forgotten along the way. Remember the boy and his broken toy, which never got fixed. In children's stories, actions are neither complete nor satisfying if they introduce characters or significant details and then forget them later on.

A good ending must take care of everything and not leave any loose threads. In Beatrix Potter's *The Tale of Peter Rabbit*, Peter loses his new jacket and shoes in his ordeal in Mr. McGregor's garden and must abandon them. But the story does not abandon them; it tells us that Mr. McGregor uses them for his scarecrow. This may not make Peter happy, but it makes for a better story. Details are important to a story, but not unless the story remembers them. Only when all the loose ends are tied up, when all the details are attended to, is the action truly complete.

In a complete action the objective introduced at the beginning is reached at the end. In *Picnic* the objective is reached when the actor has a picnic, and in *The Flea* when the actor can go back to sleep. The essence of the objective in each story is to satisfy the actor's desire or need. The objectives in *The Flea* and *Picnic* were apparent at the outset. There are, however, stories where the apparent objective

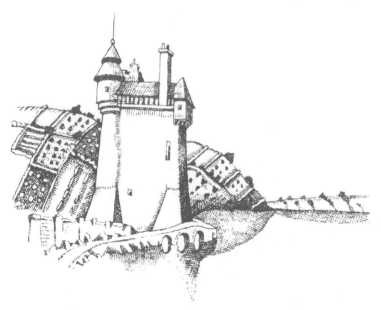

is transformed, or grows with the unfolding of the action, although the underlying essence of the objective remains the same.

In Robert Louis Stevenson's *The Touchstone*, the hero goes in search of the touchstone of truth to win a beautiful princess. When after many years he returns with the touchstone, he finds his brother has married the princess. At first he is very sad, but seeing his brother and the princess for what they are, he realizes that the truth he has found is more valuable than his initial goal, and that he is better off without the princess.

The hero's realization completes the action of the story on a deeper level than either he or the reader had anticipated. When his perception changes, when he realizes that his initial objective is no longer valid, the true essence of the story is revealed.

The action and the actor are alive, and so is the objective: it grows as the story and the actor change and grow. At first, the reader can see only the apparent objective (marrying the princess), and is not aware of the story's essence (enriching the hero's experience of life). It is in the course of the story that the hero discovers the added dimensions of the objective. By ending in an unconventional manner, seemingly counter to the hero's aspirations, the story prompts the reader to discover the essence that lies beneath appearances.

In Robert Kraus's *The Littlest Rabbit*, the bigger rabbits of the neighborhood bully the littlest rabbit. When he grows bigger and stronger, he beats up these bullies. This completes the action because the problem introduced in the beginning has been solved. The story could end right there. But it goes on to tell us about his parents' reaction, how proud they are of him and his overcoming the bullies, and about how he experiences himself and the world in a new and happy way. And then it goes on and tells how he rescues a tiny rabbit who is bullied by larger rabbits. When the tiny rabbit thanks him, he replies, "I am a big rabbit now, but once— I was the littlest rabbit." We are deeply touched because he has not forgotten how he felt in the beginning of the story, when he was in the same position. This story is satisfying because the author has fulfilled the reader's unconscious longing for a happier world.

The ending of *The Littlest Rabbit* unfolds in three stages: (1) his victory over the bullies; (2) the respect of his parents and his new experience of the world; (3) the rescue of the tiny rabbit in whom he sees himself as he was in the beginning of the story. Thus, the end reminds us of the beginning and brings the story full circle.

As the ending unfolds, the reader's understanding of the objective of the story broadens. In that sense *The Littlest Rabbit*, like *The Touchstone*, takes on a new dimension at the end.

In the course of an action, questions are raised. The quality of the story will depend on the questions that the author chooses to address. The author must understand clearly the action of the story before addressing those questions that go to the heart of the story. In deciding what these questions are, the author focuses on the story's significance.

In *The Littlest Rabbit*, when the hero grows up and beats up the bullies, there is one such suggested question: Will the hero be kind or will he, too, become a bully when he grows up? But when he is big and safe, he chooses to defend the tiny rabbit. By doing so he goes beyond fighting for his own safety and fights for a world where those who cannot defend themselves are safe as well. He has used his personal victory over the bullies to fight for a principle—justice and kindness. By answering the question in this way, the story has taken on universal significance.

In the way a story answers the questions it poses, in the way it completes its action, there lies an implied philosophy. In *The Littlest Rabbit* the implied philosophy suggests that it is important not only to defend oneself, but to go beyond oneself and fight for principles, and that the present need not wipe out the memory of the past. The essence, or implied philosophy, of any story must be valid, although the story may be fantastic and unreal. The satisfaction readers take away from a story often lies in the implied philosophy, in the meaning of the story, as much as it does in the way the details of the story unfold. Even though readers may not be fully aware of the story's philosophy, it will be alive to them on a subconscious level and will stay with them after the story has ended.

In the best of stories the end may take on a greater meaning than was anticipated in the beginning. When this happens, the story grows into a new dimension, the individual becomes universal, the specific and mundane become magical and wondrous. Even stories of the utmost simplicity can take on surprising significance from the way they complete their actions.

In *Goodnight Moon* by Margaret Wise Brown, a little rabbit is in bed in a room with various objects, animals, and an old lady whispering "hush." One by one, he says goodnight to the room, to the animals, to the objects, to the old lady, to the stars in the sky outside his window, to the air, and finally to noises everywhere. Then he falls asleep.

The action of this story is very simple: a little rabbit saying goodnight to his "friends" and going to sleep. Yet after saying goodnight to everything in his room, he says goodnight to what is outside, to the whole universe—thus pushing the story beyond its obvious boundaries. By transcending a mechanical listing of the room's contents, the rabbit is creative—he reaches beyond the private world of his room and unites with an infinite universe at peace. He can now sleep securely in his little bed.

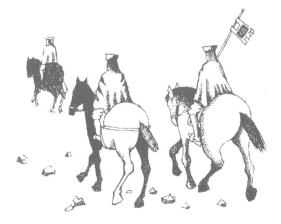

Happy Endings

Because children take stories so seriously and believe in them as if they were real life, the author must evaluate with utmost care whether a sad or unhappy ending is truly justified. Unhappiness creates a problem for the child. It is as if the action of the story had not been completed. Good children's stories are considerate of the reader *as well as* of the facts of life and the world. They offer something positive to help the child grow. They may show how life and the world are, how problems are solved, or they may teach, comfort, strengthen, inspire, entertain. But none of these goals is successfully achieved when the reader is left frustrated or discouraged. Good children's stories satisfy their readers.

Although the completion of the action brings the story to its close, it doesn't end all action. It allows the child to leave the story with confidence that the characters will continue successfully in their lives after the end of the story.

Beyond the Principles

We have encountered various principles that underlie good stories. In the unfolding of a story, we have seen the importance of a complete action, a unifying link, significant detail, fulfillment of the actor's desire or need, and an ending with a satisfying resolution. Other principles include observance of the logic of cause and effect, tying up loose ends, and an awareness of the implied philosophy. Good stories embody these principles, and original stories embody them in new ways. There is, however, no simple formula for writing a good story. It is crucial to learn the principles of good storytelling; yet, strangely enough, these are the very things you must "forget" as you write so that you can use them spontaneously.

The ultimate test of any story is what happens in the reader's mind. The reader must take pleasure from the story's gradual unfolding. There must be rewards in discovering and experiencing each new moment. But, beyond this, there should be a sense that the story is moving toward a final moment that will not only complete the action of the story but also resonate with the inner world of the reader.

There is no easy rule to follow, no simple way to explain how such an ending can be arrived at. The story must *feel* complete. And this can happen only when the reader is fully satisfied with it— only when the story affects the reader emotionally. To do this, the author must bring feeling to a story. Without it, the story will not be alive.

To write a story that is truly moving, you should take the characters and what happens to them seriously, regardless of whether the story is sad or happy, serious or funny. Don't feel remote or above your own story. On the contrary, what affects your characters affects you as well. You have to respond fully to what is in your story, and you must care about your characters, their interests, their joys and sorrows. Project yourself into your characters, so that you and your story become one. Be what you write about. You should empathize with everything in your story; nothing is insignificant, nothing is forgotten or neglected.

An author must learn the principles of good storytelling only in order to write better from the heart.

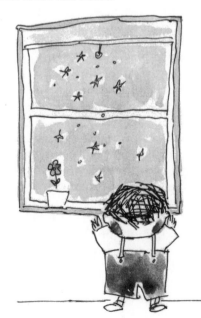

4. Story Content

Exploring content gives us a better understanding of stories. This approach also provides an important tool for writing your own stories. The six stories presented here are all very different. But they all have one thing in common: their content is about change of one kind or another.

In fact, whatever its subject matter, every story is about *change*. This change must be important to the hero, for if it doesn't matter to him or her, the reader will not care.

Cinderella

Cinderella, who is beautiful and kind, is ridiculed and treated like a servant by her arrogant stepmother and her two vain stepsisters. The stepmother makes her do all the household chores in order to degrade her. But Cinderella does her work patiently and without complaining.

One day the prince of the land gives a ball, and the two stepsisters eagerly attend it. Cinderella longs to go too, but she has no fine clothes to wear, nor a carriage to take her. As she cries, her fairy godmother appears. Through magic, she transforms Cinderella's rags into a beautiful ball gown. A pumpkin becomes a carriage; mice turn into a team of horses, lizards into footmen, and a rat into a coachman. The fairy godmother tells Cinderella she may attend the ball, provided she returns home before midnight, when the spell will end and her finery turn back into rags.

At the ball no one recognizes Cinderella, who becomes the center of attention and captivates the prince. Before he learns her name, she has to leave—it is almost midnight. While running from the ballroom, she loses one of her slippers. The prince proclaims he will marry the mystery princess to whom the slipper belongs.

When the prince's messenger brings the lost slipper to Cinderella's home, her two stepsisters try it on in vain. Then Cinderella tries it on and it fits. Everyone is astonished. She marries the prince and goes to live at the palace.

The Tale of Peter Rabbit
by Beatrix Potter

Peter's mother warns him and his sisters not to go into Mr. McGregor's garden, where their father lost his life. His sisters listen to their mother's warning, but Peter defiantly sets·off for the garden. He eats too many vegetables and becomes sick. Then, when he is about to leave, he is seen and chased by Mr. McGregor. Peter is terrified. The forbidden garden of delights becomes a nightmare when Peter cannot find his way out. After losing his new jacket, his shoes, and almost his life, Peter escapes.

Peter returns home exhausted and sick. He has to take medicine, while his sisters enjoy a delicious supper.

Dandelion
by Don Freeman

Dandelion is invited to a friend's party, but he becomes concerned about his appearance. He gets a curly haircut for the occasion, as well as a manicure, a new jacket, a cap, and a cane. When he arrives, looking like a stylish dandy, his friend doesn't recognize him and won't admit him to the party.

Dandelion paces back and forth in front of his friend's house. Suddenly a gust of wind blows away his cap. Then it begins to rain heavily; he drops his cane, his curls come undone, and he takes off his wet jacket. Eventually the rain stops, and the sun comes out again. When he dries out, Dandelion looks like his old self again.

Once more Dandelion rings the bell. This time he is recognized and welcomed to the party, where everyone is pleased to see him. Dandelion decides to be himself and never turn himself into a stylish dandy again.

The Nature of the Change

The change may affect the hero's physical environment, as in *Dawn*, or social situation, as in *Cinderella*; or the hero may learn or realize something and change, as in *Dandelion*, *The Tale of Peter Rabbit*, and *Where the Wild Things Are*.

Of the six stories examined in this chapter, the simplest kind of change occurs in *Dawn*. There the transition is from night to day. The setting of the story stays the same, but is gradually revealed in a new light.

In *The Very Hungry Caterpillar*, a caterpillar changes into a butterfly. Unlike the change from dark to light in *Dawn*, which is gradual and continuous, the change in *The Very Hungry Caterpillar* is really a series of changes: an egg turns into a caterpillar, then a cocoon, and finally a butterfly.

In spite of their differences, the changes in both *Dawn* and *The Very Hungry Caterpillar* can be viewed as simple: they both depict a predictable course of nature. Day follows night and a caterpillar ultimately turns into a butterfly.

In *Cinderella* the change is social and economic: Cinderella rises from being a lowly servant in her own home to social and economic prominence, from being oppressed and isolated from the world to becoming recognized and rewarded for her beauty and kindness. This process of change is unpredictable: not every beautiful girl marries a prince, although in a fairy tale her chances are much better than average.

Whereas Cinderella's unhappy situation at home isn't of her own doing, Dandelion creates his own problem. He is a perfectly fine-looking lion who decides to change his appearance and look like a stylish dandy.

In *Cinderella* and *Dandelion* the reader is sympathetic to the heroes throughout, but in *Peter Rabbit* and *Where the Wild Things Are* the reader is alienated at first because of the hero's unrestrained self-centeredness. Peter and Max are similar in character: they are cocky and defiant. Peter goes to McGregor's garden, and Max creates a forest in his own room. Peter is defeated in McGregor's garden and almost loses his life; Max is victorious over the wild, nightmare monsters. The plot in each story is different, but the results are similar: both heroes learn something and change as a result of it. Peter loses his foolish arrogance and Max his anger.

The Consequences of Change

The heroes of our six stories realize, experience, or achieve something that has an impact on their lives, something that helps them grow or enriches them in some way. Sometimes the change is far-reaching and permanent. Other times it is temporary or a part of an ongoing natural cycle.

The caterpillar, for instance, does what he has to do: he eats a lot so that he can grow big and fat and thus fulfill his destiny—to become a butterfly. The change is permanent and irreversible.

The sunrise in *Dawn*, on the other hand, is part of an ongoing natural cycle of change. The change from dark to light has occurred before and will occur again. But to the old man and his grandson, it is a unique and moving experience they will not forget.

Once Cinderella marries the prince, her life changes radically and permanently. As a princess, she'll never have to endure the unhappy situation at home again. Although her whole life changes, including her social situation and her environment, her character stays the same.

Dandelion, on the other hand, changes as a result of his experience. He thought that by turning himself into a dandy he would gain greater social acceptance. But, instead, he becomes a stranger to his friends. Now he realizes that dressing to please others doesn't please anybody, whereas being oneself does. Not only does he learn a lesson, but he is capable of laughing at his own foolishness.

Peter Rabbit has a terrifying experience in McGregor's garden, where his father was killed. In fact, he himself almost loses his life there. Peter returns home sick and exhausted after his ordeal. He has paid

---

Where the Wild Things Are
by Maurice Sendak

Max's wild behavior leads to an angry confrontation with his mother, and he is sent to bed without supper. Max's room changes into a forest near an ocean, and he sails away to where the wild things are. They try to scare him, but Max gains power over them and becomes their king. He orders a wild rumpus. Free to act as they please, Max and the monsters roar and jump wildly until Max gets tired of it. Feeling lonely and hungry, he longs for home, where someone loves him. Max gives up being king, sails home, and finds his supper waiting for him.

The Very Hungry Caterpillar
by Eric Carle

In the moonlight, a little egg lies on a leaf. On Sunday morning, a tiny, very hungry caterpillar emerges from it. The little caterpillar looks for food. On each successive day of the week he eats more food but is still hungry. On Saturday, he eats even more and gets a stomachache. He eats a green leaf and feels better. He's no longer hungry, and by now he has grown big and fat. He makes himself into a cocoon and emerges from the cocoon as a beautiful butterfly.

Dawn
by Uri Shulevitz

An old man and his grandson sleep through the night under a tree by a lake. A light breeze rippling the water signals the slow transition from night to dawn. Gradually, the sky and water lighten, the colors brighten, and various animals wake up. The old man and his grandson get up. They break camp and row off on the lake. As their boat moves, the first signs of the rising sun appear. When they reach the middle of the lake, they witness the magnificent spectacle of dawn.

dearly for his foolish defianace of his mother's wise advice. The story ends with a changed Peter, and well-earned sympathy from the reader.

In *Where the Wild Things Are*, Max gets tired of acting out his rage in unrestrained behavior. He realizes that the power he has gained over the fantasy monsters isn't as rewarding as the love and kindness he finds at home. He is lonely and misses his mother. He returns home, to reality and to the supper waiting for him. He's no longer angry and thoughtless toward those around him. His mother has forgiven his earlier behavior, and so has the reader.

The Stages of the Change

The change in a story unfolds in three stages.

The **beginning** presents the reason or motivation for the change. The hero and the problem (or direction of the action if there's no problem) are introduced.

In *Cinderella*, for example, Cinderella's unhappy situation at home and her desire to attend the ball are introduced. In *Peter Rabbit* we see how Peter creates his own problem by defying his mother's advice and entering Mr. McGregor's garden. Similarly, Max's behavior at the beginning of *Where the Wild Things Are* creates the conflict with his mother, and he's sent to bed without supper. In the beginning of *The Very Hungry Caterpillar*, the egg turns into a tiny caterpillar with an enormous appetite. *Dawn* shows us the landscape setting in the dark and the heroes asleep.

The **middle**, which shows the change in process, constitutes the main action of the story: what happens and how. Obstacles are overcome; there is movement toward a solution. Or—in a story that does not have problems or obstacles to overcome—events unfold, leading toward a conclusion.

The middle of *Cinderella* shows Cinderella's magical transformation into a beautiful princess who secretly attends the ball. In *Peter Rabbit* the garden of delights turns into a nightmare, until Peter finally manages to escape. Max

travels to where the wild things are, gains power over them, and does as he pleases—until he gets tired of wildness and longs for home. The caterpillar eats more and more, grows, changes size and shape, and turns into a cocoon. In *Dawn* we see the gradual transition from dark to light, from the old man and his grandson sleeping through their waking up to their breaking camp and rowing on the lake.

The **end** brings the change to a conclusion and shows its consequences. Although the change may involve dramatic or upsetting events, it is presented in a framework that is reassuring to the child. The goal stated or implied at the beginning has been reached, or the problem has been resolved.

At the end, Cinderella's true qualities are revealed to all. Her unjust treatment at home is resolved and her goodness is rewarded: she marries the prince and enjoys her new life at the palace. This is quite unlike what happens to Peter, who returns home at the end in a pitiful state, sick and exhausted. Yet even though Peter has an upsetting experience and pays dearly for his lesson, he makes it home alive and safe. This ending is reassuring to the reader. Max also returns home, no longer defiant, to find a hot supper waiting for him.

In *Dawn* the gradual transition to daylight comes to an expected, but still dramatic, conclusion as the heroes finally see their surroundings fully revealed in all their color by the rising sun. The caterpillar also fulfills an expected destiny. Throughout the story he has been self-reliant—he's his own doctor when he has a stomachache and his own architect (he builds his own cocoon). His diligent pursuit of what he needs to do to realize himself pays off, and he becomes a beautiful butterfly.

The beginning gives birth to the end, and the end remembers the beginning; none of the elements introduced at the beginning are forgotten, no loose threads are left hanging—from Peter's lost new jacket and shoes to Dandelion's cane and curls. The implied promise made to the reader in the beginning has been kept.

5. Picture Book Characteristics

As we have seen, in a picture book the pictures do much more than illustrate the text. Often they expand upon the words and provide information essential to the story. In fact, without the pictures, we might not understand the meaning of the words.

Martha Alexander's *We Never Get to Do Anything*, for instance, opens with the words:

"Mom, will you take me swimming?"
"Not today, Adam, I'm busy."

But it is the picture that really tells us what is happening. We see a woman hanging laundry and meet her little boy, Adam, and his big dog. A wordless double spread follows, showing Adam and his dog leaving while mother isn't looking.

The picture says what the words do not. And if the picture says it all, no words are used. Normally, a picture book uses a minimum of words, since most, or all, of the description—the setting, the characters, and the action—is shown through the pictures.

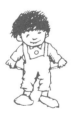

Normally, also, the words in a picture book do not repeat what is in the pictures and vice versa—unless the repetition serves a specific purpose, such as emphasis. The words and the pictures interact with or complement one another. In Chapter 1, we saw how the words serve as a soundtrack to the pictures in *Hey, Diddle, Diddle* and my own *One Monday Morning* (which is based on an old French folk song). In *Mine's the Best*, Crosby Bonsall literally uses music notes on the opening page of the story to indicate a tune the little boy is whistling in the picture.

A different kind of soundtrack occurs in Maurice Sendak's *Where the Wild Things Are*, with its rhythmic prose. We read that "The wild things roared their terrible roars and gnashed their terrible teeth and rolled their terrible eyes and showed their terrible claws." These words are neither mere description nor mere repetition of what can be seen in the picture (**Figure 1**). Their rhythmic sound augments the feeling of "terrible" activity. And the words tell us something the picture cannot fully show: the movement of gnashing teeth and rolling eyes. Unlike·film, a picture book with its still pictures cannot show certain kinds of movement. This is where the words come in; they can help emphasize a detail, clarify an action, or link two pictures together.

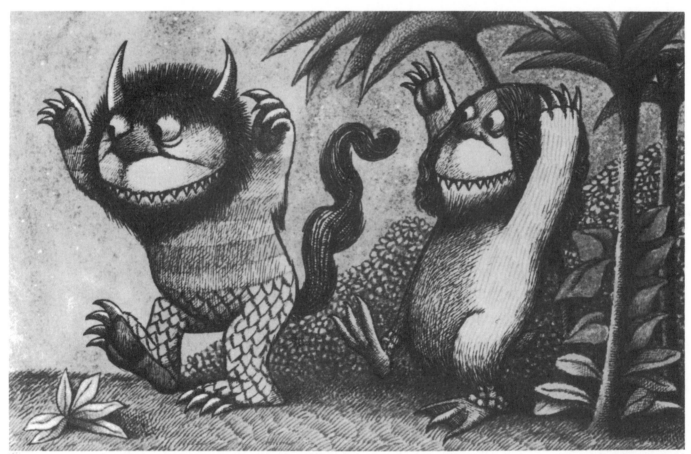

© 1963 Maurice Sendak

1

Direct Approach

A picture book favors a direct approach. A description such as "Mr. McGregor was on his hands and knees" would be either shown by a picture or avoided altogether. When an image such as this is clearly described, with the visual details presented through words, to show it again through a picture would be redundant and possibly boring. In a picture book there should be no such repetition; the visual representation takes precedence. Repetition in a picture book only lengthens and complicates a form that is best kept as simple, brief, and clear as possible.

Analogies and similes should also be avoided in picture books. Take, for example, the line: "He was *like* a mouse." If the story is about someone who may feel as small as a mouse, such an image is most effectively expressed by the words: "He *was* a mouse." The reader is perceptive enough to realize that a story with a mouse as the main character is actually about a child, who is much smaller than those around him in his family or in his class, and who may feel as small as a mouse.

Lively Hero

A story is more enjoyable when the hero is active and resourceful. If the hero, for example, is a passive plant who suffers constantly and does nothing but worry, it is hardly fun. The plant is capable of thinking, but chooses not to move a leaf. If the plant had been resourceful and done something about its problems, it could have been an interesting story.

Remember, action makes the story lively and dramatic. In Leo Lionni's *Swimmy*, for example, the hero—a little fish—is appealing because he is full of initiative. When Swimmy's brothers and sisters are eaten by a big fish, he is left "scared, lonely, and very sad." As he swims along, however, he discovers many wonderful creatures in the sea. Then he finds a group of small fish just like his lost family, but they are scared of the big fish.

Swimmy decides to do something about this. He teaches them to swim in a formation that looks like a giant fish, and they chase the big fish away. His ingenuity in solving the problem brings the reader satisfaction.

Similarly, in Pat Hutchin's *Changes, Changes*—a story told in pictures, without words—the two heroes are active. When their building-block house catches fire, the boy and girl use some blocks to create a hose and put out the fire. They then find themselves in a pool of water so they reshape the blocks into a boat. Throughout the story, whenever a new difficulty arises, the boy and girl do something to solve it.

Visible Action

Like film and theater, picture books are a form of dramatic art: they tell their story through visible action, which is concrete and easy to grasp. They contain simple actions and avoid vague or general ideas. They show the characters doing something that can be readily grasped: physical movement, such as the cow jumping over the moon in *Hey, Diddle, Diddle*, the royal retinue climbing the stairs in *One Monday Morning*, or Max sailing a boat in *Where the Wild Things Are*. The reader follows the unfolding of the same action without digressions. Thus we see Max's journey to where the wild things are without losing sight of him at any time, or switching to any events not directly related to him.

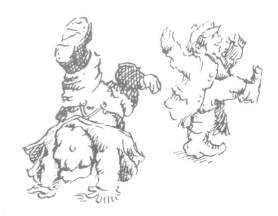

	lost
	3

found	
4	**5**

	lost
	3

search	search
4	**5**

search	search
6	**7**

search	FOUND
8	**9**

2

Linear Continuity

In order to maintain utmost clarity, the action of a picture book follows "linear continuity"; it preserves the natural time sequence of events, without subplots or digressions, flashbacks or "in the mean-times."

> Snow is falling,
> The field mice are sleeping . . .

So begins Ruth Krauss's *The Happy Day*. It continues, after presenting various sleeping animals:

> Now they open their eyes. They sniff.
> The field mice sniff . . .

The animals sniff, then they run. The action unfolds as a single, continuous thread without breaks or jumps. The scene of the animals sleeping flows smoothly, following a natural sequence of events told in the order it happened, through to their awakening.

Time

A picture book uses other means besides pictures to expand on the meaning of words. Take, for example, the concept of time in a picture book. If a picture book tells on page 3 that a child has lost his toy, and on page 4 that he found it after a year of searching, the reader will not feel that year's passage. The words "the toy has been lost for a year" do not take enough time to read or to listen to. If, however, the toy has been lost on page 3, and the picture book tells us on pages 4, 5, 6, 7, and 8 about the boy looking for it, and finally finding it on page 9, then we actually experience that length of time (**Figure 2**). Because the reader has participated in the search by turning the pages of the book, the search for a lost toy is no longer an abstract concept—it is a concrete physical experience. The turning of the pages has added weight to the meaning of the words.

Pauses

There is a close link between the physical makeup of a picture book and the natural pauses taken while reading it. When we read page 6 of a double spread consisting of pages 6 and 7, a short silence is naturally created as we move our eyes from page 6 to 7. When we turn page 7 to page 8 and the next double spread, the silence is longer, since it takes more time to turn the page than to move our eyes across the same double spread. As a result, a longer pause is established between one double spread and the next than between pages on the same double spread. This physical fact affects the silences between words and sentences, regardless of punctuation. It is important to take this aspect into consideration, as it dictates these silences in a natural way. Whereas in a story book periods and commas determine the pauses, in a picture book the pace of reading the words and the silences created by turning the pages must be in accord.

No "Loose" Threads

A picture book limits the number of themes it introduces and develops. But once introduced, no single thread is left loose at the end.

Ruth Krauss's *The Happy Day* introduces field mice, bears, snails, squirrels, and groundhogs. They all participate throughout the action of the story. By the end of the story none has been forgotten.

Margaret Wise Brown's *Goodnight Moon* introduces a room with various objects and creatures. The little rabbit in bed says goodnight to all of them, and adds:

Goodnight nobody—
Goodnight air
Goodnight noises everywhere

The rabbit forgets no one and even gives the reader more than expected. A picture book can give more than it promises, but never less. What it introduces in the beginning it must fully develop by the end. It must never disappoint the reader by presenting something and then dropping it capriciously.

Consistency

An early draft for one picture book by one author began this way:

1. Sara was a mean little girl.
2. She lay on the piano when her mother tried to play.
3. She pulled the end of her father's beard.
4. She chased the rabbits in the garden.
5. She hooted at the owls.
6. And nobody wanted to play with Sara because she was so mean.
7. One night the moon shone into Sara's dream and woke her up.

Through a series of images, lines 1 to 6 introduce Sara. But the action of the story begins with line 7, after which we learn how Sara changed and stopped being mean. The images in lines 1 to 6 are exaggerated to emphasize Sara's meanness. But when in line 7 "the moon shone into Sara's dream and woke her up," we enter into fantasy, because the same moon, which is "real" and outside her dream, cannot shine into her dream. It is inconsistent with the code of the story, which has only exaggerated reality so far.

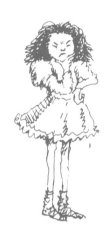

In later drafts the author changed line 7 to read: "One night the moon shone into Sara's room and woke her up." But in the end she preferred: "Sara saw the moon in her dream and woke up." This sentence was closer to her original idea; now the moon appears *in* the dream and thus is not inconsistent with reality.

What happens in a picture book is motivated from within by the elements of the story and should not be dictated by the author. Let the characters take on a life of their own and lead the story to a conclusion that is consistent with their inner dynamics.

Simple Words

When a picture book has words, they must tell the story with utmost simplicity. In *Mine's the Best*, Crosby Bonsall achieves an ease of storytelling with very unsophisticated words:

"Mine is the best."
"It is not. Mine is."
"Mine has more spots."
"It does not. Mine has."

Sometimes, however, "difficult" words—not commonly used in everyday speech—can be used in a picture book and be clear to children. In *Rain Rain Rivers* I used such words to describe waves:

Waves billow and roll,
Rush, splash and surge,
Rage, roar and rise.

The difficult words become clear to the reader in the context of the easier words—and the picture showing the waves (**Figure 3**).

Where the Wild Things Are uses words such as *rumpus* or *gnashed* ("The wild things roared their terrible roars and gnashed their terrible teeth"). Again, their meaning can be grasped in the context of the story and the pictures.

Word Images

Not only does a picture book make full use of pictures, but of word images as well. Simple, bold images are most effective. A visual image can be presented using very few words: "He was a mouse in a land of lions." A whole story is contained there. The image is vivid and concrete. Like a road sign seen at a glance, the situation and its implications are grasped instantly.

Abstract ideas can be made clear when expressed in images, as in this Japanese haiku poem by Sengai:

A white heron on snow is hard
to distinguish:
But the ravens—
How they stand out!

Show, don't tell.

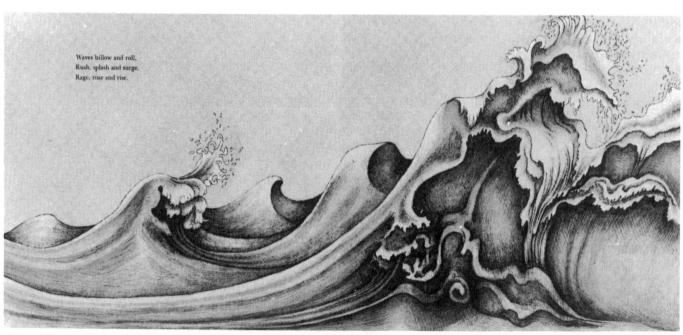

Waves billow and roll,
Rush, splash and surge,
Rage, roar and rise.

Rhythm and Repetition

In *The Happy Day* Ruth Krauss draws this picture with words:

> The field mice are sleeping,
> the bears are sleeping,
> the little snails sleep in their shells;
> and the squirrels sleep in the trees,
> the groundhogs sleep in the ground.

These five short lines are filled with repetition: various animals are all doing the same thing—sleeping—in various places. But the repetition is enjoyable because it creates a rhythm and contains variety. The lines combine sameness with diversity; although field mice, bears, snails, squirrels, and groundhogs are all animals, they are different kinds of animals. The sameness creates familiarity and the diversity, novelty. The familiarity induces reassurance and the novelty, interest. The repetition also helps the reader to understand the content. The balance of sameness and diversity has a function similar to that of the static and dynamic elements in a picture sequence.

The Happy Day also conveys movement by the simplest means.

> They sniff. They run.
> They run. They sniff.
> They sniff. They run. They stop.

The short, repeated sentences set up a satisfying rhythm. In another example—M. B. Goffstein's *Brookie and Her Lamb*—the rhythmic, vigorous prose is also very effective:

> Brookie taught the lamb to sing
> and he had a very good voice
> but all he could sing was, Baa baa baa
> so she taught him how to read
> and all he could read was, Baa baa baa
> but she loved him anyhow.

Sound and Rhyme

Margaret Wise Brown's *Goodnight Moon* opens with: "In the great green room." These words tempt the reader to say them aloud, for they are enjoyable both to speak and to listen to. This quality occurs throughout the book:

> And a comb and a brush and a bowl
>   full of mush
> And a quiet old lady who was whisper-
>   ing "hush."

Although *Goodnight Moon* uses many phrases that rhyme, some of them do not. This casual approach to rhyming leads to a less rigid and more playful kind of storytelling:

> Goodnight room
> Goodnight moon

Though lacking in rhyme, it still has rhythm.

Sound plays an important role in *Goodnight Moon*, *The Happy Day*, and *Where the Wild Things Are*, as it does in folk ballads and nursery rhymes:

> High diddle ding, did you hear the
>   bells ring?

[*or*]

> Lock the dairy door,
> Lock the dairy door!
> Chickle, chackle, chee,
> I haven't got a key!

"Chickle, chackle, chee" is fun to read. The sound is pleasing, even though the words don't represent objects or actions as words usually do. A similar use of sound occurs in *Hector Protector*, where Maurice Sendak adds sound to the pictures with both letters ("Sss-s," "Grr-r") and words ("Bow-wow").

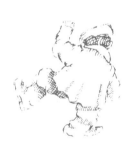

A picture book is like a musical score for reading aloud to a child who doesn't know how to read yet. The printed words in a picture book are intended not only to be seen and read, but to be spoken aloud as well. That is why it is important, as writer Jane Yolen advises, to "read each of your sentences aloud" while writing a picture book.

Rhyming can add extra enjoyment, but only if it is well done and sounds natural. It must not come before clarity of content. Poor rhyme interferes with the flow of expression and sacrifices meaning for the sake of phrase endings. The awkward phrasing in the example below unnecessarily complicates the simple content:

Three country mice came down for tea
To visit the gray turtle's home by
  the tree.
The three country mice
They said: "Indeed, how very nice."
But when the tea had begun,
Oh! How much fun!

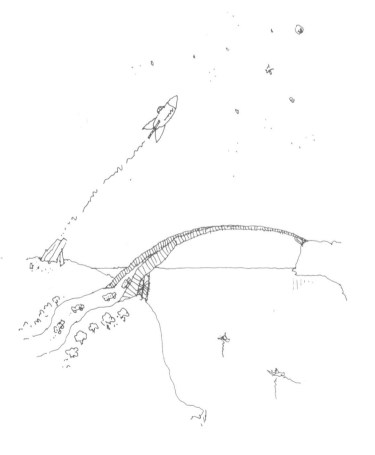

Explore Your Own Story

Read your story aloud and hear how it sounds. Enter into your own story as if it were concrete and real and everything in it were tangible. Explore it as you would a new country. Imagine that you are literally entering the world you are creating—look at it, feel it, touch it. This way you make sure everything in the story is clear and believable.

From the Familiar to the Unknown

A bridge spanning an abyss begins with a foundation on solid ground. A rocket launched into the unknown also begins its journey on familiar soil. Similarly, many stories begin with the familiar before proceeding to the unknown.

Max's room in *Where the Wild Things Are* is familiar. The room changes gradually into a forest, and as Max sails away on the ocean, the unfamiliarity increases. His journey into the unknown is over when he returns to his room.

One Monday Morning opens with city buildings, a familiar city scene. But the arrival of a king is unexpected. The daily growth of the king's retinue increases the unfamiliarity and the surprise.

When an unfamiliar situation consists of familiar components, it may be easier to follow. In *Hey, Diddle, Diddle* the cow and the moon are familiar so that, although the cow jumping over the moon is a surprise, we understand it.

This method of combining the familiar and the unknown is widely used in story books as well as picture books. The Russian tale *Soldier and Tsar in the Forest*—a story book—first describes a familiar relationship between two brothers. When the younger brother enters the army, the older brother—now a general—ignores and even punishes him. The young soldier runs away and goes to live in a wild forest. There he meets the tsar of Russia, who is alone and lost. It is no longer a familiar situation. The soldier, unaware of the tsar's true identity, saves his life and is later rewarded for his courage. This happy ending also makes the encounter with the unexpected reassuring.

The Visible and the Invisible

Let us imagine that we are flying over an ocean. We see a tiny island. But when we explore it from closer up an entirely different picture emerges. The tiny island turns out to be the tip of a huge mountain. Although you see only the small tip and not the large base, they are both part of the same mountain and are both equally there.

Just as the tip is an extension of the base, the obvious in a picture book stems from a broader, invisible base—the suggested. What you don't see affects what you do see. It is this relationship between the seen and the unseen that contributes to a good picture book. The whole picture, both the tip and the base of the mountain, have to be clear to you, for the unshown elements can be just as significant as those that are shown.

In *Where the Wild Things Are*, we never see Max's mother, but her effect on him is felt throughout. She cares about Max: she sends him to bed without supper when he makes mischief, but she also gives him supper when he comes back home. Although invisible, she is present through her effect on Max and through his reactions to her. Without the unseen mother, whose punishing and rewarding actions frame and motivate the story, Max's adventures might not have taken place at all.

Implied Philosophy

In every communication there is something unsaid that is as significant as what is said. Similarly, every story suggests a philosophy that is as significant as the story. This implied philosophy is made up of the ideas underlying the story—it is the invisible part of the story.

Imagine that the hero of one story prefers skating to learning because, in his opinion, it is more fun. He is discovered by a talent scout, who offers him a contract to perform in a show. But unfortunately, since our hero doesn't know how to sign his name—not to mention

how to read a contract—he must return to school and learn how to write. Although this story is well intentioned in that it shows the importance of knowing how to write, its implication is that learning is necessary but not enjoyable. Such an attitude may discourage some children from wanting to learn how to write.

The implied philosophy, like the unseen base of the mountain, is an integral part of the story. The author must be aware and work with everything the story says and everything it suggests. The quality of the story depends on it.

Showing a Way Out

When children are unhappy or feel misunderstood or discouraged, they may also feel helpless about doing anything to change their lives. To such children, a picture book can hold out hope that they *can* do something about their situation. To leave a child with a negative or cynical ending, without showing a way out, is needlessly discouraging.

When a fictional story ends unhappily, it is usually due to the author's choice rather than to any inevitability inherent to the story. Stories need a reassuring framework to ease the telling of distressing events. An author can suggest, without violating the story's integrity, other ways the situation could have been dealt with, or perhaps avoided. *The Tale of Peter Rabbit*, for instance, suggests a solution without spelling it out. The terrifying experience is Peter's doing—all he had to do to avoid it was heed his mother's advice. A child can learn from such an approach that not only do problems exist but solutions as well. Children take stories very seriously.

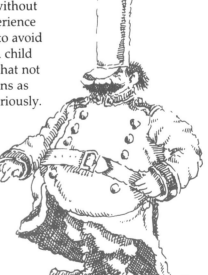

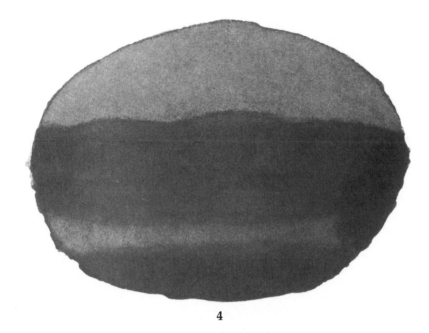

4

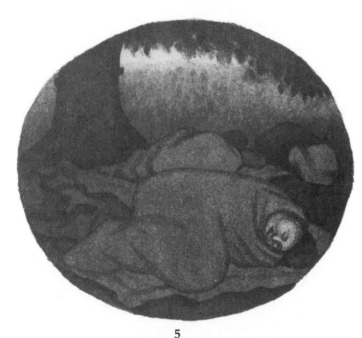

5

Content and Form

All the elements in a picture book—words and pictures, the visible and the invisible, content and form—must work together toward a common goal. How you say something—whether in words or pictures—is as important as what you say. It makes no sense to put a simple idea, fit for a picture book, into story book form. (Can you imagine *Hey, Diddle, Diddle* as a story book?) Let form be a product of content.

Applying Picture Book and Story Book Concepts

Chapter 1 raised the question: picture book or story book? It isn't that one is better than the other; they are merely *different*. In order to achieve the best results, it is essential that you understand each concept thoroughly and the difference between the two. Depending on what's best for your book, apply the picture book or story book concept, or combine the two.

In my book *Dawn*, for example, I used the picture book and story book concepts in different parts of the same book. Early in the book there is a picture of a mountain by a lake before dawn (**Figure 4**). The text reads simply: "Still." Without the picture, you would not know what "still" referred to. This is characteristic of the picture book concept.

Later, however, I describe how "Under a tree by a lake an old man and his grandson curl up in their blankets." The picture here shows them curled up in their blankets (**Figure 5**). This approach is characteristic of the story book concept. Although the words help guide the reader to where to focus in the picture, the words could be understood without the picture.

Ezra Jack Keats's *The Trip* is another book that combines the picture book and story book concepts. On page 6 the words are: "He taped a piece of colored plastic on the top of the box, and another piece on the end. He hung his plane from the top, and closed the box." The picture shows Louie closing the box, with the colored plastic on top, another at the end, and the plane hanging from the top. The text on page 7 reads: "Louie looked through the hole. WOW!" And we see him looking through the hole in the box. We can understand the action on pages 6 and 7 through the words alone. But the next spread shows what Louie saw in the box without any words at all (**Figure 6**).

To test whether a book uses a story book or picture book concept, see whether you can understand the words without the pictures and whether the pictures are merely showing what can be understood by the words alone. "Under a tree . . .," in its context, is enough for the reader to get a fairly accurate mental picture of the subject; whereas with "Louie looked through the hole. WOW!" it is not clear what he saw without the picture. Every page can be examined in this fashion to see which concept has been applied.

Applying the picture book concept can be especially helpful in simplifying the text, even when the book is not, strictly speaking, a picture book. With *Dawn*, for instance, part of my first rough draft, jotted down spontaneously one night in diary fashion, went like this:

4 A.M. By the window:
Stillness—nothing moves. Sky is light and clear. Moon is out. Landscape is dark and still. It's cold and damp. I curl up like a fetus. In the east, five stars and the moon. Stillness—nothing moves. A feeling of eternity, as if the night will never end. Moon shining over rocks and an occasional leaf. A light breeze. I am in the cradle of nature, in its womb. Stripes of dark trees. Everything is one dark mass.

4:45 A.M. By the lake:
Eastern sky: light blue appearing—the announcer of dawn. Water is light blue. Vapors rise from water. Sky is pure clear blue and still. Frogs jump into water. A lonely bat is flying in circles over water. Sky and water—same color. Phosphorescence of water. A glow. One bird sings, calls. Silence. Then another. Silhouette of trees, light blue peeping through. Water is smooth, still, like a mirror. A star is still seen. Light blue of dawn brings forth yellow-ish-orange-gold, as if coming from electric bulb. The whole sky is lighter. White flowers start glowing in the shadows, reflecting the coming light. Water—mirrorlike, still. Occasional

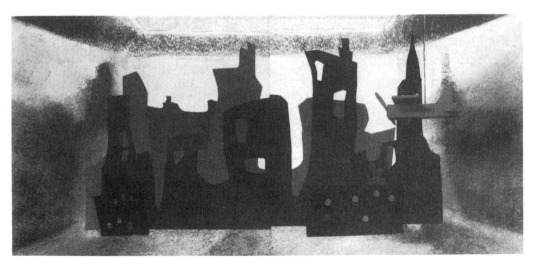

6

slight ripple. Vapors rising from water like geysers. Reflections of shadows in water lightening, to light gray. Landscape becoming greener (from noncolor), reflections in water becoming greener too. Vapors glowing, cotton, phosphorus, water light, silver blue. Gold in eastern sky, serene. Moon is still out. Mountains are blue. Cotton vapors between layers of mountains. Patches of green. Frogs jumping into water, points of moving insects. . . . Vapors moving, hovering, walking over waters . . .

The final version as it appears in the book was reached by eliminating repetitions and inessential details, substituting drawn pictures for written descriptions, and communicating silence and slowness through pauses between new lines or different pages. Throughout, I organized details in a consistent progression to reveal the gradual transition from darkness to the reawakening of nature with the coming of dawn. I also introduced an old man and his grandson so

the story would have two central characters with whom the reader could identify. In the end the first part of the text reads:

> Quiet.
> Still.
> It is cold and damp.
> Under a tree by the lake
> an old man and his grandson
> curl up in their blankets.
> The moon lights a rock, a branch,
>   an occasional leaf.
> The mountain stands guard, dark
>   and silent.
> Nothing moves.
> Now, a light breeze.
> The lake shivers.
> Slowly, lazily, vapors start to rise.
> A lonely bat circles in silence.
> A frog jumps.
> Then another.
> A bird calls.
> Another answers.

At the end of the next chapter, we'll see how the pictures and the words work together and how the story develops as you read the book.

A similar process of elimination went on when I wrote the text for *The Treasure*. The progressive stages of *The Treasure*'s opening went like this:

> *Version 1*: A long time ago in Cracow, there was a man whose name was Rabbi Eisik.
> *Version 2*: A long time ago there was a man in Cracow, and his name was Rabbi Eisik (Isaac).
> *Version 3*: A long time ago, in a different land, there was a man and his name was Isaac.

Since the pictures were going to show the period—the eighteenth century—the words "a long time ago" weren't necessary, and I removed them in a later version. The mention of Cracow was not essential to the universal content of the story, so I also left it out. Not mentioning Cracow specifically lifted possible limitations, but drawing the city accurately enriched the book (**Figure 7**).

I changed the hero's name to Isaac, since it is pronounced in the same way as

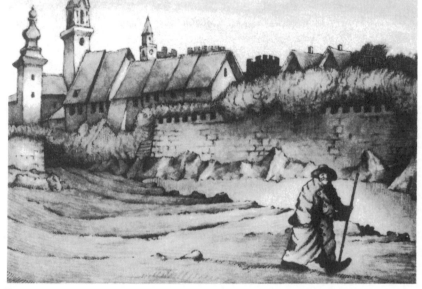

7

Eisik and is more recognizable. I also took out the title "Rabbi" because it was not meant as an occupation, but merely as a respectful way of addressing the hero. Leaving out the title "Rabbi" also made the story more universal by removing an inessential ethnic distinction.

The final version of *The Treasure*'s opening sentence reads: "There once was a man and his name was Isaac." By deciding to show the specific setting and ethnic tradition of this story through pictures instead of words, I gave myself more freedom to stress the universal content of the story while still including its particular ethnic flavor.

The story tells of Isaac's dream of a treasure and his long journey to a distant city to find it. Later in the book, after Isaac has reached the distant city, one of my early versions went like this:

> The captain of the guard had been watching him. The captain in spite of his fierce mustache (was) seemed a kindly man.
>
> Finally the captain asked what he was doing.
>
> Isaac told him of the dream that brought him on this long journey. The captain laughed.

The description of the captain is shown in the picture (**Figure 8**). His fierce mustache and friendly face did not need to be repeated in words. Isaac's long journey is shown graphically earlier so it did not need to be repeated either. As a result, the final version became:

> One day, the captain of the guards asked him, "Why are you here?"
>
> Isaac told him the dream. The captain laughed.

In these examples you can see how applying the picture book concept—eliminating descriptions in words and presenting them instead through pictures—condenses and simplifies the text.

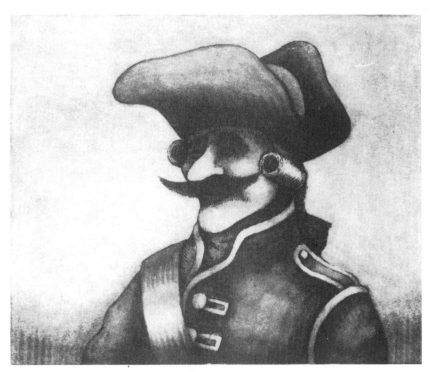

8

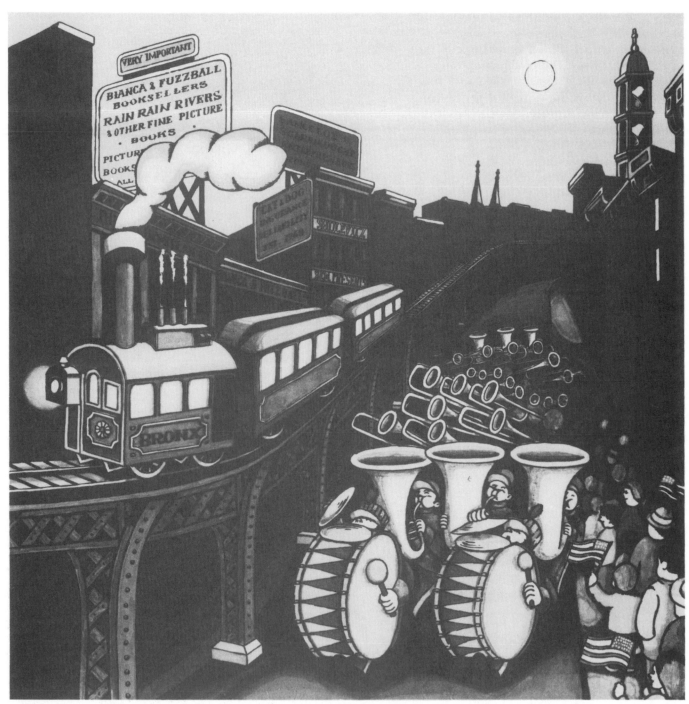

From *Oh What a Noise!*

Part Two Planning the Book

If a book comes from the heart, it will contrive to reach other hearts.

Carlyle

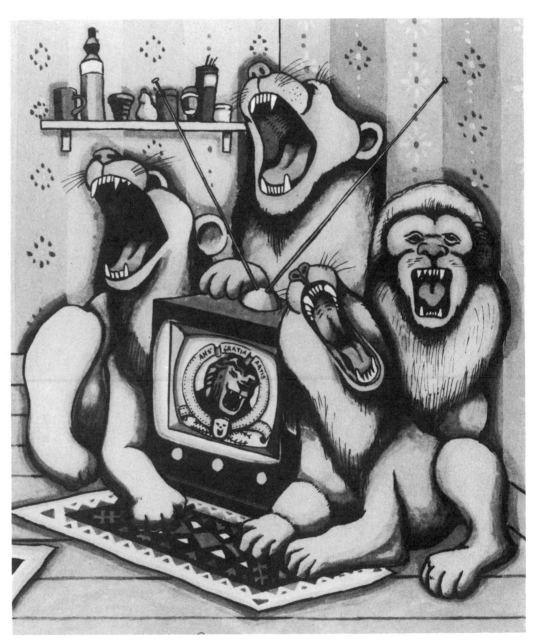

From *Oh What a Noise!*

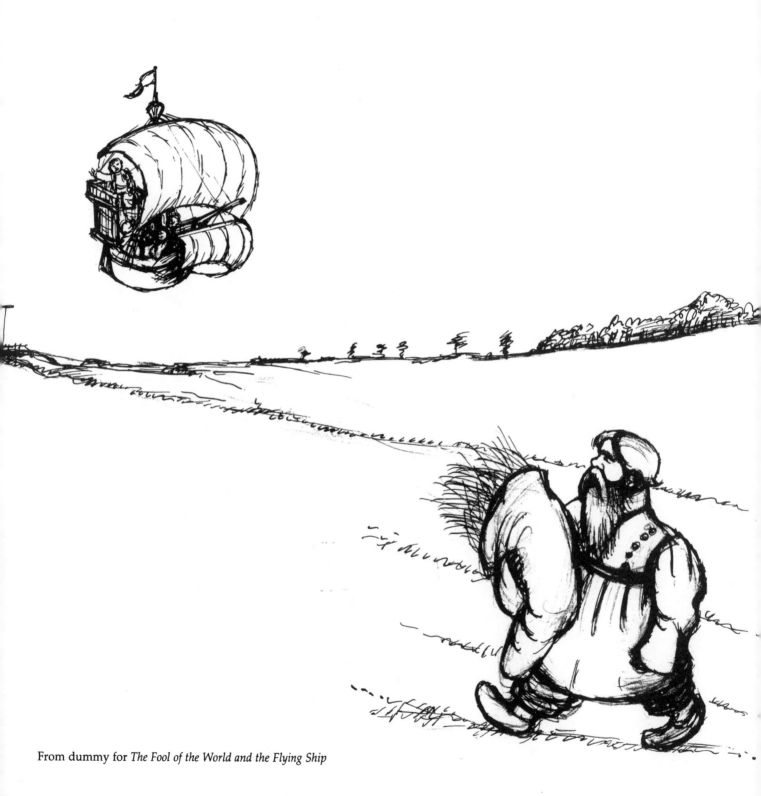

From dummy for *The Fool of the World and the Flying Ship*

6. Storyboard and Book Dummy

Without emotion art is lifeless, without intellect it is shapeless.

Charles Johnson

An outstanding picture book is a result of both spontaneity and careful planning. The tools for planning such a book are the storyboard and book dummy. The storyboard gives you a bird's eye view of the whole book: it shows all the pages of the book, greatly reduced, on a single sheet of paper. The book dummy, on the other hand, is a preliminary model of the book—with the same number of pages, either the same size or smaller.

A rough book dummy is sometimes shown to an editor or art director to help them decide if they want to publish your book, or to give them a better idea of how you conceive it, or how your project is progressing. But this is not its chief purpose. The storyboard and book dummy are primarily *thinking* tools for the author-illustrator.

Putting together the storyboard and book dummy is a necessary process—it is the foundation for your book and lies at the heart of good bookmaking. It is also enjoyable because it allows you to watch the book take shape. The thinking and planning that go into a storyboard and dummy will guide and affect the pictures, design, and mood of the completed book.

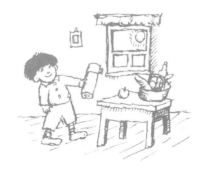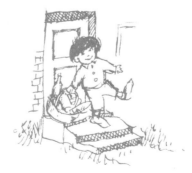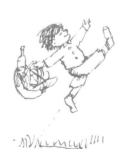

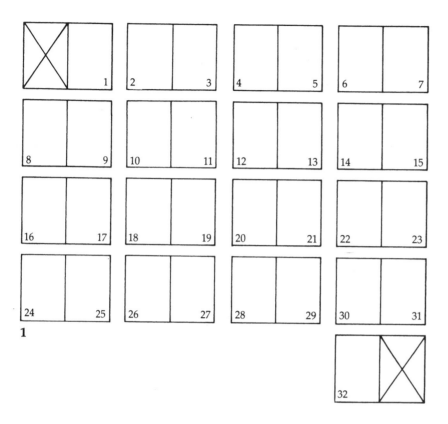

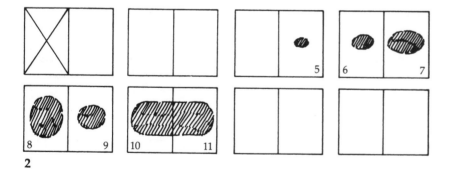

How to Make a Storyboard

Before a house is built, the architect draws a plan of the house. Similarly, in creating a book, the illustrator first draws a plan—the storyboard.

The storyboard is a two-dimensional model, with all the pages of the book laid out on one piece of paper. You can see the whole book at a glance, how each page relates to another and the whole. This overview of the entire book facilitates the planning of the main visual elements.

To make a storyboard, take a sheet of paper and draw postage-size rectangles on it to represent all the pages of the book. Remember that, except for the first and last pages, the reader will see the book as a series of double spreads—that is, pairs of facing pages. Therefore, your storyboard must also be divided into double spreads. As you can see in **Figure 1,** each larger rectangle is divided into two smaller ones.

Now mark the page numbers clearly below the appropriate rectangles. Because books always begin on a right-hand page, cross out the left-hand side of the first spread and begin on the right with page 1. Books always end on a left-hand page, so there the right side is crossed out.

In planning a picture book, stick with 32 pages whenever possible, as this is the length most publishers prefer. If 32 pages is not long enough, you can expand to 48 pages. On the other hand, if 32 pages is too long for your story, you can shorten this by using each double spread as if it were a single page, thus reducing the number of illustrations by about half.

Actually you don't have 32 pages for your story. The first two to four pages in a picture book are used to convey necessary information, called front matter. These pages contain the book title, the names of the author and/or illustrator, the publisher's name and location, the copyright notice, and sometimes a dedication or a brief author's note. Leave the first four pages blank for now and begin the story on page 5. If you are pressed for space, you can begin on page 3, but the book will look more attractive if the full four pages are used for front matter.

Taking a Bird's Eye View

The storyboard allows you to approach the book as though you were viewing it from a great distance and could see only the larger elements. You can even view the entire book as if it were one picture made up of smaller units—the double spreads.

A good way to begin is with the large elements—concentrate on the overall idea and visual concept. Sketch out the entire book with very rough black-and-white drawings, and avoid getting distracted by details or by color. Preoccupation with detail, color, and a polished appearance at the beginning stages is detrimental. It is easier and more efficient to think about one aspect of the book at a time, such as overall design, visual movement, and rhythm.

Figure 2. These four double spreads are from one of many storyboards I made for *Dawn* in order to determine the shape and size of each picture in relation to the page and to the other pictures. My aim was to establish an overall pattern and rhythm through the increasing size of the pictures. At this point I concentrated only on shape and size, without going into the

content of the pictures at all. On pages 5–7 the oval grows larger. Then, on page 8, the oval changes to a vertical oval, with page 9 showing a smaller version. Finally, on pages 10–11, the oval expands to a double spread.

Figure 3. In this more developed storyboard for *Dawn*, it becomes clear how the design of the ovals works with the pictures and the telling of the story. On pages 5–7 we gradually see more of the landscape as the oval grows larger. On page 8 we move in close on the tree in the scene, while page 9 zooms in on the figures under the tree. Then, as the oval spreads across pages 10–11, we pull back and see the entire scene. In the final version—discussed at the end of this chapter—the basic design and flow of the pictures remain the same.

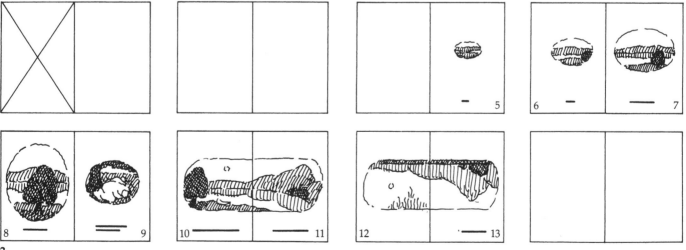

3

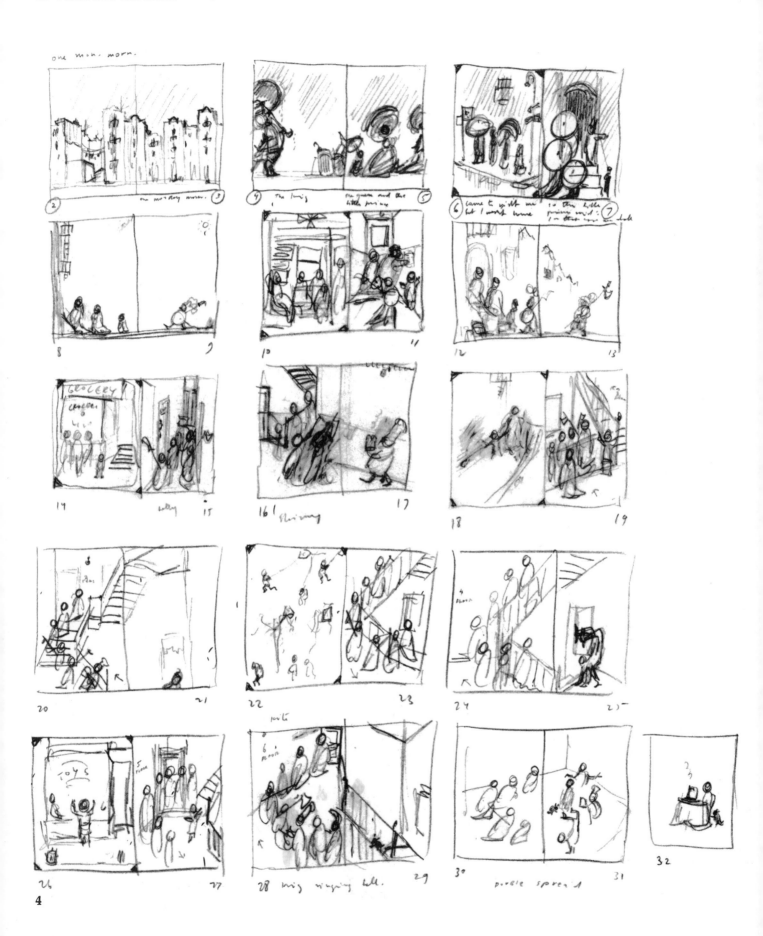

Figure 4. In this early storyboard for *One Monday Morning* the drawings are quite rough but readable. They are a means of visualizing the story. By focusing on the essential visual aspects and avoiding detail, I could see at a glance how the pictures worked together. Many elements were later changed.

Creating Visual Movement

Because the storyboard shows you all the pages together, it helps you to observe their overall visual pattern. You can plan the general progression of the double spreads and the visual movement of the book.

Figure 5. These six double spreads from *The Twelve Dancing Princesses* show the broad movement and design of the illustrations. In the story it is a mystery where the princesses go every night and why the soles of their shoes are worn out every morning. On pages 14–15 the text describes how the princesses jump out of bed every night and dress in their finest gowns. The design of this double spread guides the eye diagonally from the top left to the bottom right-hand corner. Page 16 picks up from that corner of page 15 and guides the eye up in an arc and then plunges it down again, while the text describes the descent of the princesses into a magical underground world.

Pages 18–19 and 20–21 constitute one sweep broken down into two double spreads, depicting the continuation of the underground journey. The shape at the edge of page 19 is a tree, divided in the middle—the other half appears on page 20, emphasizing the connection between the two spreads. At the end of their long walk, the princesses come to a lake, where twelve small boats are waiting for them. Pages 22–23 and 24–25 depict the progress of their boat ride, moving in a diagonal from the bottom left to the top right-hand corner. In these two spreads the direction of the action is away from the viewer, up and up, until the princesses reach their destination—a brilliantly lit castle (which is reflected in the water at the edge of page 25).

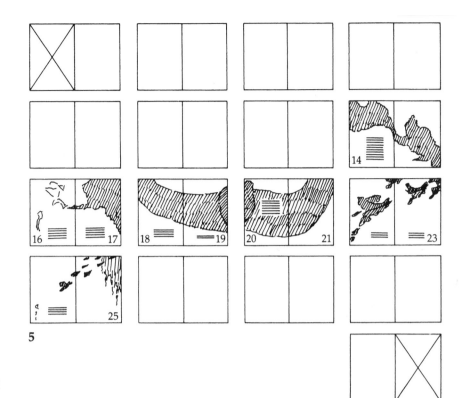

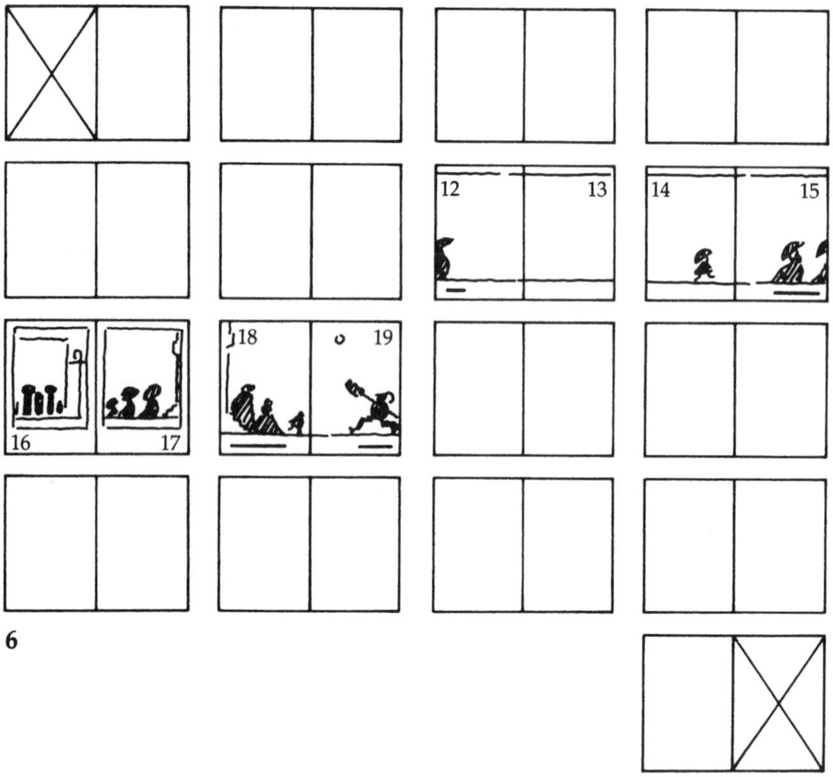

6

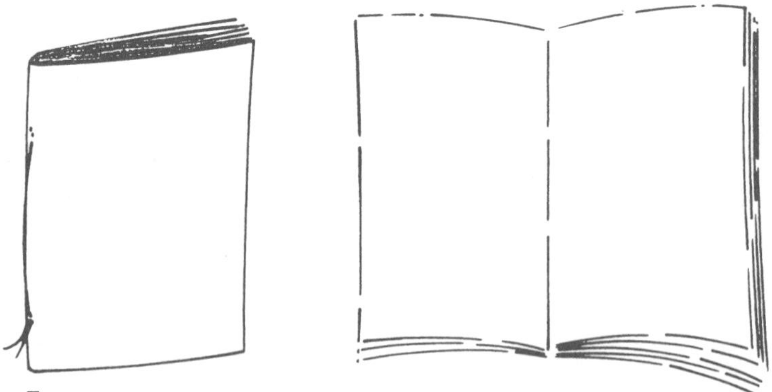

7

Checking the Rhythm

By seeing the book as a unified visual entity, you can also review and improve its rhythmic pattern. You may, for instance, decide to change the size and shape of the pictures, or the "visual beats" created by the main elements.

Figure 6. Simplifying the elements in my storyboard for *One Monday Morning* made me more aware of the rhythm, which was especially important since the story is based on a rhythmic song. On pages 12–13, the king is moving into the picture, but only half of him can be seen. Pages 14–15 show the other half of the king, followed by two other figures—the queen and the little prince. The transition between these two spreads suggests movement and the ground covered by the king and the two figures. If we think of the king on pages 12–13 as one visual "beat," then pages 14–15 have three beats, each represented by a figure. Placing the second and third figures (or beats) farther apart than the first and second creates not only a greater visual distance, but also a longer rhythmic pause between them.

Pages 16 and 17 show two contrasting pictures. On page 16 the figures are stationary, and from the words we learn that the hero of the story was not at home for the royal visit. On page 17, however, the movement of pages 14–15 continues. It is now Tuesday, and the king, the queen, and the little prince have returned. Pages 18–19 reverse the direction of the movement and add a new figure, increasing the number of beats to four. The increasing number of visual beats reflect the additional days on which the characters come back to look for the hero. Thus, rhythm is an integral part of the action.

Seeing Similarities and Differences

Once the storyboard is done, you can readily see the similarities and differences between the most outstanding components of the pictures. Although this may seem similar to what we have discussed, it is slightly different. You can decide, for instance, if there is too much repetition between pictures, or not enough. The storyboard also permits you to recognize static and dynamic elements easily. You may ask, for example: What differences do you want? When does sameness help the story, and when is some variation needed?

How to Make a Book Dummy

Like the architect, the illustrator also makes a three-dimensional model—a dummy with the same number of pages as the printed book. This dummy immediately conveys how the book will read when printed. Turning the pages allows you to experience the story's progression and the pages' relation to each other as the reader will.

To make a dummy, staple or sew 8 sheets of white paper together in the middle and then fold them in half to make a 32-page booklet (**Figure 7**). (For a 48-page book dummy, use 12 sheets of paper.) Mark the page numbers clearly on *both* sides of each leaf, from 1 to 32. The dummy's usefulness depends on the correct and clearly marked sequence of pages—otherwise, you cannot accurately evaluate the relation of one page to another.

Thumbnail Dummy

A thumbnail dummy is smaller than the actual book will be—the pages may be 3 by 4 inches, or even smaller. It may have the same proportions as the final book, but this is not necessary. A rough, thumbnail dummy is useful because its small size compels the artist to concentrate on the essentials of the pictures without being sidetracked by details.

Using the storyboard as a guide, prepare the entire dummy with rough black-and-white sketches. While drawing, imagine that you are seeing the printed book. When this is done, read your dummy as the reader will the book and make the necessary adjustments.

The distribution of words on their proper pages shows how they relate to the pictures—something you can't see so well in the storyboard, where all the text is on a single page. Alternating between storyboard and dummy, you can work out the best progression of pages, constantly changing and revising. The joy of these two planning aids is that they enable you to see and to test your future book while it is being conceived.

Figure 8. Here is a spread from one of the rough thumbnail dummies I made for *One Monday Morning*. The drawings are done roughly, to show essentials—they need only be readable. It is a kind of *functional* thinking: the intent is not to make a finished picture, but rather to put down the basic idea so that you can see where you are and determine where you want to go.

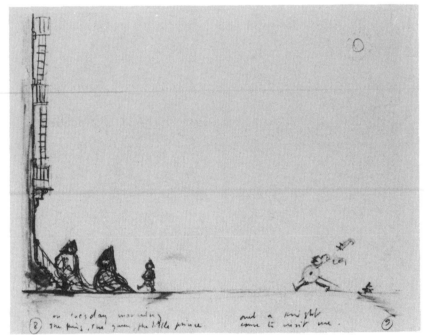

8

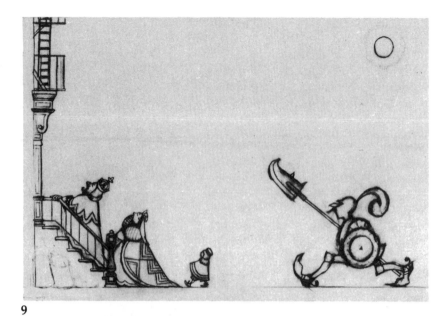

9

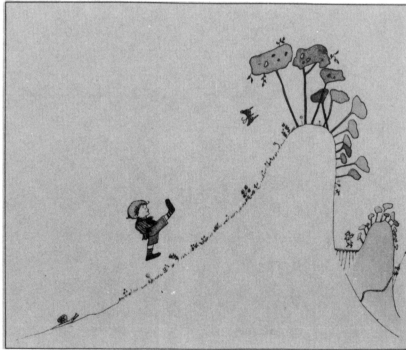

10

Actual-Size Dummy

An actual-size dummy is the same size and has the same proportions as the final book. If the final book will measure 8 by 10 inches, so should this dummy. With the actual-size dummy, you can get as close as possible to the finished book, short of seeing the final product itself. It allows you to visualize the book and experience it as the reader will when turning its pages. With this dummy you get the feel of the book in its entirety and the details that make up the whole.

Actual-size book dummies may be executed with rough sketches or with finished ones. Some artists make their dummies quite finished-looking for their own visualization or for presentation to an editor. As a beginner, I felt the need to produce a finished dummy to compensate for my lack of experience, and I took the dummy as close as possible to the finished book. Arnold Lobel, however, sees a danger in expending too much creative energy on an excessively finished-looking dummy. He feels it can make the preparation of the final art anticlimactic, with the result that the art loses the vitality of the original sketches.

Figure 9. In this spread from my actual-size dummy for *One Monday Morning*, the sketch from the rough thumbnail (Figure 8) has been elaborated. The figures have been enlarged in relation to the building, for instance. Even though this drawing was quite finished, I still made a few more changes as I prepared the final version.

Figure 10. Because *Charley Sang a Song* was an early book I illustrated, I felt the need to make a finished dummy. This picture is almost the same as the final picture, while in later books the dummy was a *stage* in the progression from idea to finished book.

Figures 11–14. In preparing the illustrations for *Hanukah Money* (a story book), I did several actual-size drawings, starting with a rough pencil sketch and progressively clarifying the image I wanted. Figure 11 shows the first step: a bold statement of the main elements. Figure 12

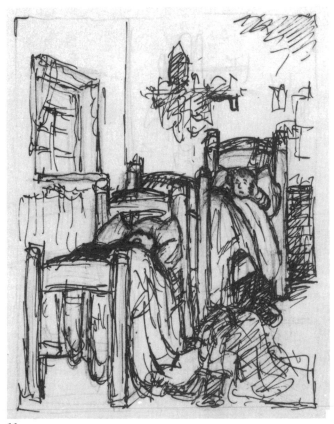

11

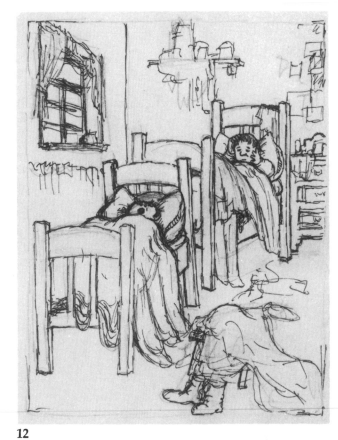

12

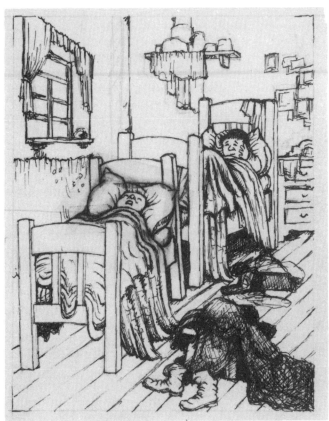

13

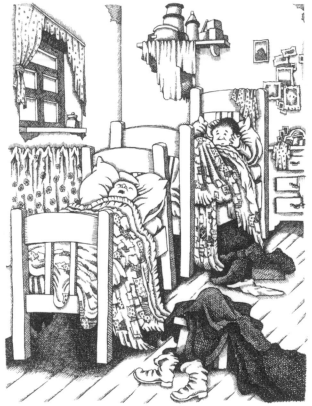

14

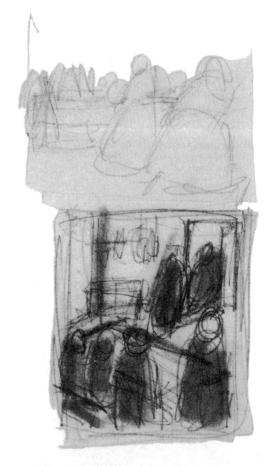

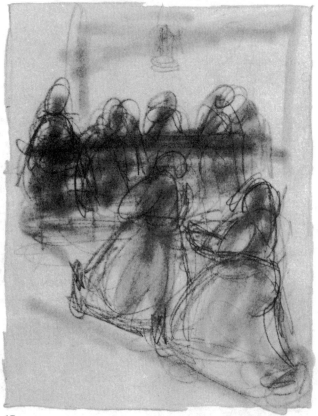

is an intermediary step. One change here involved moving the beds slightly deeper into the picture and away from the viewer. With the final dummy sketch—Figure 13—a lot more detail was added, but this was still a working sketch. Only in the final line drawing for reproduction—Figure 14—did I put in small details like the patches on the quilts.

From Rough to Finished Sketches

Like the storyboard, the rough dummy is seen as if from a distance; you can see the overall composition with its larger elements, but cannot make out the details. You perceive them as you come closer; as you progress from rough to finished sketches, you introduce and sharpen the details until everything in the picture is clearly defined.

Figure 15. In these very rough, preliminary sketches for another illustration in *Hanukah Money* only the large elements are shown. The figures are simple shapes. The emphasis is on the overall composition.

Figure 16. Here I began to explore the possibilities of the sketch at the lower left of Figure 15. You can see how the view sharpens as the previous sketch begins to come into focus. Specific items of furniture emerge and the forms become more human.

Figure 17. Now the view moves even closer. If you look at the men at the table or the women with the trays, you can see their features and the beginning indications of character.

Figure 18. The focus here has been sharpened a little more. There are also subtle changes in the composition. The man in front, for instance, is now looking in a different direction.

Figure 19. With this drawing, I made a major change. I wasn't satisfied with the composition and decided to shift the position of the door and the direction of the women carrying the food. By drawing this possibility—instead of simply thinking of it—I could actually see the effect.

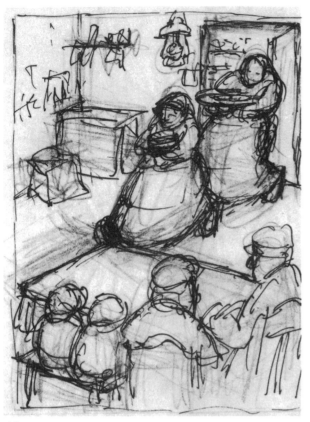

16

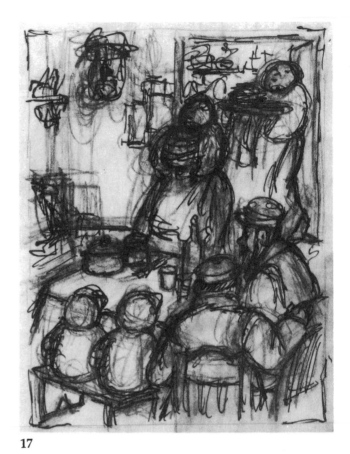

17

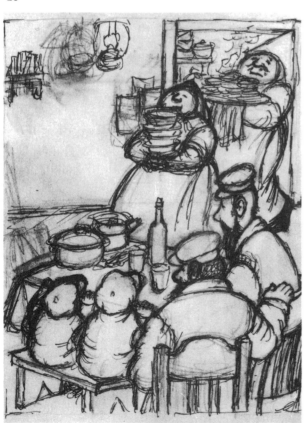

18

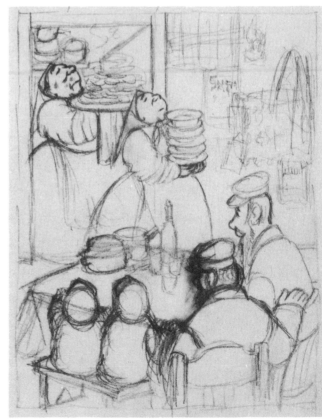

19

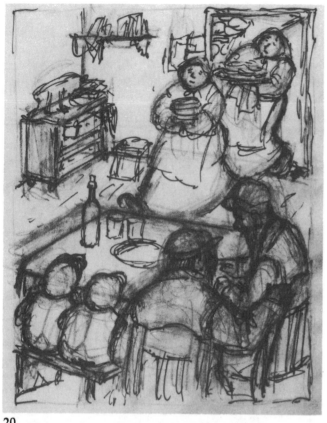

20

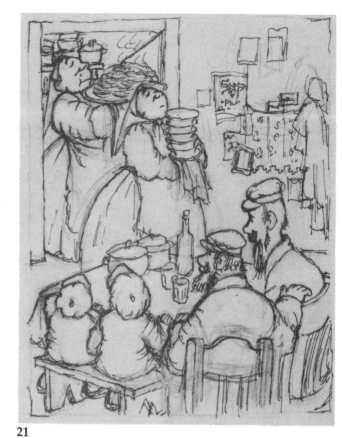

21

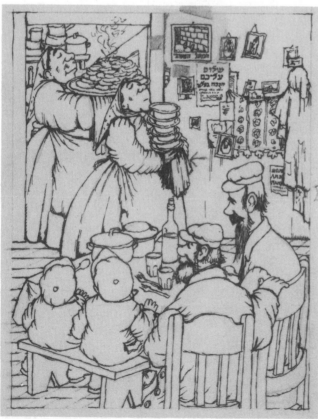

22

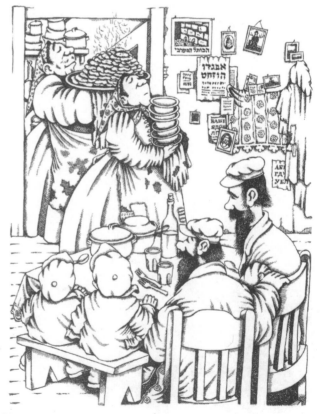

23

Figure 20. Drawing for a dummy is a concrete way of testing out different possibilities. It is hard to know the visual impact of a change unless you can see it. Here I went back to my conception in Figure 18, but I used the perspective of Figure 16. I also turned the two men at the bottom toward each other so that they appear to be conversing.

Figure 21. This composition worked best in terms of the effect I wanted. The scene is more compact, with less space than the one in Figure 20. As a result, the picture has a more intimate, homey feeling, in keeping with the story.

Figure 22. In this, the final dummy version, I focused in on the scene and added many details. If you look from Figure 19 to Figure 21 to this drawing, it is as if you were moving from far away to up close. The image becomes sharper and sharper.

Figure 23. The final line drawing for the printer brings everything into focus. It is here that finishing touches, like the men's dark hair or the women's patterned scarves, were added.

Working Procedure

Creating a picture book presents the same problems as composing a painting: how to arrange the parts into a whole. The storyboard and book dummy complement each other and allow you to transform all the pages into a unified book. Different authors, however, use these tools in different ways.

Arnold Lobel, for example, begins by making very rough, postage-size squares, storyboard style, which only he can read. They enable him to get a tangible feel for the text breakdown from page to page. From there he moves on to make the sketches. Then he makes a "flat" dummy, consisting of double spreads, by tracing his sketches onto sheets of white paper. From this dummy he goes on to make the finished art.

Jose Aruego also begins by making a rough storyboard. He shows this to his editor, who is familiar with his work. He then blows up the rough drawings of the storyboard with an enlarging machine (a "Lucy") and makes the final art. When Aruego first entered the field of illustration, however, he made actual-size dummies that looked very finished.

M. B. Goffstein, on the other hand, does something rare among illustrators: she visualizes her dummy in her mind, without actually making one. She then does the finished art and makes photocopies of it for a dummy, which she shows to an editor.

My own working procedure has changed since I first began illustrating books. For my first book I made several actual-size, finished dummies; for subsequent books I made small, rough dummies and storyboards only. Generally, I like to make as many storyboards and small, rough dummies as necessary and go back and forth from one to another as I plan the book. I prefer to start by making a storyboard, however, and I recommend that beginners start this way too.

Sometimes, after having made a storyboard and a rough thumbnail dummy for my own use, I paste down the final sketches (or photocopies of them) with masking tape onto an actual-size dummy to show to the editor or the designer. In any case, I find that a readable dummy is the most helpful tool for communicating how you see the book. For picture books, which rely so much on the visual aspect, some editors require it before giving you a contract. They also want to see how you are progressing. On many occasions, I show my dummies to the editor to convey how I envision the book. The editor can then give me criticism, which in turn enables me to go back and work on my book idea further.

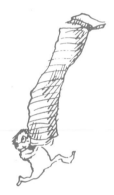

From Words to Dummy in Story Books

When you conceive your own *picture book* visually, you put it directly into dummy format—that is, you actually write the words on their respective pages while visualizing the pictures. When this has been done, a few changes or adjustments may be needed to perfect the words, and to make sure they are on the most suitable pages and the text divisions are natural.

On the other hand, when you illustrate a *story book* that is already in manuscript form, it is necessary to organize the words into a dummy format. In this case, it is appropriate to use an actual-size dummy, because you need enough space to paste down the words. (For picture books it is best to follow the method described above, but if you have written the words in manuscript form, you can follow the same steps as for a story book, but apply the picture book concept.)

Before you begin dividing the text, read it until you understand it thoroughly. Grasp the tone and the mood of the story. Live with the words for a while and let them sink in. Read them both silently and aloud. Try to visualize them; see the pictures inherent in them.

As you get to know the text, you will begin to see its structure. You will discover that it consists of units and sub-units. A unit may be a complete situation, scene, or tableau. The words describing it may suggest natural pauses that will allow readers to catch their breath. Subunits, the shorter units within the larger units, can bring out the meaning or emphasize the drama of a scene. Listen for those natural pauses and divide the text accordingly. This will help ensure that your breakdown of the text into pages is the best possible, and it will help you make better decisions about what to illustrate.

Once you have worked out your basic divisions, you then create an actual dummy. To do this, cut up the typed manuscript and attach the units or subunits to the appropriate pages of the dummy. Be sure to cut up and attach the text to the dummy pages in a way that allows you to make changes if necessary. You may have to move the words back and forth until the division and progression of the text make sense. At this point, however, if any adjustments are necessary, it is unlikely they will be arbitrary because you already have a thorough understanding of the text. This understanding makes the text breakdown more likely to be an outgrowth of its own structure, rather than an imposition from without.

Your dummy serves as a guide in planning the book. If better ideas come up in subsequent stages, you can adjust and improve once more. You may discover later on that you are unable to keep your initial subdivisions of the text; you may have to make additional changes so that the words are in accord with the dummy. This decision, however, will have been reached through an approach to the whole book and not merely as a matter of whim or convenience.

This is how I broke down the beginning of *The Treasure* into pages. Compare this breakdown—which shows sequential progression—to the way the story reads when it is placed on a single page. Notice the difference in the way it reads when pauses are created by dividing the text into pages.

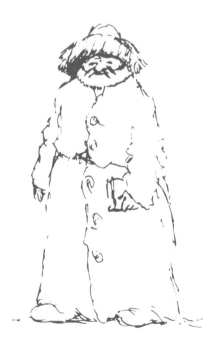

The Treasure

There once was a man and his name was Isaac. He lived in such poverty that again and again he went to bed hungry. One night, he had a dream. In his dream, a voice told him to go to the capital city and look for a treasure under the bridge by the Royal Palace. "It is only a dream," he thought when he woke up, and he paid no attention to it. The dream came back a second time. And Isaac still paid no attention to it. When the dream came back a third time, he said, "Maybe it's true," and so he set out on his journey.

	There once was a man and his name was Isaac.

5

He lived in such poverty that again and again he went to bed hungry.	(picture)

6   7

One night, he had a dream.	In his dream, a voice told him to go to the capital city and look for a treasure under the bridge by the Royal Palace. "It is only a dream," he thought when he woke up, and he paid no attention to it.

8   9

The dream came back a second time. And Isaac still paid no attention to it.	When the dream came back a third time, he said, "Maybe it's true," and so he set out on his journey.

10   11

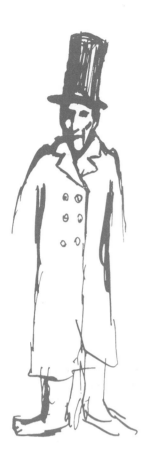

The divisions and subdivisions in the text will help you visualize the content. Look for the most crucial or dramatic elements of the story; they will tell you what to illustrate, and a natural division of the text will follow.

My decisions about where to break the text affected the way I illustrated *The Magician*. The first eleven pages of the book are actually only a lengthy introduction to the main action of the story.

Page 5. These words constitute a complete unit, introducing the magician. A pause is natural here.

Pages 6–7. There could have been a pause after "He was traveling on foot," but there was a space problem—it would have meant adding a page to the book. Also, it was not as crucial to break the text here as it was to give the dramatic line on page 11 a page to itself: "Yet he looked poor and hungry." And since the seven lines on page 6 do work together, I decided to keep them all on the same page.

The first three lines on page 7 constitute a subunit; space permitting, it could have been on a page by itself. But for the same reason that I combined the lines on page 6, I opted for including the whole unit, which calls for a longer pause than the subunit. Thus, combining the seven lines on the same page emphasizes the drama of the magician's disappearance.

Pages 8–9. Lack of space also prompted me to combine two actions—"pulling ribbons out of his mouth and turkeys out of his boots"—on page 8. My solution was to depict the magician doing both actions at once—after all, if he can do one kind of magic, why not both at the same time?

Page 9 also has two actions: (1) the appearance and dance of the rolls and loaves of bread through the air, and (2) their disappearance. The first action is pictorial, but the second would have been most difficult to illustrate in a still picture. It was logical for the text to tell of both actions here: while the picture shows only the appearance of the bread, the words tell of their disappearance.

Pages 10–11. Page 10 prepares the reader for page 11. These two pages are the most dramatic part of the book so far and constitute the climax of the introduction to the action that will take place. It was very important to give these three lines their own double spread. If the sentence "Yet he looked poor and hungry" had not been surrounded by clear-cut pauses, both before and after, its dramatic impact would have diminished considerably.

Now try to visualize *The Magician* in dummy form, and imagine what effect turning its pages would have on the rhythm of reading it.

The Magician

One day a magician came to a small village. He was traveling on foot. "Where from?" the villagers asked. "Far away," the stranger replied. "Where to?" they wanted to know. "The big city," he said. "Then what are you doing here?" they asked. "I lost my way," he replied. He was an odd fellow. He was ragged and tattered, yet he wore a top hat. He gathered people around him on the street. One minute he was full of tricks and the next, he disappeared. Just like that. He pulled ribbons out of his mouth and turkeys out of his boots. He whistled, and rolls and loaves of bread danced through the air. He whistled again. Everything vanished! He scratched his shoe and there was a flood of gold coins. Yet he looked poor and hungry.

One day a magician came to a small village.

5

He was traveling on foot.
"Where from?" the villagers asked.
"Far away," the stranger replied.
"Where to?" they wanted to know.
"The big city," he said.
"Then what are you doing here?" they asked.
"I lost my way," he replied.

6

He was an odd fellow.
He was ragged and tattered, yet he wore a top hat.
He gathered people around him on the street.
One minute he was full of tricks and the next, he disappeared.
Just like that.

7

He pulled ribbons out of his mouth
and turkeys out of his boots.

8

He whistled, and rolls and loaves of bread danced through the air.
He whistled again.
Everything vanished!

9

He scratched his shoe and there was a flood of gold coins.

10

Yet he looked poor and hungry.

11

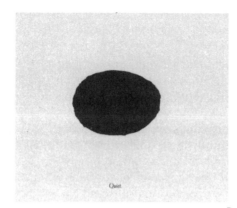

Quiet.

5

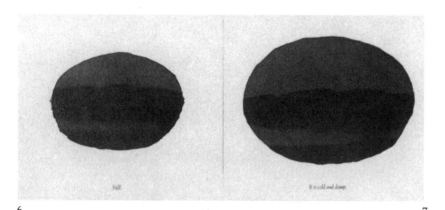

Still.

It is cold and damp.

6

7

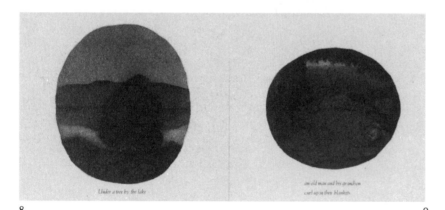

Under a tree by the lake.

an old man and his grandson
curl up in their blankets.

8

9

An Example of Planning

Dawn is an example of how important planning is to a picture book. The slightest inconsistency or deviation from its visual code would have distracted from the mood and feeling of the completed book.

The *visual code* of a book consists of the shape of the pictures; the way they are drawn; their mood, pace, and rhythm, plus any other visual means used by the artist. Established at the beginning of the book, the visual code should be adhered to consistently throughout.

In *Dawn*, for instance, the pictures are mostly oval in shape or derived from the oval. The horizontal page emphasizes both the calm of the ovals and the landscape depicted in them. The corners of the pictures are always rounded and the edges irregular, never angular or razor-sharp. Introducing a rectangular picture with sharp edges for no apparent reason would have contradicted the visual code of the book. Close attention was also paid to the relationship between the constant (static) and changing (dynamic) elements throughout.

The book opens with the words "Quiet. Still." The problem was how to portray quiet and a lack of movement without boring the reader. To depict this mood, static elements were necessary. But to keep the reader's interest, change and dynamic elements were also required. Whatever my solution, I had to make the art conform to the mood.

Pages 5–7. On these pages there are both static and dynamic elements, but I made them as subtle as possible in order not to introduce too much "visual noise." The static elements are the oval shapes of the pictures, the repetition of the same scene, and the horizontal stripes. A dynamic feeling is added by the ovals growing larger as the scene gradually comes into focus from picture to picture (similar to the way our vision increases as our eyes grow accustomed to the dark). In the third picture, a tree emerges as a result of the movement of our eyes over the landscape from left to right.

Pages 8–9. The tree becomes the center of attention on page 8. Focusing on the tree, we can start to discern figures, and we move closer to them on page 9. So far, nothing new has been added to the pictures; the only movement is that of the viewer discovering new facets of the same scene.

Pages 10–11. In this double spread the scene is fully established. As a result of the preceding pages, it is already familiar.

Pages 12–13. At this point I felt I could not continue to repeat the same scene without it becoming boring so I decided to show only the reflection in the water. It almost looks like the scene on pages 10–11 turned upside down. This constitutes a very dramatic change in the visual progression of the book, and it could have broken the quiet mood maintained so far. The shock of this drastic change, however, is softened by our familiarity with this scene from the preceding pages. As a result, this visual leap reads as a zooming in on the reflection.

Pages 14–15. The picture on pages 12–13 prepares the reader to recognize at once the subtle change on pages 14–15—caused by "a light breeze"—which otherwise might have gone unnoticed. This movement within the picture heralds a shift in pace.

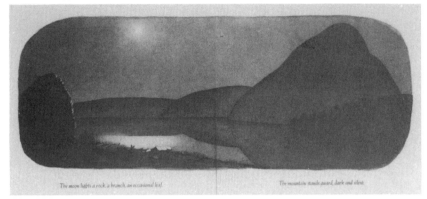

The moon lights a rock, a branch, an occasional leaf.   The mountain stands guard, dark and silent.

10   11

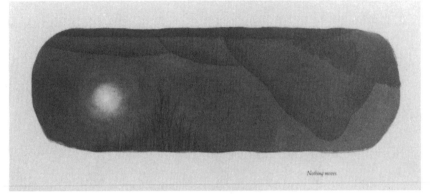

Nothing moves.

12   13

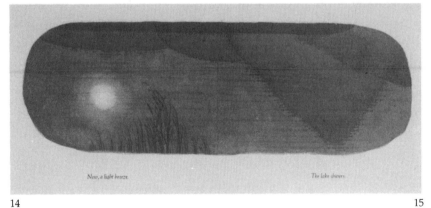

Now, a light breeze.   The lake shivers.

14   15

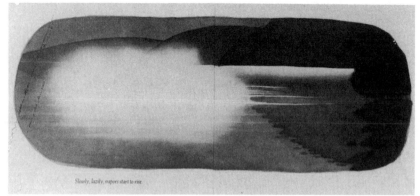

Slowly, lazily, vapors start to rise.

16   17

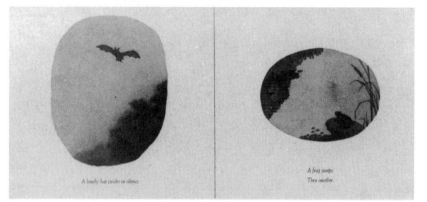

A lonely bat circles in silence.

A frog jumps.
Then another.

18   19

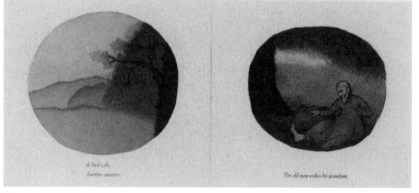

A bird calls.
Another answers.

The old man wakes his grandson.

20   21

Pages 16–17. Although there has been no noticeable change in the shape or size of the pictures on the last spreads, the slow pace established in the beginning is starting to change. The movement of the breeze begun on the previous spread continues on pages 16–17, only now vapors rising slowly over the lake are introduced into the picture.

Pages 18–19. As the day grows lighter, and as more life awakens, there is an increase in movement. This is reflected in the size and shape of the pictures on pages 18–19: the breakdown into smaller pictures helps to quicken the pace and echoes the break of day.

Pages 20–21. These pictures grow larger to reflect the increasing visibility as the day grows lighter. The movement from one scene (the bird in the landscape) to another (the old man waking his grandson) continues the movement begun on pages 14–15 and picks up the faster pace of pages 18–19.

Pages 22–23. The pictures continue to increase in size. They show the old man and his grandson moving, but at a slow pace—as is true of people who have just gotten up. The strong horizontal band of the distant mountains is static. It runs through both pictures as if attaching one to the other. The even shades of the sky and water also help to suggest the morning calm, which in turn emphasizes the slow pace. The light of the fire hints at the ball of fire in the sky—the sun—which will appear later.

Pages 24–25. This spread begins the final sequence of the action—the boat ride. Page 24 concludes the previous sequence (rolling up the blankets after the night's rest) and is the transition to the next sequence (getting ready for the boat ride). In order to emphasize their movement into a larger space, I placed the figures in the foreground of the picture in a relatively closed-in area—near the tree—on page 24. On page 25, they move away into the distance, into a more open space, which in turn suggests the spread that will follow.

Pages 26–27. Here I achieved a somewhat quicker pace by showing the old man and the boy on the lake with no land in sight, implying that they have gone some distance since the previous spread. The even color of the lake surrounding the boat suggests quiet.

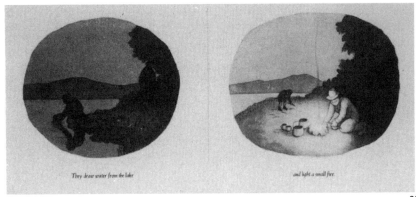

They draw water from the lake

and light a small fire.

22   23

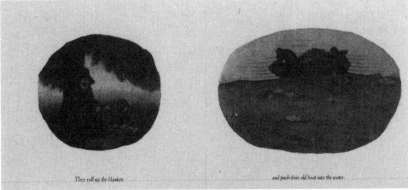

They roll up the blankets

and push their old boat into the water.

24   25

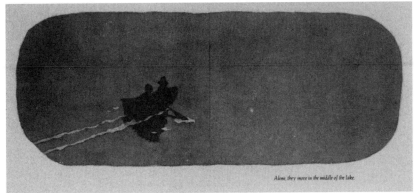

Alone, they move in the middle of the lake.

26   27

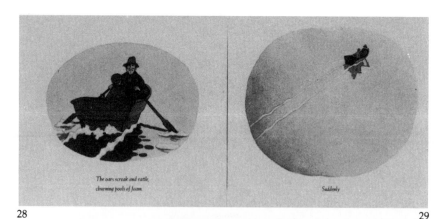

28   29

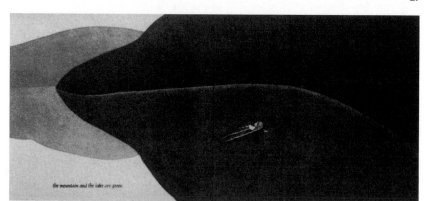

30   31

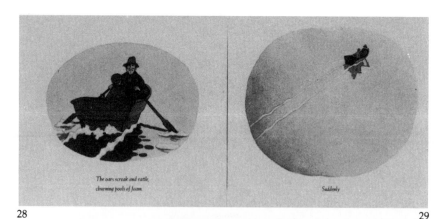

32

Pages 28–29. At this point I imagined the old man rowing, absorbed in the effort and looking down, not paying too much attention to his surroundings. That is why I chose to zoom in on the boat on page 28. This also enabled me to emphasize the pools of foam in the water. The visual movement of the foam surrounded by the quiet blue of the lake emphasizes the noise of rowing in the surrounding quiet. Page 29 reminds us of pages 26–27, but here the boat is farther away, becoming smaller—leading us into the next spread.

Pages 30–31. Here I saw the old man taking a break from rowing, lifting his head, and seeing the climactic spectacle. In the book, which is in color, pages 30–31 are a dramatic visual change. Until this point the pictures have been almost monochromatic, with only subtle color shifts. Now the scene appears in vivid yellows, blues, and greens. This sudden burst of color, however, is justified by the content of the story and does not jar the reader.

Page 32. I could have ended the book on the previous spread, but I added this last page so as not to cut off the enjoyment of pages 30–31 too abruptly. This smoother ending is more consistent with the pace and mood of the book—its visual code.

7. Size, Scale, and Shape

Trifles make perfection.
Michelangelo

When you pick up a children's book, the first thing you see is its size and shape. Before you even look at the pictures or read the text, the size and shape of a book have an impact on you. Therefore, when you plan and illustrate a children's book, give size and shape ample consideration. Let your decisions be a natural outgrowth of the content and mood of the story you are illustrating, not the result of some arbitrary whim. Consider what will work best for your book.

The size, shape, and scale of a book are closely linked and depend on one another. They are described separately in this chapter only for the sake of clarity. The examples shown point to some of the ways size, scale, and shape are used in children's books. They are not intended to represent all of the possible ideas used by artists, or all the new ways yet to be explored.

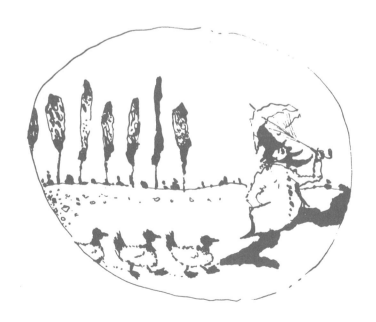

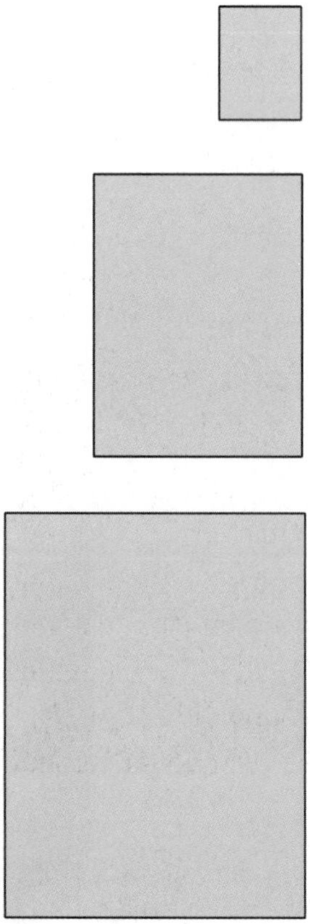

Size

The size of a book is defined by its horizontal and vertical dimensions. Does it, for instance, measure 4¼″ × 6½″, or 9″ × 10″? In the publishing business, the measurements used represent the *trim size:* they are actually the dimensions of the trimmed book page—not of the book cover, which is a little larger in order to protect the edges of the bound book pages.

Many publishers now use a few standardized trim sizes to save on production costs, if they can do so without diminishing the book's effectiveness. Standardization permits optimum use of press equipment, as well as savings on binding and paper costs. The standard trim sizes, however, vary from publisher to publisher, and some publishers are stricter about size than others. With some, an 8″ × 10″ upright trim (or 10″ × 8″ for an oblong shape) is the largest size; others may produce books up to 11″ × 8″ or even 12″ × 9″. Publishers have minimum sizes, too. One publisher's smallest trim size is 4″ × 5½″. Books for older children and for adults—especially novels and series books—are normally standardized at two sizes: 5½″ × 8¼″ and 6⅛″ × 9¼″. With picture books and story books, however, there are still a few publishers that allow greater flexibility in size.

Regardless of changing conditions in the publishing industry, it is important for you to know how to determine the best trim size for your book. Even if you are asked to conform to one of the publishing house's standard sizes, your choice should be made wisely. Looking at different children's books can help you gain an awareness of size.

Figure 1. These rectangles all have the same proportions, but different dimensions. Each has a different impact on the viewer.

Figure 2. In deciding on a trim size, you may want to draw the dimensions of the book on a sheet of paper and cut it out in order to see what the effect is.

Figure 3. Normally, a small book tends to evoke an intimate mood, and a large book projects a wider scope. Just as a solo piccolo produces a different response from a full orchestra, Maurice Sendak's *Nutshell Library*, which measures 2¾″ × 4″, affects us differently from Isaac Bashevis Singer's *Elijah the Slave* (illustrated by Antonio Frasconi), where the trim size is 10½″ × 10¼″.

Figure 4. Notice the difference between this single page and this double spread, both from my book *Oh What a Noise!* Bear in mind that when you consider page size, you are thinking in terms of a closed book. When you open the book, the two pages together will constitute a double spread.

1

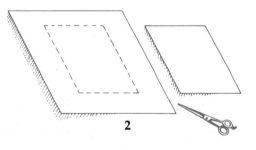

2

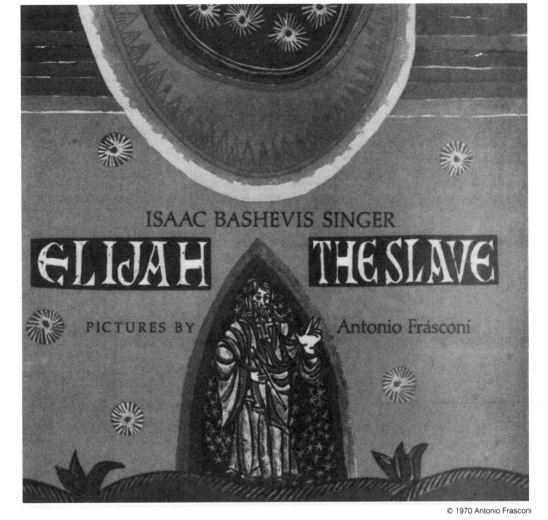

© 1970 Antonio Frasconi

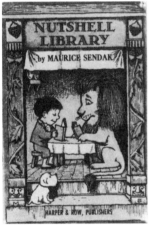

3   © 1962 Maurice Sendak

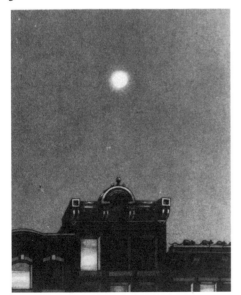

4

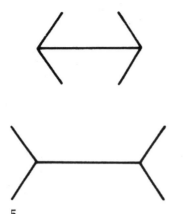

5

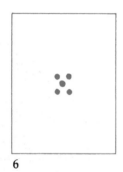 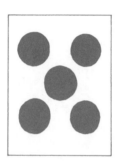

6

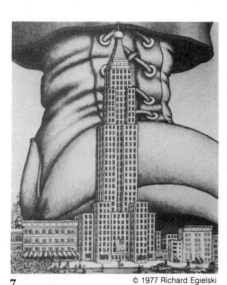

7 © 1977 Richard Egielski

Scale

Look at a children's book and ask yourself: Do the pictures appear larger or smaller than they really are? Does the book give the impression of being larger or smaller than its actual size? Sometimes you may find that the pictures in an oversize book appear smaller than they really are, thus making the book seem smaller than it is. Scale is the appearance, the illusion, of size as opposed to the real, or measured, size.

If you were to take two pictures, one very large and the other very small, and reduce them both to the same size, would they *look* the same size? They might or might not, depending on the various visual factors in the pictures. For instance, a picture will look larger than it is when the elements in it expand beyond the picture's frame, toward the viewer. The examples shown here are intended to demonstrate that size and scale are not necessarily the same.

Figure 5. These two lines, with the "arrows" on either end, represent the well-known Muller-Lyer illusion. The two lines are actually the same length, but this is very hard to see. The one on the bottom appears longer because of the opening out of the arrows at the ends.

Figure 6. These squares are the same size, but the one on the right appears larger.

Figure 7. These pictures are of equal height, although Richard Egielski's picture from *Sid and Sol* by Arthur Yorinks (left) is ⁷⁄₁₆″ wider. It looks much larger, however, than my illustration for Sholem Aleichem's *Hanukah Money* (right). Without the frame, Egielski's picture would appear even larger.

Figure 8. Although these two pictures from Walter Crane's *Noah's Ark A.B.C.* are both the same size, the page for E-F-G seems larger than the one for T-U-V. This is because the giraffe expands vertically, the elephant expands in all directions, and both animals are considerably larger than anything else in the picture. Furthermore, the background is lighter than they are, allowing visual space for them to expand. In contrast, on the T-U-V page, the tiger and unicorn blend into the background, their shapes are horizontal, and they don't look much bigger than the other elements in the picture. The tiger is squeezed in under the powerful, upper white rectangle and has hardly any space to expand upward.

Figure 9. With Marc Simont's two pictures from Ruth Krauss's *The Happy Day*, the one on the left seems smaller than the other, although it is actually slightly larger. The coiled forms of the sleeping bears circle inward, as if becoming smaller, while the awakening bears break the boundary of the picture and seem to grow out into the page.

Figure 10. Beatrix Potter's picture from *The Story of a Fierce Bad Rabbit* (left) measures 2¹⁵⁄₁₆″ × 3½″, but it feels larger than the illustration from M. B. Goffstein's *Two Piano Tuners* (right), which measures 4¾″ × 5½″. The rabbit is large in relation to the small bench and the tiny rabbit in the distance. The rabbit's relatively short ears accentuate the largeness of his head. Moreover, the picture's oval shape is without a frame and thus expands into the surrounding white of the page. In M. B. Goffstein's picture, on the other hand, the girl is small in relation to the room, as well as to the picture size. Potter's picture also appears larger than Goffstein's because of the different perspectives used. The rabbit is seen from below, as if we were looking from a position slightly below the carrot. The little girl, however, is seen from above, with the viewer's eye approximately at the same height as the top of the door, way above her head.

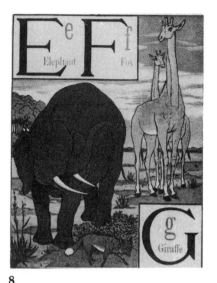
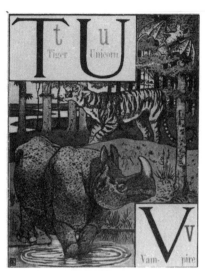
8

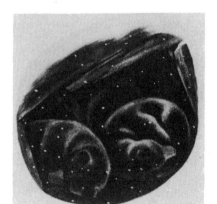
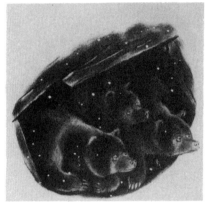

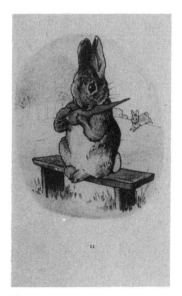
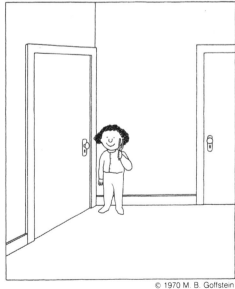
9   © 1949, 1977 Marc Simont   © 1949, 1977 Marc Simont

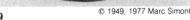

10   © 1970 M. B. Goffstein

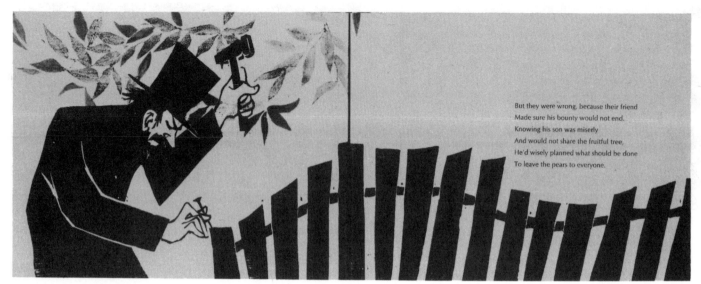

But they were wrong, because their friend
Made sure his bounty would not end.
Knowing his son was miserly
And would not share the fruitful tree,
He'd wisely planned what should be done
To leave the pears to everyone.

11

© 1969 Nancy Hogrogian

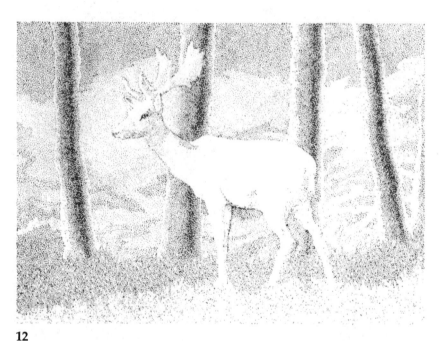

12

Figure 11. Nonny Hogrogian's double spread from *Sir Ribbeck of Ribbeck of Haveland* (a poem by Theodor Fontane) is another example of a picture that looks larger than its actual size (17¾″ × 6½″). Here the black areas expand into the light background of the picture and seem to extend beyond the edges of the book itself.

Figure 12. Donna Diamond's illustration for *The Transfigured Hart* by Jane Yolen measures 4⅛″ × 2⅞″. It does not give the illusion of being either larger or smaller than it is.

It is important to be aware of scale when you illustrate a picture book or story book, for you need to know how to achieve a scale that fits the content and mood of your pictures. There is no point in using a large trim size and unintentionally achieving a small-scale picture. This is not only a waste of space, but it would also make producing the book unnecessarily costly.

Book Shape

The rectangle of a picture book or story book is the stage or screen upon which the pictures and words will appear. The shape of a book is in itself a statement and can create a mood. An upright rectangle affects you differently from a square. A narrow rectangle moving upward evokes a different response from one that sits solidly on its base or expands sideways. Generally speaking, an upright rectangle guides the eye in a vertical direction, an oblong one guides it horizontally, and a square suggests a circular motion, since the square contains an implicit circle. (That is why a square may sometimes suggest movement inward and appear smaller than it is.)

These principles hold true when the page is a blank rectangle. As we shall see, the picture's own shape and its composition may guide the eye in a different direction from that suggested by the shape of the page alone. In general, however, it is best to choose a book shape that will enhance the overall feeling you want, rather than counteract the shape on every page.

Figure 13. Here the upright and oblong rectangles contain the same amount of space, but their proportions are different. Although technically these rectangles are the same size, the different shapes change our perception of them. The square shape is smaller than the two others, but even if it contained the same space, we would perceive it as more solid than the oblong shape, and sitting more firmly than the upright. The upright seems to be rising and the oblong, expanding horizontally.

Figure 14. You see the rectangle of a book even before you see the details of the jacket. The overall impact is that of the geometric shape determined by its proportions: Which is greater, its height or its width? Is it upright or oblong? The jacket of William Steig's *Gorky Rises* fits its title: the shape stresses vertical movement. In contrast, the shape of my jacket for *The Fool of the World and the Flying Ship* emphasizes the horizontal direction.

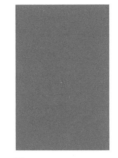

13

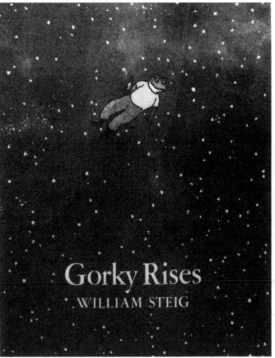

© 1980 William Steig

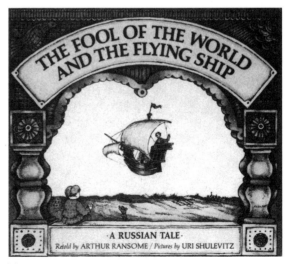

14

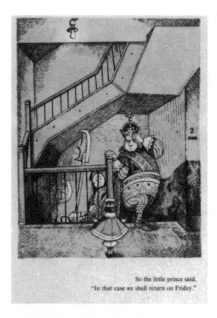

So the little prince said,
"In that case we shall return on Friday."

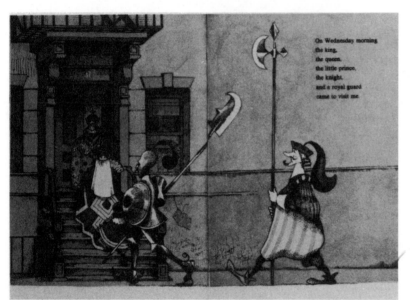

On Wednesday morning
the king,
the queen,
the little prince,
the knight,
and a royal guard
came to visit me.

15

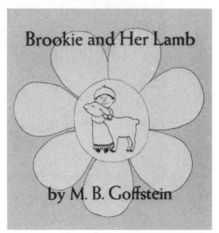

16   © 1967 M. B. Goffstein

Figure 15. Of course, just as with size, in considering book shape, you should be aware of both the single page and the double spread. A book such as *One Monday Morning* may be upright when closed but oblong when opened. Consequently, your decision on shape should take into account the effect of the double spread, regardless of whether you conceive the pictures in single-page or double-spread units.

Figure 16. Although not a perfect square—it is about 5″ × 4¾″—M. B. Goffstein's jacket looks square. Its circular design draws the eye to its center, the "heart" of the book, emphasizing its intimate scale and the warmth and affection between Brookie and her lamb.

Figure 17. This picture by Domenico Gnoli from *Alberic the Wise and Other Journeys* (written by Norton Juster) emphasizes the vertical shape of the page and its upward movement, the height of the towers being by far the most prominent feature of the picture. The texture of the bricks, however, slows the upward movement of the eye, which tends to linger on their individual details. Their unevenness hints at the precariousness of the towers and their potential for collapse.

Figure 18. This vertical picture I did for *Runaway Jonah* by Jan Wahl uses its shape to guide the eye downward. The tip of the wave points like an arrow to the falling Jonah. From there on, there is nothing to delay our eye from rapidly sweeping down the wave.

Figure 19. In this picture for *The Fool of the World and the Flying Ship*, I utilized the horizontal direction fully to emphasize the vastness of the flat landscape and the movement of the approaching flying ship.

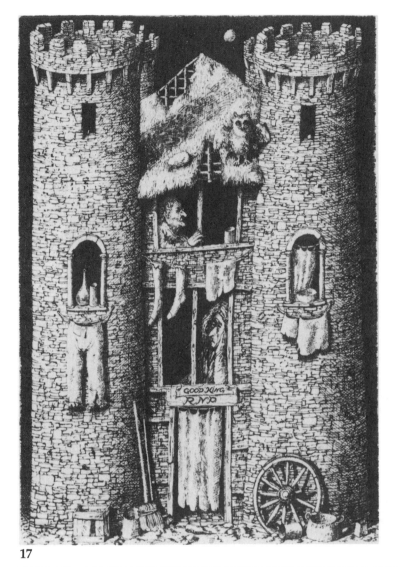

17

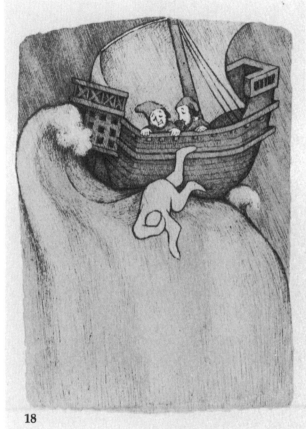

18

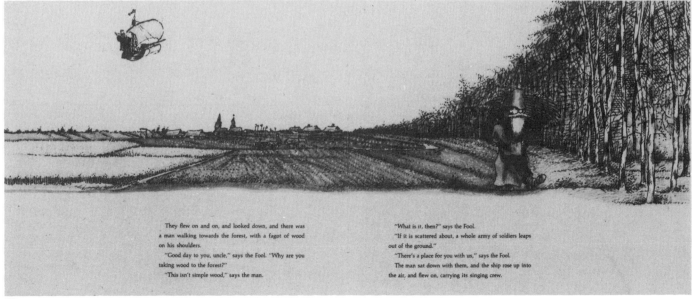

They flew on and on, and looked down, and there was
a man walking towards the forest, with a fagot of wood
on his shoulders.

"Good day to you, uncle," says the Fool. "Why are you
taking wood to the forest?"

"This isn't simple wood," says the man.

"What is it, then?" says the Fool.

"If it is scattered about, a whole army of soldiers leaps
out of the ground."

"There's a place for you with us," says the Fool.

The man sat down with them, and the ship rose up into
the air, and flew on, carrying its singing crew.

19

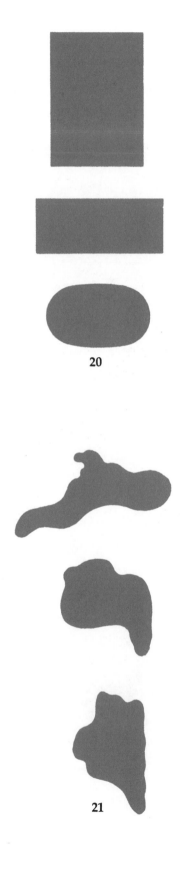

20

21

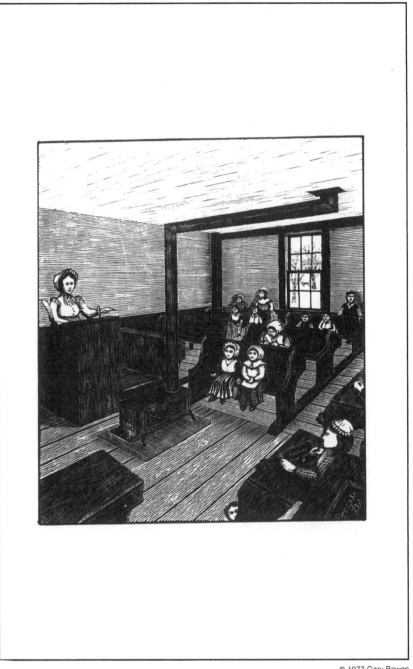

22

Picture Shape

Picture shape is an additional means of conveying the mood of the picture. When you make your decisions about picture shape, you should consider two important aspects: (1) the overall form of the picture if viewed as a silhouette with no interior details and (2) the picture's edges. Both the overall shape and the edges have an effect on the picture.

Figure 20. Symmetrical picture shapes derive from geometric figures such as rectangles, squares, circles, and ovals. Usually they suggest calm and solidity.

Figure 21. Asymmetrical picture shapes are unbalanced, irregular, and dynamic. They can have endless variety.

Figure 22. This neatly framed picture, engraved by Randy Miller for Gary Bowen's *My Village, Sturbridge*, reinforces the sharp, clearly defined lines within the picture itself. It reflects the solidity we associate with early nineteenth-century New England, when life was well ordered.

Figure 23. The straight edges of the shaded areas define the overall shape of Geoffrey Hayes's picture from *When the Wind Blew* by Margaret Wise Brown. Because the cloud on the upper right blends into the white of the page, however, the picture shape can be read two ways: as a rectangle or, due to the interrupted frame, as a slightly irregular outline, in keeping with the mood of the story.

Figure 24. The clearly defined rectangle provides a formal frame for this picture by M. B. Goffstein from *Laughing Latkes*. It creates a "stage" that contrasts with the quivering line of the two pancakes. Although the ground on which the pancakes stand is suggested by their position, there is no drawn background. In fact, there is nothing to differentiate the picture from the page except the frame.

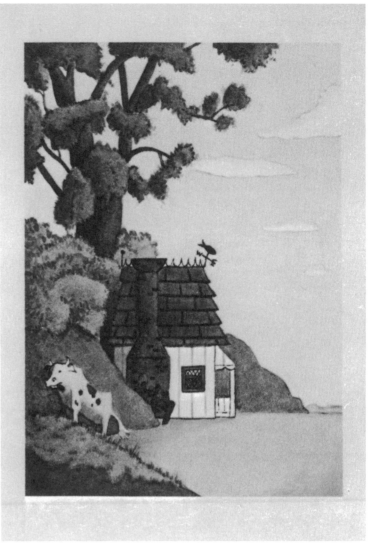

23

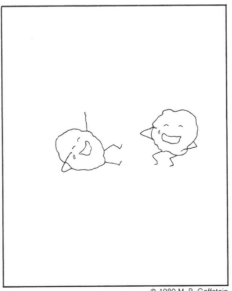

24

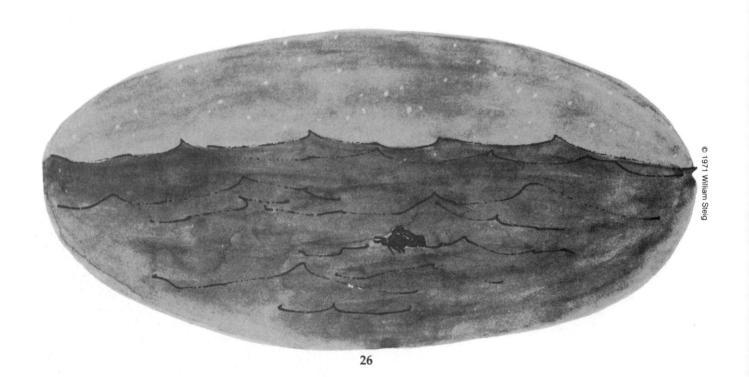

"What's the matter?" Charley said.

"It's the wind," the pine tree said.

"I don't care about the wind," Charley said.

"I'm afraid of the wind," the pine tree said.

The wind blew a little harder and all the trees ran back to where they belonged. They had to get into the ground quick. They had to hold on.

Then they began to fight with the wind. The wind banged them and they banged back. The wind knocked their leaves off. You could hear the leaves crackling and the wind puffing and puffing.

Then the wind blew over Charley's knees.

"You stop that," Charley said.

34

25

26

Figure 25. This double spread I did for *Charley Sang a Song* by H. R. Hays and Daniel Hays has a rectangle on one page and an irregular shape on the other. The sudden break in the frame emphasizes the wind blowing through the frame from one page to the next.

Figure 26. The soft edges of this symmetrical, oval picture from William Steig's *Amos and Boris* give it an informal quality. This is in keeping with the relaxed, casual way the picture is drawn.

Figure 27. The shape of Margot Zemach's picture for *Mazel and Shlimazel, or the Milk of a Lionness* by Isaac Bashevis Singer is determined by the figure's silhouette. The movement and irregular outline of the figure are in keeping with its humor.

Figure 28. This irregular-shaped picture from Beatrix Potter's *The Tale of Peter Rabbit*, with its soft edges, gradually eases into the page. In spite of the irregularity of its shape, it suggests a circle because of Peter's position at its center. Strictly speaking, however, the shape resembles half an oval.

Figure 29. The outer edges of the drawing define the shape of this picture from Robert Kraus's *Boris Bad Enough*, illustrated by Jose Aruego and Ariane Dewey. Although asymmetrical, its horizontal base and overall shape suggest a rectangle. This implicit rectangle helps to calm the dynamic outline and gives the picture weight.

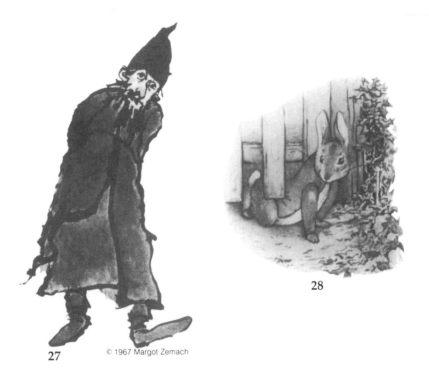

28

27

© 1967 Margot Zemach

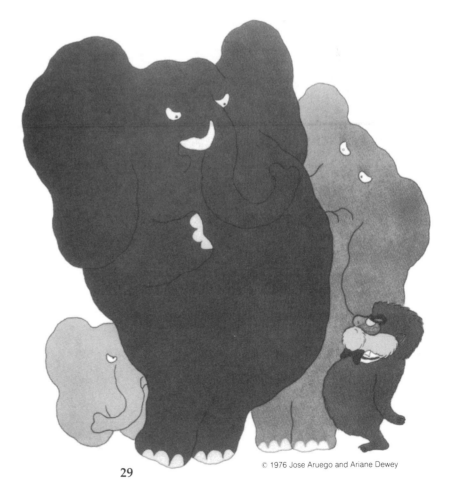

29

© 1976 Jose Aruego and Ariane Dewey

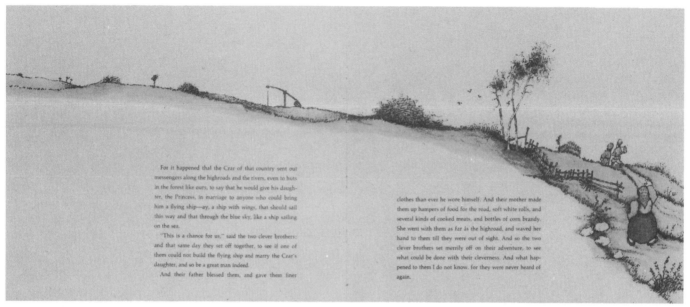

For it happened that the Czar of that country sent out messengers along the highroads and the rivers, even to huts in the forest like ours, to say that he would give his daughter, the Princess, in marriage to anyone who could bring him a flying ship—ay, a ship with wings, that should sail this way and that through the blue sky, like a ship sailing on the sea.

"This is a chance for us," said the two clever brothers; and that same day they set off together, to see if one of them could not build the flying ship and marry the Czar's daughter, and so be a great man indeed.

And their father blessed them, and gave them finer clothes than ever he wore himself. And their mother made them up hampers of food for the road, soft white rolls, and several kinds of cooked meats, and bottles of corn brandy. She went with them as far as the highroad, and waved her hand to them till they were out of sight. And so the two clever brothers set merrily off on their adventure, to see what could be done with their cleverness. And what happened to them I do not know, for they were never heard of again.

30

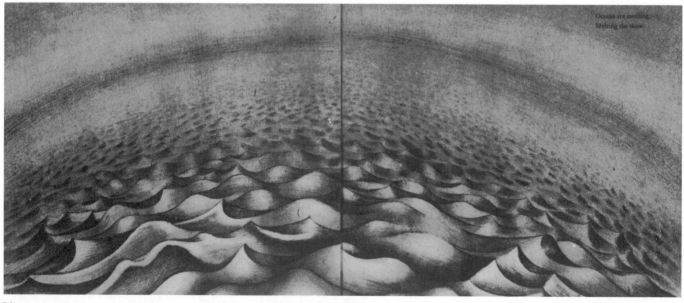

Oceans are swelling,
Melting the skies.

31

Bleeds

The largest possible picture in a book is one that bleeds. A picture *bleeds* if it extends to the trimmed edge of the page. A picture may bleed on one, two, three, or all four sides. Naturally, when it bleeds on all sides of a single page or double spread, the picture shape corresponds to that of the book page (or spread).

An artist may decide to bleed a double spread on all four sides to use the maximum amount of space available. This may be done to increase the scale of the picture or to suggest the space extending beyond what is shown in that picture.

Figure 30. My elongated, asymmetrical picture from *The Fool of the World and the Flying Ship* suggests a wide expanse. The bleeding of the picture to the edges on the upper left and lower right stabilizes the undulating landscape and "locks" it into the rectangle of the double spread.

Figure 31. A double-spread picture that bleeds on all four sides occupies the largest possible space in a book. Because of the convex shape of the ocean in this spread from my book *Rain Rain Rivers*, the picture expands beyond the borders of the page and appears larger than it is.

Figure 32. In this double spread from *What Is Pink?* by Christina Rosetti, illustrated by Jose Aruego, the right-hand page, which bleeds on the top, suggests how large the mother flamingo is. Because the facing page does not bleed, the fledgling appears even smaller.

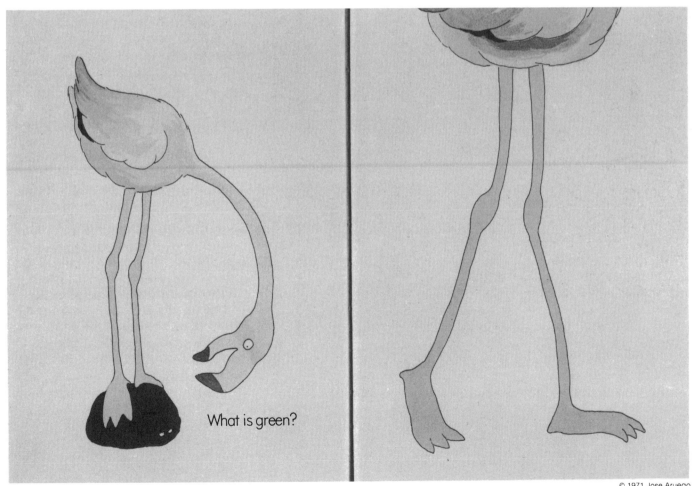

What is green?

© 1971 Jose Aruego

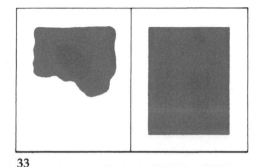

33

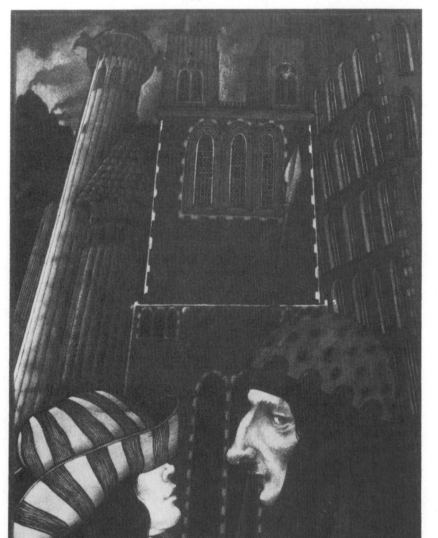

34

© 1974 David Palladini

Frames

A picture that bleeds has no white paper showing around it (except for a slight glimpse of the inside of the book's cover) and suggests expansion beyond the size of the page. In contrast, a picture smaller than the page is *framed* by the white margins of the paper. Pictures can also be framed by decorative borders or by straight-ruled lines of varying thickness and style. In all of these cases, the picture is confined on the page. Its shape, however, can relate to the trim size of the page in different ways: it can have the same proportions or different ones; it can be parallel to the trimmed edge or diagonal to it. Thus, the picture's shape also determines the shape of the frame around it.

Figure 33. When a picture is smaller than the page size, it may be framed by white space on all four sides. The irregular shape on the left here has a dynamic feeling; it also leaves room for the inclusion of text below.

Figure 34. Framed by a dark line and the white of the page, David Palladini's picture for *The Girl Who Cried Flowers and Other Tales* by Jane Yolen shows us its world as if through a window. The clear distinction between the white paper that frames the picture and the picture itself contrasts the reality of the book page and the illusion of the picture.

Figure 35. Although this picture by Beatrix Potter has no formal frame, it is still framed by the white of the paper. The soft edges, fading gradually into the paper, ease the transition from the picture to the white of the paper. As a result, the picture appears more as a vision than as a world seen through a window.

Figure 36. In keeping with its informal style of drawing, William Steig's picture for *Abel's Island* has a freely drawn double frame.

Figure 37. Antonio Frasconi used a straight line to frame this picture from *Overhead the Sun: Lines from Walt Whitman*. But because the picture is a woodcut, the line has a textured, irregular quality. This picture is also an example of how the picture's composition affects its shape. The emphatic horizon line divides the large rectangle, making it seem smaller.

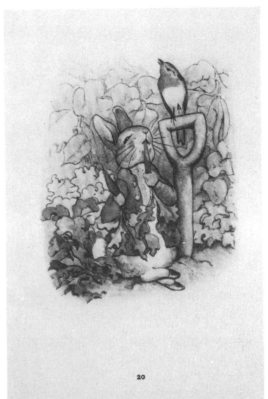

35

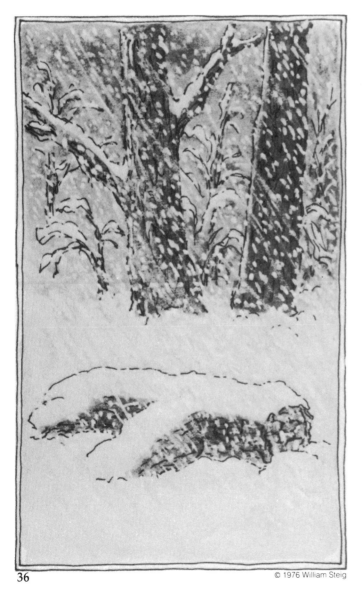

36

© 1976 William Steig

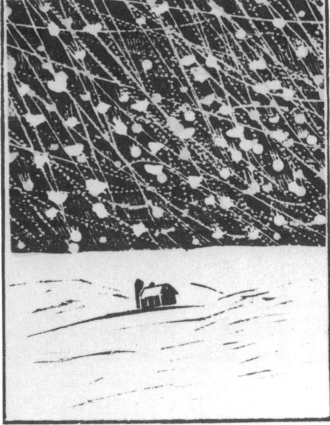

37

© 1969 Antonio Frasconi

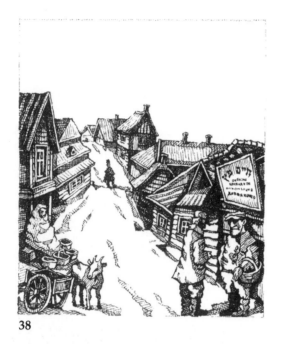

38

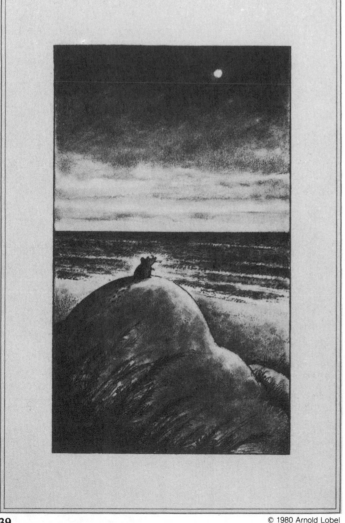

39

Figure 38. I created the frames for *The Magician* by using the outlines of the pictures themselves. The edge of the sky area is defined by irregular dots. Although I used a ruled line in my sketches, I executed the finished versions freehand to achieve an informal quality.

Figure 39. Arnold Lobel framed his pictures for *Fables* twice: once with a single line and again with two lines drawn closely together. This framing choice adds elegance and a feeling of depth. It also closes the expanse within the picture so that the scene becomes more intimate.

Edges

The edges of picture shapes vary as well: they can be hard, soft, jagged, straight-ruled, even. How you handle them should be an outgrowth of the content of the picture and mood. All the elements of the picture should cooperate and strive for the same effect. Study different picture books and try to determine whether the picture shapes and edges help or hinder the picture.

Figure 40. These are only a few of the many ways of treating the picture's edges.

Figure 41. Generally, a symmetrical picture with edges that create a regular frame (top) represents a more static, stable shape than an asymmetrical picture with sharp edges (center). An asymmetrical picture with soft, gradually fading edges (bottom), however, eases into the page more quietly than one with sharply contrasting edges.

Figure 42. The soft edges of this picture from my book *Dawn* were dictated by the mood of the story. A busy, jagged outline like the one below would have contradicted the stillness of the picture.

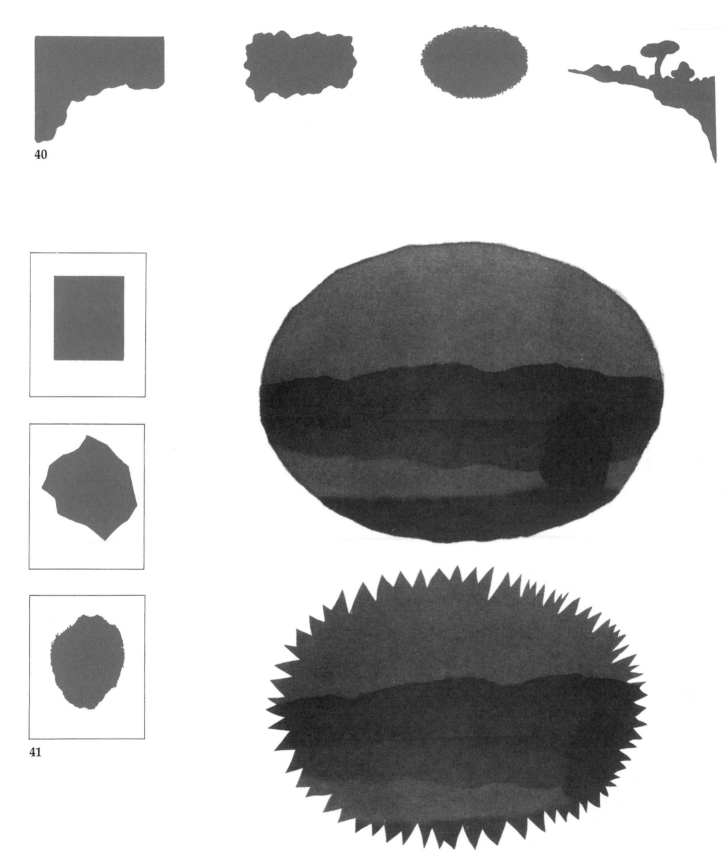

40

41

42

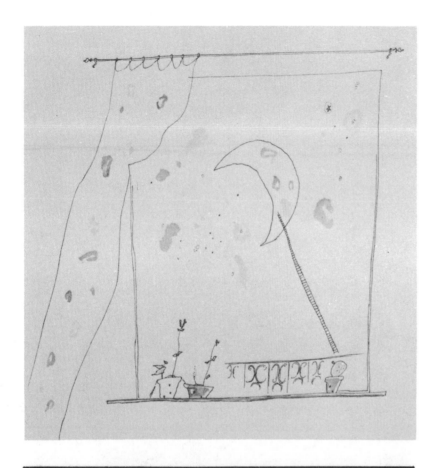

Figure 43. The heavy frame shown below would have been out of keeping with the character of my drawing for *The Moon in My Room*.

Figure 44. The delicate line of this picture I did from *My Kind of Verse* (compiled by John Smith) would have been "choked" by a heavy, ragged frame.

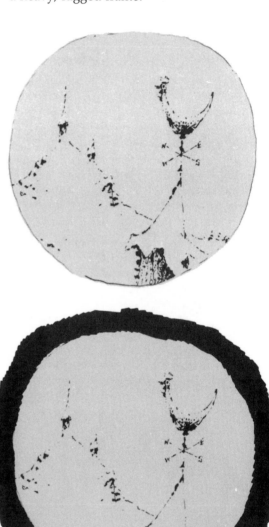

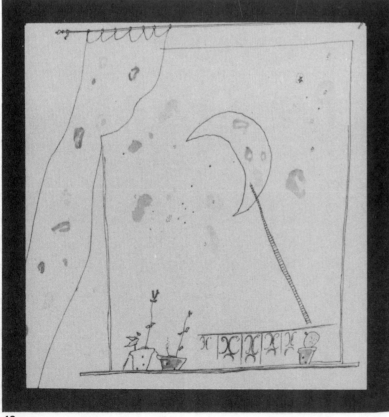

43

44

A Note on Design and Typography

It is impossible to aim for excellence without considering every aspect of book-making. Even if you don't plan on designing your books, it helps to have a basic knowledge of design and typography. Their importance in a book, especially a children's book, cannot be overstated. Although a detailed discussion is beyond the scope of this book, I encourage you to learn more about them.

Good design is inconspicuous: it does not draw attention to itself unnecessarily. Instead, it does its job quietly, enhancing the picture and making the whole highly readable. If the design becomes self-conscious, "showing off," it will take center stage and distract from the total effect of the page. The most important aspects of design to bear in mind are readability—of all the visual elements on the page—and breathing space, the white space around both the type and the pictures that provides rest for the eyes.

With few exceptions, type is more readable than hand lettering, and therefore almost always more desirable for the text of a book. Hand lettering can sometimes be used sparingly, to add a beautiful touch to a book, especially when only a little text is needed. But when too much hand lettering is used, it may wear the reader down.

Figure 45. Cynthia Krupat's design of the title page for *Toby Lived Here* by Hilma Wolitzer is readable and elegant without the help of pictures. Notice the balance between the type and the white space: although the type fills the page, sufficient breathing space remains.

Figure 46. In this woodcut page from a Japanese illustrated book, the writing and the drawing blend perfectly. The line used for the text is similar in character to the line used for the horses.

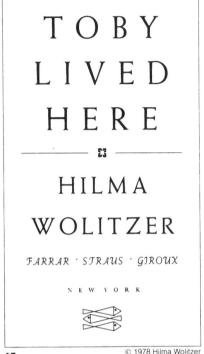

T O B Y
L I V E D
H E R E

HILMA
WOLITZER

FARRAR · STRAUS · GIROUX

N E W   Y O R K

45   © 1978 Hilma Wolitzer

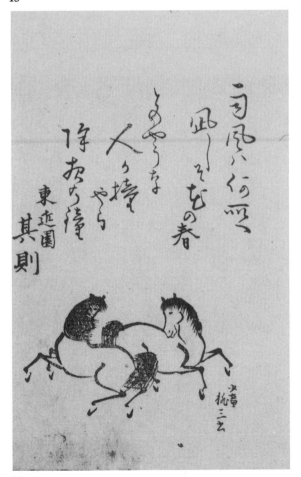

46

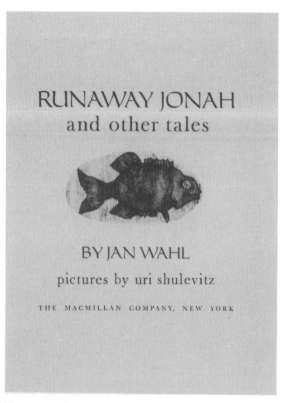

47

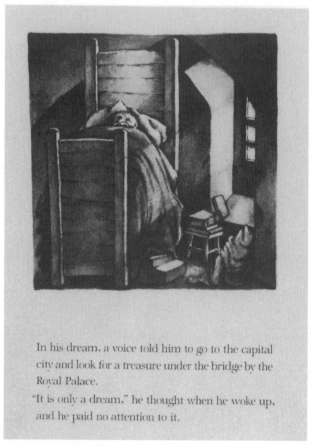

Figure 47. The title page of *Runaway Jonah*, designed by Ava Weiss, has elegance, and the type enhances the picture.

Figure 48. The varying thickness of the lines in this typeface, chosen by designer Jane Bierhorst, is in keeping with the picture's lines. It would be hard to imagine this picture from *The Treasure* with a modern sans serif type.

Figure 49. The type on this spread from Ruth Krauss's *Open House for Butterflies*, illustrated by Maurice Sendak, appears as small units, similar to the snowflakes, hats, and children.

Figure 50. Here, on another page from the same book, the bold, spread-out type emphasizes the bossiness and self-importance of the older brother.

Figure 51. On this page from *Open House for Butterflies*, small units of text are playfully scattered over the page, just as Sendak's pictures are.

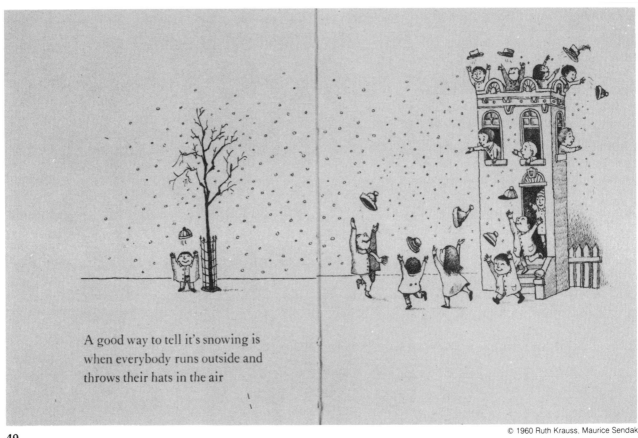

A good way to tell it's snowing is
when everybody runs outside and
throws their hats in the air

49

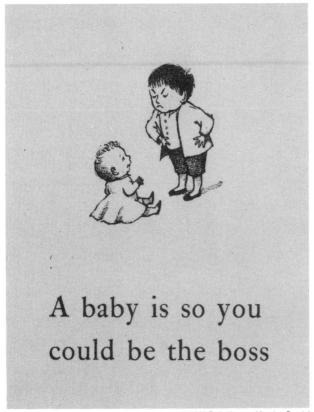

A baby is so you
could be the boss

50

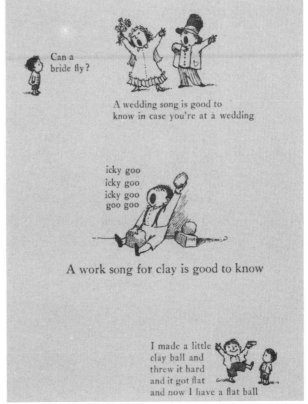

Can a
bride fly?

A wedding song is good to
know in case you're at a wedding

icky goo
icky goo
icky goo
goo goo

A work song for clay is good to know

I made a little
clay ball and
threw it hard
and it got flat
and now I have a flat ball

51

Figure 52. The hand lettering by Jeanyee Wong on this page from *The Little Humpbacked Horse* (a Russian tale retold by Margaret Hodges) is an integral part of Chris Conover's picture. It reads like a solemn announcement; thus it affects both our sense of hearing and our sense of sight. It sets the mood for the tale.

Figure 53. The handwritten words in *Some Swell Pup*, by Maurice Sendak and Matthew Margolis, are in keeping with the varying thickness of the lines of Sendak's picture. Since few words are used, the hand lettering is easy to read.

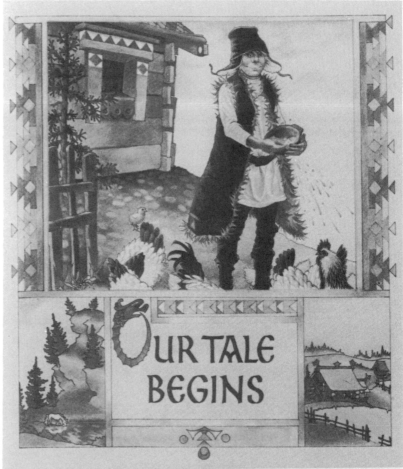

52

© 1980 Chris Conover

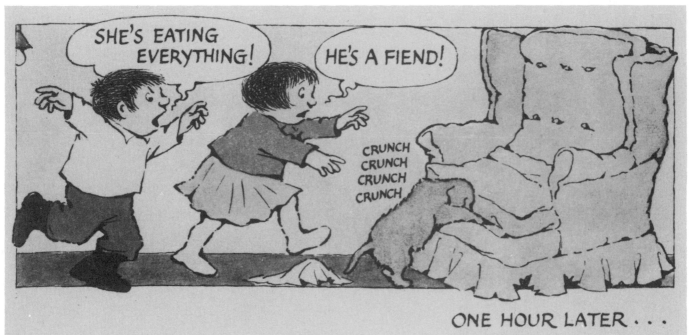

53

© 1976 Maurice Sendak

8. The Structure of a Printed Book

There are no details in the execution of a work.
Paul Valéry

In order to write and illustrate a children's book, you must take everything into consideration—including its physical structure. A well-conceived, well-executed book must be thought through to the smallest detail, from conception to production; you must leave nothing to chance. The book has to be integrated into a single organic entity whose parts are in harmony with each other and the whole. Ideally, a book grows from within: every detail of production is in keeping with the basic concept of the book.

Great books—with outstanding illustrations and stories—can be diminished by careless design, poor production, or flimsy binding. There are no unimportant parts in a book.

When you illustrate a children's book, your goal is the most beautiful book you can produce. Such a book will not only have wide audience appeal, but will also bring satisfaction to both author and publisher. Because the reader sees only the printed book, not the original art, it is important that everyone involved in the book's production do his or her best to do justice to the illustrations. To achieve this goal, to be able to plan and design a better book, artist and author must understand its anatomy and how the basic structure of the bound book can affect its design and illustrations.

This chapter is concerned primarily with the hardcover (or casebound) trade book, which consists of a stiff binding cover, holding together the printed book leaves or sheets, with a jacket wrapped around it. Most picture books and story books published in the United States have this kind of binding. Some books are also published in what is called a library edition, which is of sturdier construction and made to withstand the heavier use books receive in a library.

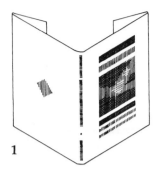

1

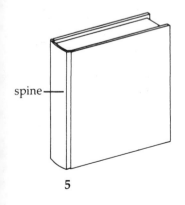

front flap   back flap

2

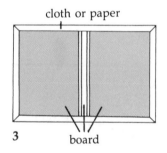

cloth or paper

3   board

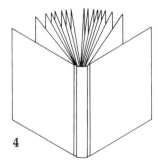

4

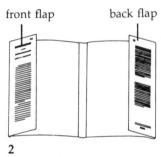

spine

5

The Jacket

The jacket (or dust cover) is a sheet of paper, generally printed with the rest of the book, that wraps around and protects the cover (**Figure 1**). Sometimes the paper is covered with a plastic laminate to protect it from dirt and water. The jacket's other functions are publicity and aesthetic appeal.

The jacket can be likened to a small poster. In effect, it advertises the book and attracts prospective buyers. Because the jacket is intended to attract buyers, it expresses the content and the mood of the book through a bold design—one that can be grasped at a glance and can be seen from a greater distance than a typical interior illustration. The jacket can be likened to a gate, or a door: it is the entrance to the book. It shouldn't promise what it doesn't deliver; it should visually represent the book in a straightforward manner.

The front of the jacket generally includes the book title, the names of the author and illustrator, and a design or illustration that visually represents the book. On the spine, or side edge of the jacket, there is again the author's name (and sometimes that of the illustrator), the book title, and the publisher's name. The back of the jacket may be illustrated. Sometimes the illustration from the front is continued on the back; this is called a wraparound jacket. Sometimes the back includes promotional copy about the book. For aesthetic reasons, it is obviously preferable to have as little publicity copy as possible because it interferes with the jacket's design. Remember, however, one purpose of the jacket is to sell the book.

When you open the jacket, it has two flaps (**Figure 2**). The front flap briefly describes the book's contents and usually carries the name of the publisher. The back flap often gives short biographies of the author and the illustrator; it may also list the author's and illustrator's other books.

In designing a jacket, consider the typography (for the title, name of author/illustrator, and any other copy) as part of the total design so that everything will be integrated. View all the elements of the jacket as a part of your composition. Because the picture for the jacket is best conceived as an outgrowth of the other pictures in the book, it often helps to design the jacket after the illustrations are done, or at least sketched out.

The Binding Case

The cover (or case) of a book consists of two pieces of stiff board connected by a strip of board or paper in the middle; all three boards are covered with a piece of cloth or paper. **Figure 3** shows how the binding looks from the inside, before it encases the book. A space is left on either side of the central strip so that the book can open easily. The edges of the cloth have been folded over the boards and pasted down securely.

The cover encases, holds, and protects the book leaves, as shown in **Figure 4**. For library editions, where more protection is needed, the binding has sturdier boards and they are often made of a durable, nonwoven material that has been treated to resist soil and moisture.

Most often, book covers are in solid colors, but sometimes the covers of library editions—and even trade editions—are preprinted with the jacket art and then covered with a clear laminate. In trade books, when a solid color is used, the front of the cover may be stamped with the book's title, a decoration, or some other identifying motif. It may be stamped with a copper, aluminum, gold, or other metallic foil or in a matte or glossy color, or blind-stamped—embossed without ink.

The spine—**Figure 5**—is where the front and back covers join. Generally it has the names of the author, title, and publisher stamped or printed on it for identification when stored on a shelf, in case the jacket is destroyed or lost. A strip of material (called *crash*) is glued along the spine and the book is attached to its binding case.

End Papers

End papers (also called end leaves, book linings, or fly leaves) are sheets of paper (sometimes of heavy weight), glued to the inside of the front and back cover boards (**Figure 6**). These sheets of paper attach the pages of the book to its case and hide the boards and the strip of crash. They are a part of the binding, and are not to be confused with the first and last pages of the book.

When you open a book, notice how the cloth of the cover "frames" the left half of the end papers (**Figure 7**). Because of this framing effect, the color of the binding cloth should harmonize with the book's mood as well as with the end papers.

The end papers can be plain white or made of attractive colored stock. They also can be printed with the artist's design. The end papers may be the only chance the artist has to use a purely decorative design in the book. They may be designed as either a double spread or a single page that can be repeated on the other half of the end paper.

When the jacket successfully expresses the book's content and mood, it arouses expectations in the reader. In a picture book, poorly designed or blank end papers may be a letdown. At their best, end papers provide a visual bridge between the jacket and the first pages of the book. Like background music, they can evoke a suitable mood while moving into the front matter, which in turn introduces the text.

Signatures

Between the end papers are the book leaves, in the form of signatures. In printing a book, large sheets of paper are used. A number of pages are grouped together on each sheet. After the sheet is printed, it is folded and trimmed to separate the pages. The group of pages made from one sheet of paper is called a *signature*.

When the book is viewed from the side, each signature looks like a separate pamphlet. The standard signature consists of 16 pages, although 8-page signatures are sometimes used. Thus, a 32-page book usually consists of two 16-page signatures. The next available standard size is 48 pages (three signatures); the next, 64 pages (four signatures); and so on.

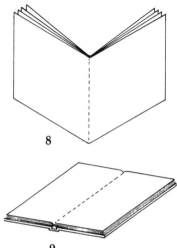

8

9

Binding Methods

The signatures of a book are bound together by two common methods: saddle stitching and side stitching.

With *saddle stitching* (or Smyth sewing), each signature is sewn through the center and the signatures are then sewn together (**Figure 8**). Saddle stitching is commonly used in trade books. It allows the book to open flat (**Figure 9**).

In *side stitching*, the book is sewn along the side of the binding edge (**Figure 10**). Because some people feel that this method holds the leaves of the book together more securely than saddle stitching, it is commonly used in library editions. It does not, however, allow the book to open flat (**Figure 11**).

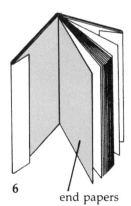

6   end papers

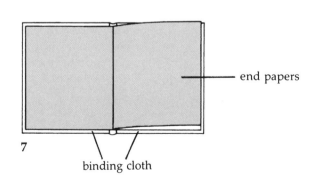

7

binding cloth

end papers

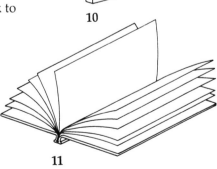

10

11

The Inside Pages

In counting the pages of a book (pagination), *all* leaves are included (except the end papers, which are part of the binding). Each side of a leaf constitutes a page. Whether or not the page number (folio) is shown, and even if the page is blank, it should be counted.

A *double spread*, as we have seen, refers to two facing pages, right-hand or left-hand. The space of inner margin where two pages meet at the binding is called the *gutter* (**Figure 12**).

The book itself consists of front matter, text, and back matter.

gutter

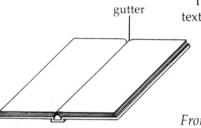

12

Front Matter

Front matter is the preliminary material necessary to identify the book. Normally the front matter consists of the following elements.

1. *Half-Title.* The half-title is usually on page 1, and consists of the title only (not the subtitle, if there is one).

2. *Title Page.* The title page includes the full title of the book and the names of the author (or translator, reteller), illustrator, and the publisher. The title page may appear on page 3 or on pages 2 and 3 as a double spread. When only one page is used, the title page appears on the right-hand side (page 3). The left-hand side (page 2) can have a frontispiece, or (less desirable) it can be left blank.

3. *Copyright Page.* The copyright page gives the copyright notice, consisting of the copyright symbol ©, the date (year), and the name of the copyright holder. It also includes the Library of Congress information (Cataloging in Publication Data). Legally, this must be found on the back of the title page, or page 4.

4. *Dedication.* If there is a dedication, ideally it should be alone on the page (page 5) facing the copyright notice. If there are space limitations, it may be on page 4, spaced so as to separate it from the copyright notice. Sometimes it may be found on the half-title page. When there is both an author and an illustrator, they can both have an initialed dedication.

Whenever possible, the text (or story in pictures) should not begin before page 5, thus leaving ample space for the front matter and conveying a feeling of elegance. It is more pleasant to be eased gradually into the book, rather than rushed right into the text. However, if you are pressed for space, you can drop the half-title, make the title page page 1, put the copyright notice and dedication on page 2, and begin the text on page 3.

Text

The text, which is the body of the book, can start on a right-hand page facing a blank left-hand page, or as a double spread. In a picture book the text may end on page 32, or a page earlier. You may tell the story in single-page units, or view a double spread as a single unit, decreasing the space you have to tell your story.

Most picture books have 32 pages, although some have 24, 40 (on rare occasions), or 48 pages, and a few have 64 pages. It is very rare, although possible, for a picture book to exceed 64 pages.

The same applies to story books, although they are frequently over 32 pages long. In selecting the number of pages in your book, your decision should not be arbitrary or capricious, but rather an outgrowth of the book's needs.

Back Matter

The back matter comes at the end of the book, following the text. It may consist of an appendix, notes, glossary, bibliography, and/or index. None of these is common in picture books or story books. If you do have back matter, however, it must be included in your page count.

How a Book's Structure Affects the Art

Every element in a book has an impact. As already noted, the feeling generated by the jacket of a book should flow through the end papers and the front matter. Some books use art in the front matter to sustain the mood. And, of course, design and typography play a crucial role not only in the front matter, but throughout the entire book.

In **Figure 13**, for instance, the blank pages of the end papers between the jacket and the title page break the flow. Then there is another jump between the title page and the opening of the text. Such disruption can be avoided by careful planning. With *One Monday Morning*, for example, I used an oval, gradually increasing in size, to lead the reader through the front matter into the text (**Figure 14**). The copyright and dedication pages, however, should have been better thought out to fit in with the rest of the front matter.

When you prepare the art for a book, it's important to keep the book's structure in mind and plan your pictures accordingly. In order to achieve the best results, you should ask the production manager or art director how many signatures the book will have, on which pages they will join, and how the book will be bound.

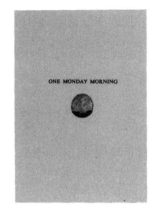

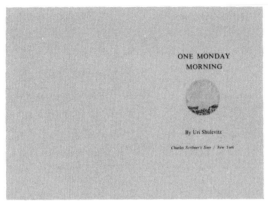

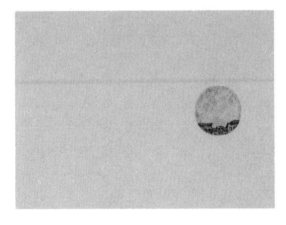

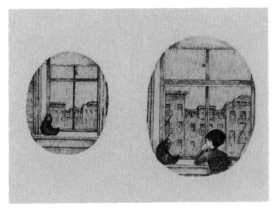

jacket   end papers

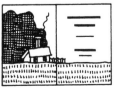
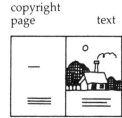

title page

copyright page   text

13

14

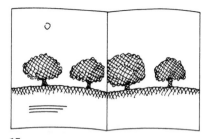

15

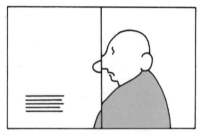

16

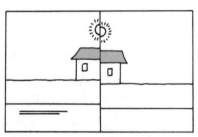

17

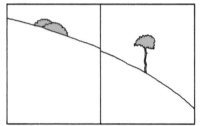

18

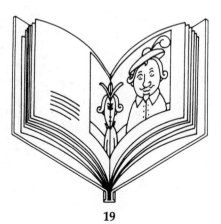

19

In a 32-page, saddle-stitched book with two signatures, for example, the signatures are glued together between pages 16 and 17. As a result, there is a slight loss of picture area near the gutter in an illustration spanning that double spread (**Figure 15**). Whenever possible, avoid using a double-spread illustration where signatures are glued. The middle of a signature (for example, pages 8–9 or pages 24–25) is better for a double spread because it will open the flattest.

At times there may be an alignment problem between two facing pages. Bear this possibility in mind when designing a book. Although any misalignment is disturbing, horizontal lines generally align better between two separate pages than do slanted or diagonal lines, as shown in **Figure 16**. When you use a double spread, keep the vital elements of the picture, especially figures, away fom the gutter, or you may end up with something like **Figure 17**. Instead, use background elements that can take a slight loss of space without damaging or distorting the picture. In **Figure 18** the disjunction would be less disturbing if the house and the sun were on one page, rather than in the center.

With books that are side-stitched to meet library specifications, there are additional problems. Unfortunately, this binding method results in a considerable loss of picture area near the gutter of *all* spreads—about ¼ inch per page, or ½ inch in all. For this reason, and because a side-stitched book doesn't open flat, ½ inch of the illustration will appear to be missing, as in **Figure 19**. One way to compensate for this loss is by keeping figures or important details away from the gutter.

By looking at books, you can learn how to judge the quality of a book's production. Examine the binding: How much glue was used. Is it neat? Look at the board on the spine: Is it strong? Is it a suitable weight? How does the cloth look and feel? Peek inside the spine: Is it cloth or paper? These factors tell you how much the publisher cares about the physical production of the book.

Part Three   Creating the Pictures

*When I am a hundred
and ten, everything I
do—be it but a line or
a dot—will be alive.*

Hokusai

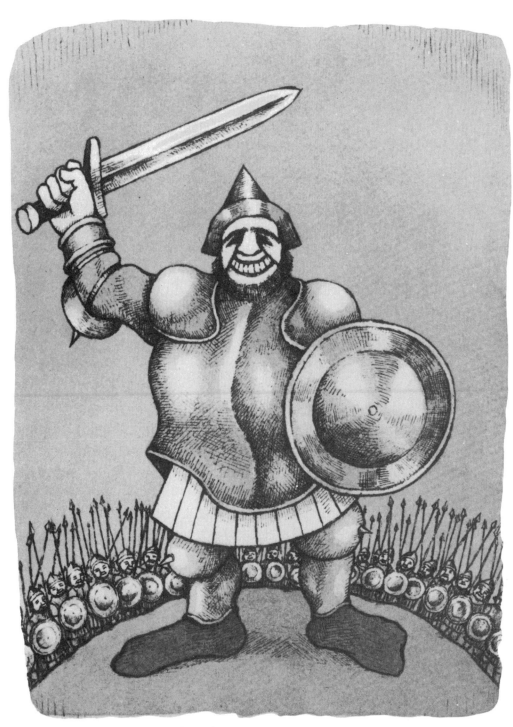

From *Runaway Jonah and Other Tales*

9. The Purpose of Illustration

The illustration which solves one difficulty by raising another, settles nothing.

Horace

The main function of illustration is to illuminate text, to throw light on words. In fact, illustration in medieval books is called *illumination* and the term *illustration* derives from the Latin verb meaning "to light up," "to illuminate."

Pictures help to clarify words because they make the subject matter concrete, closer to the way we perceive the world. This clarification comes from accurately representing the literal meaning and then going beyond that by representing the mood and the feeling of the words. The picture may also provide details the reader has missed or not fully understood and in this way throw new light on the words. The range of illustration thus extends from its most modest role as mere explanation of text to its highest possible achievement, when it enlightens spiritually and mentally.

Illustration also decorates the text. Medieval artists sometimes used gold in their pictures, literally *lighting up* the page. But neither gold nor a decorative design is necessary for a picture to adorn a text; it adorns by virtue of being visual. The mere introduction of pictures enhances the beauty of a book and provides the reader a rest from reading the words. In fact, the artist need not be concerned with decorating the text at all—it is a natural result of the process of illustration. The artist need only read the text thoroughly and concentrate on pictorially clarifying the text and on the picture's readability.

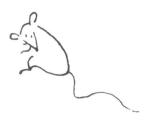

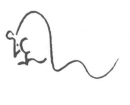

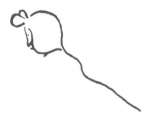

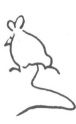

What Makes Pictures Readable?

In order to clarify the words, the picture itself must be clear. A picture's readability depends on the ease and interest with which the viewer can perceive its content and form. The viewer should be able to distinguish easily between static and dynamic elements, between important and unimportant details, between subject and background. If excessive effort is needed to understand a picture, one is less likely to be interested in it. A picture should not be a puzzle. When a picture is unreadable, it defeats the purpose of illustration.

Figure 1. My illustration for *The Wonderful Kite* by Jan Wahl aims to clarify the text by showing the scene described. It is readable because the clear outlines and the flat colors, used with sufficient contrast, enable the reader to distinguish easily between the figures and the background. There is also ample breathing space. Overall, the flat tones, distinct forms, and simple composition create a harmonious pattern that clarifies the text and decorates the book.

Figure 2. In this scene from *Naftali the Storyteller*, written by Isaac Bashevis Singer, Margot Zemach elucidates the words by showing the reader what the characters are doing, their appearance and expressions. The picture is made robust and clear through very simple means. Although the lines retain their sketchy, informal, handwritten quality, their thickness varies—giving the figures a feeling of volume. The occasional areas with multiple lines create grays (in the beards, hair, money, folds of clothing), adding "color" to this black-and-white picture.

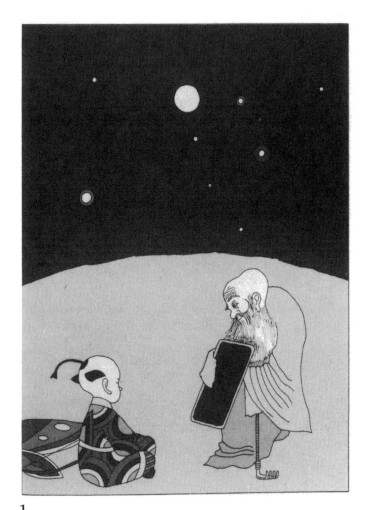

1

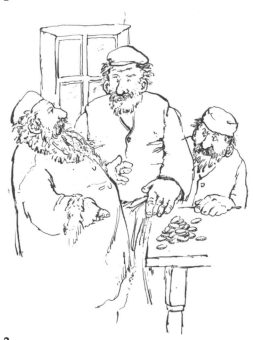

2

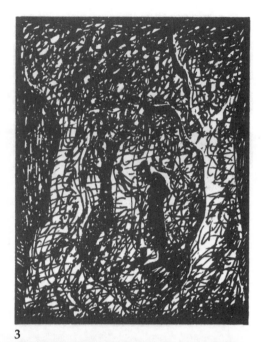

3

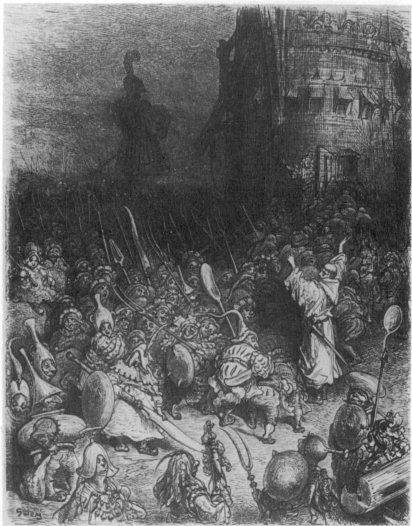

4

Figure 3. This drawing is an example of a picture that is very hard to read. The lack of contrast and confusion of lines make it difficult to distinguish the figure from the background.

Figure 4. Like Figure 3, this illustration by Gustave Doré is a dark scene with many energetic, curved lines. Here, however, the picture is very readable. The lighting and the contrasts help to focus our attention on the most important areas of the picture, which are clear.

Figure 5. Photographs can also suffer from a lack of readability. Many photographs that illustrate children's books are hard to read because they contain too many distracting details. One example is this photograph, which I took. It doesn't discriminate between the important and unimportant details and therefore both compete for the viewer's attention.

Figure 6. In contrast to Figure 5, these two photographs from Tana Hoban's *Push-Pull, Empty-Full* are selective in the details they present. The distinction between the two clocks, as well as between each clock and the background, is quite clear, and the actor-stage relationship is very readable.

Details and the Whole

Although details can enhance a picture's readability, an overemphasis on detail may overwhelm readability. In a good picture all the details are well integrated so that they do not interfere with the unity of the whole. It is the artist's job to find a balance between detail and the readability of the illustration as a whole.

Peter Hopkins, a painter with a lifelong interest in the old masters, comments:

As a general rule the old masters tended to represent objects in such a way that the viewer would have no doubts as to what they were. In this sense it can be said that they tended to explain everything in the picture.

Also they showed as much as possible of a subject. For example, given the option of depicting a figure either with one or two hands in view, they would

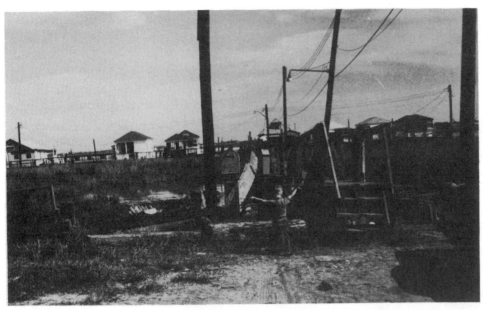

5

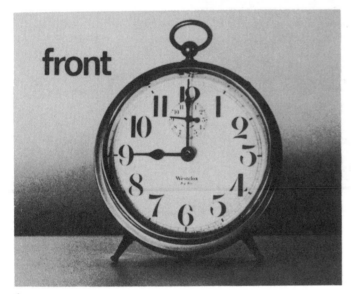

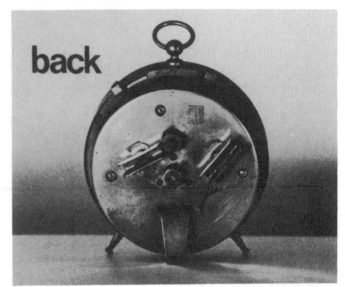

6

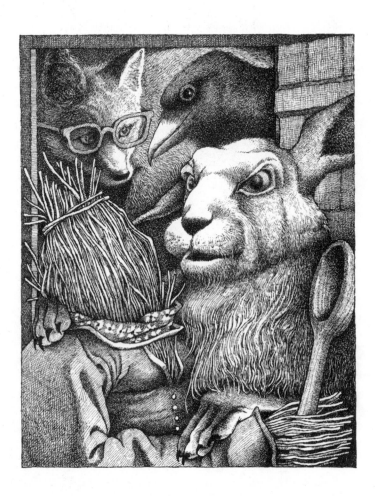

opt for two. Whenever practical, they would show both feet of a figure instead of arbitrarily hiding one or two. . . . [Yet this] general rule of revealing and visually explaining all the forms constituting a picture had to be balanced against another rule which demanded an effect of the unity of the whole.

Figure 7. Maurice Sendak's picture for "The Goblins" in *The Juniper Tree and Other Tales from Grimm* is a highly personal interpretation of the line: "There suddenly came a lot of little goblins." In the tradition of the finest fantasy illustration, it is composed of concrete, highly realistic details. But the total picture conveys the fantastic. The animal characters seem possessed by evil spirits.

This picture is a fine example of how definition of detail is balanced with overall unity. The figures are three-dimensional, and the alternating light and dark help to achieve contrasts and visual clarity. Many of the elements in the picture are both static and dynamic at the same time, as one figure becomes the background for the next.

It could have been difficult to read this "cluttered" picture, but the generous white frame of the page helps to avoid any confusion. The judicious use of white space not only makes the picture readable, but by compressing it into a smaller frame it adds drama.

Figure 8. Just as the hero of a story in Norton Juster's *Alberic the Wise* literally enters a painting at a museum, so Domenico Gnoli enables the reader to "walk into" his illustration for the text. Like Sendak's illustration (Figure 7), Gnoli's picture clarifies the imaginary world of the words by making it real and concrete. Despite the abundance of detail, the subject matter is clear and three-dimensional. In fact, the three-dimensionality organizes the details, subordinating them to the larger volumes so they become more readable. The alternating light and shadow contribute to the luminous, rich quality while creating contrasts that invite the reader to enjoy the many details.

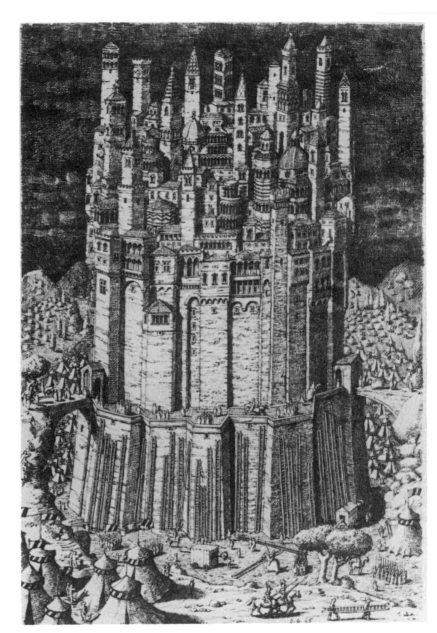

8

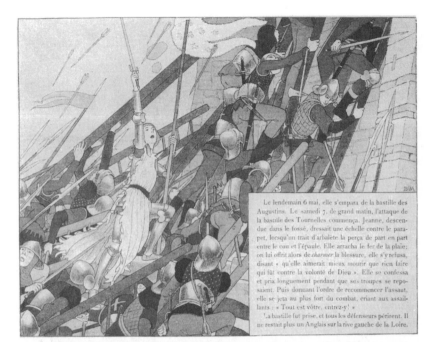

Le lendemain 6 mai, elle s'empara de la bastille des Augustins. Le samedi 7, de grand matin, l'attaque de la bastille des Tournelles commença. Jeanne, descendue dans le fossé, dressait une échelle contre le parapet, lorsqu'un trait d'arbalète la perça de part en part entre le cou et l'épaule. Elle arracha le fer de la plaie; on lui offrit alors de *charmer* la blessure, elle s'y refusa, disant « qu'elle aimerait mieux mourir que rien faire qui fût contre la volonté de Dieu ». Elle se confessa et pria longuement pendant que ses troupes se reposaient. Puis donnant l'ordre de recommencer l'assaut, elle se jeta au plus fort du combat, criant aux assaillants : « Tout est vôtre, entrez-y! »

'.a bastille fut prise, et tous les défenseurs périrent. Il ne restait plus un Anglais sur la rive gauche de la Loire.

9

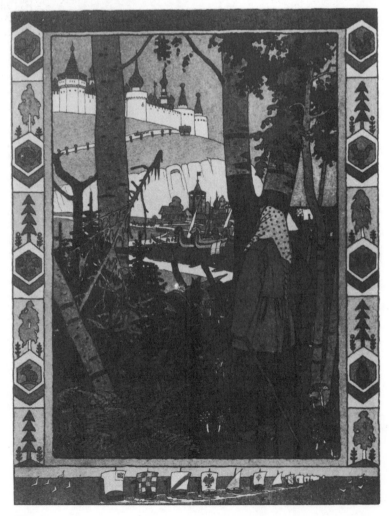

10

Figure 9. Again, despite all the detail, this picture of Joan of Arc by Boutet de Monvel is highly readable. The details add interest, but they are subordinated to the whole. The figures, weapons, and ladders are orchestrated into a powerful diagonal sweep upward. Yet the striking figure of Joan of Arc makes the viewer pause before continuing upward along the diagonal.

Figure 10. This illustration by Bilibine for a Russian folk tale is highly decorative, with a lot of detail. Even so, it is readable, because it has areas that provide rest for the eye, such as the meadow in front of the castle. As in Gnoli's picture (Figure 8), the many details are organized into units (such as the leaves in the left foreground), and they are balanced against areas that are less busy.

Varieties of Readability

Obviously, readability doesn't mean that your picture must look like a poster, full of bold elements that can be perceived all at once. A readable picture can be subtle and delicate, with the viewer slowly discovering details that linger on in the mind.

Sometimes the overall atmosphere in a picture is more important than the details, the feeling and mood more important than telling a story. This is especially true when you are illustrating certain types of poetry. Then, readability takes on a different meaning.

When it serves a specific purpose, even a slight difficulty in readability can be justified—provided it doesn't deny pleasure to the viewer. To evaluate and balance all the considerations involved in readability, you must develop sound judgment, which comes with practice.

To begin with, you must take illustration seriously, never with condescension. Understand and respect the subject matter and express it in a way that is true to the story. You also must have a vivid mental image to create a clear picture. If you understand the elements of a story and give them proper consideration, your pictures will reflect this.

In general, a picture should not be ambiguous. The subject matter should be drawn with clarity and skill, with contrasts that enable the reader to distinguish between the different elements in the picture. There also should be uncluttered areas, even in the most complex or crowded picture, to provide "breathing space" and rest for the eye.

Figure 11. Antonio Frasconi extends Isaac Bashevis Singer's text in this picture from *Elijah the Slave,* for he depicts a setting that is not described in the words. The picture throws light on Singer's retelling of the ancient legend and recalls the simple woodcuts of ancient books. Readability is enhanced by the bold outlines and colors, which contrast the clear definition of the figure against the uniform color of the sky. The sky offers rest for the eye, whereas the lines and the underlying forms suggest movement.

Figure 12. In contrast to Frasconi's illustration (Figure 11), my picture for *Charley Sang a Song* by H. R. Hays and Daniel Hays is delicate. The meandering lines, soft tones, and tiny details suggest an intimate fantasy world.

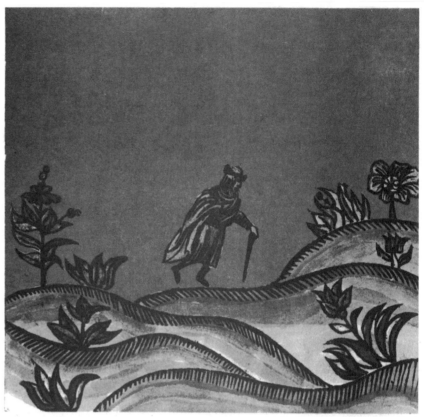

11

© 1970 Antonio Frasconi

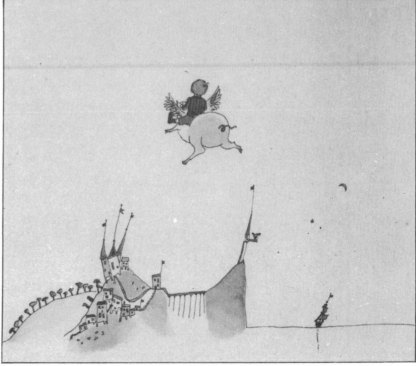

12

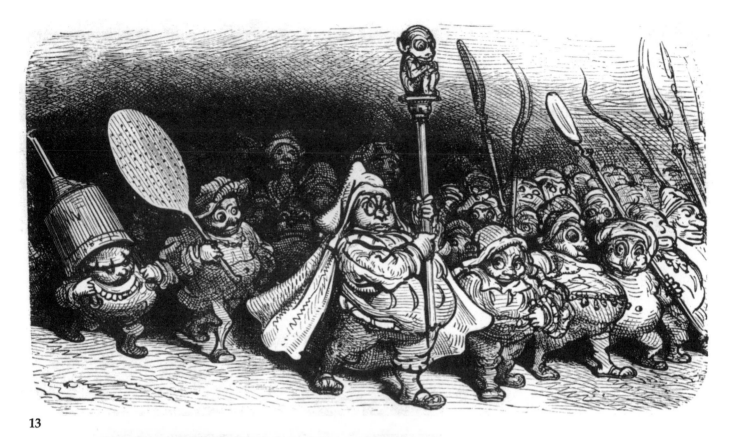

13

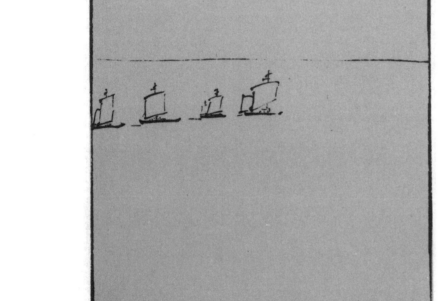

14

Figure 13. A different kind of fantasy mood is created in this vigorously drawn picture by Doré for Rabelais' *Pantagruel*. It has the quality of a caricature, but the distorted details never overwhelm the subject matter. It is a good example of an illustration that is both expressive and readable.

Figure 14. "As they sailed, they were joined by other boats, craft of every sort . . . [for] the captains of the other boats had learned that Li Po was journeying to contest the sea monster." So Jean Russell Larson tells us in *The Silkspinners*. Instead of attempting to fill in details not provided by the words, I wanted my illustration to evoke the atmosphere of the story. The picture is extremely sparse, relying on the empty, undrawn areas to suggest suspense and the movement of the boats toward confrontation with the monster. It is, however, readable.

Content and Form

Outstanding illustrations are effective on at least two levels. First, they tell us the story, portraying the subject matter accurately; and second, the abstract pattern of the picture is alive in its own right, with an underlying geometric structure that gives character and strength to the forms. Imagine a story in which a small boy stands before a giant oak tree. On the first level, a good illustration accurately portrays the oak tree and the boy. But an outstanding illustration also embodies the content in its design. The oak tree is not only accurately represented but also has life and substance as a form.

Pictures that function only on the first level are acceptable illustrations, whereas those that function only on the second level are good designs but poor illustrations. It takes success on both levels to make an excellent illustration. Although, in books, it is more important that a picture be an adequate illustration than a good design, it is more rewarding when pictures satisfy on both levels.

Always keep in mind, however, that as the artist you are a partner of the author in shaping the reader's mental image and understanding of the text. Therefore take care to interpret the text accurately in order not to mislead the reader.

Figure 15. This picture from Diderot's *Encyclopedia* accurately portrays the interior of an eighteenth-century gunpowder mill. It is as inviting to the reader as a clean, well-planned workshop is to an eager visitor. But the superb clarity of the picture helps it far exceed its modest goal, and it is enjoyable even if we don't have the slightest interest in gunpowder production. In addition to the precise representation of the subject matter, the underlying geometric structure provides a harmonious composition and adds beauty to the picture. It is a good example of a successful fusion of content and form.

Figure 16. This illustration by Phiz for Charles Dickens's *Nicholas Nickleby* succeeds in conveying the content of the story. It depicts in detail a period scene, with attention to the setting and the

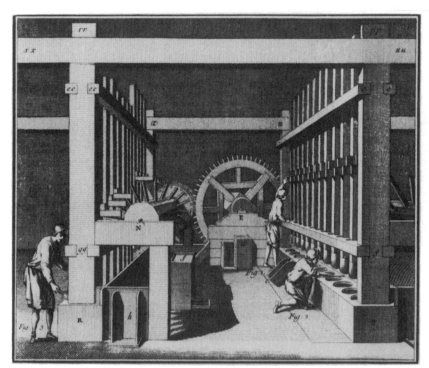

15

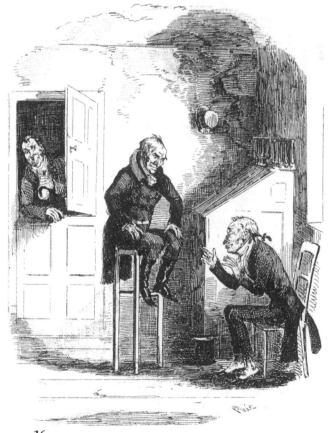

16

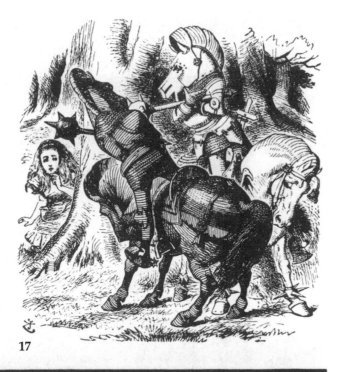

17

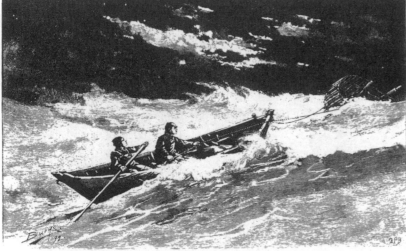

18

characters' appropriate dress. The figures' gestures and positions, however, go beyond mere description to suggest the underlying psychology. Both the subject matter and the mood are effectively portrayed.

Figure 17. This illustration by Sir John Tenniel for Lewis Carroll's *Through the Looking Glass* is different from the picture by Phiz. In addition to a detailed and accurate portrayal of the subject matter, it shows a strong awareness of form. The underlying geometric structure makes the various elements—especially the horses and the knights—seem as solid as if carved in stone.

Figure 18. This wood engraving by M. J. Burns for *St. Nicholas* magazine is very graphic. It is a fitting portrayal of the subject matter, but it doesn't have the form and structural awareness of the preceding illustration (by Tenniel) or the drama of the next illustration (by Doré).

Figure 19. In addition to its readable content and realism, this picture by Doré for Samuel Coleridge's *The Rime of the Ancient Mariner* provides a tremendous sense of drama and movement. It has the almost rhythmic quality of a musical composition. The overall design—with the swirling pattern of the waves, the helpless boat, and the powerful light in the center—enhances the portrayal of the subject matter.

A Range of Possibilities

Even the modest selection of pictures in this chapter reveals the many different possibilities for creating effective, readable illustrations. Although some of the illustrations are not from children's books and are not suitable for very young children, they are helpful to the aspiring illustrator both as models of excellence and as examples of different approaches. At times it is the *descriptive* aspect that stands out, while in other cases the effect is more *suggestive*, evoking a particular feeling or mood. Some pictures have a *decorative* quality; others may emphasize *expressive* elements. Often, in the best

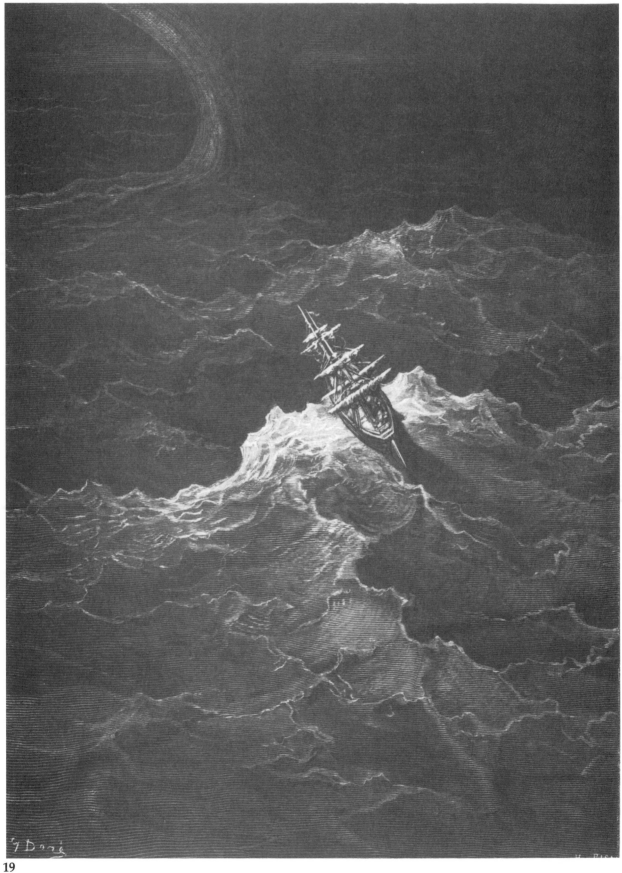

19

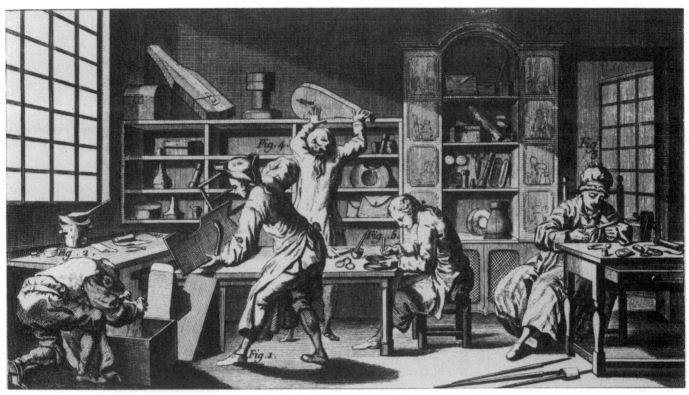

20

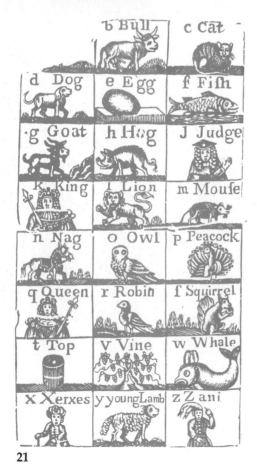

21

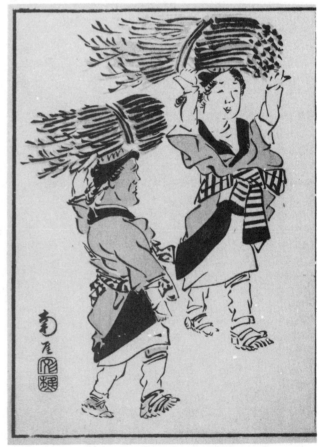

22

illustrations, several of these aspects are combined in a way that enriches the picture's meaning and our enjoyment of it.

Figure 20. This illustration from Diderot's *Encyclopedia*, like the earlier one (Figure 15), both explains the subject matter and decorates the page. The tools and the work of an eighteenth-century case-maker's shop are accurately portrayed with many details. The figures move in different directions, almost in a balletlike dance. The light from the window is like a spotlight on a stage; it emphasizes the underlying design and helps to unify the picture.

Figure 21. Thomas Bewick's illustration of the alphabet is highly decorative. It adorns by virtue of being visual. Unlike the Diderot illustration (Figure 20), it is neither realistic nor precise in its depiction. Yet it does provide description by representing the images for each letter.

Figure 22. Although this Japanese illustration is loosely drawn, with economy of detail, it is still descriptive. The essential information about the women carrying the bundles of twigs is very readable. At the same time the energetic handwriting of the lines contributes movement and an expressive quality. We can almost feel the women moving.

Figure 23. The immediate impact of Frans Masereel's illustration for *Passionate Journey* is expressive. Although the smoke and railroad track might have been descriptive or decorative only, here they are also vehicles of expression. The bold black-and-white contrasts, sharp woodcut lines, and simplified shapes create a posterlike effect, which is very readable.

Figure 24. This illustration by Gustave Doré for a tale by Rabelais is far less descriptive than the other examples, but it is still readable. The frenzied activity of a battle is clearly expressed, even though many of the details are unclear in themselves. It is the overall design and subject of the picture that suggests and explains the details. We can distinguish only a few of the soldiers on horseback, for instance, but there is enough information for us to

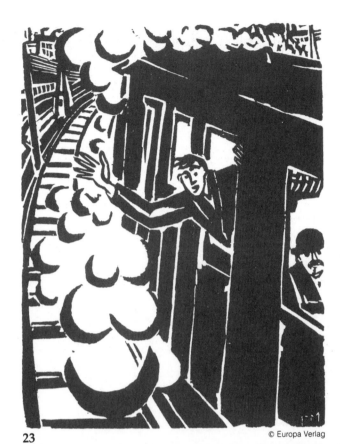

23 © Europa Verlag

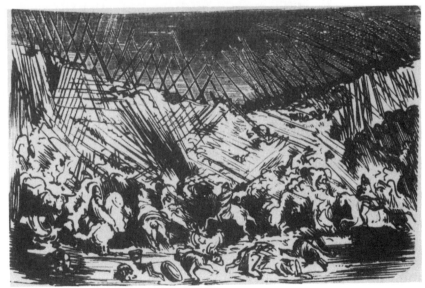

24

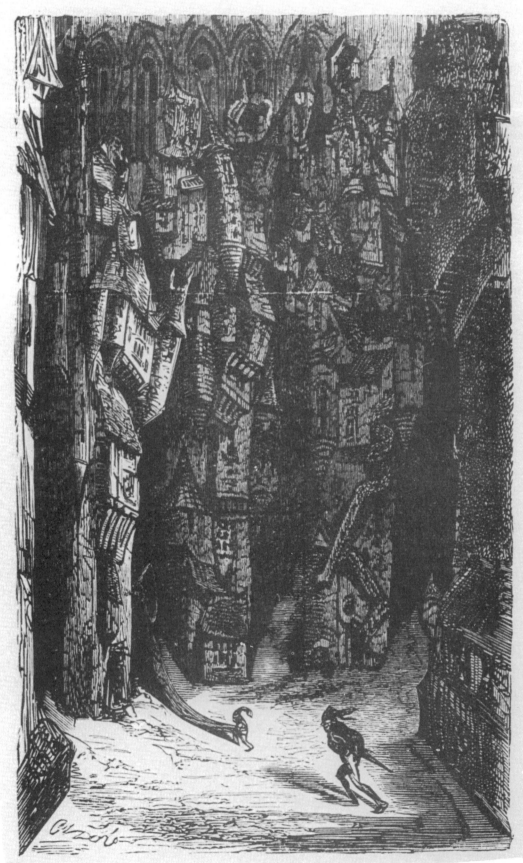

experience the chaotic fighting the text describes.

Figure 25. In this medieval scene, Doré did not draw the buildings exactly as they were, yet the subject matter appears real and believable because of his use of detail and three-dimensional space. The forms seem firm in spite of their general fluidity and movement because they are drawn with an underlying geometry. At the same time, through his use of dramatic lighting and subordination of details to the overall design, Doré has created an expressive picture with an exceptionally strong mood.

Figure 26. My spot illustration for *The Silkspinners* by Jean Russell Larson is concerned only with mood. The atmosphere of the scene is clear in spite of the sparseness of detail. The picture relies heavily on suggestion rather than full description. It decorates without being a decorative design, but only by being a picture.

Figure 27. Randolph Caldecott, in this austere picture from *A Frog He Would A-Wooing Go*, sticks closely to the essentials of the subject matter. The strength of his illustration comes from clarity of concept, vigorous drawing, and a sense of form. He achieves a poetic mood quietly, without straining for it.

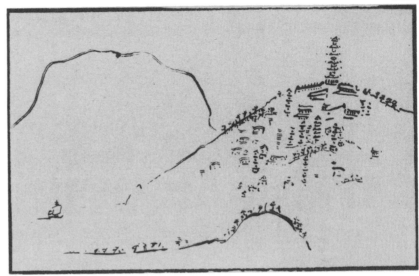

26

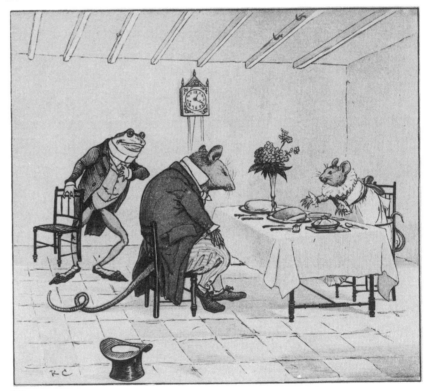

27

10. Drawing Figures and Objects

Remember: acquire accuracy before speed.

Leonardo da Vinci

Without drawing there is no illustration. It is through drawing that the artist shapes and conveys the visual content of the story. Drawing is the foundation on which the other aspects of the picture—mood or color, for instance—rest.

It is best to draw from direct observation of nature—figures, landscapes, animals, plants, inanimate objects—as much as possible. In this way you have clear references against which to compare and correct your drawings. Artists who draw exclusively from imagination run the risk of drifting into vagueness.

You should practice drawing constantly, until it feels as natural and unselfconscious as your handwriting. When you reach that stage, ideas will begin to flow more freely. I have found that drawing clarifies my vision and my thinking. Pictures that are hazy or vague in my mind gradually sharpen and crystallize as I draw. Another advantage of drawing constantly is that one drawing often triggers another, which in turn leads to yet another. But that exciting journey cannot start until you take your pencil or brush in hand and begin to draw.

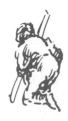
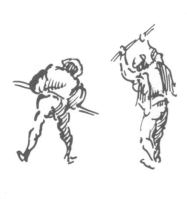
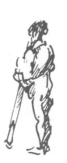
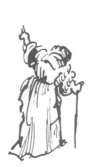
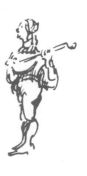

Basics of Figure Drawing

The hardest subject to draw is the human figure, because of its complexity as a form. Also, as the French poet Paul Valéry has pointed out, our familiarity with the human body makes any mistake or inaccuracy immediately apparent. There are countless ways to draw the figure. My purpose here is not to encourage any particular way, but to point out some essentials that have helped me and that can save you time.

Flat or Round Drawing

The two main approaches to drawing are two-dimensional (representing figures and everything else in a picture as "flat") and three-dimensional (representing everything as "round"). Flat drawing generally favors a hard, continuous outline, which suggests a flat surface, as in the wall paintings of the ancient Egyptians. Round drawing, on the other hand, favors soft, broken lines with shading, to suggest volume. An example is the art of the High Renaissance.

Figure 1. Because the figure on the left is drawn with an even, continuous outline, it tends to appear flat. On the right the outline is less even, with variations in the thickness of the line, so that the figure looks rounder.

Figure 2. If you take a strongly outlined figure like the one on the left and add shading, this is likely to create a contradiction between the outline and the suggested volume.

Figure 3. In contrast, when the outline isn't too heavy (as in the figure on the left), it can work well with the shading to suggest volume. In fact, the less outline there is, the rounder the figure will look.

Figure 4. To achieve a round effect in your drawings, think of the figure as if it were a sculpture. Use outlines sparingly, but don't lose them altogether. You may, for instance, want to vary the thickness of the outline or break it in places. Light and shade can also help to create an illusion of depth and three-dimensional form.

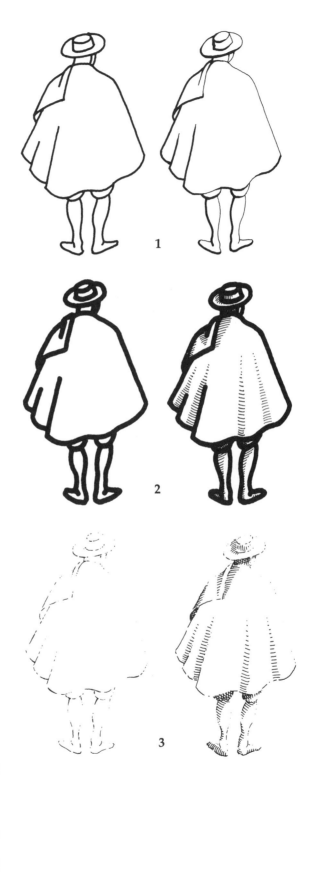

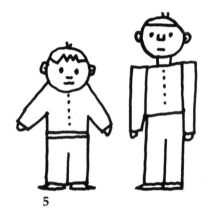

5

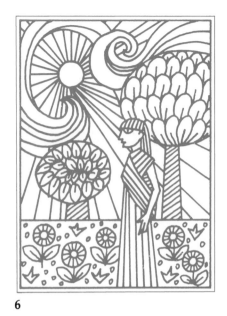

6

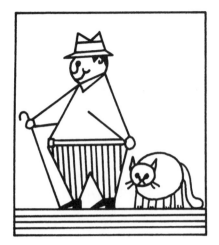

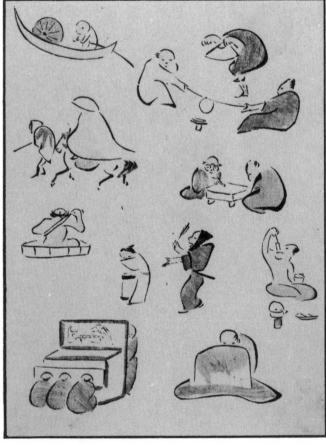

7

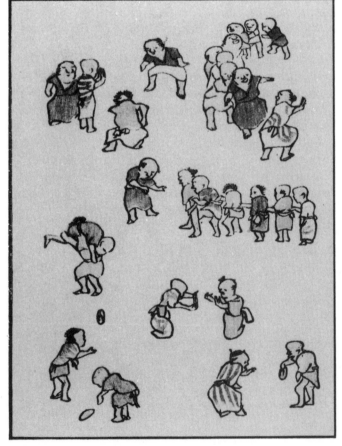

8

Figure 5. To beginners, flat drawing may seem easier than round drawing. Yet obviously there are pitfalls, as these stiff and lifeless figures show.

Figure 6. These two pictures reveal some of the common mistakes beginners make in using flat drawing. Again, the figures appear stiff and lifeless. When it is not nourished by direct observation, flat drawing may lead to simplistic and overly stylized characterizations like the ones here. In addition, although flat drawing lends itself very well to decoration and may make for a pleasing design, it may lack feeling. Sometimes, as in the picture on the left, an overemphasis on flat pattern can interfere with readability, for it becomes difficult to distinguish the figure from the background.

Figure 7. But flat drawing need not have the problems just described, as the work of Japanese old masters shows. This flat drawing by Kitao Masayoshi is full of life and emotion. Although the figures are extremely simplified, almost abstract, they are not simplistic. It takes a lot of careful observation and practice to convey so much with so few lines.

Figure 8. The lively, expressive character of these figures by Kawamuro Bumpō again stems from careful observation. The figures are simplified and boldly outlined, but the silhouette brings out the individuality of each.

Figure 9. Even though this woodcut by Jichōsai is flatly drawn, it is full of movement, with energetic lines. It is also highly readable. It avoids the pitfalls of the pictures in Figure 6. Here the lines—unconcerned with describing volume—have an exuberance and joy on their own.

Figure 10. This illustration by the French master Boutet de Monvel shows how the decorative possibilities of flat drawing have been used effectively in a Western children's book.

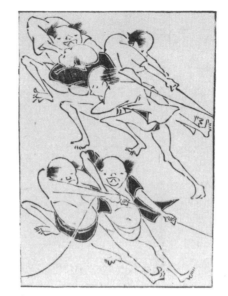
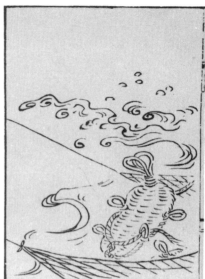

9

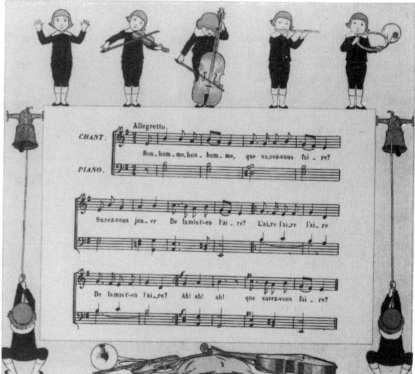

10

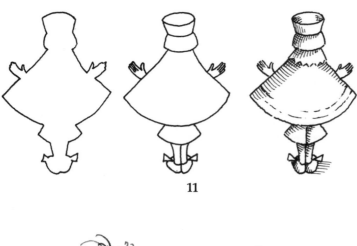

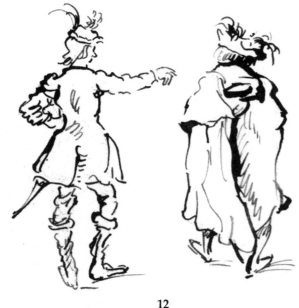

11

12

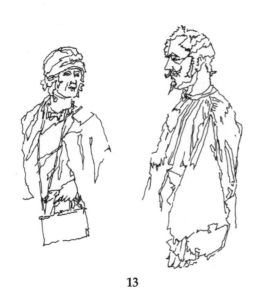

13

Combining Outline and Volume

When you draw, try to keep both the outline and the volume in mind. Even in a basically flat drawing, a suggestion of volume cannot be entirely avoided. On the other hand, in a round drawing, outline cannot be avoided entirely. Understanding how the outline and the volume relate to each other will help to improve your figure drawings.

Figure 11. Here you can see how the outline relates to the volume. If you draw a continuous line to represent the outer edge of the figure (as on the left), the result will look like a flat silhouette before it has been colored in. Should you now add lines inside the outline to describe the forms within its boundaries (center), you begin to suggest an illusion of roundness. If you add shading (right), the figure's roundness may be further emphasized, and it may gain volume as well. Minimizing and breaking the outlines would increase the roundness even further.

Figure 12. In these quick sketches, both the outline and volume are suggested.

The Underlying Form

The novice often focuses on superficial details and external appearances, overlooking the larger form. When you understand how the underlying structure affects smaller details and surface appearance, you will have gained insight into what may be one of the most important aspects of drawing. This knowledge will help you draw better regardless of whether you depict flat or round figures.

Figure 13. When you focus on superficial details and overlook the larger form, everything may seem equally important and the figures may be difficult to read.

Figure 14. Become familiar with the basic geometric volumes: cubes, cylinders, and spheres. Look for them, in various combinations, in different forms like the ones shown here. When you are able to see and use these geometric volumes in your pictures, you will have acquired a solid foundation for drawing.

Figure 15. Even more complicated forms like this have an underlying geometry.

Figure 16. As a rule of thumb, work from large to small. Begin your drawing with the largest geometric shape, followed by the next largest shapes, and so on. Look for the geometric volumes (like the cylinders here) within the larger forms. Then, observe how the details fit into the larger forms. When you subordinate the details to these larger considerations, they will contribute to the figure's readability rather than detract from it.

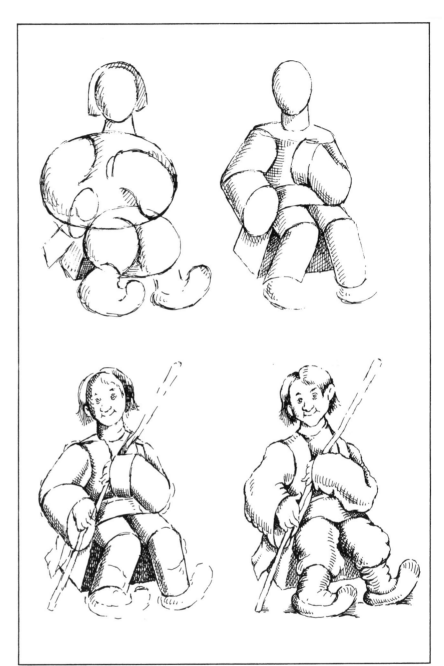

16

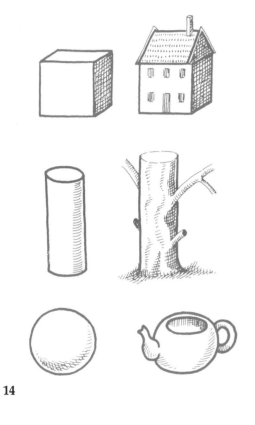

14

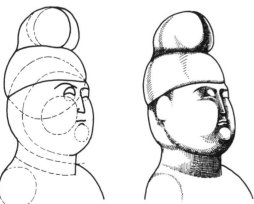

15

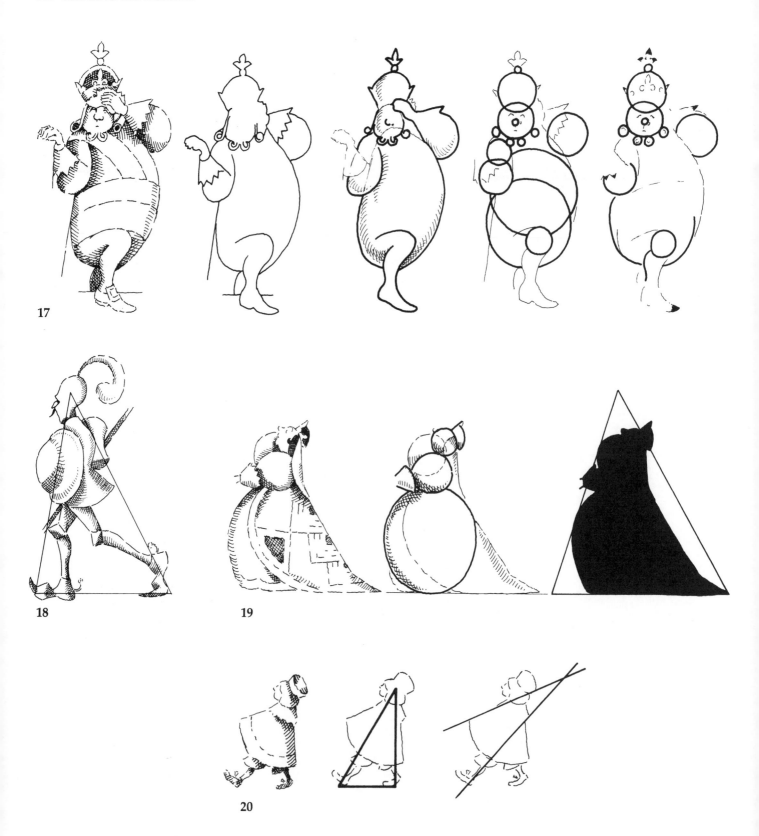

17

18

19

20

Figure 17. One way to learn more about form is to analyze the elements that contribute to a particular figure's character. If we analyze the king on the left, we can see first the outline and then the relationship between the outline and the volume. The next drawing shows how the king is composed of a series of circles, and the last drawing suggests the abstract humor in the relationship of these shapes.

Figure 18. In addition to the volume, you should also be aware of the figure's overall shape. Here the knight fits into an underlying triangle. This basic shape helps to organize the details and determine the overall character of the image.

Figure 19. In analyzing the queen, you can see how the volume is built up with a series of spheres (center) and how her silhouette relates to a triangle (right).

Figure 20. The little prince also contains a basic triangle. On the right you can see how another, implicit triangle is created by the directional lines that underlie the figure's movement.

Figure 21. Drawings by the old masters reveal the importance of understanding the figure's underlying geometry. The drawing on the left here is based on a study by Cambiaso; the one on the right is by Dürer. In both cases the artists "boxed" the figure to learn more about its form.

Figures 22–23. Dürer did many drawings like these in which he analyzed the basic shapes of the figure. This kind of understanding will help make you proficient in drawing the human figure.

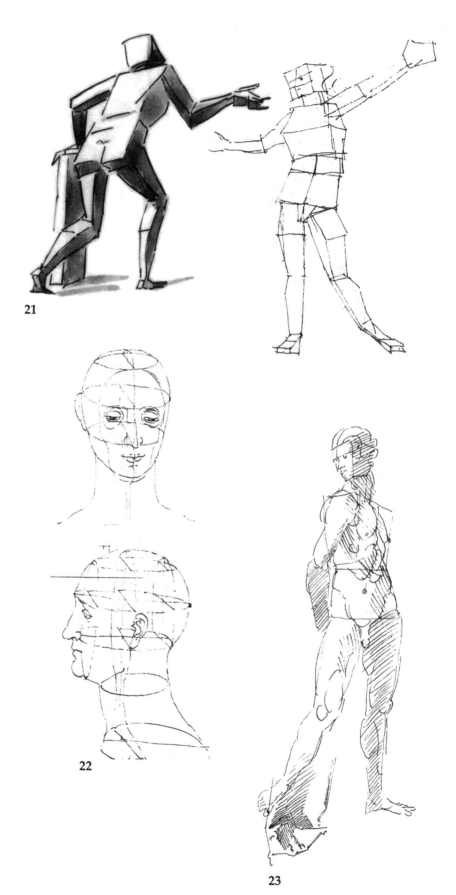

21

22

23

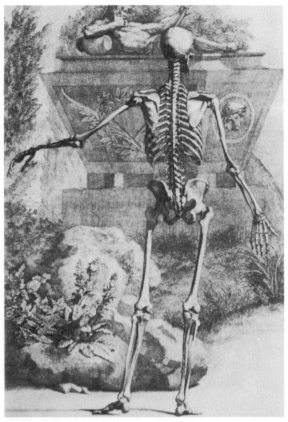

24

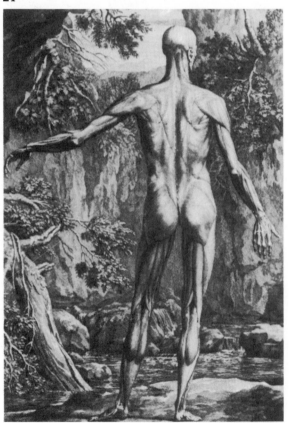

25

Figures 24–25. An understanding of basic anatomy is also important. These precise engravings by Albinus show how the skeletal and muscular systems relate.

Liveliness

The ability to depict a figure accurately is an important skill. That alone, however, is not enough; your drawing must have life—be animated—as well.

Figure 26. A good way to loosen up is to do sketches like these, which were done very quickly from life. I used a Japanese reed pen and sepia ink on inexpensive paper. I have found that my drawings have more spontaneity and daring when I'm not concerned about wasting expensive paper—I don't feel that I have to come up with a "masterpiece." I do a whole series of drawings in this way, ten to twenty, or more, at one sitting. It takes me some time to warm up and build momentum. Because I'm not concerned about a polished look, I usually find a few out of such a series aesthetically satisfying. I couldn't achieve quite the same results if I labored over my drawings.

Capturing Movement

One of the qualities of a lively figure is movement. And in illustrating children's books, you often need to draw figures or animals in motion because the characters are always doing something.

A good principle to remember in creating a feeling of movement is that when the weight of a figure is evenly distributed and the pose is symmetrical, the figure tends to be static. As Leonardo da Vinci wrote, "Motion occurs when there is a loss of equal distribution of weight."

Figure 27. Doing rapid drawings of a moving figure forces you to focus on the essentials of movement. These drawings were done during a dance recital in very dim light, again using a reed pen on inexpensive paper. I couldn't always see what I was drawing or how the drawing looked, but I didn't lose sight of the movement of the dancers. They were moving fast, slowing down only in the sitting positions. I had to observe the essence of their movement and put it down with great speed, relying as much on feeling as on sight. Only when I viewed the whole body as one unit was I able to capture the continuously changing positions, the twisting, bending, and shifting of the dancers' weight and balance.

Figure 28. Here you can see how asymmetry and an unequal distribution of weight contribute to a feeling of movement. Because the cylinder on the left is balanced and perpendicular to the ground, with its weight equally distributed, it is static, without movement. The other cylinder is not perpendicular to the ground but rather tilted to one side, so that it appears to be in motion—falling.

Figure 29. The same principle holds true for figures. The figure on the left is standing in a symmetrical pose, with the arms in identical positions. He is balanced, but static and stiff. The figure on the right is livelier and suggests movement. Although he is balanced, the balance is dynamic and asymmetrical—the parts of the body are not evenly positioned.

Figure 30. Imagine the figure as a stack of boxes. As the distribution of weight becomes more and more unequal, there is a greater suggestion of movement.

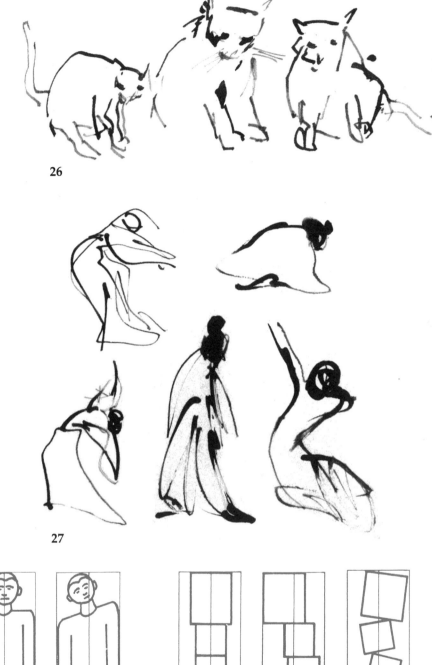

26

27

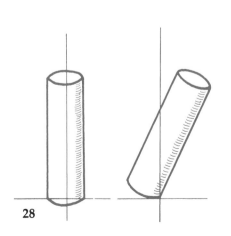

28

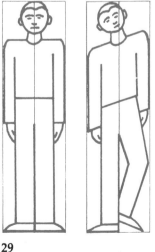

29

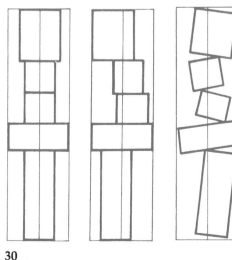

30

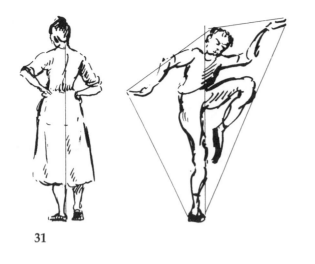

31

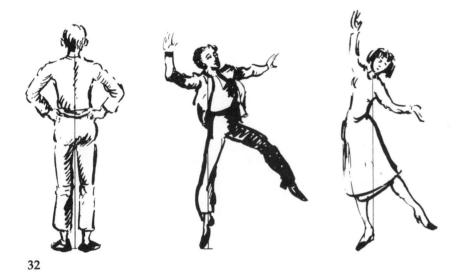

32

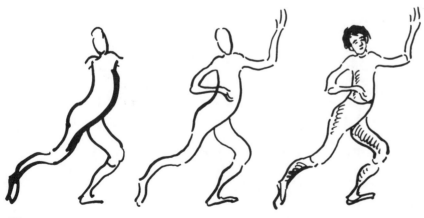

33

Figure 31. Although both these figures are balanced, the one on the right seems to be moving because the body parts have different angles and positions. The appearance of movement is increased by the variations in height and shape.

Figure 32. No matter how wild the movement, if a figure is correctly balanced one can run an imaginary straight line from the center of the neck to the supporting foot, or between the feet when the weight is equally distributed.

Figure 33. In drawing a live model in motion, view the figure as one shape or volume in space. Concentrate on the large parts—here the trunk, legs, and head. See how they relate one to another in direction and angle. Pay attention to how the weight falls by following the imaginary plumb line from the neck to the supporting foot. Once the main lines of movement are down, observe how the other parts—the arms and hand—relate. Finally add individual details like the clothing and facial features.

Figure 34. It's also important to consider the figure's overall shape. If the overall shape is dynamic rather than static, it will add movement to your drawing. The asymmetrical shape here is clearly more dynamic than the square, and this contributes to the motion of the knight.

Figure 35. Sometimes you can exaggerate the movement of a figure and achieve added drama or humor.

Figure 36. Once again, practice is important in capturing movement. Try drawing figures in a variety of poses.

Figure 37. In addition to studying the human figure, try to observe how different animals move by drawing from life or photographs.

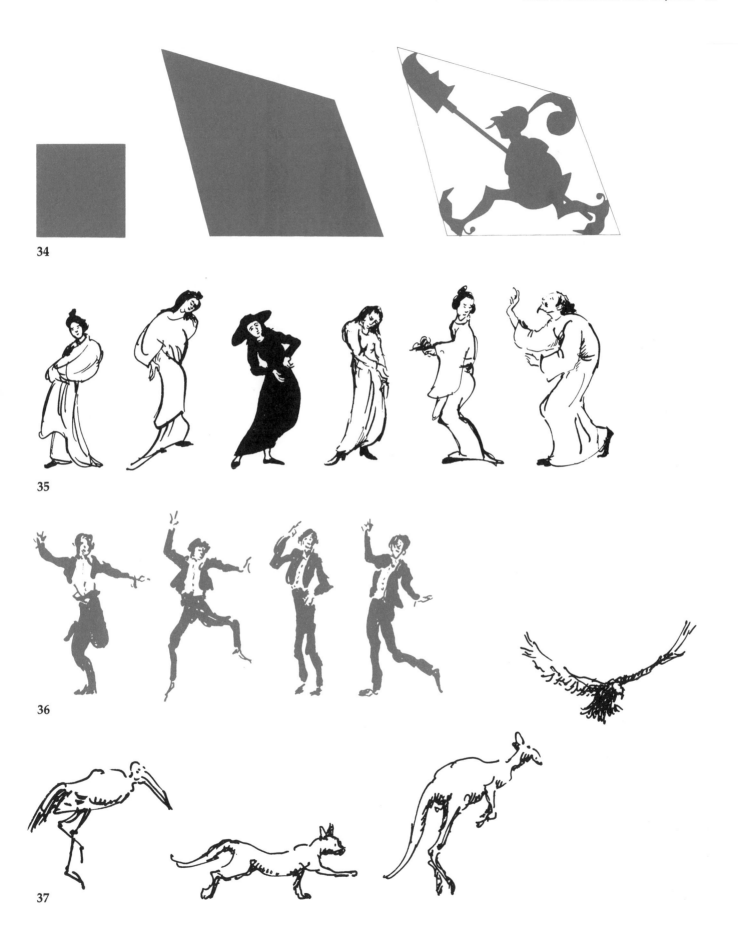

34

35

36

37

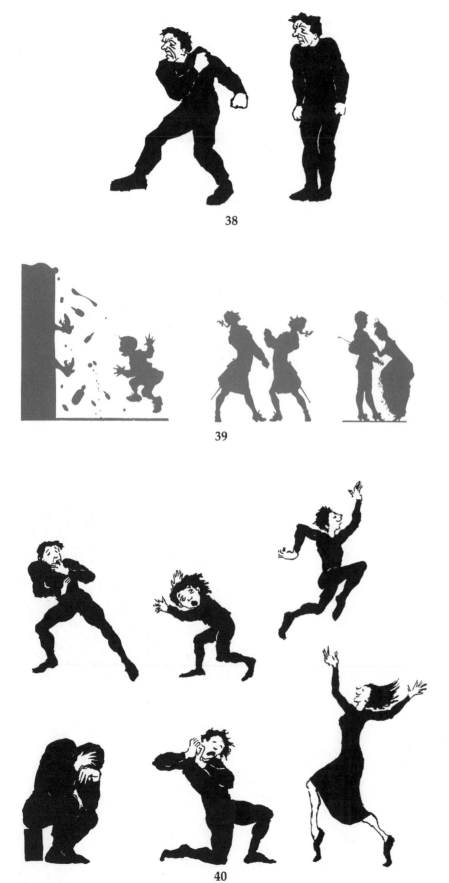

38

39

40

Using the Body for Expression

Another way to enliven your figure drawings is to use the *whole* body, not just the face, to express emotion. Think of your figure drawings as pantomime, with the whole body serving as the vehicle of expression.

Figure 38. Although you can rely on the face alone to express emotion, if you use the whole figure instead of just a few of its parts, your drawing will be more expressive.

Figure 39. Working with silhouettes forces you to show expression through the whole body.

Figure 40. There is no one way to show emotion in a drawing. Try to explore a range of possibilities. Using the whole figure as a vehicle of expression sharpens your eye. Then, when you want to express emotion subtly, without noticeable body movement, you will be able to do it better.

Cute Characterization

Some illustrators portray humans and animals as cute because they assume this will add charm and appeal. But cute figures are very unnatural and artificial, without "life." They also often lack a sense of form. Avoid cute drawings by basing your pictures on accurate observation and paying attention to form.

Figure 41. The appeal of cute figures like these tends to be short-lived because they are based on an idea or stereotype rather than honest observation.

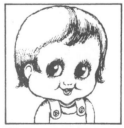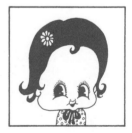

41

Exaggeration and Fantasy

The relationship between small and large elements affects the expressiveness of a picture. The same principle applies to the proportions of figures and faces.

By enlarging one part of the body and reducing another, the artist can change the character of a figure drastically. Exaggeration can be used in the face, body, or the entire picture to create amusing pictures. Make sure, however, that you don't create characters so grotesque that they scare children.

Figure 42. A change in the proportions of the face affects the physiognomy, as these studies by Dürer reveal. It can be used to create a caricature or bring out a humorous aspect of the person.

Figures 43–44. Exaggerated proportions can be used effectively to illustrate fantasy, as in Sir John Tenniel's illustration for Lewis Carroll's *Alice's Adventures in Wonderland* or the famous example of Pinnochio.

Figure 45. The distorted proportions of the figures and the contrast between large and small make this illustration by Grandville humorous.

Figure 46. Experimenting with different possibilities for exaggeration can be fun, and it can increase your understanding of expression in drawing.

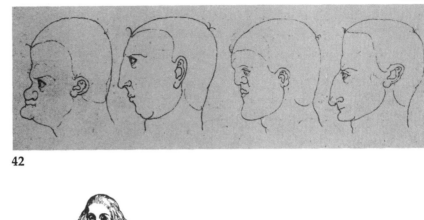
42

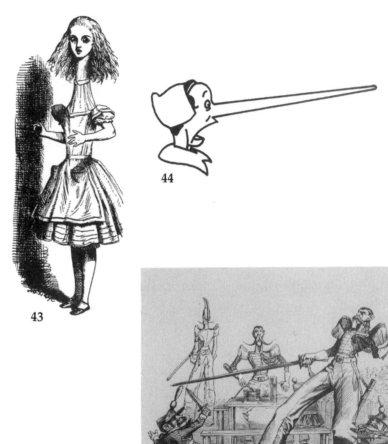
43

44

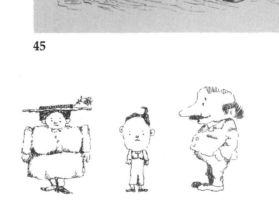
45

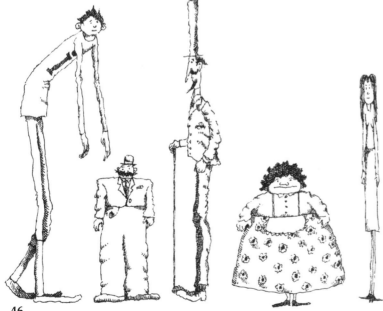
46

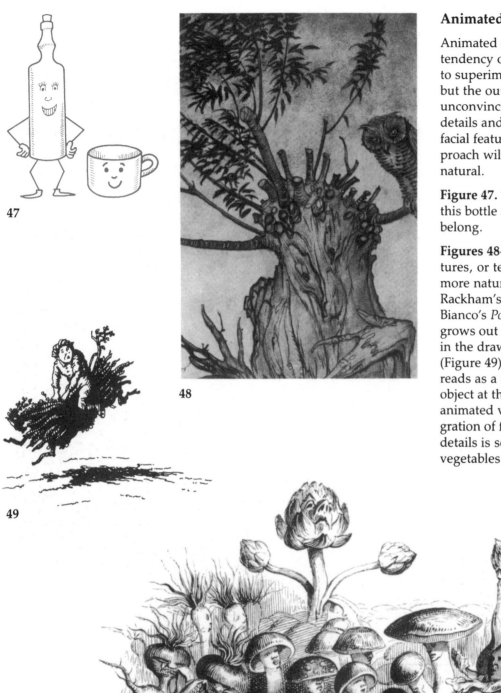

47

48

49

50

Animated Objects

Animated objects are tricky to draw. The tendency of many inexperienced artists is to superimpose facial features on objects, but the outcome is usually artificial and unconvincing. It is best to use the existing details and forms of the object to suggest facial features. In most cases, this approach will make the features look more natural.

Figure 47. The features superimposed on this bottle and cup don't look as if they belong.

Figures 48–50. Using existing details, features, or textures to animate an object is more natural and less forced. In Arthur Rackham's tree from Margery Williams Bianco's *Poor Cecco* (Figure 48), the face grows out of the tree's texture. Similarly, in the drawing after George Cruikshank (Figure 49), the horselike bundle of wood reads as a realistic object and an animated object at the same time. With Grandville's animated vegetables (Figure 50), the integration of facial features with existing details is so well done that one sees the vegetables becoming human.

Drawing Objects with Feeling

When you don't want to actually animate the objects in your illustration, you can give them life by drawing them with feeling. Try, as you draw, to consider everything—table, wall, tree, sky—as being alive, without making it human. This approach will help you put more care and feeling into drawing every element of the picture. You will be less likely to look on some parts as merely background and of secondary importance. Try to be aware of the total picture as a *living entity*, and at the same time retain the uniqueness and individuality of every element in it.

Figure 51. In this illustration by Gustave Doré, every element—from the deserted boats to the moonlit water to the eerie towers—is infused with life. The whole picture breathes.

Figure 52. With this illustration for *The Golem* by Isaac Bashevis Singer, I tried to give as much life to the buildings and sky as to the figures.

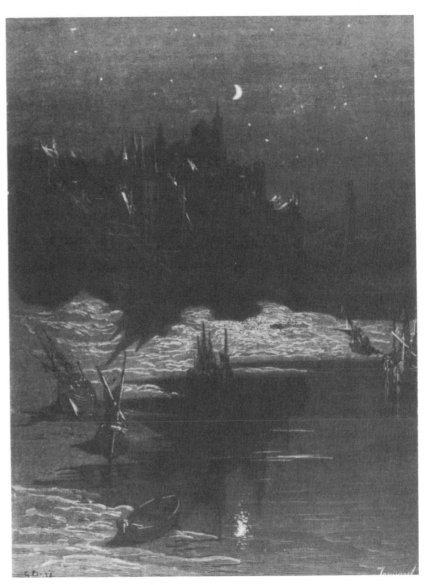

51

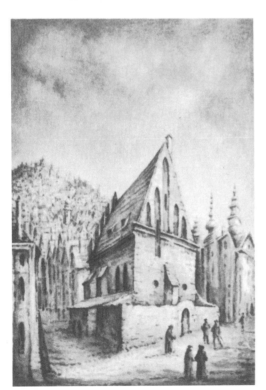

52

11. Visual References

Whether your book is set in a contemporary city, ancient China, or a world of pure imagination, you will need to depict the characters, objects, and scenery in a believable way, with details that lend authenticity and convey a sense of time and place. It is difficult to remember the exact appearance of things with which you are familiar, let alone represent people and places you have never known or visited. You can, of course, try to draw from imagination, but this can be difficult and the results are often unconvincing. True, there are illustrators who rely totally on imagination, but they are few. When you rely on imagination alone, you soon discover its limitations.

Nature, in all its aspects, is the richest source of reference material. No artist's imagination can compete with it. That is why most illustrators use visual references to aid them in creating and enriching their pictures.

Depending on the subject matter, you may choose to draw from nature directly, or you may rely on references like photographs. There are different kinds of visual references and different ways to use them.

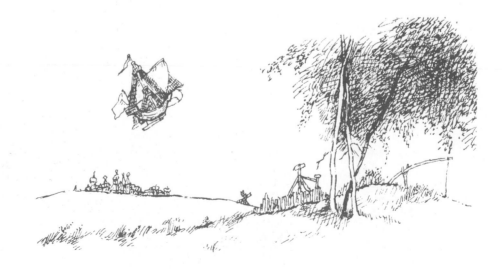

When to Use Visual References

Visual references can be used in depicting almost any element in a picture, from background details to the main character. While they are especially helpful in describing an unfamiliar setting or particular costume, their usefulness extends beyond that. At times you may want to refer to a real-life model or a photograph to draw a character's facial expression. Or you may want guidelines in capturing a kitten's playfulness.

Imagination may also be limited where manmade objects are concerned. Real furniture is often the result of hundreds of years of furniture-making experience. And once an object has been created, it has a life of its own. It is touched, moved, scratched, rubbed, polished, repainted—acquiring individual characteristics that are hard to imagine.

When you begin to create your pictures, you soon discover the need for details you never dreamed of, and for others that you had assumed you would remember when necessary. You may not always be able to find all the reference materials you need, but if you have used them wherever possible it will be easier to fill in the gaps in your information based on what you have on hand. You will be better able to make up something of your own.

Figure 1. Before I drew this illustration for *The Wonderful Kite* by Jan Wahl, I looked at a variety of photographs of Chinese buildings. Although my drawing is not a replica of the photographs, they helped me to understand the architectural style—particularly the design of the rooftops—so that my picture would do justice to the story's setting.

Figure 2. In a similar way, to create the illustrations for *Soldier and Tsar in the Forest*, I looked for pictures of Russian architecture and a sentry box. I found pictures of various buildings, but I couldn't find any of a sentry box. Finally I made up my own, based on the prevalent architectural style in the pictures I already had. Most buildings were constructed like log cabins, so I drew the sentry box as if it were constructed in this way too.

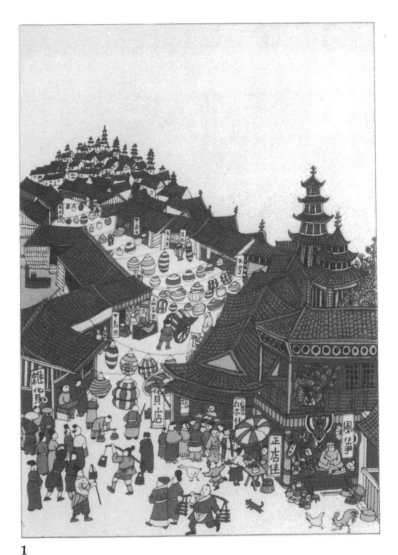

1

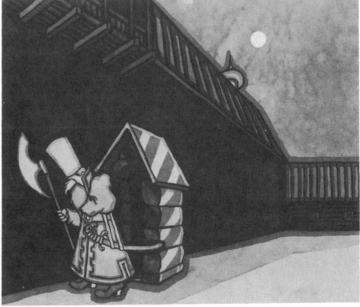

2

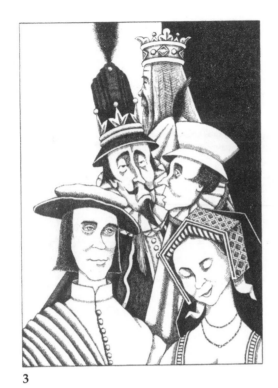

3

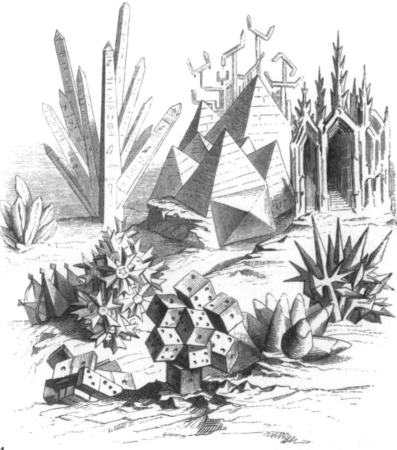

4

Figure 3. The elder brother in Robert Louis Stevenson's *The Touchstone* falls in love. To depict him accurately, I searched for a picture of someone in love. This proved to be difficult, but I finally found a model in movie stills of Cary Grant.

Figure 4. Fantasy relies much more on specific and closely observed details of reality than is commonly assumed. The best fantasy illustrations are precise and concrete, like this picture by Grandville. It is made up of real details interpreted, combined, or arranged in new or un-usual ways.

Figure 5. "A pigwee is a sort of animal that isn't there. You can't see it. It is very old. And it can talk to you. Pigwees don't like people." How could I illustrate this fantasy creature described in H. R. and Daniel Hays's *Charley Sang a Song*? To arrive at my interpretation (left), I combined features from existing animals and added a beard to make my pigwee "very old." Sir John Tenniel probably used a similar process for Lewis Carroll's *Alice's Adventures in Wonderland* (right).

Figure 6. At one point in *The Lost Kingdom of Karnica*, Richard Kennedy describes the invention of great machines to speed the process of digging for a huge precious stone the size of the kingdom itself. For this fantasy-parable, I turned for inspiration to some of Leonardo da Vinci's inventions. I found some sketches he had made of war machines, which I adapted to create my own digging machines.

Figure 7. Although most often you will want to use actual visual references, there may be times when your reference is a vivid picture in your mind. I drew the forest in Dorothy Nathan's *The Month Brothers* guided by a mental picture and a strong sense of what the trees should feel and look like: hostile and full of needle-like branches. Months later I saw trees in the Czech film *Loves of a Blond* that were very much like the ones I had imagined. This experience convinced me that strongly felt mental pictures may come from a concrete source.

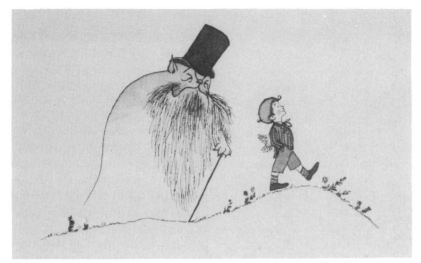

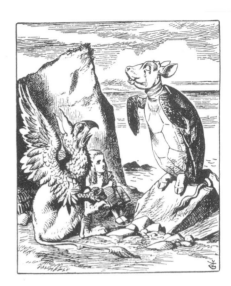

5

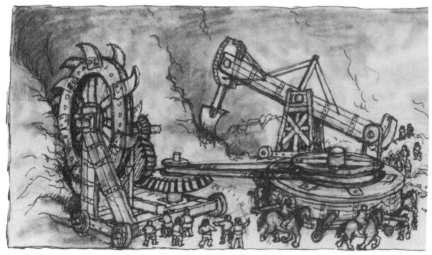

6

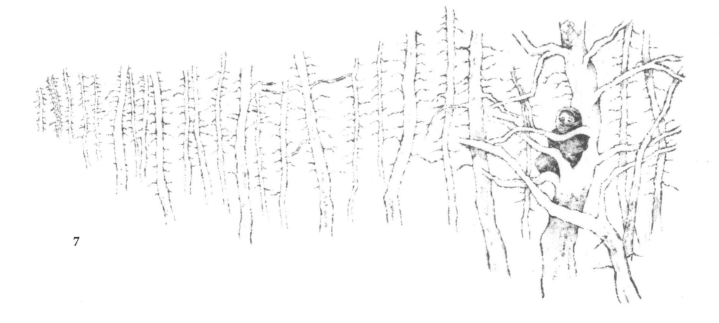

7

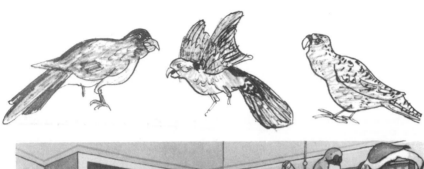

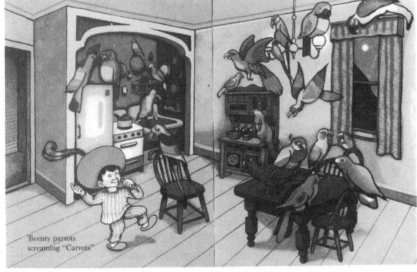

Twenty parrots
screaming "Carrots"

8

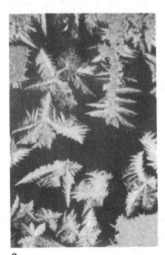

9

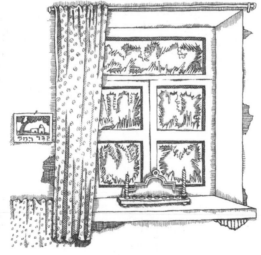

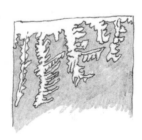

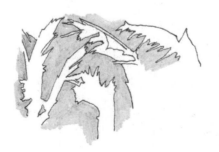

What to Use for Reference

Nature, of course, is the best reference material. When you need a human model, you can use a friend or relative, or even draw yourself while looking in a mirror. When you need an animal, you can draw your pet or go to a zoo. But when you want to illustrate something that is inaccessible to you, pictures are your next best source of information.

The best pictures to use are ones that are accurate and represent the subject clearly. Try to find readable, detailed photographs that present information objectively. You need *facts*, not *opinions*. "Artistic" or highly "personal" photos usually emphasize the photographer's special point of view, so that you may end up presenting someone else's interpretation instead of your own. You want to be able to respond to what *you* see rather than what someone else does. Try to be especially aware of subtle distortions in pictorial references.

Although objective photographs are the next best thing to nature, you should not overlook the many fine drawings, paintings, woodcuts, and engravings of the past that represent their subjects in a straightforward, factual way. In many cases they are the *only* source of visual information we have about the world before the camera was invented.

Figure 8. To create these parrots in *Oh What a Noise!*, I first did a lot of sketches at the zoo. Even the kitchen had a real-life model—it's based on my own kitchen.

Figure 9. I began working on Sholem Aleichem's *Hanukah Money* in the summertime. The book's setting is Eastern Europe, in the midst of winter. One of the first illustrations calls for delicate frost patterns on the windowpanes. I couldn't wait until winter to draw the picture and, besides, the chances that my windows would be covered with appropriate frost patterns were slim. My only recourse, then, was to use photographs such as the one shown here to study my subject. In drawing from these photographs, I selected formations that not only looked like ice but *felt cold* as well.

Figure 10. Before drawing the large, splashing waves in *Rain Rain Rivers*, I studied this detail of a photograph of water patterns. A photograph can be particularly helpful in "stilling" a moving subject so that you can observe what is really happening.

Figure 11. Photographs like these are useful reminders of how textures weather with the passage of time. They provide information on details that can enrich a picture and make it feel more real. The worn character of the stairwell, for instance, would be difficult to visualize on your own.

Figure 12. As reference material, the photograph here is preferable to my subjective drawing. The photograph presents facts; the drawing, opinion. From this photograph you can learn how the building is constructed and select the information you need. With the drawing you are limited to my personal interpretation.

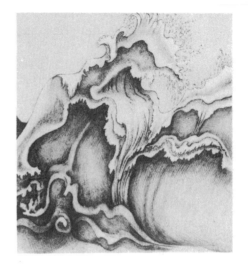

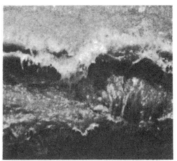

10

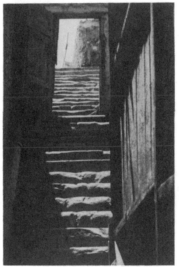

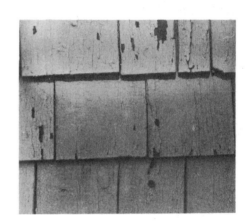

11

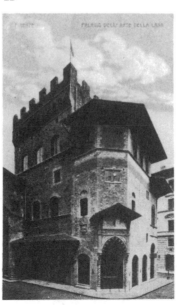

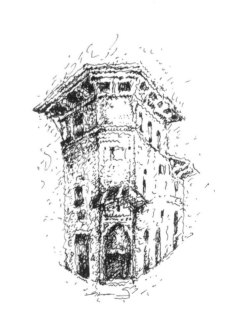

12

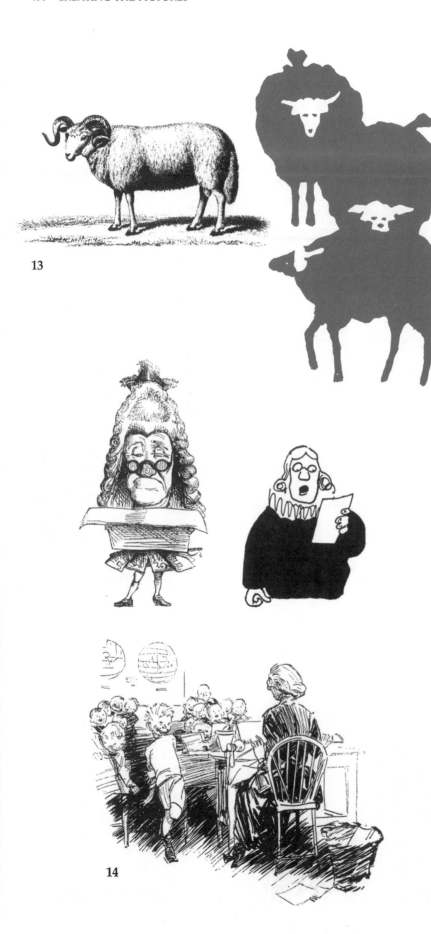

13

14

Figure 13. Other illustrations can be useful as references, but you have to be careful which ones you choose. The highly stylized sheep on the right might be fun to look at, but the engraving on the left gives you information that enables you to create your own image.

Figure 14. As references, these illustrations are obviously poor choices because they use highly personal handwriting and interpretations. If you compare the classroom scene here with the illustration of the casemaker's shop in Chapter 9 (Figure 20), you can see how differently the information is presented.

How to Use Reference Pictures

When you use a photograph (or objective illustration) as a visual reference, you need to learn how to use it without copying it. The best way is to skip the intermediary, the photo itself. Instead, view the photo as if it were the real object, not a photographic representation. Visualize it as tangible and three-dimensional. If the object is a house, walk around it in your mind and see how it looks from all sides. Concentrate on its *structure*, and use this information as your guide. Don't allow yourself to be distracted by the play of light and shadow in the photograph, except to understand how it describes form. If you need shadows in your illustration, add them later, based on your picture's own requirements. If you need to represent the interior of the house and have no reference materials available, enter the house in your mind and imagine what it looks like inside, or find another pictorial reference suited to the interior.

Remember that visual references are a tool, not a model cast in stone. It isn't necessary, or always possible, to find the "perfect" reference, with all the elements you want. Often I use elements from several different references, plus variations of my own, in developing the final picture. Visual references are not a substitute for imagination. Their usefulness lies in helping you to make an imaginary scene richer and more real.

Figure 15. In drawing from this photograph, my main concern was to understand the form of the goat. This understanding of structure is necessary before you develop your image of the goat.

Figure 16. With photographs it's important to select the most useful information. My drawing focuses on the substance, the architectural form, and ignores the fleeting play of light and shadow.

Figure 17. You can use a photograph to visualize something that isn't in the picture itself. Here, after studying the form of the building in the center of the photograph, I imagined entering the rounded entranceway on the right. Although my picture of this is "fictional," it is based on an understanding of the building's structure.

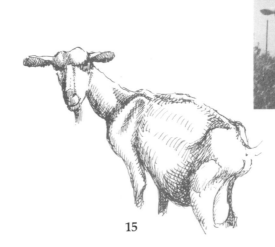

15

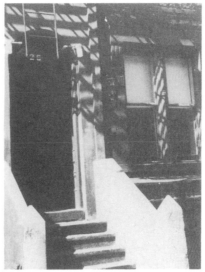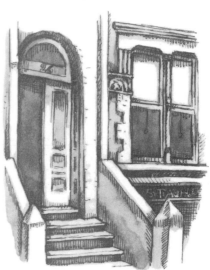
16

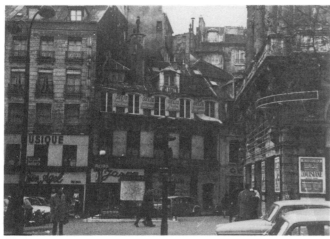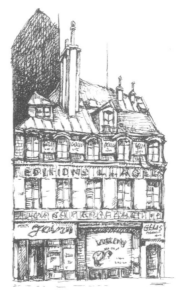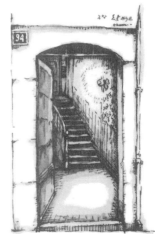
17

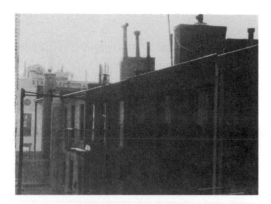

Figure 18. This photograph was my original reference for the background buildings in my illustration for *Rain Rain Rivers*. Notice how I selected information and adapted it to fit the requirements of the final picture.

Figures 19–24. Pictorial references can enrich your imagination, thus improving the pictures you develop. The setting for one of my illustrations for *The Touchstone* (Figure 24) was modeled on a photograph of a road by the Danube, leading toward a castle (Figure 19). I couldn't have imagined a more perfect setting, and in my drawing (Figure 20) I indicated the features that appealed to me. (When I borrow a photograph like this one from a library collection, my drawing serves as a reference after I return the photograph.)

For the castle, I decided I wanted something different. To gain a better understanding of how to construct a castle, I sketched a variety of castles from photographs, including those in Figures 21 and 22. I liked the form of a castle in Scotland best (Figure 21), and I used this as the basis for my own picture.

You can see how I incorporated my sketches into my preliminary drawing (Figure 23). In the final picture (Figure 24), I made some additional changes—moving the horses and riders slightly to the right and the castle slightly to the left, making the castle itself larger, and giving the tower on the left another roof. These adjustments were more in keeping with what I wanted.

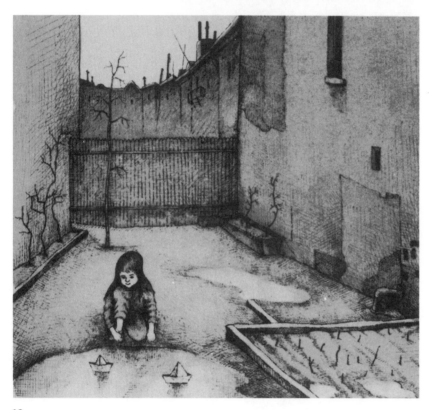

18

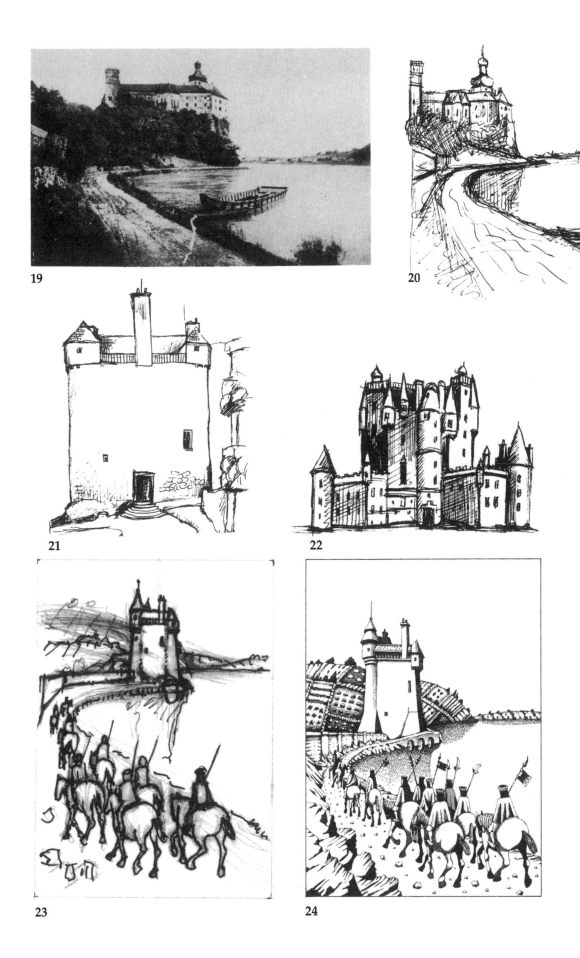

19

20

21

22

23

24

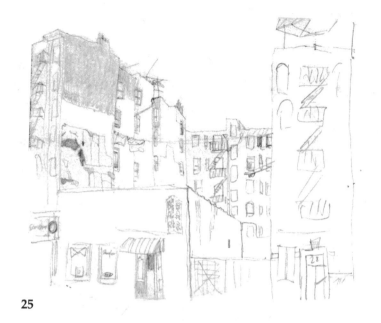

25

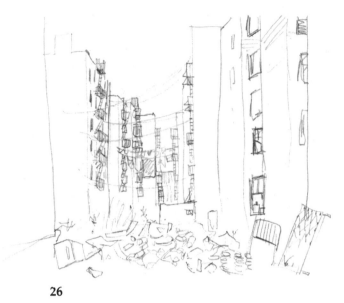

26

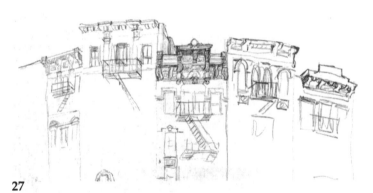

27

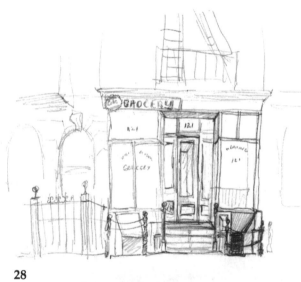

28

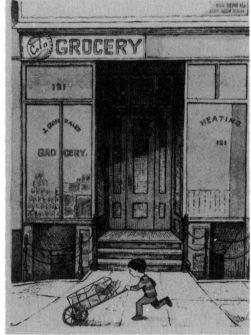

29

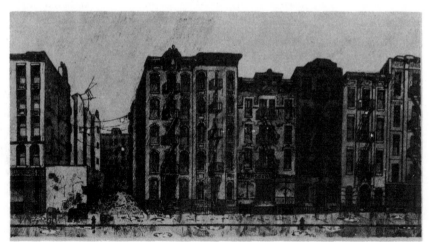

30

Figures 25–30. For the city scenes in *One Monday Morning*, I did many sketches on the Lower East Side of New York City—a few of which are shown here (Figures 25–28). Aspects from these sketches were incorporated into my panoramic double spread near the beginning of the book (Figure 30). Later in the book I showed closeups of this view—for instance, the grocery store in Figure 29 (which is based on the sketch in Figure 28).

Figures 31–35. In illustrating *The Touchstone* I did many studies of costumes from different periods before deciding on the ones I wanted. The informality of the early-seventeenth-century costume in Figure 31 seemed appropriate for the young hero, and I sketched it, as well as other, similar costumes (Figure 32). Doing these drawings enabled me to envision the costume from the back, as it appears in the final illustration (Figure 33).

To contrast the king's pompous personality with the hero's simple honesty, I wanted a "bloated" look. Again, by drawing from a photograph (Figure 34), I gained the understanding of structure necessary to create the costume in my final illustration (Figure 35).

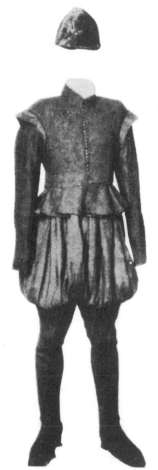

31

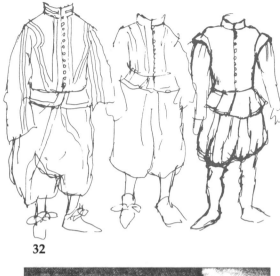

32

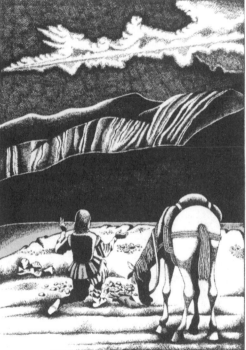

33

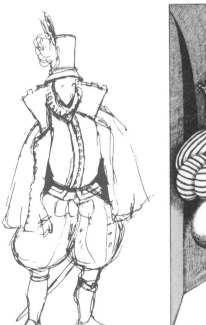

34

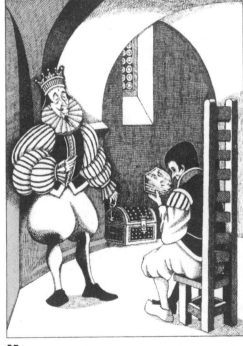

35

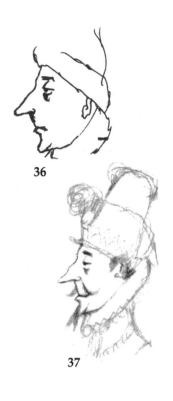

36

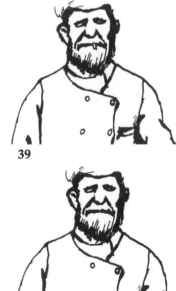

37

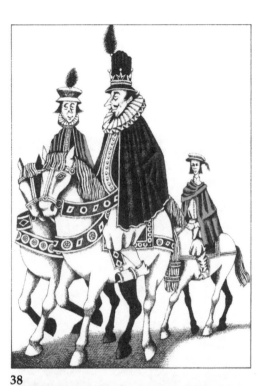

38

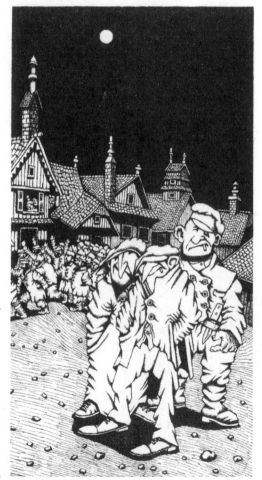

41

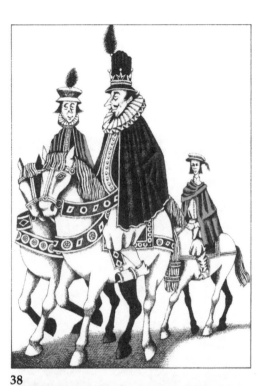

39

40

Figures 36–38. In *The Touchstone* Robert Louis Stevenson describes the king as "a man that stood well before the world, his smile was sweet as clover, but his soul withinsides was as little as a pea." Before I began drawing I studied historical pictures of various kings and rulers. Finally, I settled on a picture of one of the kings of France. I modeled the first sketch (Figure 36) on his main features and expression; in the second (Figure 37), I retained his cold and unsmiling eyes but added a smile to his face. Figure 38 shows how the king appears in the book. Notice how I adapted the costume in Figure 34.

Figures 39–41. To create the characters for Isaac Bashevis Singer's *The Fools of Chelm*, I studied photographs of people in traditional Eastern European settings and began to make sketches. I paid particular attention to the small details that make an individual believable—details that I couldn't possibly have invented, such as the cigarette butt in the corner of the carter's mouth (Figure 39). Without the cigarette butt (Figure 40), he is nowhere near as "tough." In the final illustration (Figure 41), I exaggerated certain details to give the caricatured figures a lively quality in keeping with the story.

Figures 42–51. These drawings show how I developed some of the other characters in *The Fools of Chelm*. For Gronam Ox—the main character—I first drew a sketch from imagination (Figure 42). This figure, however, seemed too grotesque and unconvincing. I then found an appropriate reference photograph and did a sketch, slightly exaggerating the features (Figure 43). In my next sketch (Figure 44), I changed the proportions somewhat. Then, for the book itself (Figure 45), I decided it fit his character to have his eyes looking in different directions.

For another character (Figure 50), I began with a drawing from a photograph (Figure 46) and then explored various possibilities for caricature (Figures 47–49). The other characters in this scene (Figure 51) were developed in a similar way. Although their features are distorted, they are based on observations of reality.

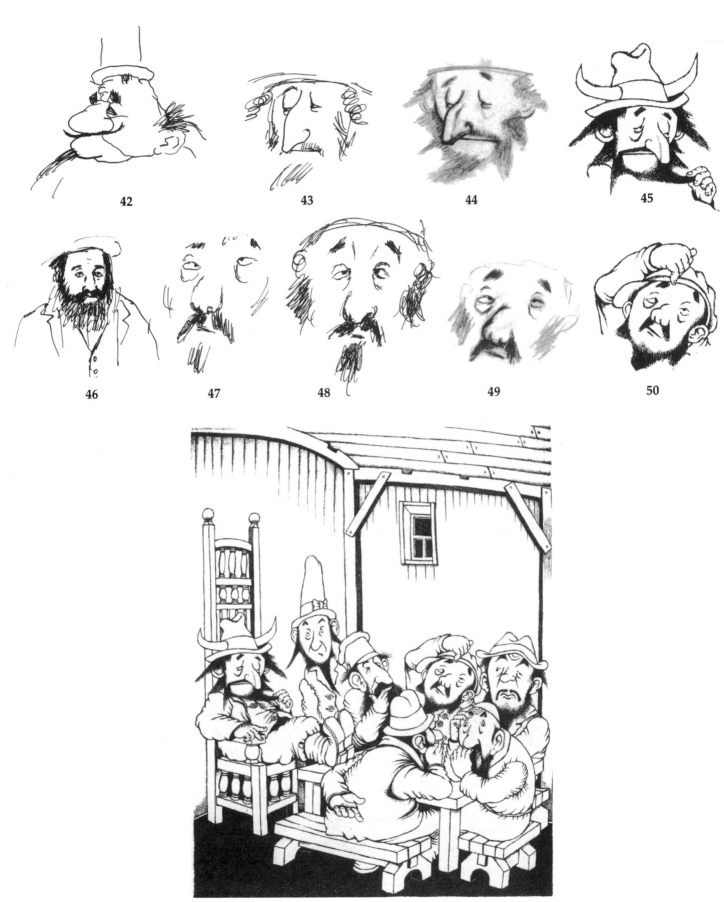

42

43

44

45

46

47

48

49

50

51

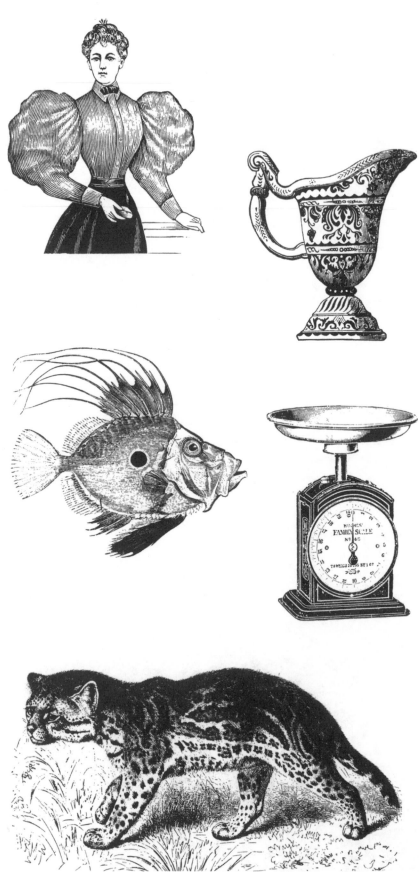

Start Your Own Picture Collection

Many large municipal, university, or museum libraries have picture collections that can be invaluable sources of visual information. But if you are not fortunate enough to live near such a library, it is vital that you start your own collection. In fact, many artists who do have access to large picture collections also have their own collections. The least expensive way to do this is to cut out pictures from magazines or newspapers and file them by subject. You can also collect other material such as posters, postcards, and snapshots. In time you will have a substantial number of pictures. Do not underestimate the significance of any picture, as it may turn out to be a valuable source of information later.

You can supplement your collection with profusely illustrated books on various subjects, from costumes to architecture to transportation vehicles. Pictorial encyclopedias, filled with informative engravings from the past, are particularly useful. Mail-order catalogs can also provide visual information. There are inexpensive paperbound field guides to birds, flowers, seashells, and other natural objects. And don't overlook the many special-interest magazines published for automobile and motorcycle devotees, sports enthusiasts, dog and cat fanciers, antiques buffs, and travel fans.

Figure 52. This sampling of images—from a pictorial encyclopedia—is just to give you an idea of the rich variety available and to encourage you to start your own collection.

12. Picture Space and Composition

We make doors and windows for a room; but it is these empty spaces that make the room livable. Thus, while the tangible has advantages, it is the intangible that makes it useful.

Lao-tzu

As a child, when I drew a picture I was aware only of its visible aspect, the objects in it. When I drew a tree, I saw the tree, but not the empty space around it and between its branches. Nor did I see exactly where in the picture the tree stood. I also packed an assortment of objects into the picture. I wasn't quite sure how to arrange them to avoid confusion and to help the picture as a whole. Gradually I learned that the invisible space, the "nothingness" around the tree, was as important as the tree itself. And I learned that there was a hidden understructure that organized everything in the picture.

These two hidden aspects of a picture are the *picture space* and *composition*. Picture space is the depth of space represented within the picture frame, including both objects and the space around them. Composition is the way all the elements in the picture are organized into a unified whole.

Every element, visible or hidden, works for or against the picture. No aspect can be ignored.

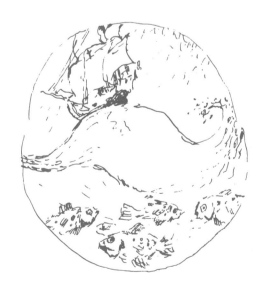

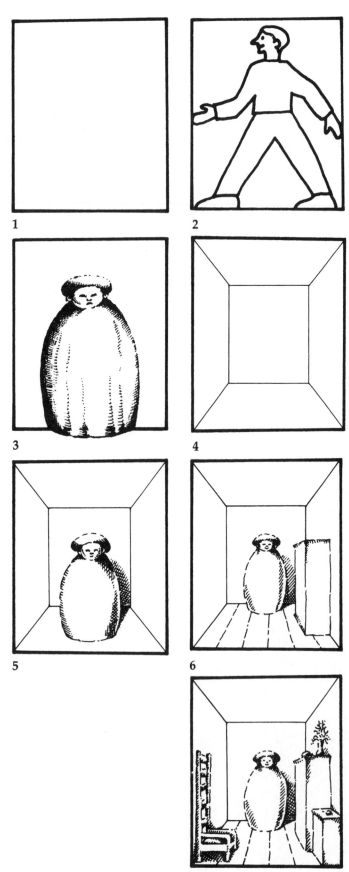

Flat or Deep Space

Paper is flat. When you draw an empty frame on paper, the frame is as flat as the paper (**Figure 1**). If you draw a figure using an even, continuous outline, the figure is also flat (**Figure 2**). You have a flat figure within a flat frame on flat paper. The space in the picture is flat as well.

So far so good. But what if you want to draw a round figure in the flat frame? By itself the round figure looks out of place (**Figure 3**). It seems heavier than the frame, as though it were sticking out of the paper, or falling out of the frame. The figure needs to breathe.

How do you create breathing space? You make the frame into an imaginary box (**Figure 4**). Actually, the frame was the border of the front of the box all along. You just didn't see it.

Now you have an appropriate space for the round figure, and you can place the figure anywhere in it. But the figure looks lonely in its empty box (**Figure 5**).

You can draw the floorboards, begin to move furniture in, and create a room (**Figure 6**). As you continue to draw the room, or when you look at it after it's done (**Figure 7**), you forget the flat surface of the paper. You are busy "exploring" the room. In a flat picture, however, you never forget the flat paper.

Your frame, then, is like part of a transparent wall. You look through that wall and what you see is the picture space. In our example the picture space is the inside of a room (Figure 7). Although the paper is flat, we have created an illusion of depth on it. This illusion of depth is a new kind of space, which deepens and extends the space of the paper.

Figure 8. We can clearly see the "space box" in this picture of Max in his room from Maurice Sendak's *Where the Wild Things Are.*

Figure 9. We can see the "space box" in this room by Domenico Gnoli for Norton Juster's *Alberic the Wise* as well, but it is seen from a higher viewing position.

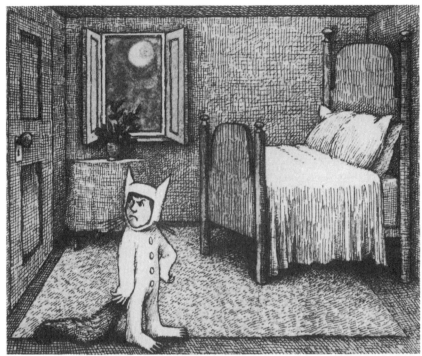

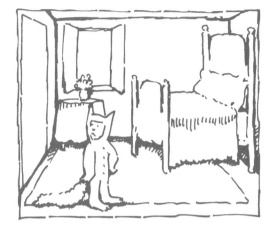

8

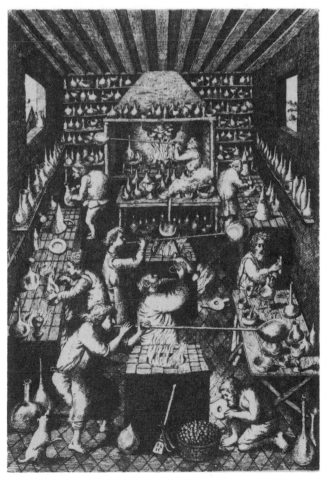

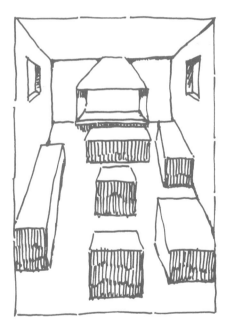

9

10

11

12

13

Differences in the Illusion of Depth

Actually, anything you draw on paper, flat or round, creates an illusion of depth. Even our flat outline figure (Figure 2) appears to stand in front of a background and thus does not seem absolutely flat. The difference between the illusion of depth in flat pictures and ones with deep space is one of degree. When we call a picture "flat," we are referring to a relative flatness. Because you cannot avoid seeing some elements in front of others, there is always an illusion of space. With deep space, however, you deliberately create the appearance of three dimensions.

Figures 10–11 illustrate this difference in the illusion of depth in a flat picture and one with deep space. If we were to look at the side view of the flat picture, we might see cardboardlike cutouts of the figure and the wall, one in front of the other, with almost no perceptible distance between them (Figure 10). In contrast, a side view of the picture with deep space might show distance between its elements (Figure 11). The figure would have volume, and there would be considerable space between the figure and the wall.

Emphasis on Two or Three Dimensions

Different pictorial elements are used to create flat and deep space. With flat space, for instance, the contour or outline of forms may be used to emphasize two dimensions. With deep space, however, the emphasis is on volume and three dimensions. This difference can be seen in a comparison of the wall paintings of the ancient Egyptians and the art of the Renaissance.

As the painter Peter Hopkins points out: "The ancient Egyptians in their wall paintings used hard, continuous outlines to represent and emphasize the two-dimensional plane." **Figure 12** suggests how this two-dimensional emphasis works. When a box is drawn behind the picture frame, the figure appears to remain in front, on the surface.

In contrast, Peter Hopkins says, "in order to represent the illusion of three dimensions in their drawings, the Renaissance artists used broken lines and perspective, both linear and atmospheric."

Figure 13 shows the difference in this approach. When the imaginary box of the picture frame is drawn, the figure seems to walk *into* its deep space.

Hopkins goes on to explain the difficulties for the artist in representing deep space on a flat surface such as a wall or a piece of paper. There is a contradiction between the illusion of three-dimensional space and the fact that the picture is drawn on a flat, two-dimensional surface (which is sometimes called the picture plane). For the picture to be unified, the artist must learn how to depict three dimensions without disrupting or breaking the flatness of the picture's surface.

Figure 14. Although traditional Western art tends to emphasize three dimensions and the illusion of deep space, flat space can be used very effectively, as this Japanese woodcut shows. The choice between flat space and deep space is only a choice. One is not inherently better than the other.

Figure 15. In contrast to Figure 14, this engraving by Bruegel creates the illusion of deep space. Notice, however, how the artist has resolved the contradiction between the illusion of deep space and the flat picture surface. For instance, the perspective lines lead back, into the picture, but the woman in the middle left, watering the plants, stops the eye and directs it forward again to the picture surface. Also, to avoid a claustrophobic feeling, Bruegel provides an escape for the eye by leaving empty space in the sky.

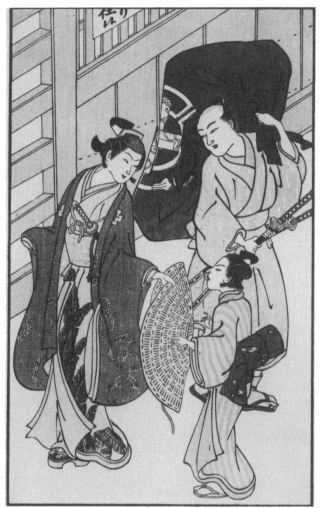

14

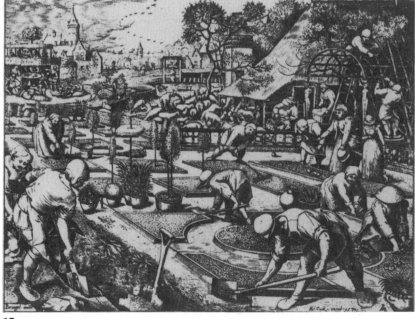

15

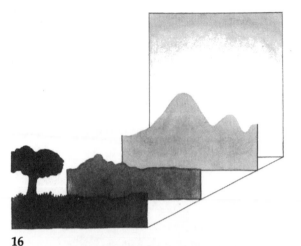

16

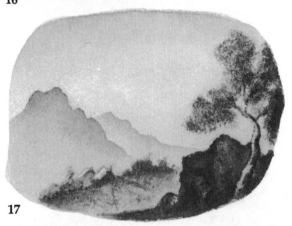

17

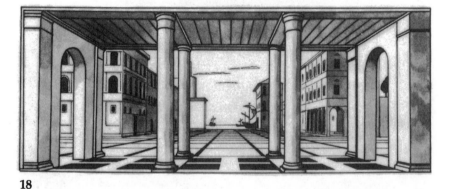

18

Figure 16. One of the ways to create the illusion of space within a picture is by distinguishing between the foreground, middle ground, and background, as in this diagram.

Figure 17. This picture uses atmospheric perspective so that as the eye moves from the foreground to the background, the view becomes hazy and less distinct.

Figure 18. In this drawing done after a painting attributed to Piero della Francesca, you can see the use of linear perspective to create the illusion of deep space. Yet even though there is a push into the picture space, there are also vertical and horizontal lines that pull our eyes back to the picture surface.

Figure-Ground Relationship and Readability

We tend to organize, simplify, and interpret what we see. Thus, the four dots in **Figure 19** are seen as a square (**Figure 20**). Were we to place this square within a frame (**Figure 21**), we might read the small square as being on top of or in front of a larger square (**Figure 22**). Or we might see the whole as a large square with an opening (**Figure 23**).

Given two elements, such as the two squares, we perceive one as closer than the other. We organize them into two opposing elements, interpreting the smaller one as a figure in front of the larger background. This is called the *figure-ground* relationship.

When clear differentiation between the figure and the ground is interfered with,

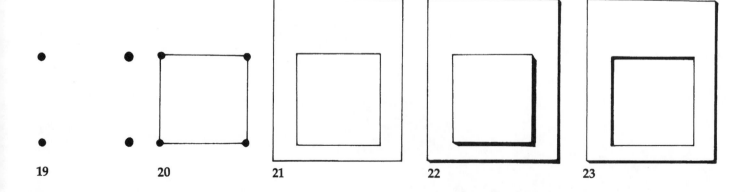

19   **20**   **21**   **22**   **23**

confusion or frustration may result. Flat pictures can be hard to read if elements meant to be close recede, and elements meant to be in the background come forward. Sometimes flat pictures can be hard to read if at first you see the overall pattern and then have to search for the subject matter.

Figure 24. How the elements in a picture either come forward or recede in relation to one another can be seen in these diagrams. In the first example, the larger square appears closer. In the second, the upper square overlaps the lower one and thus seems to be on top of it. Finally, in the third, the black square moves back while the white one comes forward.

Figure 25. In the picture on the left, the figure-ground relationship is clear: the chair is seen as the "figure"; the floor and the wall as the "ground." On the right, however, the figure-ground relationship is ambiguous: the black and the white shapes take turns in appearing closer—they alternate as figure and ground.

Figure 26. Although the first picture uses deep space and the second flat space, both are equally hard to read because there is not enough contrast between figure and ground.

Figure 27. Unclear differentiation between figure and ground makes the first picture hard to read. In the center picture, with the greater contrast between figure and ground, readability is increased. The picture space is even clearer in the last picture, and the improved readability allows for greater enjoyment.

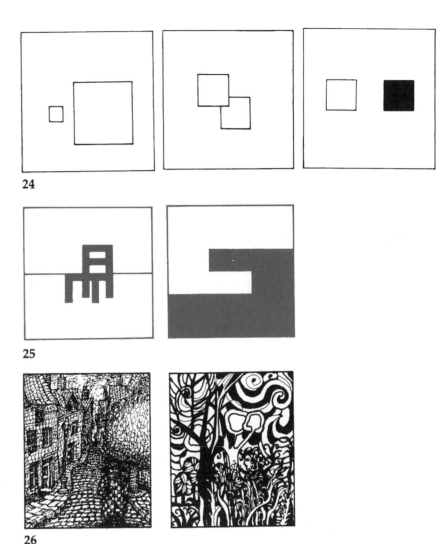

24

25

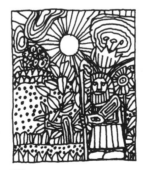

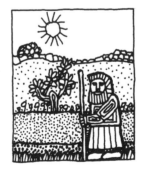

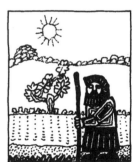

26

27

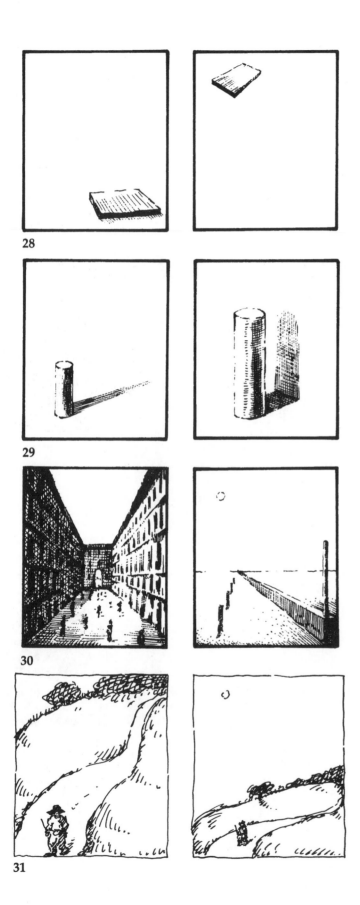

28

29

30

31

Picture Space and Expression

To put feeling into a picture, you need a vehicle. Just as the entire body—not only the face—expresses a character's emotion, every element of the picture—not only its subject matter—contributes to its emotional quality. Space is an important means of expression in a picture. Each way of depicting space has a different impact on the picture. And every area in the picture—even empty space—is important.

Figures 28–29. Although the object is the same in each paired figure, the space suggested is different and thus elicits a different response.

Figure 30. Here the space described in the first picture is "closed" while in the second it is "open," even though the perspective is similar. As a result, the pictures have a different feeling.

Figure 31. Both pictures here have the same subject matter, but the emotional quality is different. In the first there is a feeling of drama. Because of the vertical presentation, the landscape and the road seem to move toward the viewer and "push" out the figure. In contrast, the other scene is more open; it is seen from a great distance and seems peaceful. The figure appears to be part of his surroundings.

Figure 32. In the first picture, seen from a distance, the castle looks modest, as if it were a home in the country. It is an integral part of the setting, and the picture's ample empty space creates a restful feeling. As we move closer in the second picture, there is less empty space, but we become curious and want to enter and explore the castle. In the next picture there is even less empty or open space, and the massive wall "hits" the eye. The last picture is mysterious and possibly threatening because we are "boxed in" and don't see enough; there is room for the unexpected. Since there is almost no empty space, we are forcefully led into the dark entrance—the only "escape" for the eye.

Figure 33. The first picture is enclosed; there is no "exit." The second is open; the eye can escape into the distance through the door and the window.

Figure 34. The picture on the right seems to have more space than the one on the left, in part because there is more space around the figure.

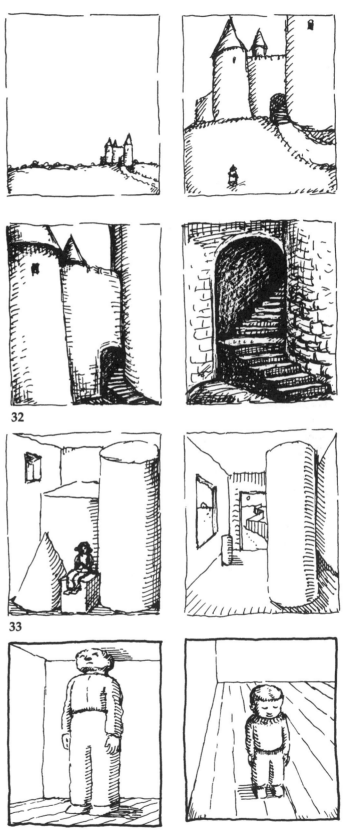

32

33

34

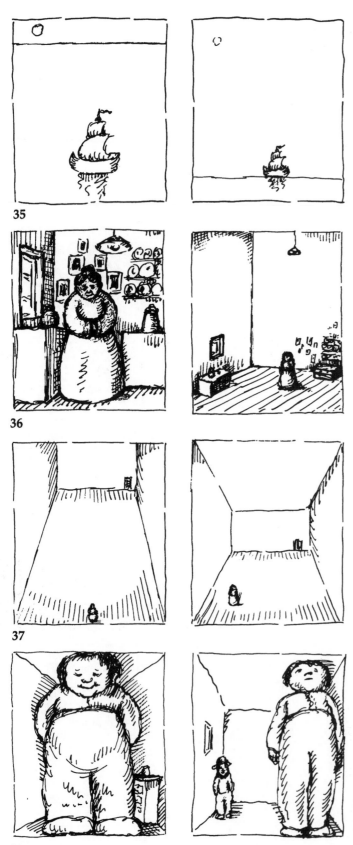

35

36

37

38

Figure 35. Although both pictures have the same subject matter, again the feeling is different. In the first the focus is on the ship and the water; it is peaceful. In the second the small ship seems almost lost against the vast sky. We may wonder if the water is safe, if there is any possible threat of danger.

Figure 36. Both pictures contain the same figure, but the first is intimate while in the second the figure seems lost and the room bleak.

Figure 37. The space on the left seems unfriendly. Because the floor is rising like a wall, it "throws" the figure out of the picture. If the figure wished to move back, it would have to climb up the floor. Although the other picture is not very friendly either, at least the figure can move easily in the space. It has the freedom of movement that is lacking in the first.

Figure 38. Although the character on the left seems pleased, the viewer may not be, because the picture offers little rest for the eye. On the right there is rest for the eye and the viewer can breathe more easily. Still, the figure does seem uncomfortable standing up straight.

Figure 39. In this picture great speed is conveyed by the angle of the train, the curving track, and the running figure.

Figures 40–44. Study these pictures to see how the space in each affects you. Although all are of equal size, some may feel more spacious than others. Why do they give you that impression? Which make you feel more comfortable and why?

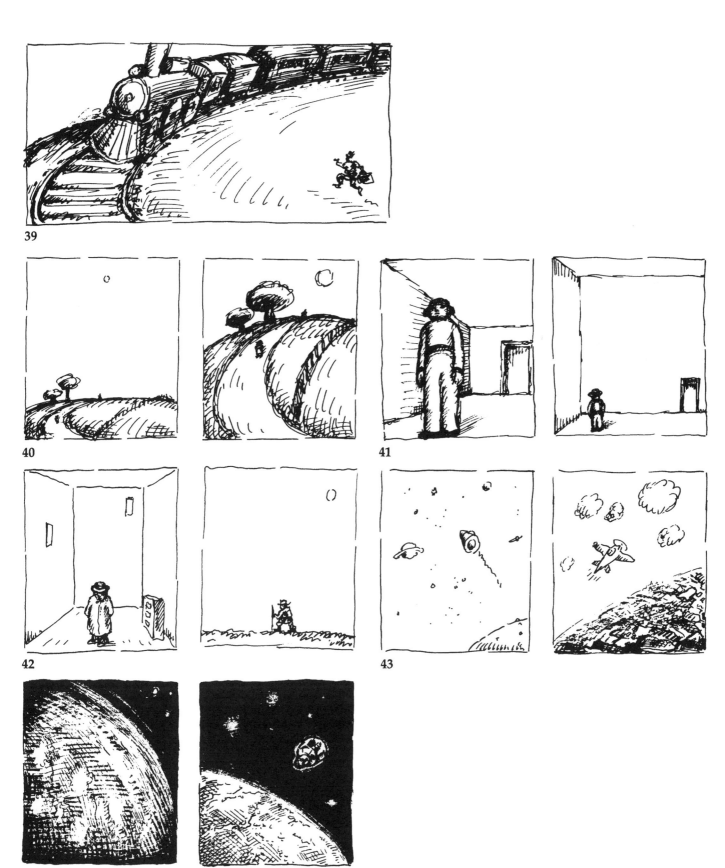

39

40

41

42

43

44

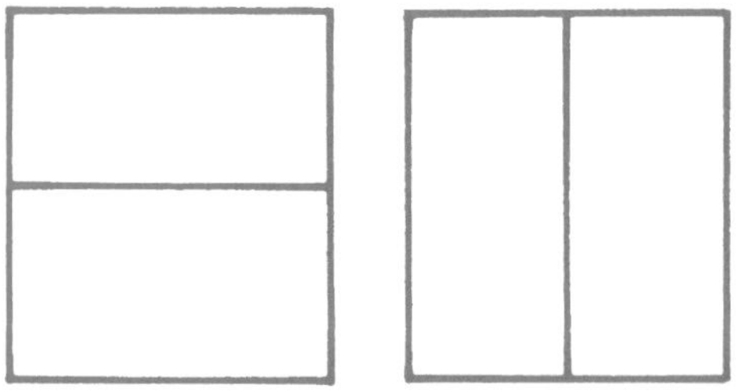

45

46

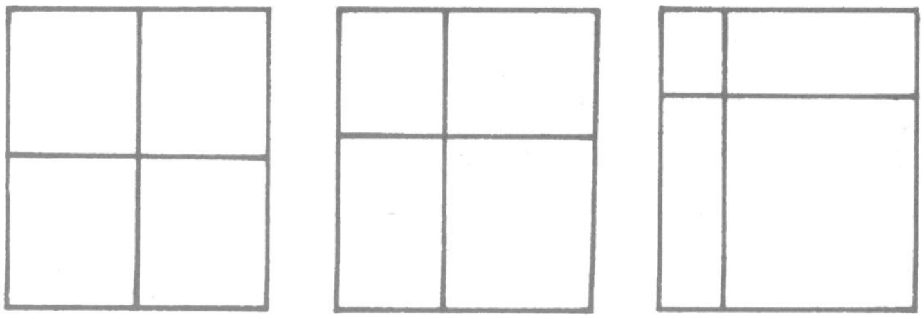

47

Composition

A picture is made up of various elements: size, shape, texture, space intervals, and so on. These elements may not necessarily be compatible, and in some cases they may even be antagonistic. The artist needs to arrange—to compose—these elements deliberately rather than at random to create a visual pattern that gives the viewer a meaningful experience rather than a confusing one.

When we look at a picture, we immediately see the subject matter and its concrete details; we do not immediately see the composition. The composition, however, is *felt*. It is to a picture what the unseen skeleton is to a human being. It structures what and how we see.

Good composition enables the picture elements to coexist on the same picture surface. It satisfies our need to organize and simplify the elements of a picture into a unified whole. When all the elements are arranged into a coherent overall pattern, we can better understand and enjoy the picture.

Dividing the Picture Surface

The following figures are a sampling of some possible ways in which a picture's surface can be divided. These divisions result in various compositional patterns, which in turn have varying impacts on the viewer. The examples below are highly simplified; when these "picture skeletons" are fleshed out with details, color, texture, and so on, it may alter the visual impact suggested here. Nevertheless, these figures are a starting point for understanding the underlying geometry in pictures.

Figure 45. A symmetrical composition, where the divisions are evenly balanced, appears stable but static, without movement.

Figure 46. An asymmetrical composition, with its unequal divisions, seems dynamic.

Figure 47. The first arrangement is symmetrical and static. The second is hesitant, even a trifle irritating, because we are unsure whether the intent is symmetry or asymmetry. It looks like a mistake. In contrast, the third composition is committed and dynamic.

Figure 48. Diagonal lines "move," seeming to fall or rise. In the first frame, however, the diagonal is "stuck"; it appears to be caught in the corners and doesn't move. In the other two compositions, the diagonals move more freely.

Figure 49. On the left the diagonals form four equal-size triangles and a firm structure, but there is little movement. The other two arrangements have movement and drama.

Figure 50. The first composition is stationary, frontal, and direct. The second has drama: the square seems to be falling. The third is solid and balanced, with the triangle sitting firmly on its base. Because of the asymmetrical placement in the fourth frame, however, there is more movement than in the third.

Figure 51. The triangle coming down in the first frame is threatening and dramatic. Although the other arrangement is also dramatic and threatening, the movement downward is delayed by the "support" of the side of the picture frame.

Figure 52. The first rectangle is standing firmly, or growing upward. The second is beginning to fall. The third may be falling down, or it may be flying.

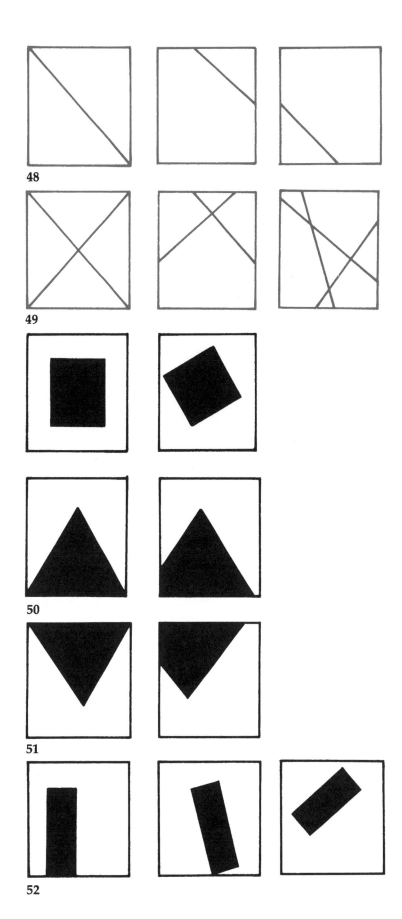

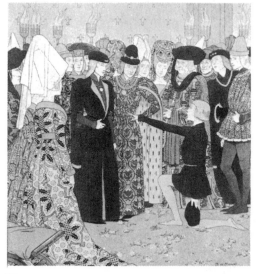

53

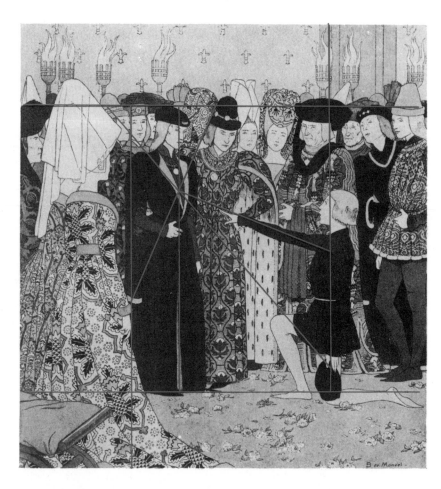

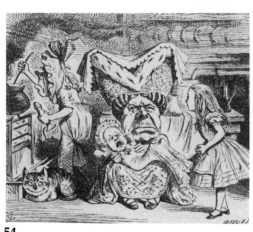

54

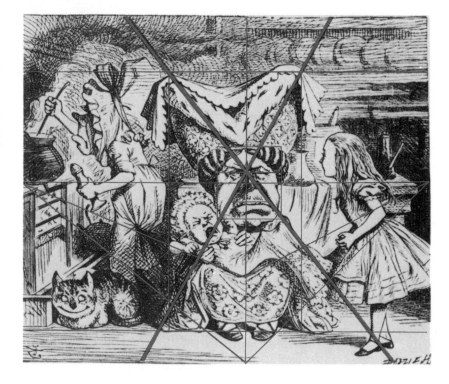

Using an Underlying Geometry

In *Geometry in Pictorial Composition*, Brian Thomas points out that the old masters often used an underlying geometry to increase the readability and expression of their pictures. This geometric pattern can be found in the main visual elements guiding the eye, which create directional lines leading to focal points in the picture.

By studying and analyzing the underlying geometric structure in the works of great artists, you can develop an awareness of composition. Through extensive practice and looking, the use of a geometric understructure can become second nature, almost instinctive. You do not have to think out every detail beforehand. Instead, you may have a basic shape—a triangle or rectangle, for instance—in mind. Or the composition, with its underlying geometry, may emerge spontaneously from the drawing process itself, as you develop the picture's content.

Figure 53. In this illustration from Boutet de Monvel's *Joan of Arc*, Joan, who has never seen the king before, recognizes him immediately, even though he is trying to remain unnoticed among his courtiers, who are dressed in flashier clothes. An analysis of the composition shows the main directional lines converging at the king's chest, leading the viewer's eye to the focal point of the picture. The composition strengthens the picture's intent. We may never know whether the artist planned it that way, but it is there nonetheless.

Figure 54. In this picture by Sir John Tenniel for Lewis Carroll's *Alice's Adventures in Wonderland*, the duchess is the center of attention. We cannot help but notice the pronounced X that underlies this composition and guides the viewer's eye to her.

Figure 55. Even in this seemingly casually drawn picture by Daumier, there is an underlying geometry. It lends the picture strength and a feeling that nothing in it is haphazard, that everything is exactly as it is meant to be.

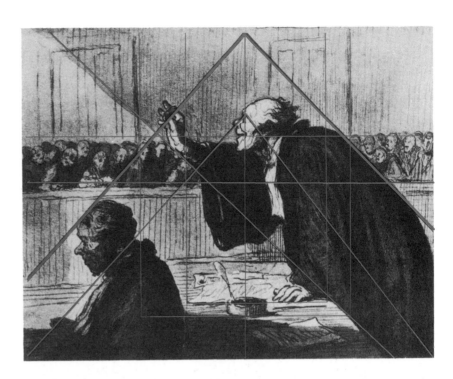

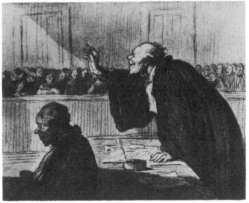

55

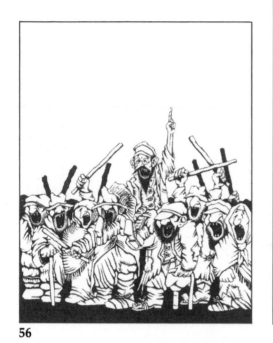

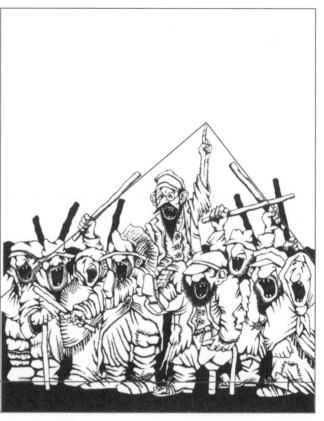

56

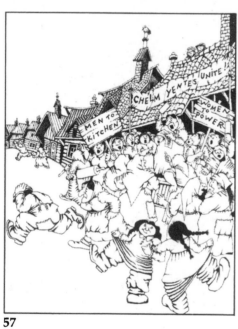

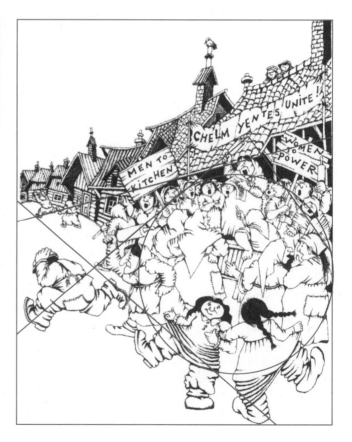

57

Figure 56. A triangle underlies my illustration for Isaac Bashevis Singer's *The Fools of Chelm*. While drawing it, I didn't think about the geometric shapes; they only became evident later. Once you understand composition thoroughly, you don't have to think about it much—it will be there when you need it.

Figure 57. Again, I didn't "plan" the circle that underlies the movement in this illustration for *The Fools of Chelm*. It was an outgrowth of a feeling for composition gained from years of looking and drawing.

Figures 58–68. These drawings for an illustration in Sholem Aleichem's *Hanukah Money* suggest how I develop a composition. When I begin, I sketch the main elements very roughly and focus on the largest forms (Figure 58). I may view a figure as a single form, or a group of figures as a single figure, or the whole picture as a single unit. I try to place the elements in the picture space in a way that seems most fitting to the spirit of the subject.

In the many sketches that follow, I move the elements around in the picture space to best convey the picture's meaning, subject matter, and mood (Figures 59–60). I keep trying different arrangements and make many changes. I work so roughly that the early stages may look like incomprehensive scribbles to somebody else. Yet these early stages might be described as forming the picture's "skeleton." It is at this first stage that the geometric pattern emerges.

When I am satisfied with the basic arrangement of elements, I begin to explore details. Individual figures appear in a group of figures, or a figure begins to have facial features or clothing (Figures 61–63). As the picture takes shape, I observe how the main visual elements suggest directional lines that guide the eye—for example, the diagonal placement of the table in Figure 63 (see next page). I continue to experiment with different arrangements, as in the double spread in Figure 64. I also consolidate and bring out the aspects of the composition that seem

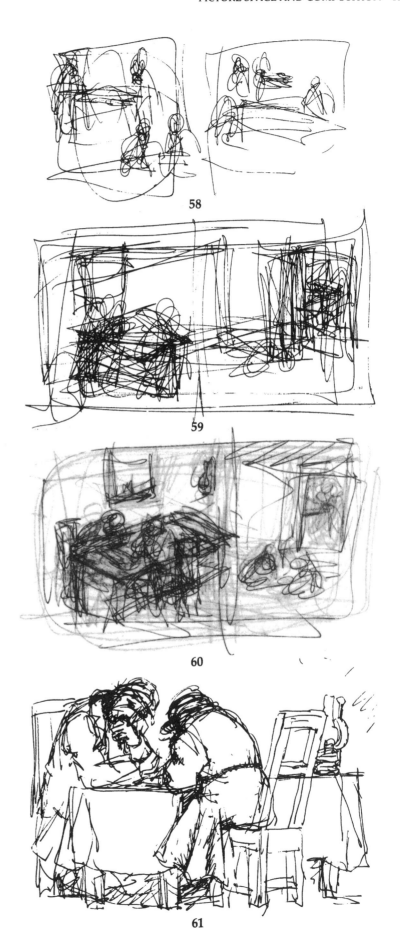

58

59

60

61

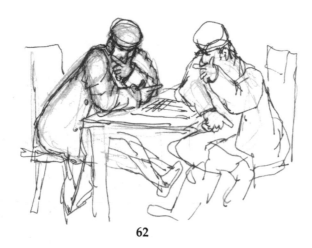

62

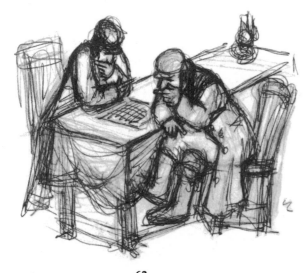

63

most important to the spirit of the picture—for instance, enlarging the figures and reducing the floor space from Figure 65 to 66.

Gradually the understructure of the picture—the composition—emerges. In Figures 63–68, for example, you can see how the diagonal of the table is crossed by the main figures. Generally I favor a dynamic rather than a static composition because it creates more movement, liveliness, and drama. I also prefer dividing the picture space or picture surface unevenly or placing small elements against large ones, instead of using symmetrical divisions or equal-size forms, which are static. In fact, when I look at this picture now, I see a weakness I overlooked at the time: in the final version (Figure 68) the lines of the tabletop parallel the corners of the floor and make the picture more static than I would like.

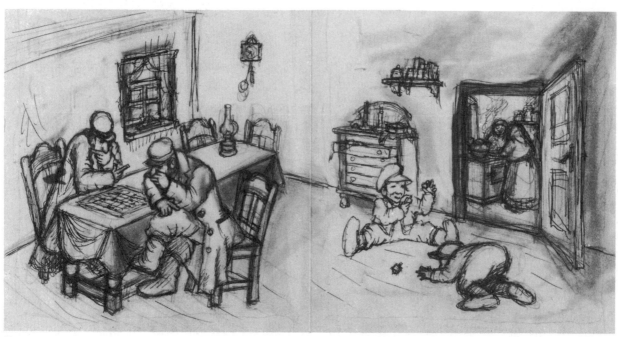

64

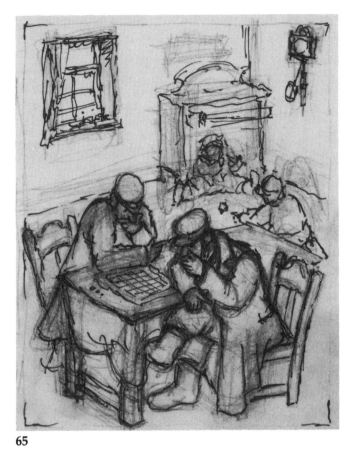

65

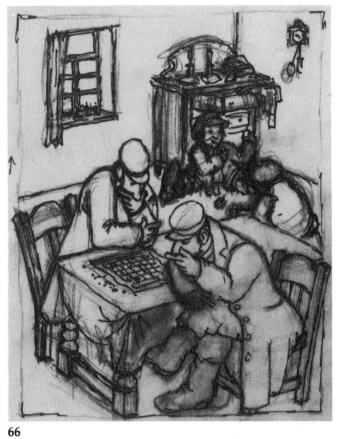

66

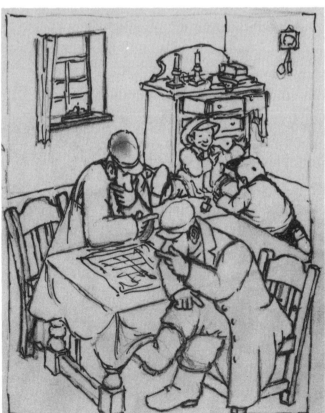

67

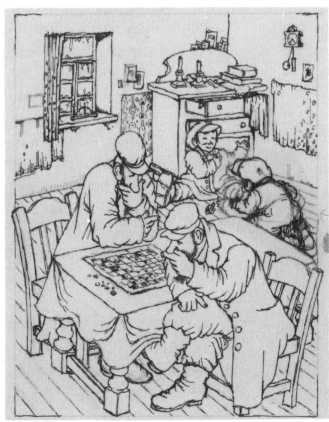

68

13. Principles of Technique

He who overdoes anything, spoils it.

Lao-tzu

In creating a picture, the artist infuses it with life. While drawing, he or she looks for the moment when the picture begins to shimmer, to sing. Not only do the figures or animals seem alive, but the whole drawing seems to breathe.

The great masters were remarkable in their ability to blend freedom and discipline. They came to drawing with a thorough knowledge of anatomy, perspective, and technique; they also had clear objectives in mind and knew how to achieve them. Yet the great masters didn't have to think about technique, because for them it had become second nature. To reach this state, to make your drawing as natural as your handwriting, requires a great deal of practice.

Technique is an important tool, but it is not an end in itself. It is a means to communicate content—it should enhance without distracting from content. Like good design, sound technique is inconspicuous.

Imagine that you are drawing a picture of a tree. If you "forget" the tree and turn your attention to embellishing the picture, you may destroy the life of the picture. Instead of depicting the tree or expressing its spirit, your lines may become only decorative lines on paper. Try not to think of lines as mere lines, but as a means to describe or express content. True, whereas a house collapses and endangers lives if it is carelessly built, carelessly drawn lines do not endanger lives. Nonetheless, you should try to draw them as if you were building a house. It is important not to confuse the "look" of a picture with its substance. Sound technique gives life to the picture; it is not embellishment.

Sensitivity and Resoluteness

Good technique is quite simple—it combines sensitivity with resoluteness, which can be summarized in the age-old precepts: *Let the paper breathe* and *Draw boldly, without hesitation*. These two principles suggest the Chinese dual principle of Yin (feminine, passive) and Yang (masculine, active). *Let the paper breathe*, stressing sensitivity, resembles Yin, whereas *Draw boldly*, stressing vigor, resembles Yang. Together, they produce a technique that is both delicate and strong.

Let the Paper Breathe

Whatever medium you choose, respect your tools and materials. Be attentive to their natural properties, to what they can and cannot do. With transparent watercolor, for instance, let the white of the paper be the source of the picture's light—as if the thin film of paint were a piece of semitransparent colored glass. When the paper is overloaded with paint, it stops breathing because the white of the paper doesn't show through. Overly tight or heavy crosshatching can also choke a picture.

Similarly, overworking colors by excessive brushwork, too much rubbing, or a lot of intermixing results in a loss of freshness, in a tired or lifeless look. With experience, you can tell when colors are overworked, just as you can tell when vegetables are overcooked. Try to apply paint as few times as necessary; don't overdo it. Use and do less, if less will do the job well.

Draw Boldly

Think, meditate, or debate in your mind as long as you wish on what and how you are going to draw, but once you take the plunge, draw resolutely. Concentrate on the subject matter, being aware of the paper and your tools, yet working without hesitation. Although they are an integral part of the picture, your lines or washes must have a life of their own. Each stroke has to have vigor and character, with no ambiguity.

While you draw, be confident but not careless, precise but not fussy or tentative, for this may irritate the viewer or distract from the content of the picture. Hesitation, like driving a car with the brakes on, stops the momentum and results in vacillating lines. If the lines in your sketch aren't right, don't erase them; draw again, without hesitation, over the previous lines.

Practicing Techniques

No discussion of how to draw freely can ever be a substitute for training acquired at an art school or through independent practice. The present discussion is no exception, but it does present a personal point of view on how to arrive at sound technique.

Since I cannot cover all techniques, I have chosen some that are frequently used in illustrating children's books—line, crosshatching, pencil, and wash. I have used all but pencil for finished illustrations with satisfactory results. From these basic techniques, you can derive others, and they show you how to apply the principles: *Draw boldly* and *Let the paper breathe*. Ultimately, however, you must find your own way of working.

Among the illustration techniques not discussed here are Chinese and Japanese brush techniques, as well as techniques for markers, reed pens, technical pens, batik, collage, oil paints, tempera, woodblock, linocut, etching, and scratchboard. By all means explore as many as possible, but whichever technique you use, apply the two principles—and also be guided by a third: *readability*.

Practice the exercises here as you would musical scales, keeping in mind that this is only one approach. Also bear in mind that, for the sake of exercise, we shall draw lines and lay down washes in isolation, when normally they would be an integral part of a picture.

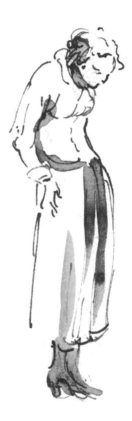

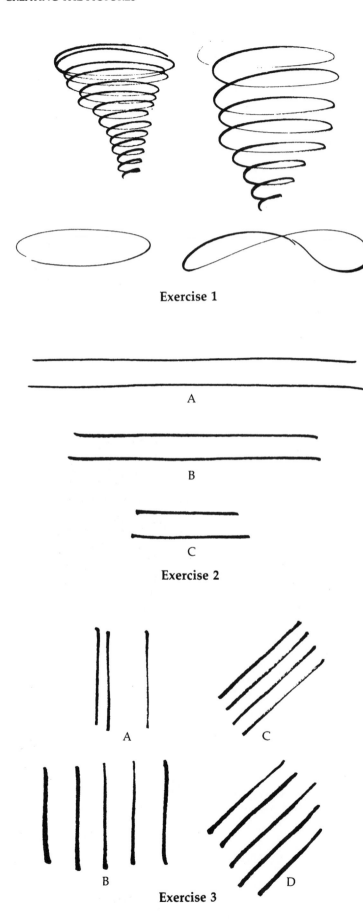

Exercise 1

Exercise 2

Exercise 3

Line

Line is the foundation of illustration. It is the most basic element and the one most often used. Through line alone, you can create successful pictures, without adding shading or color.

Whether you work with a pencil, marker, brush, stick of charcoal, or pen, line requires total commitment and clear decisions. Embellishment will not hide badly drawn lines. The goal is to draw lines with freedom and without hesitation—lines that are bold yet light of touch, firm yet not belabored, spontaneous yet disciplined.

To learn about the use of line, study the drawings of the great masters. Then begin to explore the use of line on your own. For the first four exercises here, choose an inexpensive paper such as newsprint, no smaller than 11" × 14". Use different tools that produce broad, soft lines and that move with ease over the paper, such as charcoal, graphite, conté crayons, or soft pencils. (For the examples shown here, I used a quill pen.)

Exercise 1. First standing up, then sitting down, draw circles, ovals, figure eights, and spirals. Draw with continuous, unbroken lines. Let them flow from your whole body, not just your wrist. Try different thicknesses of line and vary the pressure, drawing light, then heavy lines. Explore your tools, using them playfully, in any way that enters your mind.

Exercise 2. Now draw straight horizontal lines. Let the point of your drawing tool be the only thing to touch the paper (A). Then use the fingers of your drawing hand as a pivot point, to support your hand as it slides over the paper. Begin on the left and draw to the right (B); reverse direction (C).

Exercise 3. Experiment with different parallel lines: vertical and diagonal, as well as horizontal. Move upward (A, C), then downward (B, D).

Exercise 4. Draw at different speeds, from slow (A) to fast (B). Draw long, then short lines. Observe the effect of inhaling and exhaling on the steadiness of long lines, and the effect of speed and resoluteness on their straightness.

Exercise 5. This exercise and the two that follow are a preparation for crosshatching. Sitting down, rest your wrist on the table and draw short, parallel strokes with pen and ink on suitable paper. In my experience, the length of the lines you can draw without hesitation depends on how far your pen reaches before you have to move your wrist. First draw short, vertical strokes by pulling the pen toward you; then experiment to find whether another way suits you better. Pause between strokes, but never in the middle of a stroke—once you begin, draw resolutely.

When the strokes are properly drawn, they look determined and you may even hear a clean "zap" sound while drawing. Maintain equal pressure, equal speed, equal distance, and the same direction for all the strokes to achieve uniform character. Although some strokes may vary, you will achieve an overall unity. Work as fast as you can without getting into a frenzy and without losing control over your lines. When your lines are firm, practice using a light touch without losing the resoluteness.

Exercise 6. Follow the instructions in Exercises 3 and 4, but use short, parallel, curved lines.

Exercise 7. Now draw a row of short, straight lines. Then draw another row below the first, connecting them to form longer lines.

Exercise 8. Before going on to the next set of exercises, try to apply what you have learned. Experiment with different kinds of line for different kinds of sketches.

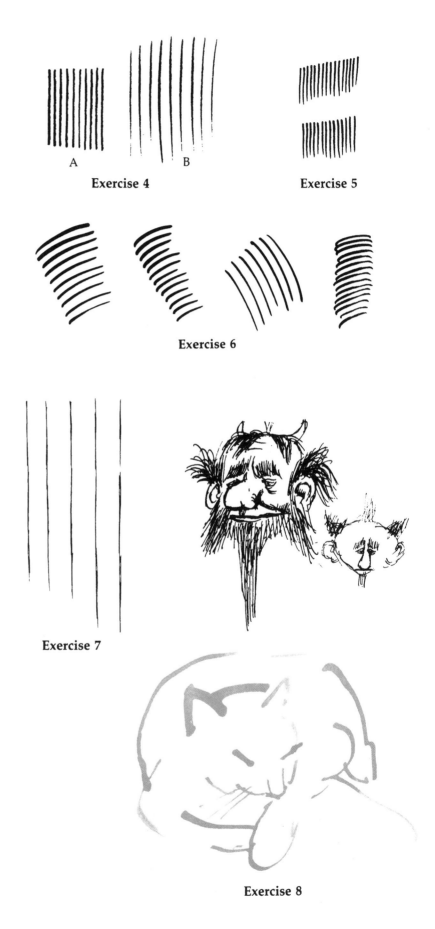

Exercise 4

Exercise 5

Exercise 6

Exercise 7

Exercise 8

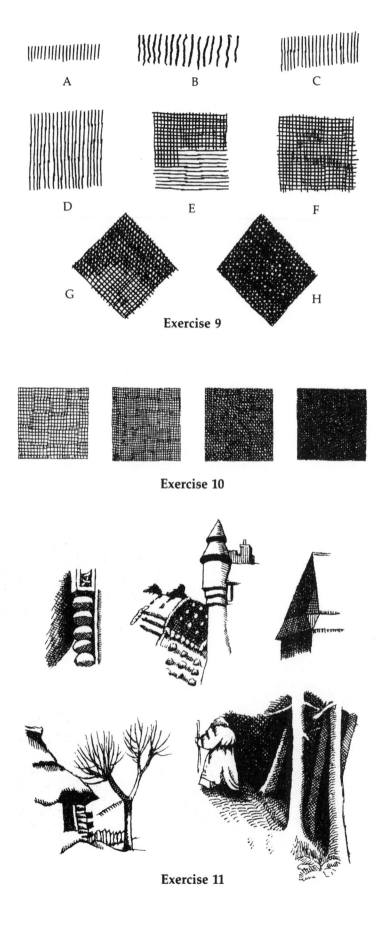

Exercise 9

Exercise 10

Exercise 11

Crosshatching

Crosshatching is a means to achieve tone, or different "colors" of gray, with line. It can be used for shading, modeling round forms, strong light and dark contrasts (chiaroscuro), or decoration.

The word *crosshatching* describes the basic process. Essentially you draw parallel strokes in one direction (*hatching*) and then *cross* them with rows of parallel strokes at a different angle. By superimposing additional layers, you darken the tone. You can also increase the darkness by tightening the space between the lines so that less of the white paper shows through. Remember, however, to let the paper breathe and draw boldly. Put each stroke down without hesitation; and, even with a tight crosshatch, avoid clogging up the tiny openings that show the paper.

Exercise 9. Begin by drawing short, parallel strokes in pen and ink as described in Exercise 5. Keep the strokes as parallel and uniform as possible (A). Again, don't hesitate—if you draw with a lack of purpose, the strokes will seem wobbly and lacking in conviction (B). You will create excessive movement, which can interfere with and distract from the content of the picture.

After drawing a row of short, parallel strokes, make another row below it, to extend the length of each stroke (C). Don't leave gaps between the extensions; instead, join the strokes into one continuous line. You don't have to give the impression of using a single stroke, but make sure the strokes touch each other. Continue with additional rows (D).

Now turn the paper 90 degrees and crosshatch the hatched lines, pulling the strokes toward you at a right angle to the previous rows (E). Follow the same procedure as above, connecting row upon row of short strokes (F).

Next, turn the paper 45 degrees and crosshatch another series of lines directly over the previous ones (G). By hatching one layer on top of another this way, you can achieve different values of gray. Make the tones as dark as you wish, but let the paper breathe (H).

Exercise 10. After you have mastered Exercise 9, make a scale of four gray rectangles, progressing from light to dark in equal steps.

Exercise 11. Now practice crosshatching by drawing simple subjects at first, such as a cube with a shadow on the ground, then a sphere. Gradually move on to more complicated subjects. Try to maintain equal pressure and equal distance between strokes, keeping them parallel and crosshatching at a constant rate. Work as fast as you can, as long as speed doesn't detract from the quality.

Pencil

The difference between pencil and pen is that pencil has variation in tone, which can be enhanced by varying the pressure on the pencil. Lines drawn by pen have no variation in tone, although they vary in thickness according to the pressure applied.

When shading with pencil, you can use hatching to achieve gray tones, or you can use a stump or tortillon (made of tightly rolled paper) to blend the pencil lines together and achieve varying or uniform tones similar to a wash. Unfortunately, many beginners think that smudging is the proper technique for shading with pencil. Also, they often press too hard on the pencil, overwork the dark tones, and fail to let the paper breathe. Avoid these bad habits: don't misuse the pencil and don't torment the paper.

The exercises that follow are done with a soft pencil, but experiment with various grades of pencil (from soft to hard) to find which is most suitable for your particular project. Soft pencils (the B range) are good for rough sketches because they encourage drawing large masses without going into details.

Exercise 12. Repeat the various exercises for crosshatching in pencil. Notice the tonal quality that pencil gives.

Exercise 13. Explore what happens when you vary the pressure on your pencil (A). Try to create gradations in tone in this way (B).

Exercise 14. Experiment with blending. First use a pencil (A), then a stump (B), to blend the pencil lines into a smooth consistency. Take care not to torment the paper with too many lines or excessive pressure (C)—let it breathe.

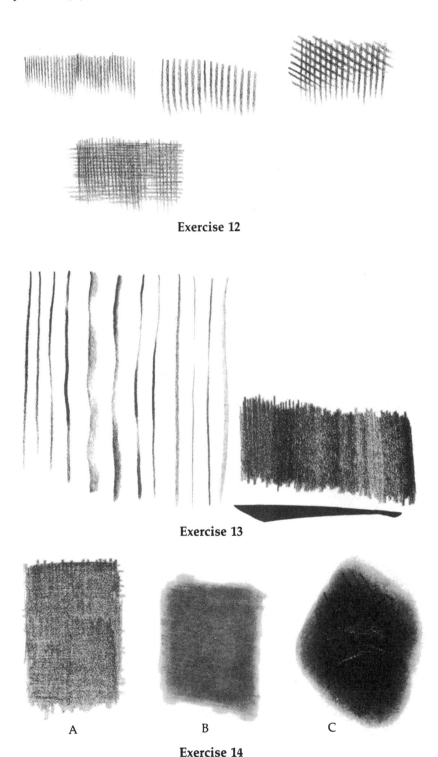

Exercise 12

Exercise 13

A   B   C

Exercise 14

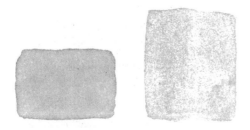

Exercise 15

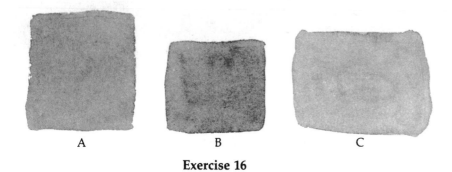

A   B   C

Exercise 16

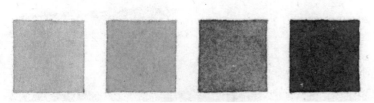

Exercise 17

Exercise 18

Wash

A wash is prepared by mixing water with water-soluble paint or ink and is then applied in translucent layers on a ground. The best ground is white watercolor paper, or a paper of equivalent quality that can withstand wetting without shredding or changing shape too much. India ink, colored inks or dyes, Japanese or Chinese drawing inks, or transparent watercolors can be diluted with water to form a solution suitable for wash.

The more water you use, the lighter the wash will be. Since the essential quality of wash is transparency, be sure the white of the paper shows through, even with dark tones. If the wash is too thick, the white of the paper will disappear and the paper won't breathe.

Exercise 15. Prepare a wash by mixing black transparent watercolor (in tube or cake form) with water in a clean paint dish. Use a generous amount of water. (For ease in mixing, you can use an eye dropper to add the water to the paint; observe how each drop lightens the paint.)

Once you have mixed a very light wash (10% black or lighter), load a good-quality watercolor brush generously with the wash. Work on watercolor paper, making small rectangles, about 1 to 2 inches wide. Paint evenly, holding the brush at approximately a 60-degree angle from the paper. Be sure to apply a generous amount of wash, spreading it throughout with as few brushstrokes as necessary. Work swiftly, but calmly. Be precise, but not too fussy or slow.

When the wash begins to settle, but before it is dry, pick up the excess that accumulates at the bottom or corner of the painted area with a brush rinsed in clean water and wiped dry. If you don't, this area will dry unevenly, leaving a blob.

If you are working on a slanted drawing surface, make this work to your advantage. Try to direct the wash to the desired areas by turning the paper on the drawing surface.

Exercise 16. Paint the same gray value on different papers and compare the different results. Here I used Arches watercolor paper (A), Strathmore drawing paper (B), and bristol board (C).

Exercise 17. Now practice painting rectangles of flat, uniform grays in different values. Keep practicing until you achieve smooth, uniform tones. When you can paint perfectly flat washes, you'll be better able to paint irregular, textured washes as well.

Exercise 18. Once you master uniform tones, paint a scale of four gray rectangles that progress from light to dark in equal steps.

Exercise 19. Use washes to add tone to your drawings. Put the washes down boldly, in relatively broad strokes. To get a darker tone, mix a batch of darker wash or try laying one wash on top of another once the first wash is dry. Remember, however, to preserve the transparency of the watercolor medium—avoid using too many layers and always add water to your paint so that it doesn't become too thick.

Tools and Materials

The choice of art supplies is strictly a personal matter. There is no better way to find out what you like than by trying out different kinds for yourself. By all means try as wide a range as possible. That is what I did when I was starting out. I bought each pen nib I came across, different pencils, papers, inks, erasers. I tried them and found the tools and materials I like to work with. I keep experimenting, however, because every book has its own requirements (see Chapter 17). Moreover, exploring new tools and materials, plus new ways of using them, keeps me from falling into a routine.

Sketching Paper

My favorite surface for sketching in pencil is Superior tracing vellum distributed by Art Brown in New York, followed by Vidalon tracing paper produced by Canson. I like the heavy tracing vellum

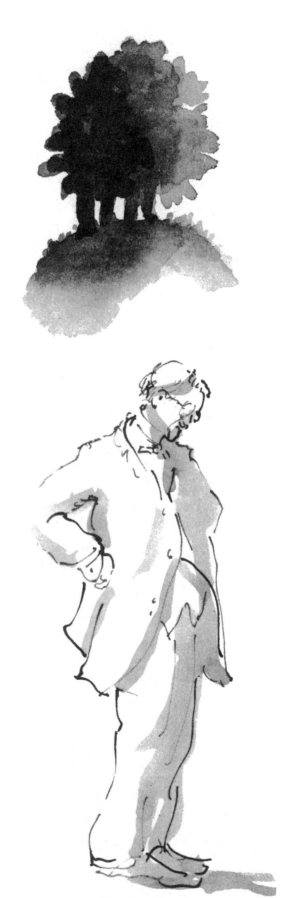

Exercise 19

because often I erase and rework the same sketch several times, going over the pencil lines with pen and ink to define them better. (The pen lines have the advantage of being more visible so that you can trace over them on a light box in preparing the final art.)

Paper for Finished Art

The paper must be sufficiently strong and heavy to withstand reworking, corrections, and erasures. For wet techniques such as watercolor, the paper must be stable and buckle as little as possible when moistened. I have used Arches 90 lb. cold-pressed, semirough paper (for both wash and line), as well as Strathmore medium-surface drawing paper (primarily for line) with good results.

It's best to use acid-free, 100% rag paper if you want your art to last. I stopped using illustration board, for instance, because I found that the glue between the layers caused it to deteriorate with time. It's also better to use a flexible surface, just in case the printing method requires the art to be wrapped around a drum.

I test a paper surface to find out whether I enjoy working on it, whether I like the way the pen or pencil moves, the quality of the lines drawn, or its texture when I am using wash.

I also look for paper that is as white as

1

possible, without any red or orange in it, to avoid reproduction difficulties.

Pencil Drawing Tools

In making my preliminary sketches for a book illustration, I like to use Faber Castell 2H leads in a lead holder. I find that this lead—in between hard and soft—is appropriate for the relatively small size of my sketches. To keep the lead pointed, I sharpen it periodically with a lead pointer while drawing. I also use a Staedtler Mars plastic eraser, which is gentle on the paper's surface.

Ink Drawing Tools

Most often I use Hunt no. 104 pen nibs or softer ones. I am not particular about the pen holder—I use whatever is comfortable and works with the nib I plan to use.

For final illustrations, I normally use Pelikan black drawing ink or, when a thinner ink consistency is appropriate, Higgins black drawing ink.

Watercolor Brushes

My brushes consist of Winsor & Newton Series 7 sables, nos. 0, 1, 2, 3, 5, and 8. I use these mostly with transparent watercolor—for India ink, which ruins brushes, I use cheaper ones. If, however, I do use a quality brush with India ink, I rinse it immediately afterward and wash it thoroughly with mild soap and water, making sure the base of the hair is clean. While it is moist, I bring it to a sharp point and let it dry standing up in a jar (**Figure 1**).

Before buying a watercolor brush, ask the salesperson for water to test the brush. When it's wet, the hair of a quality brush should come to a single point. A good brush will retain a sharp point and its original shape throughout its life.

Studio Arrangement

Arrange your work area so that it is convenient and pleasant. Make sure that you can sit upright comfortably while working and that the lighting is adequate and doesn't cause eye strain.

My own working arrangement is shown

2

in **Figure 2**. My *drawing table* is adjustable, but I usually keep it tilted at 20 degrees. It is covered with a sheet of gray chipboard, which doesn't cause glare and is therefore easy on the eyes. Since I'm right-handed, to prevent shadows from my drawing arm, I've set up my drawing table so that daylight comes from the left.

Even in daylight I use direct *lighting* for my work: a combination incandescent-fluorescent lamp with a maneuverable arm fixed at my left to avoid shadows from my drawing hand. A regular ceiling bulb provides additional overall area lighting at night or whenever it gets dark.

In front of me, over the table, I have a *bulletin board*, which allows me to pin up drawings or picture references. My *drawing tools*, including paints and inks, are on a table with a level top, to the right of the drawing table.

To my left is a *light box*, mounted on a small typing table with casters. The light box is hinged and can be tilted at an angle. When using the light box, I cover the lit surface around the art with black paper, which concentrates the light on the work area and eliminates glare (**Figure 3**).

I sit on an office swivel *chair*, which can be adjusted for height. Casters underneath allow me to move over to the light box whenever necessary.

Sitting and Hand Position

When I'm working on illustrations, I sit firmly on the chair, trying to keep my back straight and my feet planted firmly on the floor. My relaxed right forearm rests on the drawing table (**Figure 4**). When I am working on a small area of an illustration or on fine details, the side of my hand and little finger rest on the paper (**Figure 5**). For sketches that require quick, broad hand movements, I use my little finger as a pivot point that slides over the paper. With soft drawing tools such as B pencils, chalk, graphite, and conté crayons, I frequently draw with one or more fingers as a pivot point (**Figure 6**). When I am drawing vigorously, creating large masses rather than details, especially in a large picture, I sketch the overall composition with a free hand and arm.

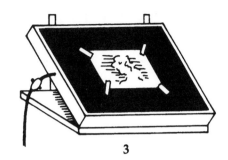

3

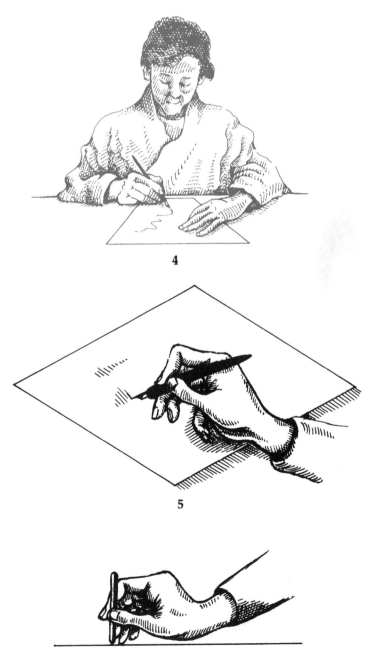

4

5

6

The Place of Technique

Practicing techniques and finding the materials you like to work with are part of the learning process. Western masters such as Rubens, Rembrandt, Daumier, and Monet show us what to strive for. In their paintings technique is never the goal, but it is an indispensable foundation. Remember that before you can run, you must learn how to walk. There is no freedom of expression without mastery of technique and a thorough knowledge of drawing. Think of technique as a receptacle—one that must be ready to receive the content and emotion of the subject.

Once technique becomes as natural as walking, however, you can "forget" it, for it will be there when you need it. Instead, try to capture what's truly important in an illustration—the life and emotion of the story. Learn to listen to and trust your first reaction to the subject. Empathize with the story, feel it, and let it come through in your picture. Don't dilute your emotions with compromises in an attempt to make the picture "look" good. *What* the picture says is more important than *how* it looks.

Give up the idea of the "perfect," flawless picture, and aim for one that is alive instead. Don't be afraid to make mistakes. And stop as soon as you begin to lose freshness. Never overdo it. It doesn't matter if the picture looks unfinished, as long as it is readable, conforms reasonably to the other pictures in the book, and is an honest portrayal of the story.

Keeping the Final Illustration Fresh

All too often there is a loss of emotion and freshness during the progression from first rough sketch to final illustration. The finished picture may be more resolved, polished, and readable, but the spontaneity of the first sketch has almost disappeared. Readability is essential to good illustration, and some compromises to achieve it are justified. If, however, the price of readability is lifelessness, the result can be viewed as a failure.

The problem has been of great concern to me. My first sketch is often more alive than later versions. In **Figures 7–9**, for instance, you can see the progression from rough sketch to finished illustration for one of the pages in *The Moon in My Room*. Although the final version is more readable and polished, it seems "tired" compared with the earlier sketches. The lines no longer have the same energy.

I've noticed that in the beginning I concentrate on capturing the subject matter of the story, which I do in one or more preliminary sketches. But during subsequent stages, when I'm busy getting rid of excess lines, clarifying, sharpening, making it more elegant and readable, the picture loses vitality. That is also when thoughts that were of no concern to me in the initial stage arise. I wonder: How will the picture look? Will it be liked? That is when I gradually begin to lose sight of the primary goal—*what* I'm illustrating, the picture and its requirements, how it will best relate to the words—and shift my attention to an imaginary audience, and *how* the picture will look and be accepted. The emphasis shifts from the purpose of the picture to its outward appearance or surface look.

In some ways the progression from rough to finished work resembles the game "telephone relay," in which a child whispers a sentence to another child, who then whispers it to someone else, and so on down the line. By the time the words reach the last child, they bear little or no resemblance to the original sentence.

Preliminary sketches help us to gain a better grasp of the subject and to solve pictorial problems. But dependence on too many preliminary sketches is the result of weak technique and poor drawing skills. When a picture is overworked, it resembles overprocessed food—vital ingredients have been lost along the way.

Far Eastern artists of the past made only a few preliminary sketches or none at all. They thought a long time about a painting, but once they painted it, they did it quickly, only once. They even avoided sketching from nature, lest unnecessary details distract from their vivid mental picture. To be able to do this, however, they developed an unusual capacity to remember mental pictures and they became masters of their craft.

When you use preliminary sketches to plan your picture (as discussed in Chapters 6 and 12), keep them to a minimum. As you work, try not to refer constantly to your previous sketch in each successive stage, because you may end up merely copying or embellishing it, not improving it. Even when you are moving in closer on a scene and sharpening the focus, try to bring to it the freshness of the first sketch.

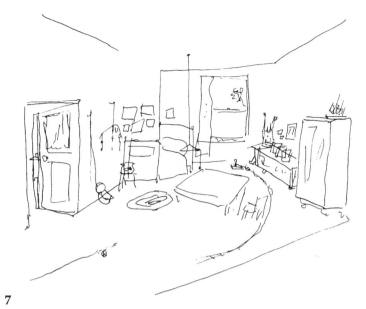

7

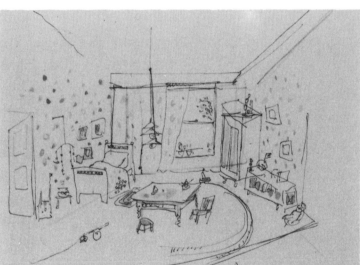

8

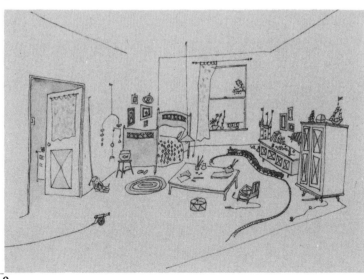

9

14. Style

Personal style is the distinctive manner of expression characteristic of an artist's work. We can recognize someone's style by his or her particular way of using composition, space, technique, line, color, or other picture elements. Such choices reflect the artist's temperament, ideas, and feelings. Even the choice of a story to illustrate is a part of personal expression.

Personal style, then, is the sum total of ability, skill, inclination, and the choices made. When you draw a picture with integrity and character, it will inevitably bear your personal style. In other words, let personal style flow from your work; don't let your work be dictated by style. Learn your craft thoroughly, so you don't have to think about technique. And forget style. Just draw the picture suggested in the words. Draw in a manner appropriate to the picture's content—this is more important in children's books than appearance, or style.

The best way to attain a personal style is by doing all you can to make your pictures communicate clearly. As the sculptor Auguste Rodin commented: "No style is good except that which effaces itself in order to concentrate all the attention of the reader upon the subject matter treated, upon the emotion rendered."

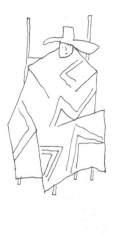

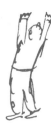

The Elements of Style

The same letter of the alphabet in different type styles conveys different feelings to the reader (**Figure 1**). A book designer chooses the most appropriate typeface for the content of a given text. Similarly, the artist must choose the appropriate elements of style for a picture.

Only a few of the many choices available to the artist have been singled out in the examples that follow. Try to use the questions and accompanying figures as a starting point in understanding how different picture elements affect the reading of an illustration. Remember, however, that although the choices are presented separately here, in a good illustration they work together as an integral whole and form the personal style of the artist.

Space

What kind of pictorial space is used, and how is it achieved?

Is the space flat (**Figure 2**)?

Shallow (**Figure 3**)?

Deep (**Figure 4**)?

Is an illusion of depth and volume conveyed through linear perspective (**Figure 5**)?

Or through atmospheric perspective (**Figure 6**)?

Demarcation

How has the artist used outline?

Are the elements of the picture separated by sharp outlines (**Figure 7**)?

Or are they subtly defined with soft outlines (**Figure 8**)?

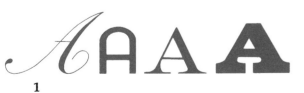

1

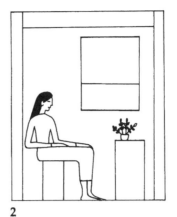

2

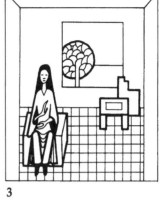

3

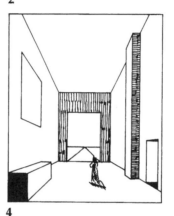

4

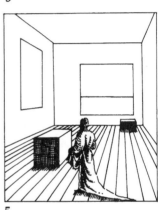

5

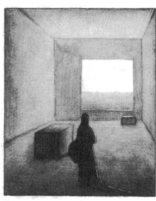

6

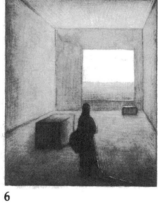

7

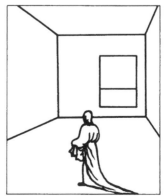

8

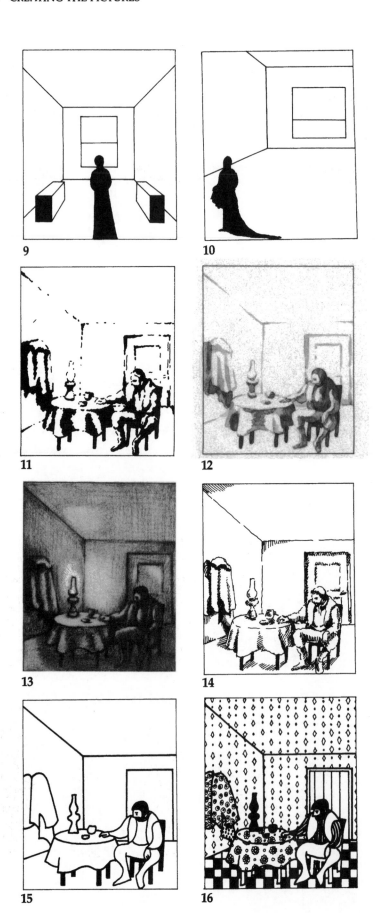

9

10

11

12

13

14

15

16

Composition

What is the underlying composition?

Is it, for instance, symmetrical and static (**Figure 9**)?

Or is it asymmetrical and dynamic (**Figure 10**)?

Technique

What graphic tools and techniques has the artist used? How do they help to convey the content and mood of the story?

Is the scene drawn in high contrast with a brush (**Figure 11**)?

Or is it suggested by delicate washes (**Figure 12**)?

Or has the artist chosen soft pencil shading (**Figure 13**)?

Representation

How is the subject matter presented?

Is the treatment lifelike and representational (**Figure 14**)?

Stylized (**Figure 15**)?

Or stylized and decorative (**Figure 16**)?

Handling of Figures

How are the figures represented?
Are they realistic (**Figure 17**)?
Stylized (**Figure 18**)?
Or simplified (**Figure 19**)?
Are they lively and full of movement
(**Figure 20**)?
Or stiff (**Figure 21**)?
Have the proportions been distorted so
that the figure is either elongated or squat
(**Figure 22**)?

Line

What is the character of the line in the
picture?
Is it continuous (**Figure 23**)?
Or broken (**Figure 24**)?
Heavy (**Figure 25**)?
Or light (**Figure 26**)?
Soft (**Figure 27**)?
Or hard (**Figure 28**)?
Descriptive (**Figure 29**)?
Or sketchy (**Figure 30**)?
Bold (**Figure 31**)?
Or hesitant (**Figure 32**)?
Or bold and delicate combined
(**Figure 33**)?
Does it define geometric shapes
(**Figure 34**)?
Or is it mannered (**Figure 35**)?
What happens when it is part of a
silhouette (**Figure 36**)?

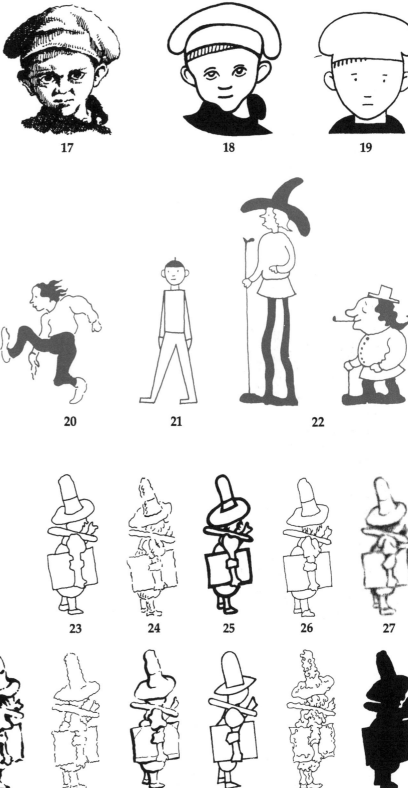

17 18 19

20 21 22

23 24 25 26 27

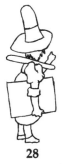 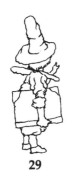 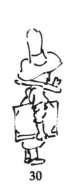 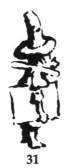 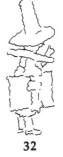 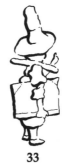 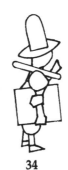 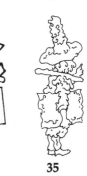 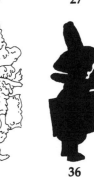

28 29 30 31 32 33 34 35 36

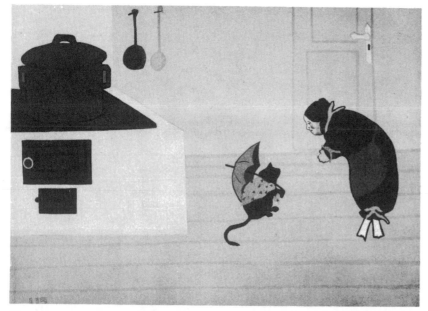

37

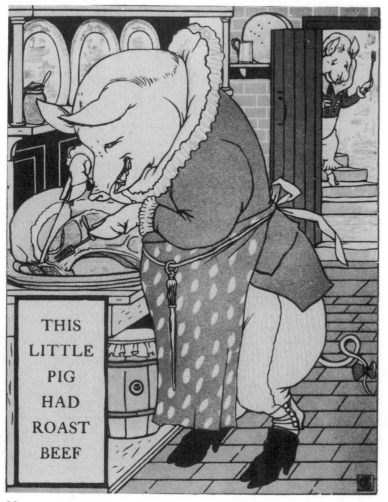

38

Varieties of Style

Although not all the illustrations in this section are for children's books, they suggest different ways in which the elements of style can be combined. Observe to what extent you can tell the mood and feeling of the story by the manner of depiction and expression in the illustration. What are the specific elements of style that contribute to this "reading"?

Figure 37. This picture by H. Jozewskij illustrates a Polish children's story. The figures appear as cutout shapes with bold outlines and precisely defined silhouettes. Yet they have a feeling of movement. What kind of space does the artist use? And how do the empty areas work with the figures?

Figure 38. Although this picture by Walter Crane is more crowded than Figure 37, with almost no empty space, there is still rest for the eye. How is this achieved? Also notice how Crane has made the pig look round without using any modeling.

Figure 39. In Phiz's illustration for Charles Dickens's *Nicholas Nickleby*, the characters are like actors on a stage. Both their facial and bodily expressions suggest the content of the story.

Figure 40. Boutet de Monvel's figures seem to dance across the page. Which elements contribute to the feeling of movement and why? How do these figures differ from those by Phiz (Figure 39) or Crane (Figure 38)?

Figure 41. The calligraphic line in Joseph Low's picture for Natalia Belting's *The Land of the Taffeta Dawn* gives the horse movement. Its loose, handwritten quality has a different feeling from Boutet de Monvel's clearly defined line (Figure 40).

Figure 42. Ludwig Richter's illustration for *The Grateful Sparrow and Other Tales* by Angela Thirkell shows the bustle of activity with the coming of spring. Try to figure out how your eye moves around this busy scene. Where can you "rest"? And which elements lead you on to explore the picture?

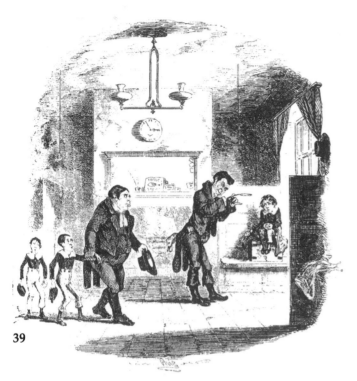

39

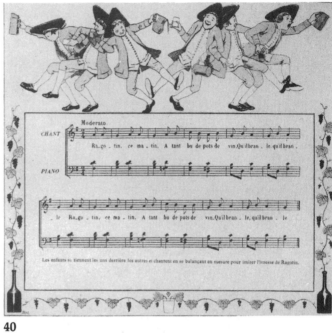

40

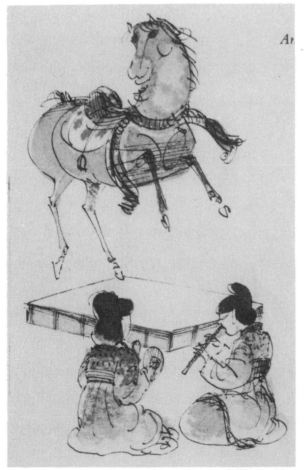

41

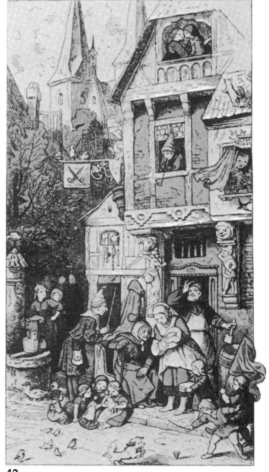

42

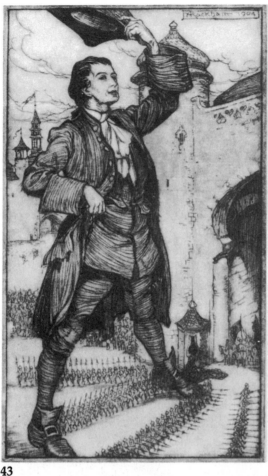

43

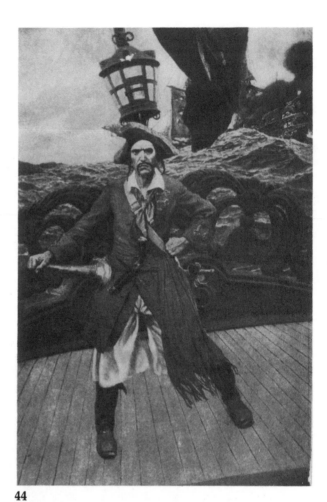

44

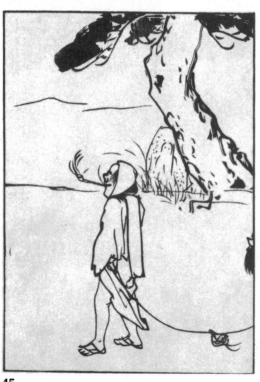

45

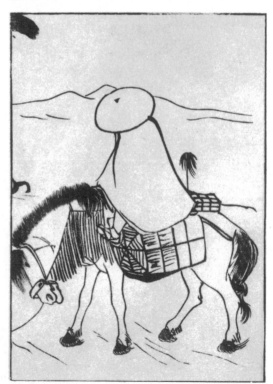

Figure 43. In this illustration by Arthur Rackham for Jonathan Swift's *Gulliver's Travels*, scale is very important. Notice also the personal handwriting of Rackham's lines. The "nervous" outlines of the sleeves, for instance, are very different from the bold outlines in Figure 37. In Gulliver's clothing, Rackham has used the lines to describe the figure's roundness and at the same time create a feeling of movement.

Figure 44. Howard Pyle's illustration for *The Ruby of Kishmoor* is highly expressive even though the approach is representational. Which compositional choices heighten the feeling of drama? Although Boutet de Monvel's illustration (Figure 40) is light and humorous, can you find any similarity between the two?

Figure 45. When you compare this Japanese picture by Yamaguchi Soken with Figure 46, you can see similarities and differences. Both illustrations use flat space and woodcut techniques, but the artist's "hand" in each is distinctive. In this picture the woodcut lines succeed in reproducing the elegance and character of the original brush drawing—to the extent that you "forget" this is a woodcut.

Figure 46. This woodcut by Jacob Pins for Heinrich von Kleist's *Michael Kohlhaas* is expressive, but the way this is achieved is different from Figure 44. Notice the economy of means in the facial expressions and the rugged outlines.

Figure 47. Gustave Doré's illustration for *Tom Thumb* provides an interesting contrast to Figure 46. Although both are expressive and suggestive, in Doré's illustration the mood is more mysterious, with a deeper space and more dramatic lighting. Notice the contrast between the small figures and the huge trees, and the snakelike movement of the figures into the dark unknown.

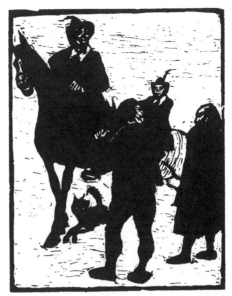

46

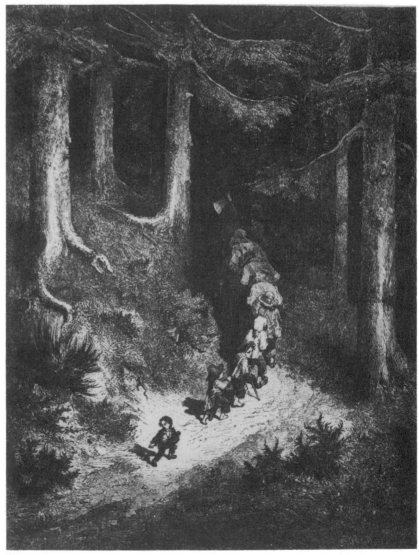

47

Advice to the Beginner

Considerations about personal style should not interfere with your spontaneous response to a story. If you do all you can to capture the story's subject matter, its emotion and mood, the style will emerge. In the beginning I read and think about the story, which leads to a clarification and visualization of it in my mind. Feelings and ideas arise. Gradually, the concept of the book takes shape in my mind and on paper.

The concept determines the technique, which in turn affects the style. When I created the pictures for *Dawn*, for instance, I realized that the soft outlines one sees at daybreak precluded the use of sharp pen-and-ink techniques and I chose to paint watercolor tones with a brush (see Chapter 17). After deciding how to approach the pictures, I executed them to the best of my ability. Since I am the artist who did them, the pictures inevitably bear my particular "handwriting."

In selecting the visual concept and the elements of style I would use, I was guided by the pictures' requirements as well as my own preferences (or affinity to a particular style of art) and temperament. I kept in mind, however, the importance of not letting my personality prevail over the content. With *Dawn*, style is to a great extent the result of solving the visual problems of the pictures (see Chapter 6). And this should hold for all illustrated books.

When the artist's personality, rather than subject matter, is the focus of attention in a children's book, personal style becomes a substitute for what is vital to the picture—the content. Excessive preoccupation with style can lead to affectation. It can divert the reader's attention from the picture to the artist, from the content to the packaging. It can also interfere with the readability and enjoyment of the picture.

Don't limit yourself to a single personal style. Using a style consistently throughout a book makes sense, but consistency becomes a straitjacket when an artist tries to force very different books into the same stylistic mold.

Before you decide to illustrate a book, make sure you like and care about the content of the story. You should also agree with its ideas and philosophy, as well as the imagery used. You cannot do your best if you have a negative or indifferent response to a story. Without true feeling, there is no genuine personal vision or style.

Illustrate a story honestly, the way you see it through your own eyes. Then execute the pictures as best you can, with the most suitable means. With each additional book you illustrate, your technical ability will increase, and so will your means of expression. Personal style will become as natural as your own handwriting. So don't force it. Remember, every artist is unique and ultimately your imprint is bound to show up on your work.

Part Four

Preparing for Reproduction

*He who thinks
everything easy, will
find everything
difficult.*

Lao-tzu

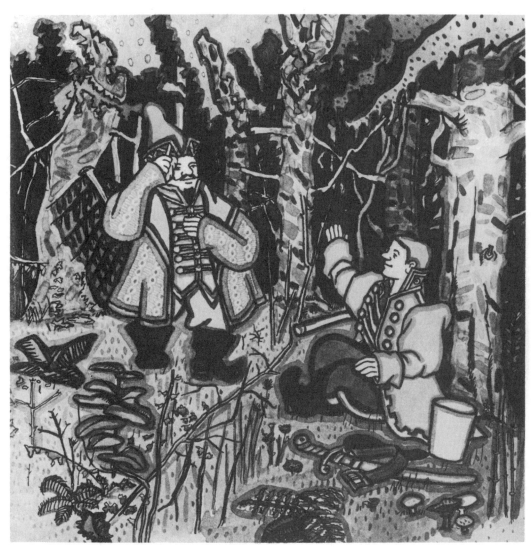

From *Soldier and Tsar in the Forest*

15. Printing Basics

*Chance will not do
the work . . .*

Sir Walter Scott

A basic understanding of printing can help you in preparing
your art for reproduction so that the printed book will come as
close as possible to what you envision. A reproduction is never
exactly the same as the original, and some kinds of art will
reproduce better than others. By becoming familiar with what
printing can and cannot do, you will be better able to choose
tools, materials, and techniques that will give the best possible
reproduction. None of these choices, however, should inhibit
your basic artistic decisions.

Most publishing companies have both an art director and a
production manager who can advise you in preparing your art
for reproduction. Although their responsibilities vary from
company to company, it is usually the art director who
supervises design and the production manager who contacts
the printer.

Usually the artist has little control over the production of his
or her book once it goes to the printer. You should, however,
discuss with the art director and production manager the
qualities you hope to achieve when your work is printed. They
will then work with you and the printer to get the best possible
reproduction within the necessary limitations.

Basic Terms

The following terms are the most common ones you will encounter in the printing of children's books. To learn more about the processes involved, you might consult *Production for the Graphic Designer* by James Craig.

Copy. Copy is any material to be printed: illustrations, photographs, type. It is referred to as *camera-ready* when it is complete and ready for reproduction without requiring additional work by the printer. Copy is generally classified as either *line* or *continuous-tone*.

Line Copy. This kind of copy is made up of solid black areas, such as dots, lines, or type, and is reproduced without any gradation of tone (**Figure 1**). A pen-and-ink drawing, for instance, can be treated as line copy because each individual line is the same color black, even though groups of lines may create a tonal effect. Pencil drawings, however, are best treated as continuous-tone copy.

Continuous-Tone Copy. Here the image has a range of tones that blend into each other, as in a photograph, pencil or pastel drawing, painting, or wash. It cannot be reproduced as it is, but must first be converted into line copy by means of the *halftone* process. With pencil, for instance, there are tonal variations in the lines themselves, depending on the pressure and type of pencil used. If a pencil drawing is treated as line copy, you will lose this tonal quality—all the lines will print the same black.

Halftone Reproduction. When continuous-tone copy is converted into line copy, it is photographed through a halftone screen, which consists of a grid of very fine lines (**Figure 2**). The image is broken up into dots of various sizes, which together convey the illusion of varying tones. These dots can be clearly seen, for example, in reproductions of photographs in a newspaper (**Figure 3**).

The coarseness or fineness of halftone screens is determined by the number of lines per inch. The more lines, the finer the screen, the smaller the dots, and the more detail captured. The choice of screen is dictated by the paper. A 65-line screen is used for newsprint, or coarse paper, whereas books are usually printed on smooth paper with 133- or 150-line screens.

Strictly speaking, the term *halftone* refers to the means of reproducing continuous-tone copy. When applied more loosely, it refers to copy to be reproduced by such means or the resulting printed image. According to James Craig in *Production for the Graphic Designer*, it is believed that "the term 'halftone' comes from the idea that the screening eliminates half the original image, which could be considered a 'full-tone,' and that only half of this full tone remains."

Flat Tints. Solid colors, including black, can be screened to produce a wide range of tones, referred to as flat tints. Flat tints are considered line, however, because unlike halftone reproduction, each flat tint has a single value and no illusion of blended tones. Although you may use several flat tints in one picture, within each tint area, the tone will be uniform.

The lightness or darkness of the flat tint depends on the screen used. The finer the screen, the lighter the tone; the coarser the screen, the darker the tone. Each tone is a specific percentage of the solid color: for example, gray can range from 90% to 10% of solid (100%) black in increments of 10% or 5% (see p. 216). Any line copy can be converted into a flat tint and print in any color.

Printing. Printing is the process of transferring an image from an inked surface (the printing plate) to another surface (such as paper), by means of pressure, for the purpose of making multiple copies. Of the many printing methods, the two most common ones in bookmaking are *letterpress* and *offset lithography*.

Letterpress. This is a direct printing method similar to the relief printing done with a rubber stamp or a woodblock. The image area is raised, as on a rubber stamp (**Figure 4**). When the ink is rolled on the surface of the printing plate, only the raised areas receive ink. The other (lower)

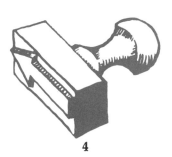

1

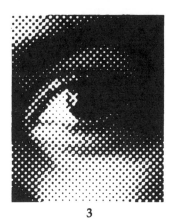

2

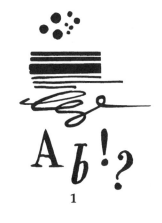

3

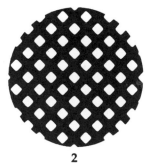

4

areas don't receive any ink and thus will not print. Once the image has been inked, it is transferred directly to the paper by means of pressure.

Offset Lithography. In contrast to letterpress, offset lithography—called *offset*, for short—is an indirect printing method, in which the image is first transferred from the printing plate to an intermediate surface (a rubber blanket) and from there to the paper. The printing plate is made photographically and then chemically treated. Once the plate is made the process is similar to that used in making a lithograph. The basic principle is that oil and water don't mix. The plate is covered with a water solution that adheres only to the non-image area. Then, when the plate is inked, the oily ink is received only by the image area. It is this inked image that is transferred to the rubber blanket and then printed. Offset lithography is the most common method of printing children's books today.

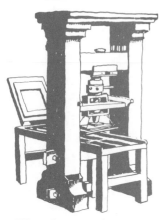

Fifteenth-century letterpress

One-Color Printing. One-color printing is the reproduction of an image in a single color, whether red, blue, some other hue, or black. (In printing, black is considered a color.) The image may be printed solid, as a halftone, as one or more flat tints, or all of these. Any color paper may be used.

Multicolor Printing. As the term implies, multicolor printing is printing with more than one color. Normally, multicolor printing uses two, three, or four colors. Many children's books are printed in two or three colors, as this is less expensive than four colors.

Two- and three-color books can be printed in a variety of ways to achieve colorful images. The colors can be used at full strength or as lighter values; flat or with blended tones. They can also be combined (surprinted) to create new colors. For instance, yellow printed over blue will create green.

More and more children's books are printed in four colors. Four-color printing may be done in one of two ways: by the *four-color process* or by *color preseparation*. (Color preseparation is also used for two- and three-color books.)

Four-Color Process. With the four-color process, the full range of colors and values in an image such as a painting, color photograph, or color slide is reproduced by means of four separate printing plates. Each plate prints one of the four standard printing inks, called *process colors*—process blue (cyan), process red (magenta), process yellow, and process black.

The colors of a full-color illustration are separated by means of filters on the camera, with each filter shutting out all but one color. Or this may be done by means of a computer. The plates are then carefully positioned to make sure the colors are in register when printed one on top of another with the four transparent process inks.

Color Preseparation. Unlike four-color process printing, which is done mechanically, color preseparation is done manually by the artist. The artist, for instance, prepares all the blue areas in the picture on a single sheet and then uses another sheet for all the yellow areas. Because color preseparation is widely used in children's books, the process is described in detail in the next chapter.

Reproduction Considerations

The printer and the artist employ totally different means to achieve a visual image; there are thus differences between the original artwork and its printed form.

Although the printer's intent is to come as close as possible to your original art, within the limits of technology, printing is better viewed as an *interpretation*, not as an exact replica. Lines drawn with pen and ink on paper don't look quite the same when printed. The printer cannot achieve the exact tones of your wash either. The best the printer can do is translate them into solid dots that convey an optical illusion of tone. And, no matter how many colors you use in a full-color picture, it will nearly always be reproduced using only four colors.

In preparing your art, then, remember that it is only a means to achieve the best reproduction possible. The reader will see the book, not the original art. That doesn't mean you should disregard the artistic qualities of your original. On the contrary, keep both aspects in mind: strive for pictures that will reproduce well and also be beautiful when exhibited. But when, for some reason, you cannot achieve both, remember the priorities: *the book must stand as art in the printed medium.* The following advice can help you enhance the reproduction of your illustrations in a book.

Paper for Camera-Ready Art

For the best reproduction results, use paper as white as possible for your final art, to provide maximum contrast to the drawn or painted image. Use stable paper that doesn't shrink, such as watercolor paper and, when possible, a paper heavy enough to reduce warping. Don't use black ink on bluish paper, or brown ink on yellowish paper, or black and red together. In black-and-white reproduction, red photographs as black.

The rougher the texture of the paper, the greater the possibility of losing light tones. Also, it is difficult to reproduce an image painted on rough-textured paper because the surface irregularities cast shadows, which can distort the image.

Avoid illustration boards; use flexible boards instead, in case the art is reproduced by computer, which requires wrapping it around a drum. Also, avoid huge boards with very large margins. They take up a lot of space and make it difficult for several pieces of art to be photographed at once (ganged up).

Line or Halftone?

In deciding on whether to use line or halftone reproduction, you need to be aware of the advantages and limitations of each method. With line reproduction, you achieve greater contrast and sharpness of definition, but halftone art gives you tonal gradations and texture.

The main limitation of line reproduction is that it lacks tonality; it can reproduce only a solid, flat image. Halftone, however, tends to reduce contrasts, flattening a picture. Dark areas tend to lighten because they don't print perfectly solid, whereas highlights are not pure white (they contain a faint dot pattern, unless the dots are removed by hand retouching on the film, or unless the camera is set to drop dots out of these areas).

Overall, there are fewer reproduction problems with line art than with halftone art. Because of this, I prefer to use line whenever possible. Everything being equal, you can expect pen and ink to reproduce better than delicate pencil or wash. Remember, however, that very delicate lines and lines with variations in value are often reproduced as halftone. Delicate pen-and-ink crosshatching, for example, will be reproduced as halftone to retain as much detail as possible, at the cost of reducing sharpness.

Preparing Line Art

As mentioned earlier, when you prepare line art for reproduction, use paper as white as possible. Also use ink as black as possible for maximum contrast. (A flame red without any blue in it is interpreted by the camera as black and can, if necessary, be used instead of black.)

Draw sharp, dense lines; avoid fine, faint, or gray lines. When crosshatching, it is best to space the lines widely enough to prevent the ink from filling in on press. If you need guidelines, draw them lightly in pencil or use a nonreproducing blue pencil. (Blue without any purple in it is interpreted by the camera as white.) Whatever you use, try not to press down too hard so that you can erase the guidelines completely when your art is finished.

Preparing Halftone Art

Generally speaking, the halftone process will reproduce the range of tones the eye sees. You can draw halftone art any way you like, but use paper that gives contrast for your medium. Also keep in mind that delicate pencil art—where the tone is barely darker than the color of the paper—is hard to reproduce.

Many printers recommend not painting tones of any color lighter than 10%. Some feel that even 10% won't reproduce well. At some point the camera can no longer differentiate between the painted tone and the color of the paper.

Enlargement and Reduction

As a general rule, it is advisable not to reduce or enlarge your art excessively. Some printers advise that enlargement should not exceed 150% to 200%. Excessive enlargement exaggerates the graininess and irregularities of the art; lines become much coarser.

Reduction is less likely to distort the character of the art than enlargement. But keep in mind that too much reduction kills detail. Some printers feel that a reduction of more than 50% will cause too much loss of detail: the openings created by crosshatching, for instance, may clog up. Others feel that it depends on the nature of the copy.

For the best reproduction results, prepare same-size art, or art to be reduced only 10% to 15%. Try not to exceed 50%. Make all the pictures in one book the same scale: it is less costly to the publisher and the effect will be more consistent. Also bear in mind that, everything else being equal, small pictures are more economical to reproduce than large ones.

Identification of Art

The art director or production manager can give you specific information on how best to identify your art for the printer. In general, try to leave 1-inch to 2-inch margins or borders around the art for identification, any necessary directions to the printer, and protection. In the bottom margin, outside the picture area, write the book title, page number, picture number, and so on. Indicate where on the page each picture belongs and clearly communicate the size you want—that is, the percentage your art is to be enlarged or reduced, or if it is to be kept the same size (100%).

Test-Proofs

It is important for the art director and production manager to examine halftone art carefully in order to anticipate any possible reproduction problems. They may decide to have the printer make a test-proof if their examination of the art raises any questions. A *test-proof* is a sample printing of a piece of camera-ready art, which allows you to see what happens when the image is reproduced. Although not all publishers do test-proofs, if possible it is best to have one done before you proceed with all the illustrations. In this way the printer can advise you, through the publisher, on what will work best.

At the Printer

A good printing job cannot save a poorly illustrated book, but poor printing can be detrimental to a well-illustrated one. Surprisingly, however, many problems in printing have little to do with the printing equipment or other technical matters. Instead, they arise from a lack of communication between the artist and the printer. If you communicate clearly what is important for your art, the abilities of everyone concerned—art director, production manager, printer, and the cameraman responsible for shooting the art—can be directed toward achieving it. Clear communication requires clear thinking, which will help you in creating better pictures as well as getting better printing results.

Remember that the printed illustration cannot be an exact replica of your art; there is always some loss in the process of reproduction. Explain to the art director or production manager what your priorities are so that he or she can tell the printer what to aim for. What is most important to retain in your art when it is printed—brightness, details, highlights, middle tones, contrasts?

In many cases, before a book is printed, the publisher will receive a complete set of *proofs*—preliminary samples of all the printed pages. These are usually checked by several people at the publishing house (including the art director, production manager, and editor); sometimes the artist will also be allowed to look at the proofs. At this stage the publishing staff makes sure that the art is correctly sized and positioned, and that the color is accurate. They check the registration of each illustration, as poor registration affects sharpness in multicolor printing. In addition, they look for any printing flaws, such as broken lines or white spots on printed areas (called *hickies*).

Once the proofs have been corrected and approved, the book is ready for a preliminary press run. The purpose of this step is to obtain a satisfactory printed sheet (*press sheet*), which can be used as a model for the entire run. Some publishers send a representative to the printer at this time and—in rare cases—the artist may also be invited. If you are given this opportunity, take it by all means and learn from it. I have been fortunate in having had the chance to be at the printer while my books were on press. Even at this stage, there are some limited adjustments that can be made.

When the initial press sheets are run off, they are usually checked against the proofs for color accuracy. It's important to consider how the press sheet, fresh from the press, will look when it's dry. Ink dries much lighter on uncoated paper than on coated paper (which has been treated to improve the finish). There is a loss of sharpness, intensity, and luster by absorption with uncoated paper; on coated paper the ink retains more of its initial value and luster. The difference between a wet sheet, fresh from the press, and the same sheet when it is dry can be considerable.

Because offset printing tends to reduce contrasts and flatten out a picture, the printer should keep an eye on the contrasts in the gray tones if a book is in black and white, or between the colors if a book is in color. To compensate for this loss in contrast, I sometimes ask that my book be printed darker than my originals.

When I go to the printer, I look at the press sheet in different ways. First, I look at the entire sheet to see if all the pictures are well balanced and have a unified character. Then I fold a sheet and look at one picture at a time to give myself a better idea of how the individual pictures will look in the final book. It's important to remember, however, that during the actual press run, the printing gradually sharpens up, and the image will look cleaner. That is why normally it is better not to delay the press run unreasonably.

Another way to look at a press sheet is through a magnifying glass. What can be seen through a magnifying glass is what determines the look of the printing: the dots have to be clean. "Hairing"—tiny hairlines around each dot—indicates too much ink. If the paper shows through, it is underinked. Type printed evenly indicates that the black plate is inked properly. If the type is gray, there is insufficient black ink.

The pressman can vary the amount of ink to a certain degree, and this can result in a considerable difference in the final appearance of the printing. It is amazing how a tiny difference in the amount of ink can affect the quality of a picture.

After a press sheet has been approved and the actual press run begins, the successive press sheets can be compared to one another and to the one that has been approved. One way to do this is to number each successive press sheet and compare the same picture on each by putting the sheets side by side. I have found that focusing on the same part of each illustration, after having looked at the overall sheet, helps me to see if there are any differences in printing and whether the same quality has been maintained.

Since, however, you may not go to the printer, remember to communicate your concerns clearly to the publisher, who will in turn communicate them to the printer.

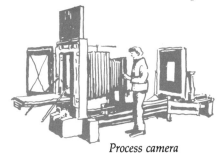

Process camera

16. Color Preseparation

Unlike color separation, which is done mechanically by means of a camera or computer, color *pre*separation is done manually by the artist. In preseparation the artist separates the color by preparing a keyplate (or master preseparation) and one or more overlays. Although the keyplate and overlays are usually painted in black or in grays, each represents a different color specified by the artist. The printer follows these instructions so that each keyplate or overlay is reproduced as a one-color image. When printed together, they form a multicolor picture.

Because preseparation is more economical than four-color process printing, many children's book publishers ask artists to do preseparated pictures rather than full-color paintings. There are other advantages to knowing how to preseparate. When thoroughly mastered, color preseparation can achieve results as good as or better than those of average four-color printing—certain textural effects or greater clarity and sharpness, for example. In addition, the discipline that color preseparation requires may help sharpen your sense of color and improve your artistic resourcefulness.

There are, however, disadvantages to color preseparation. Often the publisher will restrict the number of colors the artist can use for budgetary reasons. Moreover, preseparation requires careful planning and considerable work of a painstaking nature, which may limit spontaneity. The keyplate and overlays are prepared in a single color (usually black), even though they will print in different colors. This means that you have to *visualize* the color scheme of the end result.

The best way to learn about color preseparation is by doing it, which is why I have included preseparation exercises later in this chapter. But before you can proceed with the exercises, you must become familiar with the basic guides to use in visualizing and planning your color scheme, as well as the materials.

Color Study

Again, one of the major difficulties with color preseparation is visualizing how your picture will look when printed while you are working with black or grays only. The first step is to make a color study, which is simply a painting of your illustration in the colors you want. This study then serves as a guide in preparing the more complicated forms of color preseparation. It also reduces mistakes and guesswork.

If you are asked to use the standard process colors (discussed in Chapter 15), select paints that closely approximate the four-color process printing inks. No art paints match printing inks exactly, but a good approximation can be made with Grumbacher's Academy Watercolors—lamp black, Thalo crimson, cadmium yellow pale, and Thalo blue.

Once you have made your color study, you must use a color chart. With this guide, you will be able to determine the percentages of printing inks needed to get the colors you want.

Color Charts

The color charts used in color preseparation consist of rectangles printed in solid colors along with their progressively lighter values, or flat tints (see the example on p. 240). They also contain various combinations of flat tints. The value of each flat tint is measured in percentages of the solid color. For example, a light pink would be 10% of solid (100%) red.

Many charts show values progressing in increments of ten, from 10% to 100%. Other color charts use a different system and omit 40%, 60%, 80%, and 90%. A multicolor chart may have from two to four colors. Standard color charts consist of the four process colors.

Color charts are printed on paper, frequently on both coated and uncoated stock, or on transparent plastic sheets. The color charts most useful for preseparation purposes are cleanly printed on paper in approximately 1-inch-long rectangles. It is a good idea to have color charts on both coated and uncoated paper.

Although many children's books are printed on uncoated paper, matte coated paper may be used for picture books.

Where to Get Color Charts

Many publishers have a selection of color charts, which may be available to the artist who is preseparating a book for them. Standard color charts of the four process colors are also available from engravers' associations and from printers. Most printers' charts, however, are not fully satisfactory, because the colors are not cleanly printed, or because the color rectangles are too small. An exception is the four-color process chart, which is available on either coated or uncoated paper for a nominal fee from Federated Lithographers-Printers, Inc. (369 Prairie Avenue, Providence, RI 02901). This is the least expensive useful chart for color preseparating.

Among the commercially available color charts, by far the best at a moderate price is the CA Color Guide in book form, which comes cleanly printed on either coated or uncoated paper. It can be ordered from Communication Arts magazine (PO Box 10300, Palo Alto, CA 94303) and is also available at some art supply stores.

The CA Color Guide consists of a selection of 65 two-color charts of different nonstandard colors (colors other than the four process colors). These colors are shown in varying values. The CA Color Guide also includes process color charts of two and three colors. The drawback is that the process color charts are printed on both sides of the page and are thus more likely to become soiled after extensive use. Also, the process color charts do not show four-color combinations. Nevertheless, this guide is a very valuable tool; it is my personal preference for use in preseparating.

The Pantone Color/Tint Overlay Selector, printed on transparent film, is available at art supply stores. This and other Pantone charts are based on the Pantone Matching System (PMS)—a color-matching guide used by most printers.

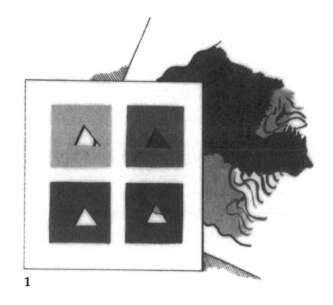

1

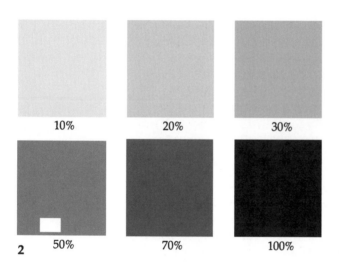

10%   20%   30%

2 50%   70%   100%

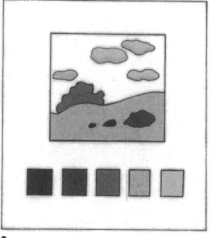

3

When you want to use colors other than the standard process colors, or nonstandard colors not included in the CA Color Guide, you will need custom-made charts of these colors, which are sometimes provided by the publisher.

How to Read Color Charts

In the CA Color Guide, a color chart combining blue and yellow reads as follows: on top, horizontally from left to right, are the yellow tints in increasing percentages (10, 20, 30, 50, 70, 100); vertically on the left, from top to bottom, are the blue tints in increasing percentages (10, 20, 30, 40, 50, 60, 70, 100). To figure out the composition of a given green tint on the chart, you locate the yellow tint contained in this green by ascending vertically to the top of the chart, to find out that it has, say, 70% yellow. You then locate the blue tint, by moving laterally to the far left, to find that it has 50% blue. Thus, the green tint is composed of 70% yellow and 50% blue.

The Federated color chart is comprised of a series of color rectangles, under which are printed formulas for the various color combinations. The abbreviations used for the four process colors are: BK for black, BU for blue, R for red, Y for yellow. When an abbreviation is not followed by a percentage, it stands for the solid color, or 100%. For example, a color rectangle labeled "Y75% BU75% BK50%" is made up of a combination of 75% yellow, 75% blue, and 50% black. "R BU BK25%" means 100% red, 100% blue, and 25% black, while "R BU BK50%" means 100% red, 100% blue, and 50% black. "Y R" means 100% yellow plus 100% red.

How to Use Color Charts

It is best to cut the Federated chart into smaller sections and to take the CA Color Guide book apart and use single sheets. Then cut out small rectangular or triangular openings within the color rectangles of the chart (**Figure 1**). Use a very sharp blade to avoid hairy white edges.

Now superimpose the chart over the

tone you wish to identify in your color study and press down firmly to eliminate any possible shadows between the chart and your art. Look through the opening to evaluate whether the tone on your art approximates the tint on the chart. This process makes identifying a tone considerably easier. You can also use these openings to see how two or more different colors relate by superimposing one sheet from the color chart on another. In this way you can visualize your color scheme.

Do not mix the various color chart systems in evaluating the different tones. Although theoretically they are supposed to be uniform, there have been instances when the process colors have varied from chart to chart because of the amount or the quality of the inks used in printing them.

In the exercises later in this chapter, you will practice evaluating the colors in a color study with the help of color charts. You also need a gray scale to complete the camera-ready preseparations.

Gray Scale

The gray scale, which is contained within some color charts, gives a range of black flat tints printed in varying screen percentages (**Figure 2**). It is consulted by the artist to determine the correct gray values to use for camera-ready preseparations. If the precise percentage of a tone is unclear, check it against the two closest tints on the gray scale, to see which one it most closely approximates.

The CA Color Guide gray scale contains the following percentages of black: 10%, 20%, 30%, 50%, and 70%. The Federated color chart has 10%, 25%, 50%, 75%, and 100% black. Again, do not mix the various color chart systems. In most cases, either the CA or the Federated gray scale is sufficient to complete a project.

Some art directors may ask you to paint a gray scale on each overlay of a piece of preseparated art for a test-proof of the same picture (**Figure 3**). You may not, however, need to do a complete gray scale, progressing in even increments

from 10% to 100% black. Instead, the art director may suggest using only those values contained in the picture.

Keyplate

Once you have decided which colors on the color chart you want to use, you are ready to make the keyplate. The keyplate is the master preseparation, which contains most of the image; it is thus more readable than the overlays of the same picture. Normally, the keyplate represents the black color of the picture. It is then referred to as the black keyplate. The black keyplate is important: not only is it the guide for preparing the overlays, but, as the darkest color, it also shows up the most in the printed picture.

To prepare the keyplate, choose a sturdy white paper. I like to use Strathmore drawing paper (called *drawing board* by the manufacturer), with a medium surface (kid-finish), two-, three-, or four-ply. It is best to use a heavy paper to provide a good support when you attach overlays to it. If you want to trace a sketch on a light box, however, you cannot use very heavy paper. In this case, I use paper no heavier than two-ply, medium-surface Strathmore drawing paper or Arches 90 lb., cold-pressed watercolor paper.

Leave 1-inch to 2-inch margins around the picture on the keyplate for information and handling. The extra margin is also a precautionary measure, in case you need to enlarge your picture. In the bottom margin, write the following information: color (e.g., black), name of book, page number, picture number, size, and picture placement. Also include any special instructions to the printer. Give the tint percentage and include a color swatch if you are not using one of the four process colors.

Overlays

An overlay is meant to "lie over" the keyplate, whether or not it is physically attached to the keyplate. It represents a color that will either overprint (surprint) or print with the keyplate. An overlay

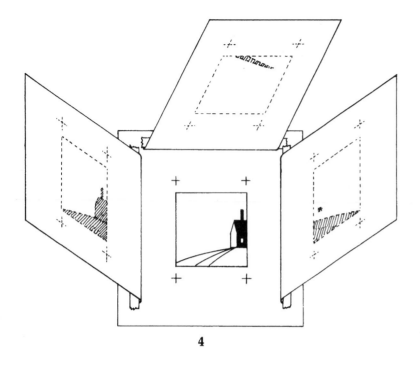

4

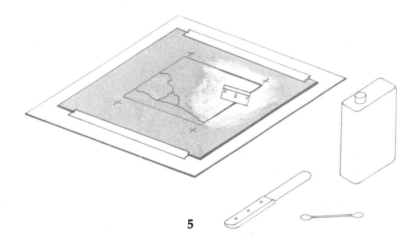

5

may also be used for protection or for conveying information or instructions to the printer. Our discussion, however, will concentrate on its function in color pre-separation. In **Figure 4** you can see how you might attach three overlays to the keyplate so that you could view any combination of colors simultaneously.

Overlays can be *transparent* (acetate, vellum, or Bourges Colotones) or *opaque* (paper or blue-bristols). For color pre-separation, I prefer to use an overlay that is white and that doesn't chip when painted. In general, choose an overlay that is suitable for reproduction and that you are comfortable with.

Acetate

Of the various transparent overlays, cellulose acetate (or acetate, for short) is the most commonly used. This transparent plastic sheet comes in matte (frosted on one side) and clear forms. I prefer matte acetate for preseparation work because it takes paint and ink better than clear acetate does.

Choose a medium or heavy weight matte acetate and make sure you work with the frosted side up. Although regular drawing ink can be used, special acetate inks are available, designed for use on film. An opaque type of acetate ink will cover an acetate surface faster than ordinary drawing ink.

To learn how to use acetate, look at Exercise 2 (p. 226). In covering the acetate with ink, you want the painted areas to be opaque. Don't, however, apply the ink too thickly. Instead, paint once and wait until this dries: then, place a sheet of white paper underneath to see whether you have left any gray areas. Paint over these areas—several times if necessary—until they are opaque.

In general, I find acetate most suitable for line reproduction. Acetate overlays can, however, be used for preseparations done with blended tones (tonal pre-separation), using a medium such as pencil. But there must be adequate contrast to differentiate the gray in your drawing from the grayish tone of the acetate. When properly prepared—with strong contrasts—acetate overlays should pose no problems in reproduction.

An *advantage* of acetate is its ready availability. In addition, its transparency simplifies the preseparation process, because you can easily see where to paint without the help of a light box. It doesn't stretch, warp, or buckle significantly when painted with a wet medium. You should, however, place an additional sheet of a transparent or semitransparent material, such as tracing paper, over the completed art for protection.

Among the *disadvantages* of acetate is that it allows only a limited range of tonal and textural effects. It can also be difficult to draw on and is an inadequate surface for transparent watercolor. Nevertheless, some artists do work with transparent washes on acetate; others use oil paints. You should also be aware that acetate lacks the warmth of paper. Remember that frosted acetate has a grayish tone, so there may not be enough contrast for delicate tones to be picked up by the printer's camera. That is why some printers prefer white paper overlays (which have no gray in them).

Vellum

Vellum, a very heavy tracing paper, can also be used as a transparent overlay. Because it buckles when wet, it is best to use vellum for pencil rather than a wet medium such as watercolor. Some artists, however, have used vellum successfully with gray markers.

Bourges Colotones

Bourges Colotones are transparent plastic sheets that come in a wide variety of colors and values. Since Colotones are transparent, you can combine them to get additional colors. For example, by overlaying a blue and a yellow Colotone, you can get a third color—green. Colotones are thus an ideal material for learning color preseparation: they enable you to visualize the color of the preseparated picture while working.

Before you use Colotones for camera-ready preseparations, however, check with the publisher's production manager or art director, because some printers have refused to reproduce from Colotones. Use values 70% and 100% only—nothing lighter. (The manufacturer recommends 70%.) If you cannot use the actual colors you want, use any of the warm red Colotones to represent other colors.

To learn how to use Colotones, look at Exercise 1 (p. 224). Essentially, you scrape away the emulsion on the matte side of the sheet and expose the clear, transparent film wherever you don't want a particular color (**Figure 5**). If, for example, you were doing an overlay for *blue*, you would scrape away all the areas of the image *without* blue. The unique coating of Colotones is fine for any scratchboard and line techniques.

The best way to get Colotones is to order a packet of assorted sheets directly from Bourges Color Corporation (20 Waterside Plaza, New York, NY 10010). The packet contains nonadhesive sheets, which are best to use for your overlays. You can also ask for some sheets with adhesive backing, for corrections.

Paper Overlays

Paper overlays—considered opaque overlays—are used to achieve tonality and texture in color preseparation. Choose a 100% rag paper that doesn't shrink or buckle excessively, such as a watercolor paper. It should be as white as possible, without gray or pink in it, especially if you are preparing art for halftone reproduction. Make sure the paper is not too light in weight, or excessive buckling may occur with a watercolor wash. On the other hand, the paper shouldn't be too heavy, and thus too opaque, to be used for tracing on a light box.

Remember that a good, heavy paper will take corrections better than a light paper. When the areas to be painted are not very large, Strathmore single-ply drawing paper, with a medium surface, may be used. When large areas are to be painted, and the outlines on your keyplate are bold enough to be seen over a light box, you may be able to use Strathmore two-ply drawing paper or Arches 90 lb., cold-pressed watercolor paper. If there is risk of buckling, however, it is advisable to use acetate (see my discussion of the problems I encountered with *Dawn* in Chapter 17).

Blue-Bristols

Blue-bristols are white bristol boards on which the black keyplate has been printed in a nonreproducing light blue ink (which is invisible to the camera). These light blue lines provide ready-made guidelines for preseparating, eliminating the need to trace them manually. A publisher may supply a limited number of blue-bristols for each picture.

Blue-bristols are time-saving and enjoyable to work with. Since they are expensive to make, however, they are not made for every book. Discuss the possibility of getting blue-bristols with the art director or production manager.

Drawing and Painting Materials

In addition to different kinds of overlays, there are different kinds of materials you can use to paint your overlays. The most important ones are described here.

Black Watercolor

Although black transparent watercolor is recommended primarily for painting tonal preseparations on paper overlays, it can also be used in preparing flat preseparations—that is, preseparations done with even tones. Black is supposed to be a neutral color, but some blacks are actually "warm" (with a trace of red in them), whereas others are "cool" (with a trace of blue). Generally, ivory black is warm and lamp black is cool, although this must be tested, as brands vary. Most gray scales within charts are printed with process black, which is cool. Therefore, the following brands of lamp black transparent watercolor, which come reasonably close to the process black printing ink, are

recommended: Permanent Pigments Watercolors, Grumbacher Academy Watercolors, Winsor & Newton Artists Watercolors, and Talens Watercolors.

You should also be aware that a wash painted with lamp black on paper with even a faint trace of pink in it will look warmer than one painted on totally white paper. Arches cold-pressed watercolor paper, for example, is warmer than Strathmore drawing paper. The farther off the paper is from pure white, the more difficult it will be to match your tone to the gray scale.

The main reason for using cool black is to match the gray scale, and it poses no major reproduction problems if you use white paper with no pink or gray in it. It is true that a warm black is easier to reproduce than a cool one (because red is easier to reproduce than blue). But if you decide to work with warm black, first find out from the publisher if it is possible to obtain custom-made color charts printed in warm black. Whether you use a cool or á warm black, be consistent—don't mix the two.

Pencil

Instead of preparing preseparations with a wash, you can use a soft pencil on paper or on frosted acetate. To blend or spread it, you may want to use a stump or tortillon. (A stump or tortillon, which is made of rolled paper and pointed at one or both ends, is used to smooth, shade, or blend charcoal, pastel, and pencil drawings as described in Chapter 13.)

The drawback to using pencil in preseparating artwork is that unless the tones are uniform, with as little texture as possible, it is difficult to measure the values against the gray scale.

Markers

Dye markers with felt tips are available in various cool or warm grays. Be sure to check whether the marker contains a water-based or an oil-based dye—do not use the two together.

Experiment with markers to find out

whether you like to work with them. You can try them on vellum, on special paper for markers, or on regular paper. They dry fast, but watch out for spreading and soaking through. The oil-based dyes tend to soak through the paper more than the water-based ones. Also find out if you can get uniform tones without streaks.

Despite the problems in using markers, books have been successfully preseparated with them. Some artists have used warm blacks on special paper for markers and have found them to be a quick way to preseparate. You might want to explore the different kinds of new markers that are available, or try various marker tips. Bear in mind, however, that the dyes are not permanent and are likely to change color over time.

Opaque Gray Paints

Several kinds of cool or warm gray paints are available. Use the cool grays, whenever possible, because they come closer to the gray scale of standard color charts. The gray paints described here can be used on paper or acetate to paint preseparations done with more than one flat tint per color (multivalue flat color preseparations).

Cel-Vinyl Cartoon Colors. Cel-Vinyl Cartoon Colors are vinyl-acrylic copolymer colors used in animation. The gray tones are most suitable for painting flat values on acetate overlays. Martha Alexander, for instance, has used them on matte acetate to preseparate more than ten of her books and has found them most satisfactory. (See her book *Nobody Asked Me if I Wanted a Baby Sister*, in which the colors were painted in flat tones and reproduced as halftones.)

Cel-Vinyl Cartoon Colors are stable and flexible; they won't peel, chip, or crack, unless too many layers are applied. When a correction is necessary, Cel-Vinyl can be removed from the acetate with a razor blade. Also, with a cotton swab and water, you can moisten the part you wish to remove and peel it off. Alexander recommends that when the gray paints dry out in the paint cups, it is easier to add more

paint on top of the old than to keep the old paint wet. If it gets too thick, mix in some rubbing alcohol, followed by water. Use more water than alcohol.

At present, in addition to black and white, twelve tones of gray are available. Of those available, the following Cel-Vinyl grays match the gray scale: no. 4 (10% black), no. 6 (20%), no. 8 (30%), no. 10 (40%). To match the other percentages on the gray scale, you must mix your own.

Gold Label Artist Colors. Ann Schweninger has found another brand of gray paints similar to Cel-Vinyl, which she has used with satisfactory results in preseparating her illustrations for Alan Benjamin's *Ribtickle Town*. They are Gold Label Artist Colors, made by Magic Touch Company in Anaheim, California. Schweninger painted her own gray scale with the Gold Label paints, based on the Federated chart. Before preseparating the book, however, she had the scale proofed by the printer. She found that the following Gold Label grays approximate percentages on the Federated chart: no. 3 (slightly lighter than 10% black), no. 6 (slightly lighter than 25%), no. 10 (close to 50%), no. 16 (close to 75%). Although she didn't use them, she suggests that no. 4 and no. 7 or 8 may come closer to 10% and 25% of the Federated chart, respectively. Whenever possible, it is best to use the ready-made grays, because sometimes the colors you mix will streak.

Grumbacher's Gamma Retouch Grays. Grumbacher's Gamma Retouch Grays are normally used for retouching photographs, but they have been used by some artists to paint on acetate overlays. Ariane Dewey has used them on matte acetate to preseparate many of her books (for instance, *Mushroom in the Rain* by Mirra Ginsburg, illustrated by Jose Aruego and Ariane Dewey, which was done in flat tones but reproduced as halftone art). The Gamma Retouch Grays are available in six tones of gray, plus black and white. Dewey suggests the following approximations to the gray scale: no. 2 (close to 10% black), no. 3 (about 25%), no. 4 (about 50%), no. 5 (about 75%), and no. 6 (about 90%). She suggests that you get a large-

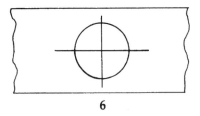

6

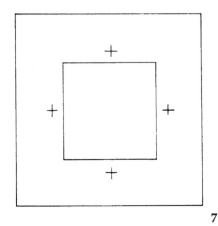 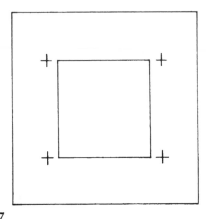

7

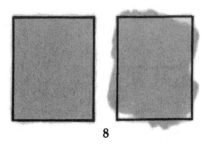

8

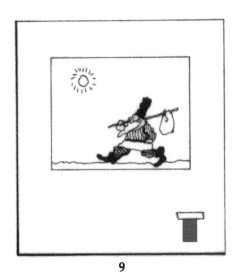

9

enough supply to last for the entire book, because a new batch may vary in tone, and then you must mix your own grays.

Some artists find that Gamma Retouch Grays do not dry flat, and when humidity is high, they can take up to two weeks to dry. If for some reason the book's printing has been delayed, after an extended period the Gamma Retouch Grays may flake, making it necessary to match the grays once more. You may have to add a medium such as Non-Crawl, Color-Flex, Flex-Opaque, or Cel-Grip to make the paint more flexible and thereby prevent chipping and flaking.

Register Marks

In preseparating your picture on the keyplate and one or more overlays, you need to show clearly how these pieces should be positioned in relation to one another to form a single image. This is done with register marks. Ready-made register marks, available in art supply stores, consist of a cross within a circle, printed on a roll of self-adhesive, transparent plastic tape (**Figure 6**). They are also available on sheets that can be cut up.

The register marks are first attached to the keyplate and then to each overlay so that the pictures line up exactly when the register marks are superimposed (see Figure 3, p. 228). The printer takes apart the overlays to prepare the printing plate, and unless they are accurately registered and identified, the printer won't be able to reposition them correctly for printing.

To position register marks, first place four of them ⅛-inch to ¼-inch from the outside edges of your illustration on the keyplate in either of the ways shown in **Figure 7**. If the art runs across two facing pages, however, it is better to use three register marks on each half. With transparent overlays, it is fairly easy to superimpose the register marks. To reduce the difficulties of accurately "registering" overlays of heavy paper, when you can't see through, cut small square holes in one overlay at a time at the center of each register mark. This will enable you to view the corresponding register marks on the overlays underneath.

Although ready-made register marks are easy to use, you can also draw your own register marks with pen and ink, if you can do it with precision. Use a T-square, triangle and, on acetate, a ruling pen or a flat or round Speedball lettering pen, size B-6. Draw a 90-degree cross—you don't need the circle. On paper, you can draw register marks with a fine black ballpoint pen.

Although the register marks should always be positioned accurately, you can develop an illustration technique that will tolerate some fluctuation in registration during printing. If, for instance, you apply the color loosely rather than neatly within your lines (**Figure 8**), it will not be as noticeable if the registration of the different overlays is slightly off.

Color Swatch

Whenever a color other than black or a standard process color is desired, a color swatch should be attached to the keyplate of your preseparated art (**Figure 9**). The color swatch serves as a guideline for the printer in matching a nonstandard color. Be sure to discuss the color choice with the art director or production manager before you begin. It is best to choose a color swatch from the ready-made Pantone Matching System (PMS), for which the printer will have specific ink formulas. You can, however, make your own painted color swatch.

In any case, the color swatch should be clean and no smaller than $1'' \times 1''$. Make sure it has a flat, even tone, as a color swatch with texture or tonal fluctuation is difficult or impossible to match accurately.

Overview of Color Preseparation Exercises

Color preseparation can be divided into two main methods: *flat* color preseparation and *tonal* color preseparation. Flat color preseparation includes *single-value* and *multivalue* color preseparations. It is best to begin with the simplest kind of flat color preseparation, using two solid, flat colors. Rely heavily on your black keyplate by including in it most of the picture's image. Add your second color on a single overlay, applying it sparingly in bold areas and avoiding too many small spots.

After mastering two colors, move on to three-color preseparation. Next, add tints; for example, in a two-color preseparation, use black and one color, with one or two tints per color. After that, you can tackle multivalue three-color preseparation, with an additional but limited number of tints. Progress gradually from three to four colors, and then finally move on to tonal color preseparation.

Single-Value Flat Color Preseparation

We shall begin with single-value flat color preseparation, which is done with uniformly flat colors without blended tones. The first exercise uses Bourges Colotones, transparent sheets of various flat colors, which enable you to see the colors during the process of making the preseparations. It is therefore the clearest way to learn color preseparation. This exercise will then be used as a color study for Exercise 2. We shall not use Exercise 1 as a means in itself of producing camera-ready art.

Exercise 1: Colotone Preseparation

Materials: (1) Two Bourges Colotone sheets. Although any two colors can be used, we will use blue and yellow. Colotones come in different values as well as different hues, but for the purpose of this exercise we will consider any value as 100% solid color. Select a blue and a yellow that suit your picture and that, when combined, create an appropriate green. If possible, select Colotones that approximate blue and yellow on a process color chart. (2) Strathmore three-ply, medium-surface drawing paper, or an equivalent white drawing paper, about 10" × 12". (3) Black India ink. (4) Rubber cement thinner. (5) Register marks with adhesive backing. (6) Masking tape.

Tools: (1) Pen. (2) Brush (optional). (3) Pencil. (4) Eraser. (5) Cotton swabs. (6) Scraping tools.

Black Keyplate (Figure 10):

1. Draw a very simple picture in pencil on the drawing paper and then execute it in pen and ink. If you wish, you may paint solid black areas as well. Avoid faint, delicate lines, as well as pencil or wash techniques.
2. When you have put in the ink, erase the pencil lines and clean up all unwanted marks and smudges. This is your black keyplate.
3. Write "black" below the bottom margin on your keyplate. Black, which requires a separate printing plate and a separate ink, is considered a color.
4. Place the register marks as described earlier.

Yellow Overlay (Figure 11). Although you can begin with either color, we will begin with yellow.

1. With masking tape, fasten a piece of Colotone large enough to cover the register marks and the picture on the keyplate. Center it over your picture, emulsion (matte) side up.
2. Scrape away the areas over the register marks to see through them better. Attach another set of register marks on the overlay, superimposed precisely over the keyplate register marks.

3. Scrape away the areas you want white or blue. Leave the yellow where you want yellow, or where you want yellow combined with blue to produce green. You can remove the emulsion from the Colotone to obtain clear areas, or you can leave remnants of yellow, or use scratchboard techniques, hatching or crosshatching lines with a scraping tool. If you have never done this before, it is best to keep it simple and avoid scratchboard techniques. Should you decide to try them, however, keep the texture very simple and the hatching to a minimum.

In order not to diminish the film's transparency by excessive scraping, first soften the color emulsion with a cotton swab dipped in rubber cement thinner (available from art supply stores). Spread the thinner over the color area to be removed before proceeding with the scraping. For large areas, it is best to use a rounded or broad scraping tool—one with a hard but not a cutting edge. I have used a dull knife or a single-edge razor, however. For hatching, use a fine point, such as the corner of a single-edge razor. Before hatching, apply a small amount of rubber cement thinner. Some artists have used scratchboard scraping tools to remove broad areas or hatch fine lines.

Blue Overlay (Figure 12):

1. Superimpose the blue sheet of Colotone over the first and tape it down to the keyplate.
2. Superimpose register marks over the register marks of the yellow Colotone. Carefully scrape the areas over the register marks as before so that you can match them exactly.
3. Remove the emulsion where you want white or yellow and leave it where you want blue or blue combined with yellow to create green.

Now you have a three-color preseparated picture: a black keyplate with two color overlays (**Figure 13**). This will serve as a color study, or guide, for the next exercise.

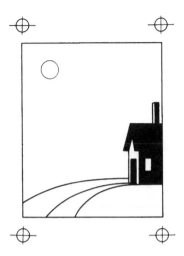

This reduced image of the black keyplate shows how to place the register marks. Each overlay will also need register marks, placed to match the ones on the keyplate exactly.

10

11

12

13

Exercise 2: Acetate Preseparation

The aim of this exercise is to duplicate the Colotone preseparation of Exercise 1. The difference is that black ink will substitute for both the blue and yellow Colotones. When the preseparation is complete, you will have a keyplate and two overlays—all done in black. Since you won't be able to see the colors while working, your Colotone preseparation from Exercise 1 will be your only guide. Follow it closely, for you must depend entirely on it to achieve successful results. As you can see, **Figure 14** repeats the black keyplate from Exercise 1 (Figure 10), but here the colors are marked BK (for black), BL (for blue), and Y (for yellow), so that it is easier to use as a color guide.

Materials: (1) Matte acetate (frosted on one side). (2) Drawing paper. (3) Black India ink. (4) Register marks. (5) Masking tape.

Tools: (1) Pen. (2) Brush. (3) Pencil. (4) Eraser. (5) Single-edge razor, or some other scraping tool of your choice.

Black Keyplate (Figure 15):

1. Copy the picture in Exercise 1 on the drawing paper. (An alternative is to use your keyplate from Exercise 1 for this exercise as well.)
2. Place your register marks and label the keyplate "black."

Yellow Overlay (Figure 16):

1. Following the same procedure as in Exercise 1, secure a piece of matte acetate, frosted side up, in position over the picture.
2. Place a set of register marks on the overlay, precisely over those on the keyplate.
3. Mark clearly at the bottom of the overlay the color it represents—"yellow."
4. Attach the color swatch—a piece of the same yellow Colotone used in Exercise 1—with masking tape.
5. Paint with black ink, duplicating the shapes of the yellow Colotone used in Exercise 1. The painted areas (including those that will be hatched or scraped) should be solid—completely covered with

black ink, without any gray. To double-check your work, slip a piece of white paper under the acetate—if the paper shows through, the area is not completely black. Go over the painted areas as many times as necessary to correct them. They have to be dense black without any gray, but they need not be opaque when viewed through light.

If in the previous exercise you used a crosshatching technique, or created texture by scraping the Colotones, match this in Exercise 2. By repeating the techniques used with the Colotones—hatching or scraping—you can achieve the same effect with the acetate. In order not to lose track of the outlines of your picture on the keyplate, paint on the overlay only half of any one color area at a time, hatching or scraping it before painting the second half. (If it is impossible to duplicate the hatching, try at least to maintain the same overall character of Exercise 1.)

By the way, if you intend a color to neatly fill a shape within a black outline, without showing any white gaps between the color and the outline, you need to extend the paint to the middle of the outlines.

Blue Overlay (Figure 17):

1. Secure the second overlay over the first and tape it to the keyplate.
2. Place the register marks.
3. Mark the color of the overlay at the bottom—"blue."
4. Attach the color swatch—a piece of the same blue Colotone used in Exercise 1.
5. Now paint the acetate, duplicating the shapes of the blue Colotone overlay. Check whether the black areas are properly covered with ink. Scrape or hatch, where necessary, to duplicate the effect of the blue Colotone.

If executed correctly, Exercise 2 will result in a camera-ready preseparation suitable for line reproduction. When printed, the picture will come as close to Exercise 1 as you have been able to duplicate it (**Figure 18**). The printer will match the color swatches with the printing inks, and print the preseparated picture with those specified colors.

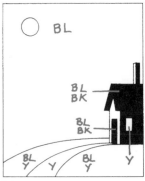

14

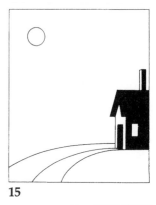

15

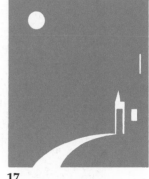

16

17

These reduced images show how the black, yellow, and blue preseparations will print.

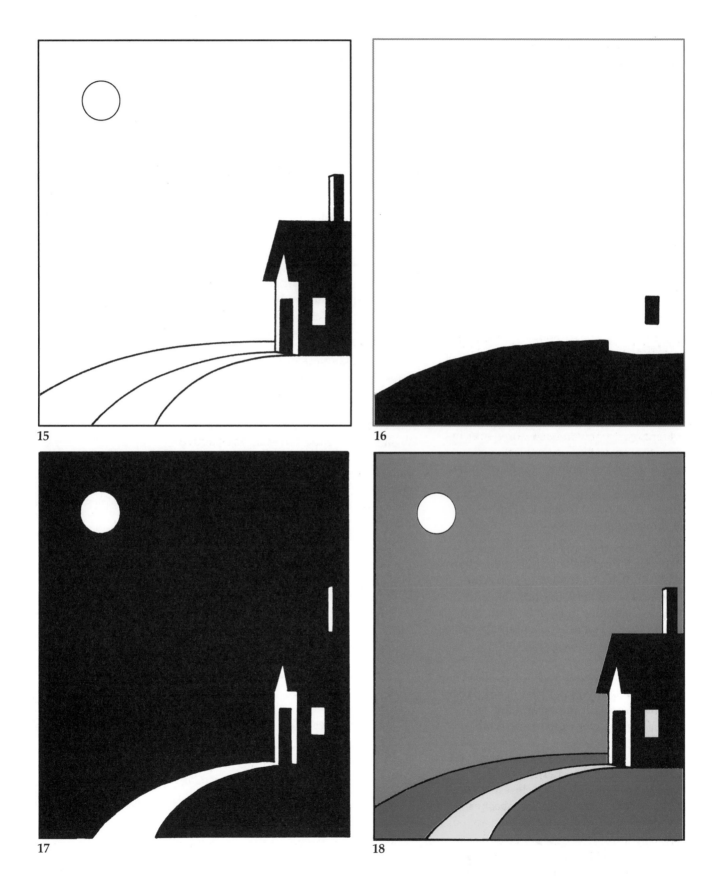

15

16

17

18

Multivalue Flat Color Preseparation

Up to now we have preseparated with single-value colors only, using black, yellow, and blue at full strength. You can, however, get different values of flat colors by using different percentages of each color.

Multivalue flat color preseparation can be achieved by painting with grays that match the gray scale, or by what we shall call flat tint preseparation. Both can be done on either transparent or opaque overlays. But before proceeding with either kind of preseparation, you must make a color study to serve as your guide.

Exercise 3: Flat Color Study

Materials: (1) Arches 90 lb., cold-pressed watercolor paper (use the smooth side) or Strathmore two- or three-ply drawing paper, medium surface. (2) Grumbacher's Academy Watercolors—lamp black, cadmium yellow pale, Thalo blue. (Instead of watercolors, you can use colored inks or dyes that approximate the black, yellow, and blue process colors.) (3) Black India ink.

Tools: (1) Pen. (2) Brush. (3) Pencil. (4) Eraser. (5) Light box.

Color Study (Figures 19–20). To make a flat color study, use a process color chart and complete the following steps carefully and accurately. (If your blue and yellow Colotones in Exercise 1 approximate process colors, you can use Exercise 1 to guide you in preparing this color study.)

1. Using a light box, trace the picture from Exercise 1 lightly in pencil on your paper.
2. Now execute it in pen and ink. (It is better to paint your picture on a table than on a light box.)
3. Find 100% black, 100% blue, and 100% yellow on the color chart.
4. Select paints that come closest to these process colors (e.g., the Grumbacher Academy Watercolors mentioned above). Since printing inks are transparent, use transparent paints.
5. Next, select on the color chart a limited number of flat tints derived from these process colors.
6. Match these flat tints with your paints. Dilute them with water and paint in thin layers of transparent tones, one on top of the other. It is easier to achieve the desired tones by superimposing very thin layers of color, one at a time, on the paper than by premixing several of them on your palette before painting. It is a good idea to practice painting flat, even tones, to approximate the flat tints of the chart, until you feel ready to tackle your color study. Then paint your color study (Figure 19). Your color study is finished when all its tones approximate the color chart flat tints that you have selected.
7. With the help of the color chart, identify the colors and the percentages of each flat tint in your color study. Say, for instance, that a tone in your color study corresponds to a color chart flat tint that consists of 10% black, 20% blue, and 10% yellow. Write this "formula" down on your color study accordingly (Figure 20). When you have identified all the painted areas of your color study in this manner, you can use it as a guide in preparing the camera-ready preseparation.

Because you have identified the tones and percentages, you no longer need your entire color chart. The keyplate and overlays of the preseparation are all painted in grays (percentages of black), so all you need is the gray scale.

Exercise 4: Multivalue Gray Tint Preseparation

One way to prepare a multivalue flat color preseparation is by using gray paints that match the flat tints on the gray scale. The paints are applied on the overlays in even, flat tones and the various tones of one color are all painted on the same overlay. The blue overlay, for example, contains all the blue tones, painted in grays that match the various desired flat tints on the gray scale.

A multivalue gray tint preseparation is not intended for line reproduction; it is meant to be reproduced as halftone art. It is classified under flat preseparation here because of its flat effect, not because of how it is reproduced.

Multivalue gray tint preseparation has several *advantages*. It is economical to reproduce, and you can use as many flat tints as you wish. Moreover, because there are a limited number of overlays, it is relatively easy to check whether any preseparated areas have been overlooked.

There are, however, *disadvantages*. Unless you use commercially ready-mixed grays, mixing your own and matching them to the gray scale can be very frustrating. When you paint with your own mixed grays, you have to wait until they are dry before you can find out whether they match the gray scale, or whether you should apply another layer. Sometimes you may have to paint them several times to get them right. On the other hand, only a few brands and percentages of premixed grays match the gray scale, and they may not be readily available. Sometimes one batch of commercially mixed gray that matches the gray scale doesn't match another batch purchased earlier.

Materials: (1) Matte acetate, frosted on one side (as used in Exercise 2). (2) Strathmore, two-, three-, or four-ply drawing paper, medium surface. (3) Commercially mixed gray paints, such as Cel-Vinyl or Gold Label (described on p. 221). (4) Black India ink. (5) Register marks. (6) Masking tape. *Note*: Although these materials are recommended for this exer-

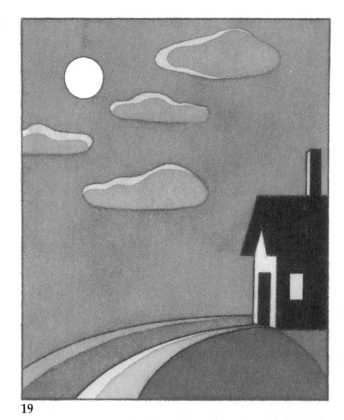

19

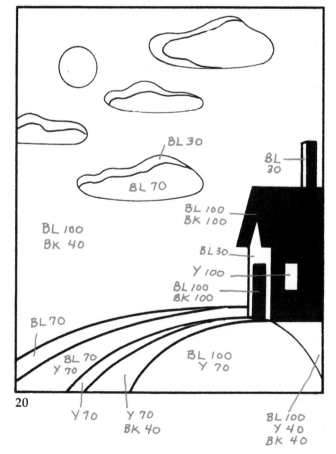

20

cise, multivalue gray tint preseparations can also be done on paper, heavy vellum (if the painted areas are small), or blue-bristols. Some artists have used gray markers instead of gray paints.

Tools: (1) Pen. (2) Brush. (3) Pencil. (4) Eraser.

Black Keyplate (Figure 21):

1. Draw the picture of your flat color study (Exercise 3) in pencil on the drawing paper.
2. Execute it in pen and ink; then erase all unwanted pencil lines and marks.
3. Place the register marks.
4. Label the picture "black keyplate."

Black Overlay (Figure 22). For the gray areas in your color study, you need to do a separate black overlay, which will be reproduced as halftone art.

1. Secure a sheet of matte acetate, frosted side up, in position over the black key-plate.
2. Place the register marks on the overlay, precisely over those on the keyplate.
3. Mark clearly at the bottom of the overlay the color it represents—"black halftone."
4. Select the premixed grays that best correspond to the flat tint percentages for black (other than 100% black) on your color study.
5. Using the color study as your guide, apply the gray paints to the appropriate areas. In order to achieve a flat effect, the paint must be applied evenly, with no light or dark streaks. This will make it easier to see whether you have come close to the gray-scale values.
6. Check periodically against the gray scale to make sure that all the painted grays come as close as possible to the desired percentages of the gray scale.

Yellow Overlay (Figure 23):

1. Secure a sheet of matte acetate, frosted side up, in position over the black overlay and tape it to the keyplate.
2. Place the register marks.
3. Label it "yellow."
4. Following the same procedure as in steps 4–6 for the black overlay, paint the grays that approximate the percentages

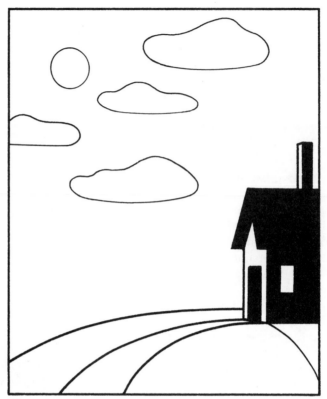

21

for yellow on your color study. Keep checking against the gray scale to make sure that you are approximating the desired percentages.

Blue Overlay (Figure 24):

1. Secure this third overlay over the other two and tape it to the keyplate.
2. Place the register marks.
3. Label it "blue."
4. Following steps 4–6 for the black overlay, paint the grays that approximate the percentages for blue on your color study.

When all the steps have been properly executed—using your flat color study as your guide and making your painted grays a good approximation of the desired values on the gray scale—your color preseparation is complete and can be considered camera-ready. The keyplate will be reproduced as line, whereas the overlays will be reproduced as halftone. **Figure 25** shows the finished result.

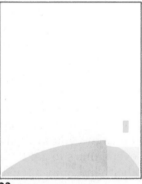

23

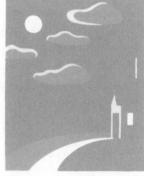

24

These reduced images show how the yellow and blue preseparations will print.

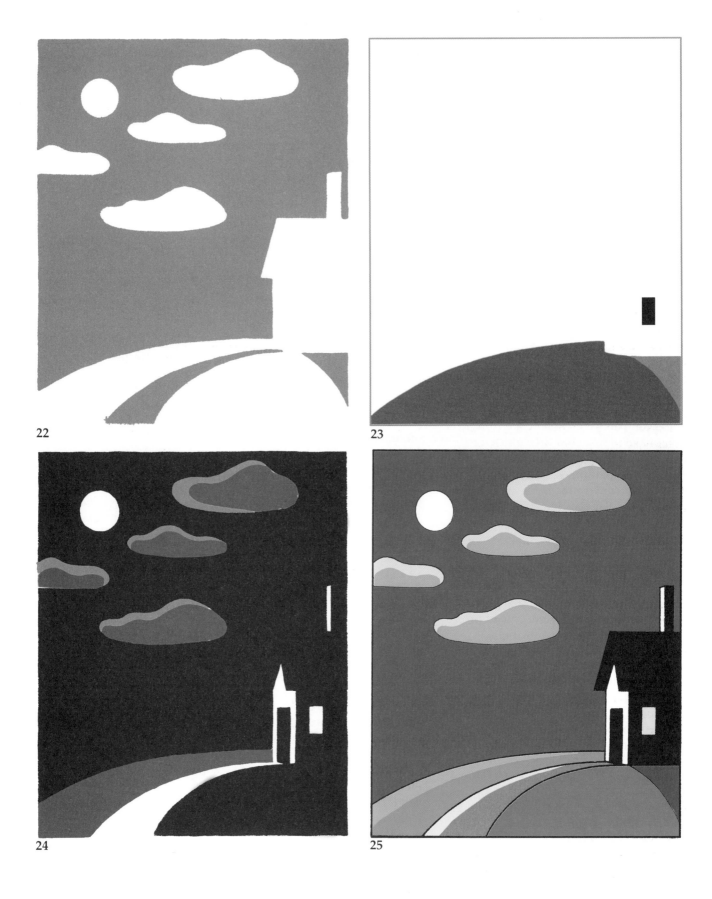

22

23

24

25

Exercise 5: Flat Tint Preseparation

(For figures, see pp. 234–235)

In flat tint preseparation, each flat tint is painted in solid black on a separate overlay. The printer screens these solid areas, converting them into the flat tints specified by the artist. The printer then combines the various percentages of each color on a single printing plate. In preparing camera-ready art, therefore, write "solid black" or "black 100%" on one overlay, if it is intended to print at full strength. On another overlay, one intended to print as a 50% black flat tint, write "black 50%." On a third overlay intended to print as a 30% blue flat tint, write "blue 30%"; and so on. In other words, every flat tint has its own separate overlay (although there are shortcuts to this method.

An *advantage* of flat tint preseparation over multivalue gray tint preseparation is that it is easier to match the gray scale. Since you paint with solid black only, you don't have to mix your own grays, or make sure that they match the gray scale. The results are more accurate because the printer can convert the black areas into the required flat tints mechanically, with greater precision than you can paint them, saving you time as well.

A major *disadvantage*, however, is that when too many flat tints are used (more than three flat tints per color), flat tint preseparation increases the cost of reproduction and defeats the purpose of preseparating. Also, when a picture is preseparated on opaque overlays into many very small areas, it is awkward and time-consuming to ensure that all the necessary flat tints have been painted and that none have been forgotten. Since each picture consists of an increased number of overlays, this means the use of more materials and creates more bulk, which in turn takes more time for you and the publisher to handle and store.

Nevertheless, depending on the book and its budget, flat tint preseparation may be used if it is simply executed, with a very limited range of flat tints. In some instances, in a two- or three-color pre-

separated book, the art director may allow for two flat tints in addition to each solid color. For example, if in your book you use 100% blue, you can also use 20% blue and 50% blue, or any other two percentages of blue you wish. The same applies to the other colors in your book.

Materials: (1) Frosted acetate. (Acetate is recommended for this exercise to save you the need to trace the image each time over a light box. You can, however, use paper for your overlays.) (2) Strathmore three- or four-ply drawing paper, medium surface. (For paper overlays, you can use Arches 90 lb., cold-pressed watercolor paper or Strathmore one- or two-ply.) (3) Black India ink. (4) Register marks. (5) Masking tape.

Tools: (1) Pen. (2) Brush. (3) Pencil. (4) Eraser. (5) Light box (for tracing, if paper is used).

Black Keyplate (Figure 26):
1. Copy the picture in Exercise 3 in pencil on drawing paper.
2. Execute it in pen and ink.
3. When the picture is complete, erase all unwanted pencil lines and marks.
4. Place register marks.
5. Label it "black keyplate."

Black Overlay (Figure 27). In addition to the black keyplate, you will need to make a black overlay(s) for any gray areas—areas that are not solid (100%) black (for example, in our picture: the areas that are 40% black).

1. Follow the same procedure as in Exercise 4: secure a piece of matte acetate, frosted side up, in position over the picture on the black keyplate. (If you use paper instead of acetate, secure a piece in position over the keyplate and place them both over the light box. Lightly trace the outlines of all the gray areas of the same percentage on the overlay.)
2. Place a set of register marks on the overlay, precisely over those on the keyplate.
3. Mark at the bottom of the overlay the color and the percentage it represents. In our example, "black 40%."

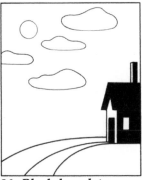
26. Black keyplate

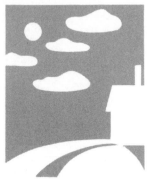
27. Black 40%

28. Yellow 70%

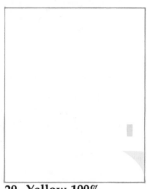
29. Yellow 100%, Yellow 40%

4. Paint the areas for that percentage in *solid* black.

5. If you have more than one value of gray, repeat this process and make a separate overlay for each different value.

Yellow Overlays (Figures 28–29):

1. Use the same materials as for the black overlay—acetate or paper—and follow the same procedure: secure the overlay over the black keyplate (not over the black overlay) and trace the outlines of all the areas of a single yellow percentage.

2. Place register marks.

3. Label the overlay correctly—for example, "yellow 70%" (Figure 28).

4. Paint the outlined areas in solid black. Make sure that the black ink covers the areas completely. If there are any gray areas, go over them with a thin layer of black ink until they are dense.

5. Repeat this procedure for each percentage of yellow until you have preseparated all the yellow flat tints in the picture. You should have several yellow overlays, one for each percentage of yellow—for example, in our picture: 100% yellow, 70% yellow, and 40% yellow. You can, however, take a shortcut and combine two percentages on one overlay—as shown here in Figure 29. Be sure to label the different percentages clearly for the printer.

Blue Overlays (Figures 30–32):

1. Secure the overlay over the black keyplate (not over the yellow overlays) and trace outlines of all the areas of a single blue percentage.

2. Place register marks.

3. Label the overlay correctly—"blue 70%," for example.

4. Paint the outlined areas in solid black.

5. Repeat this procedure, using one overlay for each percentage of blue—for example, in our picture: 100% blue (Figure 30), 70% blue (Figure 31), and 30% blue (Figure 32).

Figure 33 shows the printed result.

Shortcuts. When you are using this method of preseparating for the first time, paint every percentage on a separate overlay. After mastering this method, however, you can take the following shortcuts:

1. If the same area combines different colors of the same percentage—for example a house that is a combination of 100% blue and 100% black—you can include both on a single overlay and mark it "prints blue 100%, black 100%." The printer will photograph the painted area twice—once for each color and will include each color on its respective printing plate.

2. If the same area combines different colors of different percentages—say, a night sky that is 100% blue and 40% black—you can include both on a single overlay and mark it "prints blue 100%, black 40%." This way you have a single overlay for both, painted only once.

3. If different areas are not adjoining or overlapping (with at least ¼-inch space between them) and are different colors of the same percentage—say, one is 70% blue and the other 70% yellow—both can be included on a single overlay. But they must be clearly marked so the printer will know where to position them on their respective printing plates. You can use a nonreproducing light blue pencil on the overlay, or identify the percentages on a separate overlay of tracing paper.

4. If different areas are not adjoining or overlapping and are different colors of different percentages (100% yellow and 40% black, for example), they can both be included on a single overlay if they are marked clearly.

When you have mastered these shortcuts, you may discover other ways of cutting down the number of overlays and achieving the same results with less work.

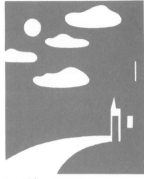

30. Blue 100%

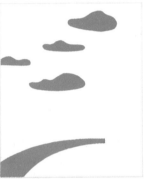

31. Blue 70%

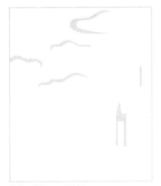

32. Blue 30%

The reduced images on this double spread show how the black, yellow, and blue preseparations will print.

26. Black keyplate

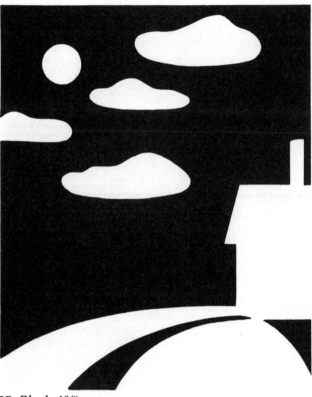

27. Black 40%

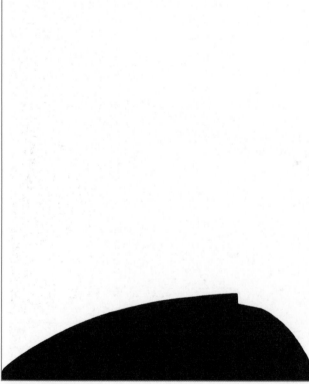

28. Yellow 70%

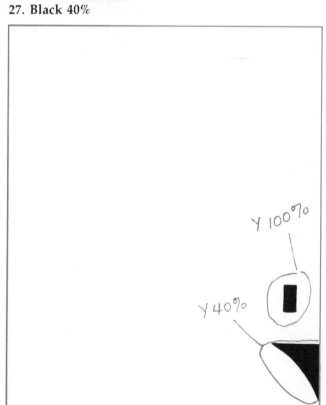

29. Yellow 100%, Yellow 40%

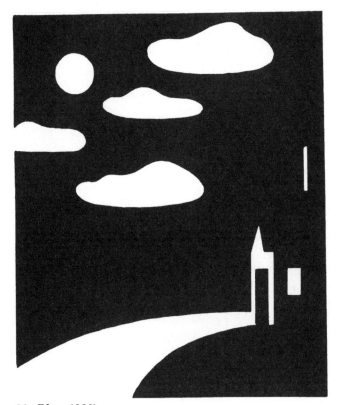

30. Blue 100%

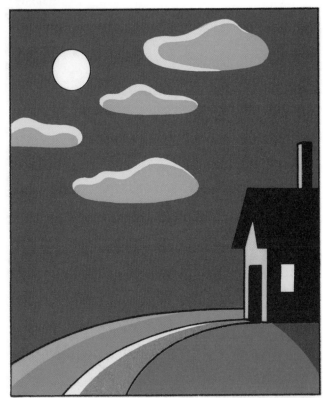

31. Blue 70%

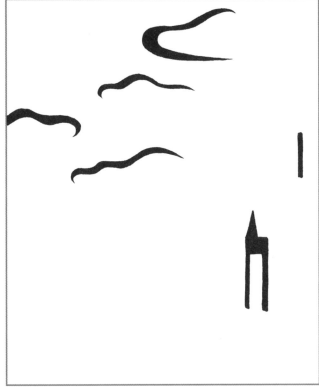

32. Blue 30%

33. Printed result

Tonal Color Preseparation

Whereas in flat color preseparation you must use flat tones only, in tonal color preseparation you can use continuous tone—that is, you can blend various tones without breaks or lines of demarcation. You can also use varying textures.

The best way to learn tonal color preseparation is by progressing gradually. At first, keep it as simple as possible—using only two colors. When you feel confident with two, use three colors, and finally move on to four-color tonal color preseparation.

The addition of continuous tone and texture makes tonal color preseparation the most interesting method of preseparating. You can achieve richer effects and come closer to the look of full-color painting by choosing this method over flat color preseparation. The chief difficulty is the lack of a gauge by which to measure with total precision the continuous tones. Consequently, you must rely on estimates and interpretation to achieve the desired results. It takes some time to master this way of preseparating.

Exercise 6: Tonal Color Study

To do a tonal color preseparation, you must first make a color study. It is prepared in essentially the same way as in Exercise 3, but you can use texture and tone variations. In order to get satisfactory results, utmost care must be taken to bring the color study's colors and tone range as close as possible to the colors and flat tints that you have selected on your color chart.

Materials: (1) Arches 90 lb., cold-pressed watercolor paper or Strathmore two- or three-ply drawing paper, medium surface. (2) Grumbacher's Academy Watercolors (as listed in Exercise 3, p. 228). (3) Black India ink.

Tools: (1) Pen. (2) Brush. (3) Pencil. (4) Eraser. (5) Light box.

Color Study (Figures 34–35):

1. Trace on a piece of watercolor paper the picture used in Exercise 3.

2. Locate 100% process black, 100% process blue, and 100% process yellow on the color chart.

3. Use Grumbacher's Academy Watercolors or approximate the process colors with paints of your choice.

4. Select on the color chart the flat tints that you plan to use.

5. Now, using tonality and texture, paint your color study, making every effort to come close to the tints that you have selected (Figure 34). If, for instance, you have chosen a green flat tint made up of 30% blue and 50% yellow, approximate it in your color study. Apply light, thin washes of blue and yellow, one on top of the other in opposing directions until you come as close as possible to the green flat tint on the chart. Don't try to approximate the percentage of each color separately by first painting 30% blue and then 50% yellow over it.

6. Write down the color percentages that make up each tone; for the green area, for example, you would write "blue 30%, yellow 50%" (Figure 35). However, unlike the flat color study, in this study, a color may vary in value throughout a painted area, making it difficult to determine the exact color percentages. Since the only gauge for determining the values of your colors is the flat tints on the color chart, you have to estimate the *range* of percentages of a tone, from the lightest to the darkest. For example, a tonal area may consist of a blue ranging from 20% to 30%. Write down "blue 20%–30%" on your color study. When preparing the camera-ready preseparation, interpret the range of tones and paint them so as to achieve the same character in the printed picture as in the color study. An exact imitation is rarely attained.

Exercise 7: Camera-Ready Tonal Color Preseparation

When you have identified the tones of your color study and have written down their percentages, you are ready to proceed with preparing the camera-ready preseparation. Again, since the keyplate and overlays are all painted in grays, you need only the gray scale, consisting of black percentages.

Tonal color preseparations are best done on paper with the help of a light box, or on blue-bristols. Use cool black paint because it comes closest to the process black printing ink used on the gray scale. Choose a transparent watercolor such as Grumbacher's or Permanent Pigments' lamp black.

When your picture is printed, the texture in your preseparation will show up more in a dark color than in a light one. Black shows texture the most, blue next, and yellow the least. To achieve a rougher texture, use a rougher-surface paper. For example, Arches cold-pressed has a rougher finish than Arches hot-pressed or Strathmore medium surface and will give you more texture. But keep in mind that too much texture may make the picture seem too busy, and it will be more difficult to measure the tonal percentages. You may find that the paper's transparency is more important to you than its texture because you must see details while tracing over a light box. In that case, Strathmore single-ply, medium surface, is a better choice than Arches 90 lb. cold-pressed because it is thinner.

Your color study is your only guide to successful results. Follow it as closely as possible and don't make any changes in preparing your preseparation, unless you change your color study first.

Materials: (1) Arches 90 lb., cold-pressed watercolor paper (use either side; the rough side for more texture); Strathmore one- or two-ply drawing paper, medium surface; or another paper of equivalent quality, weight, and surface. (You can also use blue-bristols, if they are available.) (2) Lamp black watercolor (Grumbacher's Academy Watercolor or Permanent Pig-

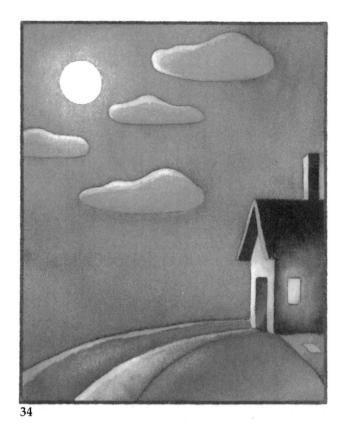

34

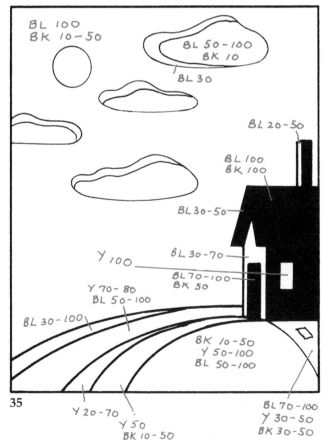

35

ments' Watercolor). (3) Black India ink.
(4) Register marks. (5) Masking tape.

Tools: (1) Pen. (2) Brush. (3) Pencil.
(4) Eraser. (5) Light box.

Black Keyplate (Figure 36):

1. Use lamp black watercolor and a brush on paper to copy the picture in the tonal color study of Exercise 6 (but see the note below).
2. Place the register marks.
3. Label the drawing "black keyplate."
Note: When you combine lines, solid black areas, and washes on the keyplate, they will be reproduced by the halftone process and will look somewhat softer when printed. If, however, you wish your lines to retain their sharpness and the black areas their density, you can separate the solid areas and lines from the washes so that the first will print as line and the second as halftone. To do this, include the solid areas and lines on the black keyplate for line reproduction and paint all the washes on a separate overlay for black halftone reproduction. You will then have a black keyplate for line reproduction and three overlays (black, blue, and yellow) for halftone reproduction. The printer will combine the black keyplate and the black halftone on one black printing plate.

Yellow Overlay (Figure 37):

1. Unless you use blue-bristols, secure a piece of watercolor paper with masking tape over the black keyplate and trace over a light box, with very light outlines, all the yellow tones of your picture.
2. Place register marks.
3. Paint the outlined areas with washes of lamp black watercolor. Approximate your gray scale by repeated applications of light watercolor washes. When they are dry, check them with the gray scale. Consult your color study as well, to make sure that you are interpreting it accurately. If you find that an area is too light and doesn't come close enough to the gray scale, go over it with an additional thin wash. Proceed in this manner until your tone comes as close as possible to the desired tint on the gray scale and your color study. You can control your tones and achieve the desired tints better with

successive light washes because it is much easier to darken them, if necessary, than to lighten them.
4. Erase all unwanted pencil lines.
5. Identify the overlay as "yellow halftone."

Blue Overlay (Figure 38):

1. Proceed in the same way as for the yellow overlay: with masking tape, secure a piece of watercolor paper over the black keyplate and trace with very light outlines all the blue tones over a light box.
2. Place register marks.
3. Paint the outlined areas with light washes of black watercolor until you achieve the desired values. Check your tones against the gray scale and consult your color study periodically to see whether you are interpreting the desired tonal range.
4. Erase all unwanted pencil lines.
5. Identify the overlay as "blue halftone."

Figure 39 shows the printed result.

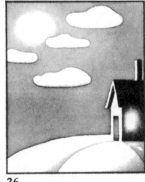

36

37

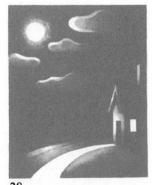

38

These reduced images show how the black, yellow, and blue preseparations will print.

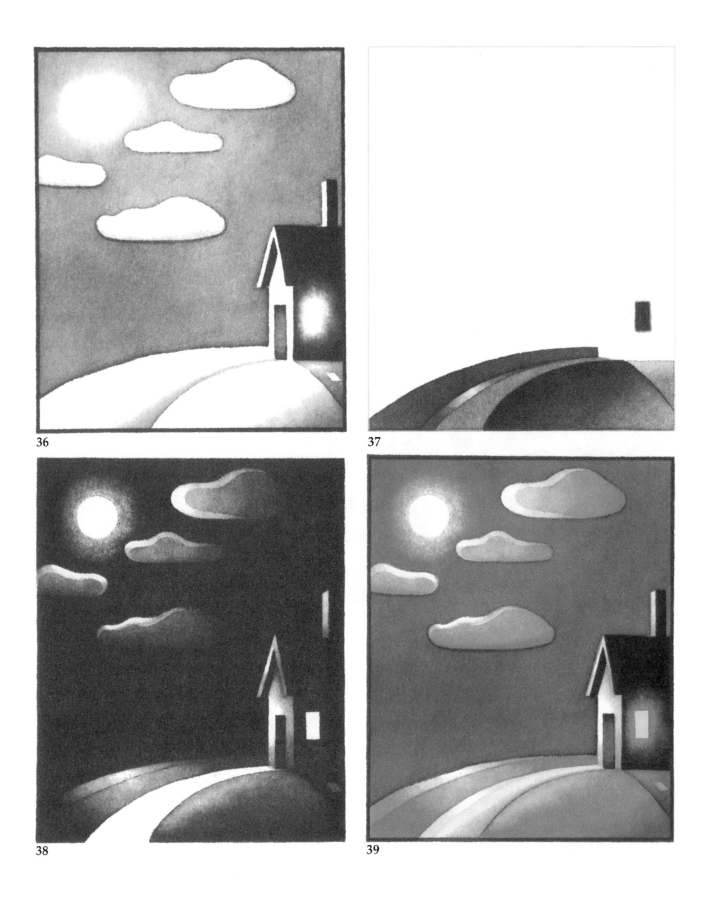

36

37

38

39

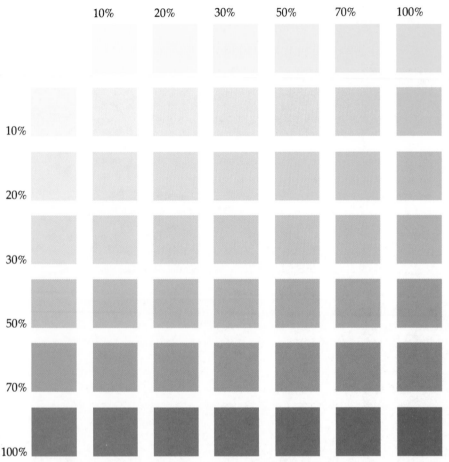

	10%	20%	30%	50%	70%	100%
10%						
20%						
30%						
50%						
70%						
100%						

Sample Color Chart for Process Yellow and Process Blue

Other Ways of Preseparating

The different exercises present the color preseparation methods that I have used. Although the principles are the same, there are other ways of preseparating. When using a maximum of two colors, some artists draw their black lines on one side of the keyplate, to be reproduced separately as line. Then, using a light box, they paint a black wash on the reverse side of the keyplate, to be printed as a black halftone or as any other single-color halftone. The wash area is reversed photographically by the printer and reproduced by the halftone process.

By placing black line on one side of the paper and full-color on the other, you can combine color preseparation and four-color printing. In this way you ensure the sharpness of the lines in four-color reproduction.

Finally, some artists use mixed media in preseparating art. They may paint some areas with water-based colors and other areas with oil paints, or they may mix crayons or pencils with watercolor washes, or some other combination.

Advice to Beginners

To get the results you are looking for, it is *essential* that you rigorously follow your color chart, the gray scale, and your color study. In the beginning, limit yourself to process colors; they are standard, and color charts including them are readily available. Don't approach color preseparation casually and don't take unnecessary chances, because too much is at stake: the publisher's budget and the quality of your work.

Whenever possible, have a test-proof made of a sample preseparated picture, as well as a scale of the colors and tones that you used in preseparating that picture. Wait until you see the printed results of the test-proof before proceeding with the rest of the illustrations. A test-proof can tell you if you need to make adjustments in the percentages derived from a color chart. For instance, some printers recommend painting the lighter tones of yellow (yellow in the 10% to 30% range) about

10% to 20% darker than the desired printed results. Other printers, however, suggest making any such adjustments only after seeing a test-proof, and not exaggerating the tones for the test-proof.

For each book that you preseparate, you may encounter different requirements or limitations in the use of color. Projects vary, according to the nature of the book, the publisher, and available budget. There is no single answer to how many colors you can expect to use or what preseparation method you should adopt. This must be a book-by-book decision.

Keep in mind that a limited range of colors and tint combinations can be beneficial: it makes the work easier to execute, and the discipline required when working within limitations can help sharpen your color skills. Remember, too, that using many colors doesn't necessarily guarantee an increased feeling of color.

A Concluding Note on Tone and Color

How you use color is more important than how many colors you use. Experience has convinced me that the feeling of color in a picture depends on tone no less than on hue. Yet too many beginners diminish the picture's feeling of color by stressing hue and overlooking tone. Whereas *hue* denotes the different colors—red, blue, yellow, and so on—*tone* denotes the value, or the degree of lightness or darkness, of a color. A judicious use of tonality has helped me to get the feeling of many colors from a limited number of hues.

Consider, for example, how you use color with paint. By mixing the primary colors—red, blue, and yellow—in different proportions, you can get a range of new colors. For instance, when you mix blue and yellow in different ratios, you get different kinds of green. Red and yellow will give an orange; red and blue, a purple.

In art, black and white are also considered colors. Even though you don't use white directly in printing, it is present as the color of your paper (assuming, of course, that you use white paper). Black and white can be used as solid colors in their own right or mixed together to produce a range of grays, from light to dark. White can also be used to lighten other colors, and black to darken them. Many outstanding Chinese paintings of the Sung Dynasty were painted in black and white only, skillfully using a wide range of grays. Many of the Renaissance masters used a limited number of colors, taking full advantage of their tonality.

To enhance the feeling of color in your picture, then, use *both* hue and tone. Sometimes your picture may need sharp contrasts, such as bright (intense) color areas alternating with subdued color areas, or light color values next to dark color values. Or your picture may require subtle, gradual transitions of colors and tones. At other times it may need both sharp contrasts and subtly blended tones, in which case you must balance and harmonize these two opposing ways of using color. Another variable to consider is the perception of colors as "warm" (for instance, red) or "cool" (for instance, blue). There is also the contrast that occurs with complementary hues (for instance, red versus green). While working on individual areas, however, don't forget the *overall* color scheme of your picture.

Color is not to be learned in a hurry. There is no substitute for constant practice. A picture develops step by step, and it is difficult to generalize on how to proceed in each case. If you have had little experience painting with colors, you are better off limiting the number of colors you use and studying the different aspects of one color at a time. Explore the range of tonality and how one hue affects another in different situations.

17. Techniques for Reproduction

Instruction does not prevent waste of time or mistakes; and mistakes themselves are often the best teachers of all.

James Anthony Froude

In preparing the final art for your book, you need to decide which techniques will give your illustrations the character you want when they are printed. Your publisher may set certain limitations—telling you, for instance, how many colors you can use and whether the art needs to be preseparated. But the choice of materials and how best to use them is yours.

To suggest a few of the possibilities, this chapter describes how I worked on the final art for four books: *The Magician*, *Soldier and Tsar in the Forest*, *Rain Rain Rivers*, and *Dawn*. In addition, my step-by-step account of how I created the illustrations for *The Magician* serves as a review of the planning stages discussed in earlier chapters—although it is not meant necessarily as a model to follow. Every book, as well as every artist, is different. The technique you use should be one that feels comfortable to you and is appropriate for the book.

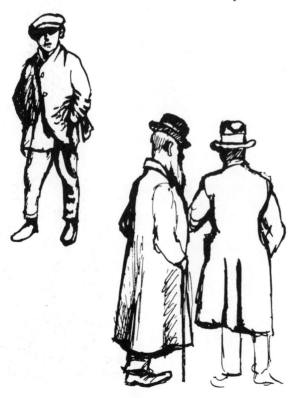

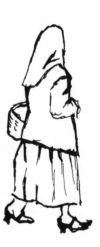

The Magician

The Magician is an adaptation of a Yiddish tale by I. L. Peretz. It tells how the prophet Elijah, disguised as a traveling magician, appears in a small town on the eve of Passover. He asks an elderly couple if he can be their guest, but they are so poor they have nothing to offer. The magician then conjures up all that is needed for a feast. The old man and woman are worried that this might be evil magic, but their rabbi reassures them that if the food is real, the magic is good. When they return home, however, the magician has disappeared. They know then that it was the prophet Elijah.

As I described in Chapter 6, I began by reading the story several times and dividing the text into sections, which I pasted into a small book dummy to see how the words read when placed on separate pages. At this stage I didn't draw any pictures. I read the dummied story many times, silently as well as aloud, thinking about it and evaluating each word. I continued to change the words until they described the story accurately and felt right, all the while getting visual ideas for the pictures to come.

I began working on the visual aspect of the book by gathering picture references for the story's setting—Eastern Europe. Making pen-and-ink sketches from these picture references allowed me to study details of buildings, people, and clothing (**Figures 1–2**). These sketches served as a warm-up and point of entrance into the pictures' world.

The next step was to create the main character—the magician. I made several studies of him—some with pencil on drawing paper (**Figure 3**), some on tracing paper (**Figure 4**), and others with pen and ink on all-purpose paper (**Figure 5**).

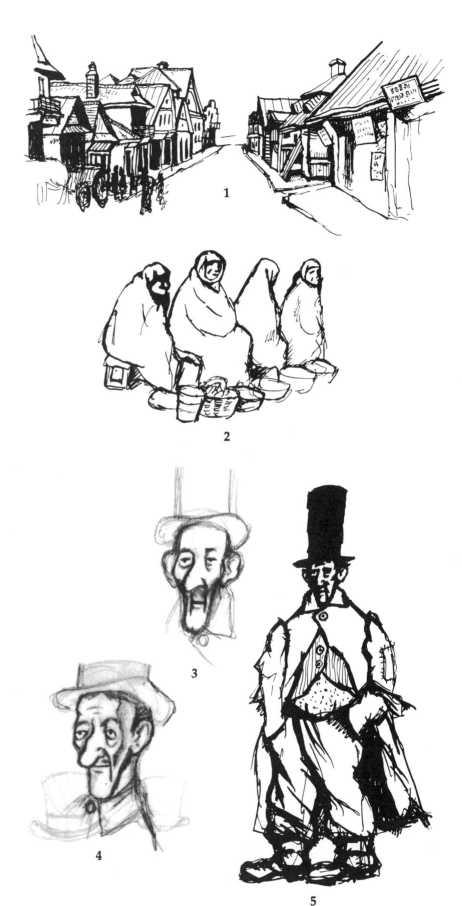

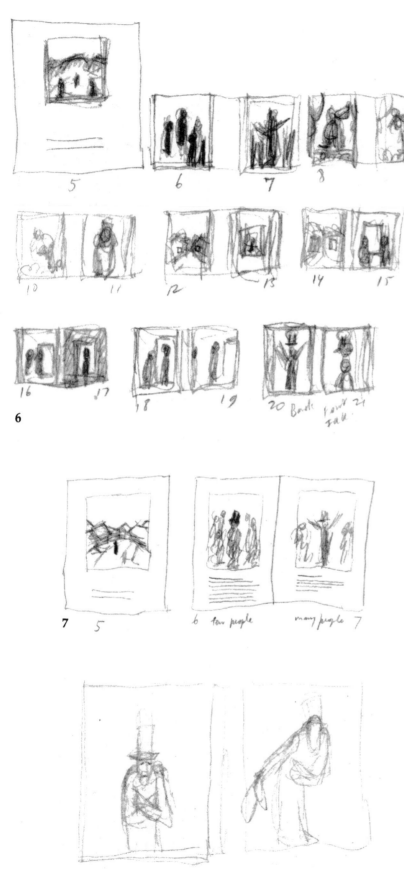

6

7

8

To visualize the story and picture sequence, I made a rough storyboard on tracing paper (partially shown in **Figure 6**). I saw the pictures as small rectangles surrounded by wide margins, with the text at the bottom of the page (**Figure 7**). Each picture would be a window or stage on which the story's action would unfold. This concept felt right because the story reads like a drama on stage.

Before moving on to the sketches for the book dummy, I experimented with different trim sizes by drawing rectangles in different proportions and cutting them out. I also sketched different layouts to determine the size of the pictures and the overall design of the page.

I made the first rough sketches postage-stamp size on tracing paper to work out the composition (**Figure 8**). The small size forced me to stay with the essentials, without being sidetracked into details. These tiny sketches served as models for the actual-size dummy sketches. At first I did preliminary sketches to work out the visual concept (**Figures 9–10**). But as the work progressed, I moved directly from a few postage-stamp-size rough sketches to the actual-size dummy.

The final sketches were done on tracing vellum with 2H leads. I kept drawing and redrawing on the same piece of vellum until the results were satisfactory. Sometimes I quickly went over the rough pencil sketches with pen and ink, which enabled me to consolidate the numerous pencil lines into one line, without erasing (**Figure 11**). I like this way of working because it doesn't stop my momentum and has the added advantage of making the lines more visible for tracing over a light box in preparing the final art.

When the final sketches were done, I attached them to actual-size dummy pages and then fastened a cut-up photocopy of the typewritten text in its approximate position (**Figure 12**). This final dummy enabled me to study the continuity of the book and to make further improvements in the text, art, and layout. When this was done, I showed the dummy to my editor.

The next step was to find the appropri-

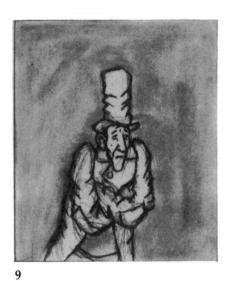

9

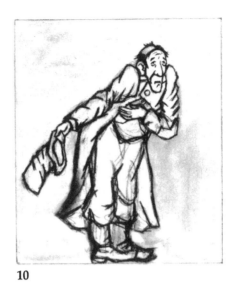

10

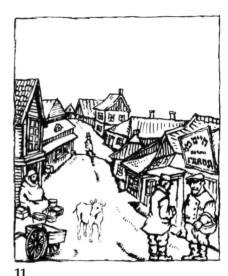

11

12

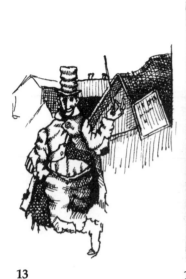

13

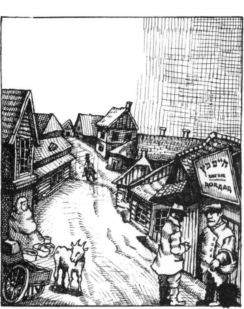

14

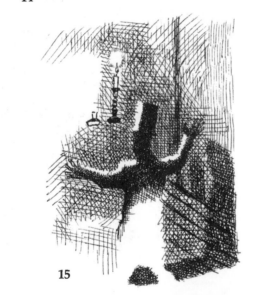

15

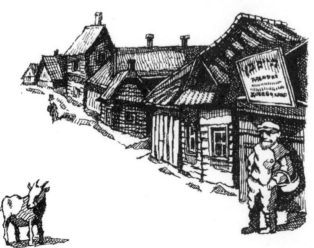

16

ate technique for the book. I experimented with various papers and different pen nibs. I tried several tracing vellums (**Figure 13**); a smooth paper; a thin, semi-transparent 100% rag paper (**Figure 14**); and Arches 90 lb., cold-pressed watercolor paper (**Figure 15**). Theoretically, after completing the sketches, it would be smooth sailing to the end of the book. But as happens so often, I experienced uncertainty and sometimes anxiety as I searched for the final form of the pictures.

With every new project, I must begin from scratch by trying different approaches and various materials until the most suitable ones finally emerge. As I progress, anxiety and uncertainty subside. I don't know of any shortcuts to finding the appropriate technique for a particular book. Even when I have a clear mental picture of the technique I wish to use, it still takes considerable effort and time to work it out on paper.

I had envisioned *The Magician* as a black-and-white book because of the starkness and drama of the text, and I knew I would use crosshatching. That is why I didn't use the two colors allowed by the publisher in the pictures themselves. The second color was ultimately used for the end papers, the title page, the large initial on the first page of text, and the folios.

After experimenting with various papers, I chose Arches 90 lb., cold-pressed watercolor paper, a Hunt no. 104 pen nib, and Pelikan black drawing ink. After numerous studies, when the crosshatching became more transparent and lighter, when it began to sing, as it were, I knew I had worked out the technique for the pictures (**Figure 16**).

Next, I taped down one final sketch at a time on the light box. I positioned a piece of the Arches paper over each sketch, also taping it down. When turned on, the light box enabled me to see through the Arches paper and to trace the drawings with faint, thin lines, using a 2H pencil.

Once all of the pictures were traced, I was ready to begin inking. After dipping the pen in ink, I first tested it on a piece of scrap paper to make sure the lines were clean and the pen nib hadn't picked up any paper fibers, which might thicken or distort the lines. If it had, I removed the fibers with my fingernails (**Figure 17**). From time to time I rinsed the pen nib in water and wiped it dry with paper tissue. While drawing the lines, and especially in doing the crosshatching, I kept turning the picture so I could pull the strokes toward me. (My hand is less steady when I draw the lines away from myself, sideways, or on a diagonal.)

After the inking was done, I erased the pencil guidelines with a plastic eraser. For minor ink mistakes, whenever possible I used a single-edge razor to remove them rather than painting over them with white paint, in order to preserve the quality of the original. I then went over the razorblade erasures with the plastic eraser and dusted off the corrected area. To flatten out any consequent roughness, I burnished the corrections with a hard, smooth, rounded object of glass or metal. If, however, numerous corrections were required and the picture began to look belabored, I made a new one.

I marked the finished art (**Figure 18**) clearly with page numbers and any other information the printer might need. (I had left approximately 2-inch margins around the picture for handling and information.) I made sure the art was clean, because the slightest dirt mark or scratch can show up in reproduction.

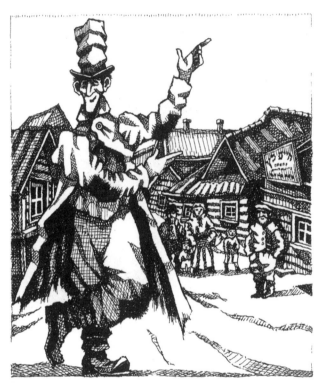

18

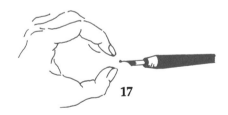

17

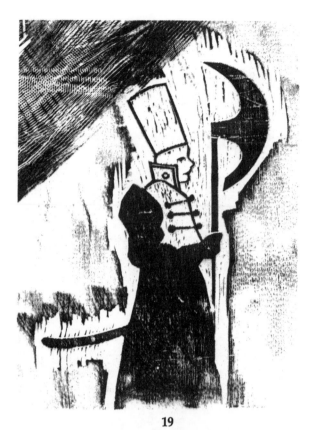

19

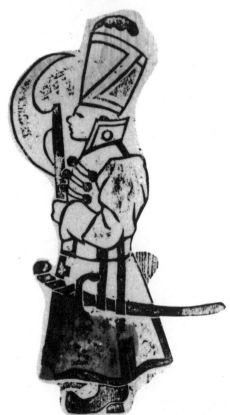

20

Soldier and Tsar in the Forest

For *Soldier and Tsar in the Forest*, I used a different technique. This Russian folktale describes the adventures of a young soldier, who is mistreated by his older brother but then becomes a hero by rescuing the tsar from the forest (see Chapter 5). I felt that a bold line would be suitable for this robust tale. At first I experimented with woodcut and related techniques (**Figures 19–20**), but I got nowhere. I also tried etching (**Figure 21**) and a Chinese brush on rice paper (**Figure 22**). Finally, I decided on a soft pen nib, which enabled me to draw heavy ink lines resembling lines done with a brush (**Figure 23**).

The book was to be printed by the four-color process. To retain sharp definition, however, I preseparated the black lines for line reproduction by drawing them on a thin, semitransparent, 100% rag paper (**Figure 24**). All the colors were then painted with colored inks on a single blue-bristol for full-color reproduction. If the black lines had been drawn on the blue-bristol with the other colors, they would have been reproduced by the half-tone method and thus softened. The black oulines of the finished illustrations were reminiscent of woodcut lines. My early woodcut experiments for the book were not wasted, after all.

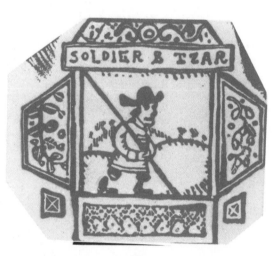

21

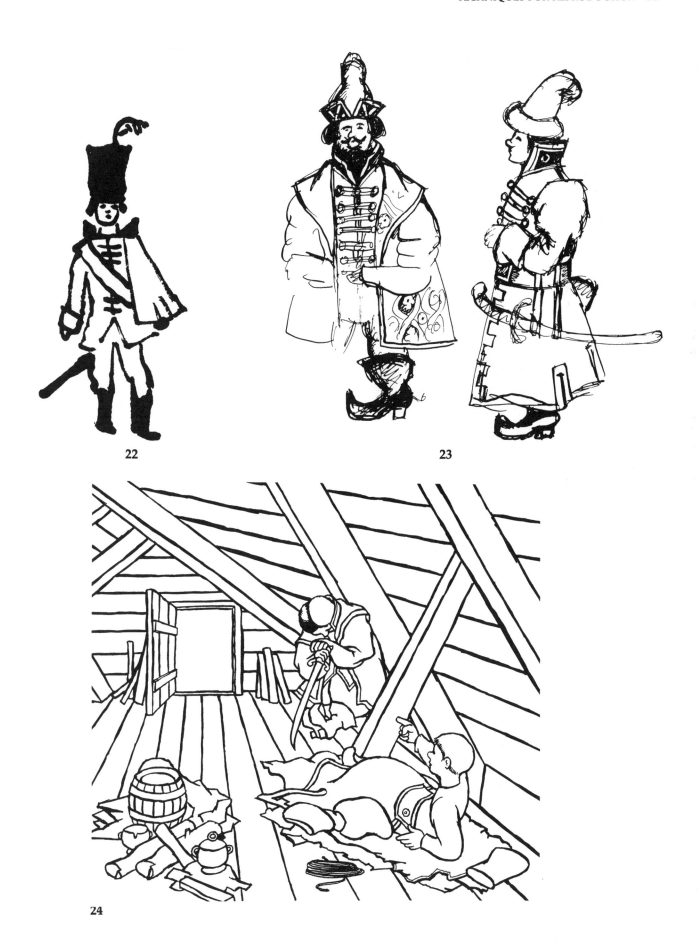

22

23

24

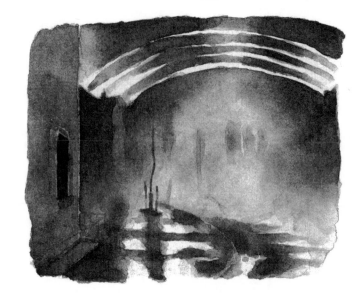

25

26

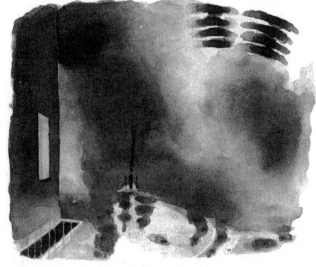

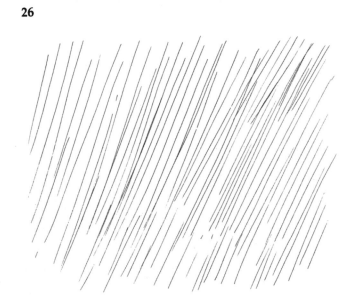

27

28

Rain Rain Rivers

In *Rain Rain Rivers* a little girl hears the rain pattering on her window and imagines that it is raining all over town, over fields and hills, with the water flowing into streams, rivers, oceans. I wanted the pictures to convey the feeling of rain.

For this preseparated book, I used three colors—black, blue, and yellow. Essentially each color was prepared as a black watercolor wash, to be reproduced as halftone art. The black keyplate was painted on Arches 90 lb., cold-pressed watercolor paper (**Figure 25**); the blue and yellow overlays were painted on two separate blue-bristols (**Figures 26 and 27**, respectively).

I executed the black keyplate by drawing light outlines with a Hunt no. 104 pen nib on the Arches paper and modeling the forms with crosshatching. Then I scraped the whole picture with a single-edge razor blade. Partially removing the ink lines in this way made them considerably softer. After cleaning the picture with a plastic eraser, I added a light wash of black watercolor to redefine the forms that were too pale; I also added gray tones. When the picture was dry, I retouched the ink lines with pen and ink to darken the accents or shadows that needed further definition. Whenever necessary, I repeated the procedure, scraping with the razor blade, painting with wash, and retouching with pen and ink. Sometimes I repeated this process three or four times, until I achieved the desired results.

Because line and wash were combined on the black keyplate, when it was printed as halftone, the lines looked soft, blended with the wash, and came close to conveying the fogginess of a rainy day. But I also wanted to show how some raindrops stand out and don't blend with the background. To do this, I drew lines representing rain on a separate blue overlay (**Figure 28**). They were reproduced as line, to retain their definition. If I had combined these rain lines with wash on a single blue overlay for halftone reproduction, they would have lost their sharpness and blended with the rest of the picture.

I was concerned, however, that the rain lines might be too dark as solid blue, so I requested they be reproduced as a lighter, 70% blue. These considerations were intended to enhance the picture's appearance of depth as well as to convey the character of a rainy day. When the picture was printed it resembled an etching (**Figure 29**).

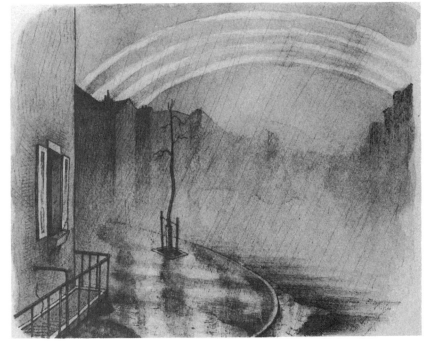

29

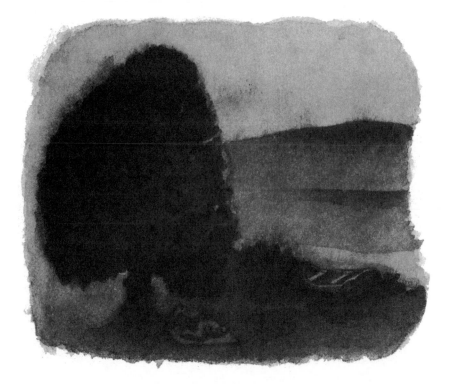

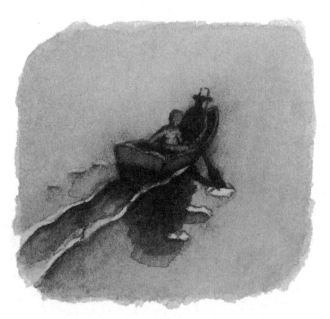

30

Dawn

The extensive planning that went into *Dawn* has been described in Chapters 4, 5, and 6. The book was preseparated into four colors—process yellow, process blue, process black, and red (a warmer red replaced the process red that was initially planned). For each picture, the black keyplate was prepared on Arches 90 lb., cold-pressed watercolor paper. Some of the overlays were done on Strathmore single-ply, medium-surface drawing paper, for ease in tracing over a light box. All were painted in black with transparent watercolor washes. An additional overlay was ultimately prepared on acetate and painted in black with opaque watercolor.

I felt it inappropriate to use pen and ink and sharply defined outlines in a book that depicts a time of day when edges are blurred and light is dim. I made several wash studies (**Figure 30**) and found that by painting with a brush, I could reduce the contrasts of the outlines and produce a misty effect whenever necessary.

In preparing the final art, I had to keep in mind that the black keyplate was my guide for the overlays. If the outlines were too misty, I wouldn't be able to trace them. Therefore, I painted the keyplate carefully so the soft outlines would not lose their definition (**Figure 32**). I traced the overlays with faint pencil outlines, then painted them with a black transparent wash.

To avoid "visual noise" in this quiet book, I painted the water and sky with as uniform tones as possible. I had to deal with one problem, however: after an area of wash is dry and another is painted next to it, the edges where they join create a line. To avoid this, both areas must be painted before they dry. I worked as quickly as I could, but when I had to paint around large and complicated forms, I knew that the wash in one area might dry while I was painting the other. Therefore, I worked on both areas simultaneously, going from one to the other, to keep them wet until I finished painting.

I took other precautions as well: before painting, I moistened the whole area by applying clear water with a brush, to extend the drying time. Also, I began by painting each area with a considerably lighter wash than the desired end result. When the first application was dry, I superimposed a second, light wash in a direction counter to the first. Gradually weaving the light layers of wash into a smooth surface, I painted as many as I needed to reach the desired value.

Paper may buckle and create serious registration problems when large areas of wash are painted. The risk of buckling increases when the wash spans large areas of a double spread (**Figure 31**). To reduce buckling, some artists soak the watercolor paper in water, then stretch it and let it dry before use. I have never tried this, however.

I had a serious buckling problem with the yellow overlay for the last double spread of *Dawn*. I solved it by using a frosted acetate overlay instead of paper and painting it with black opaque watercolor. I was concerned that the acetate overlay might have a different effect from the others, perhaps distracting the eye and breaking the book's consistency. But because yellow was the lightest color, the texture of the other colors dominated the painted picture so that its character was in keeping with the rest of the book.

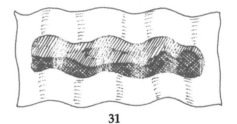

31

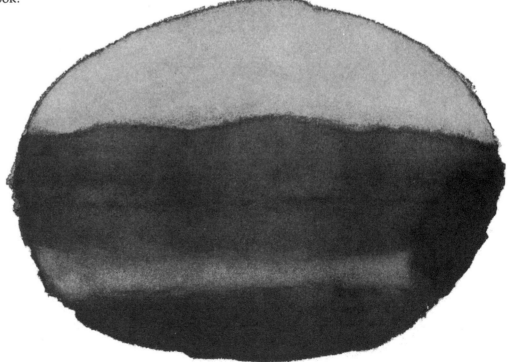

32

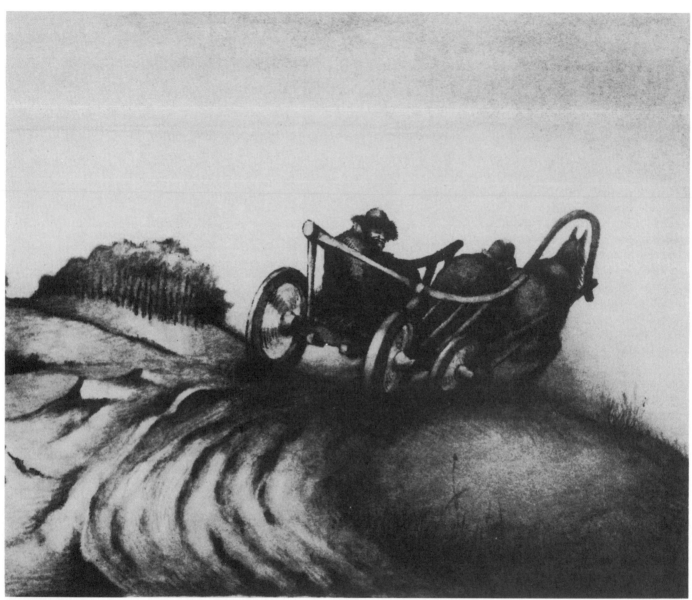

From *The Treasure*

Envoi

I am not a teacher: only a fellow-traveler of whom you asked the way. I pointed ahead—ahead of myself as well as of you.

George Bernard Shaw

An ancient tale tells of a student who had the desire to go to a certain place but didn't know the way. He asked his teacher to help him get there. The teacher took his cart, and together they set out on the wide road. The journey was pleasant and fast. Traveling by cart with the teacher saved the student ample time. But after a while the road came to an end. Now there was only a narrow path, too narrow for the cart to continue. In fact, the path was just wide enough for a single person to walk. There the teacher had to turn around and go back, while the student continued by himself on the path where one must walk alone.

This book, like the cart, has taken you as far as it can. I hope it has helped you save time and avoid paths that lead nowhere. Now, to find your own way, you must continue on your own.

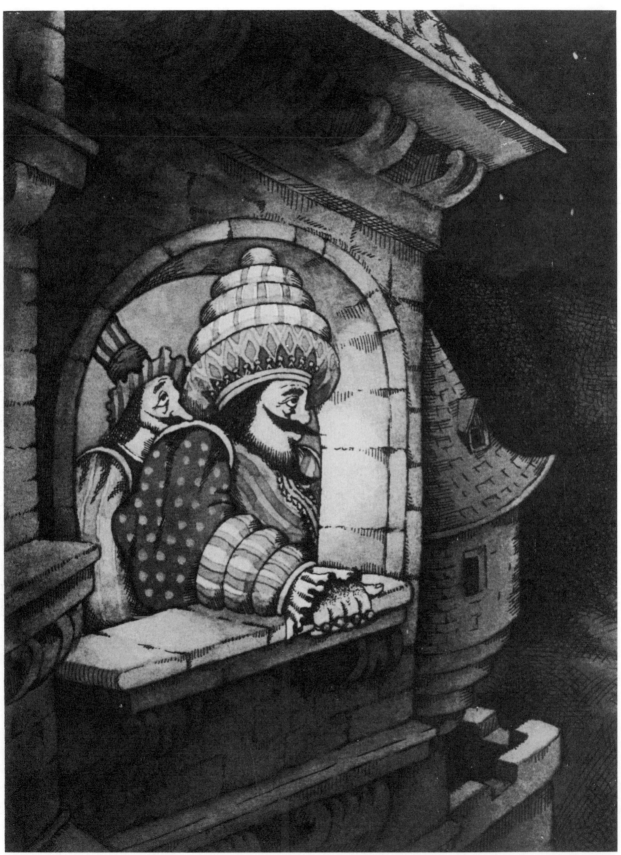

From *The Lost Kingdom of Karnica*

Appendices

This morn, as sleeping in my bed I lay, / I dreamt (and morning dreams come true they say).

W. B. Rhodes

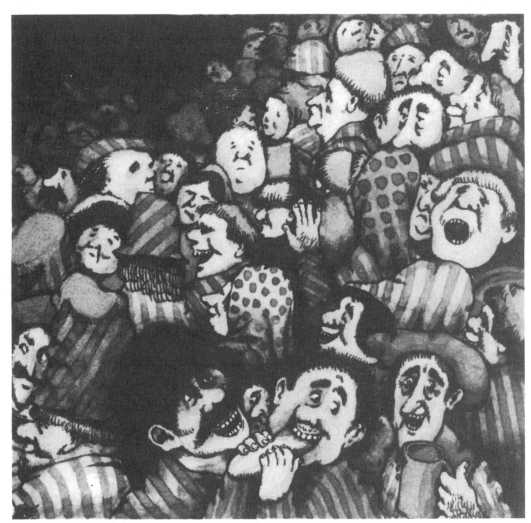

From *The Lost Kingdom of Karnica*

Finding a Publisher

The first step in selling your work is finding out which companies publish the kind of book you are interested in making. You can get to know the different publishers by looking at the books they publish. Go to libraries and bookstores, decide which books you like, and check who their publishers are. You can get a list of publishers of children's books with their addresses and their editors' names from the Children's Book Council (67 Irving Place, New York, NY 10003). Go to publishers' exhibits at annual conventions of the American Library Association (ALA), American Booksellers Association (ABA), and the International Reading Association (IRA) when they are held in your area. Get publishers' catalogs at each booth and examine the books on display. Also study publishers' ads and listings in publications that cover the field of children's books—for instance, *School Library Journal*, *Horn Book* magazine, *Publisher's Weekly*, and the special children's book issues of the *New York Times Book Review* that appear in the spring and fall. If these publications are not on sale at newsstands or stores in your area, you may be able to locate them at your public library.

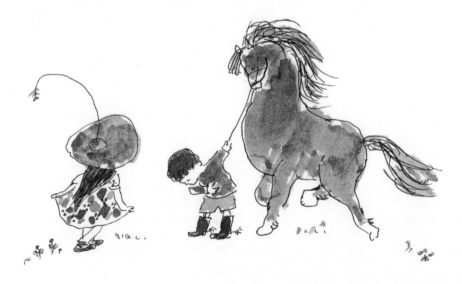

How to Contact a Publisher

Publishers of children's books are very approachable. You can contact them by letter or by telephone, but make your inquiry brief and to the point.

If you are an artist and live in or near the city where the publisher's editorial office is, call and ask for an appointment to show your portfolio. If you live out of town but plan to make a trip to the city to see publishers, call or write in advance to arrange for an interview. It is best to ask for an interview at least two or three weeks ahead of time. When you call or write, give the dates that you will be in the city.

You may also send a publisher samples of your work, but don't risk mailing originals. Instead, send black-and-white or color photocopies of pieces that are representative of your work. A publisher who is interested can then request to see the originals.

If you are an author of nonfiction, you can write a query letter, briefly describing your manuscript and its intended age group, to find out whether the publisher is interested. If, however, your manuscript is fiction, mail the story itself—clearly typed, double-spaced, on non-erasable bond—with a brief cover letter and a self-addressed, stamped envelope. (Remember, mailing an original is risky; keep a duplicate for yourself.) In the cover letter, you can request to see an editor after he or she has had a chance to read your manuscript.

Multiple Submissions

When an author submits a manuscript to more than one publisher at the same time, it is called a multiple submission. This used to be frowned upon in the publishing industry, but now editors generally are understanding—given the five or six weeks it normally takes to respond to a submission. Many editors, however, do feel very strongly that the author's cover letter should state clearly that the manuscript is a multiple submission, and that if the manuscript is accepted by a publisher, the author should *immediately*
notify the other publishers who are considering it.

I spoke to many editors about their feelings on multiple submissions. Some of them were indifferent. One said it would induce her to read the manuscript sooner. Other editors said they don't like multiple submissions or wouldn't even bother to read such a manuscript. One editor would rather just be reminded by the author of the need to reply quickly.

Meeting with an Editor

Most editors feel no need to meet with the author in considering a manuscript. They find it sufficient just to read the text. (Allowances may be made if either the editor or the author feels a special need for it. But the author shouldn't expect a response before the editor has read the manuscript, nor will an editor read a manuscript during an initial meeting.) Later, if the editor is interested in the manuscript, a meeting may be set up to discuss the manuscript and possible revisions. These meetings are usually friendly and relaxed.

Where artists are concerned, however, editors feel that it is helpful to communicate with them directly. Although deserving out-of-town artists sometimes get positive responses when they mail in their portfolios, whenever possible, it is best to show your portfolio at a meeting. Unlike the author, the artist can expect an immediate reaction to his or her work. The editor may suggest that you leave your portfolio at the publishing house for a while to enable other editors or the art director to see it.

Editors also seek a responsible attitude in the prospective artist—one that inspires trust and indicates reliability in keeping appointments and meeting deadlines.

Preparing Your Portfolio

The purpose of a portfolio is to show representative samples of an artist's work, including different styles and techniques that you like to do and feel comfortable with. A portfolio case—one that is not so

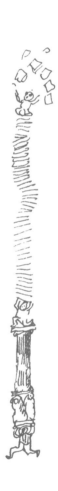

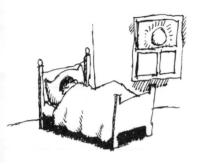

large that it is unwieldy or awkward—is a wise investment. One editor I spoke with said a neat portfolio case shows a caring, serious, professional attitude. She said that about ten leaves is an adequate length, neither too short nor too long. The more examples it has the better, provided they are not repetitious.

Another editor said that out-of-town artists who have to mail their portfolios can send photocopies, if they represent the artist adequately. Although she said that transparencies are acceptable, another editor said she prefers originals, or even color prints, to slides.

When you mail your portfolio, always include return postage. But remember, mailing a portfolio can be risky.

What to Include

Your portfolio should include examples of black-and-white art suitable for both line and halftone reproduction. Some of your color art should have a limited color range, suggesting the potential for doing preseparated art. If you know how to make color preseparations, you may even want to include some samples of preseparated art. You may also include two or three sample jackets you have designed for well-known stories. Or you can make up your own. Show a full-color jacket and another that could be preseparated.

Art directors and editors are skilled at reading pictures. They are not interested in seeing the same illustration repeated over and over again with slight changes. Show a wide range of subject matter, not merely different techniques. You should have pictures demonstrating an ability to illustrate different kinds of stories. Show adults, children, and animals engaged in various activities, in different settings, situations, and moods. Show groups of people relating to one another, not just single figures. You can illustrate well-known stories in order to show your approach: choose a fairy tale or another story you like and make two or three samples to show how you would develop the action and sustain the characters.

Your work also should reflect an under-standing of book format and size. Art directors and editors want to see that you can think realistically about the finished book. Include a sample of a book dummy, even if it is rough. Make the samples actual size or close to it. Your examples should demonstrate your sense of sequence and continuity. Include, for instance, a sequence of pictures, with the same characters, which reveals an awareness of the direction in which they are moving. Show that you can illustrate the same person or setting in three or four different pictures. Also show how the pictures relate to the content of the words, and how type might be used in planning a page—not necessarily by choosing the type (since you may have no part in this decision), but by making it an integral part of the page's composition.

Besides artistic quality, editors look for the artist's vision, for how he or she sees things, for *who* the artist is.

Should You Emphasize Variety or a Specialty?

Include in your portfolio as wide a range of your work as possible, but don't include anything you wouldn't like to do. If you're versatile, include samples that emphasize your strengths. Don't, however, force yourself to include variety unless it feels natural to you and you enjoy, or find it interesting, to work in more than one way. But bear in mind that if you draw in one way only, it narrows your chances of getting more work, whereas versatility increases them.

An editor once remarked to me that when she sees a variety of work by an artist, she gets a better feel for the person. It is important for her to like the person, to have a good feeling about both the artist and the artwork.

Presenting an Idea for a Picture Book

A picture book is best presented in dummy form because editors like to see how the text reads as a book. Although they usually don't insist on a dummy at this stage, it can only help. The typed manuscript can be pasted into the dummy, or if the text is very brief, it can be clearly printed by hand. Don't submit your manuscript in dummy form unless the dummy has been properly done and shows a clear grasp of the pacing and flow of the book.

The dummy can be prepared with rough drawings in pencil or any other medium. You don't have to finish the art for the whole dummy—it can have just one finished picture, or the entire dummy can be rough—because you may want to make revisions later. In addition to the dummy, you can submit one or two more finished-looking sample pictures, either in black-and-white or color. In fact, some editors like to see a dummy that has two or three pages done more carefully than the rest—though not necessarily finished—to indicate the style and techniques the artist intends to use. You don't need to include any preseparated art, however.

Send a photocopy of the dummy, and if you are also including a couple of samples of the finished art, send black-and-white or color photocopies of them.

Leaving Sample Pictures

Since editors and art directors see many artists, one way to help them remember you is to leave reproductions of sample pictures with them. Editors and art directors keep these samples on hand in special artists' files. Decide carefully which pieces to leave because they will identify and represent you long after your visit.

The samples are normally kept in manila file folders approximately 11″ × 9″. Don't make your samples too large to fit the folders, or so small that they get lost, as a calling card would. (One editor I spoke with, however, does prefer a 3″ × 5″ file-card size.) A page containing two or three pictures is better than one with many small, hard-to-read ones. If you can afford to reproduce your samples by offset printing, that is fine. But even inexpensive photocopies—provided they give an adequate idea of your work—are

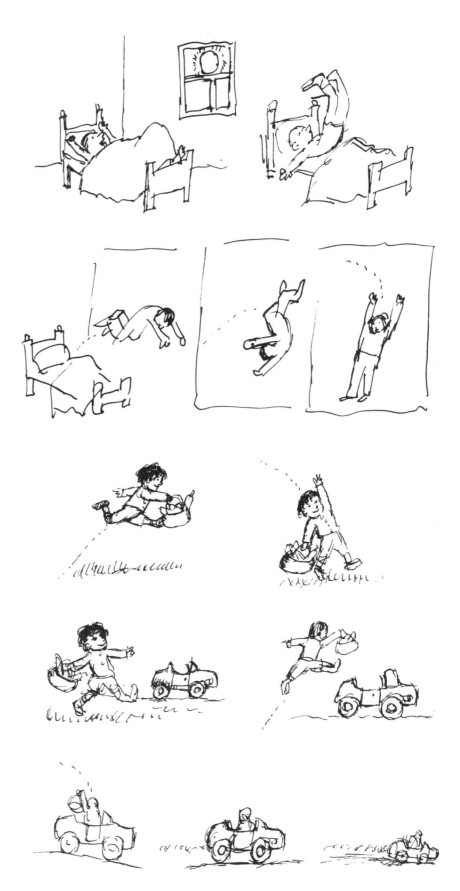

preferable to leaving no samples at all. Don't include a résumé; only your work matters. But be sure to include your name, address, and telephone number.

Sometimes an editor or art director may ask for permission to photocopy some samples from your portfolio. You may want to keep a few photocopies—in color, black-and-white, or both—in your portfolio so that you can leave more than one sample.

How Editors Choose a Book to Publish

Publishing is a personal matter. Editors listen to their instincts and publish what they like and respond to. They are guided by their individual tastes and sense of quality. Economics are an important factor, too, so decisions may be based on what the publisher thinks it can sell and what seems to be lacking on its list. One editor commented that she chose a book if she experienced a shiver, if something touched her—provided there was no conflict with other books on the list and it fit the house's needs. But she said that for her, a strong subjective feeling outweighs all. Another editor, Liz Gordon, summed it up as follows: "Intuition raised to power of technique based on experience of what is good or not."

Here is a sampling of comments from some editors I have interviewed about what they look for when they read a manuscript or look at an artist's portfolio.

Liz Gordon (Harper & Row): "In writing I like to see a fresh approach, an eye that sees the world differently. I look for good writing, and for an artist who draws well, but good technique alone isn't enough. A book has to have feeling, something that speaks to children without condescending to them. A children's story should be interesting and have internal consistency, cohesion. I look for a book that works—not that it must be finished or flawless, but it needs to have spirit, talent, or potential. Publishing is personal, and editors publish what they like, but the author or artist should not try to second-

guess the editor. Don't concentrate on a 'professional' look, but on what you really like to do."

Lee Deadrick (formerly at Charles Scribner's Sons): "When I review a potential children's book, my mind is a clear slate. Am I going to be impressed, pleased, feel good, be turned on? Is the story wonderful, funny? Does it have strong emotional appeal; will it make me laugh? Will I be pleased with what happens to the characters? Does it get a response from me; does it communicate anything on an emotional level? I see many good pictures, but most stories I read are unsatisfying—I get no reaction out of them. It is hard to find good picture book texts. It's hard to find good books to publish, period."

Margaret McElderry (Atheneum): "I look for quality, and for an individual way of telling or drawing or painting. I look for originality, but not necessarily an original idea. I like to see a person who has some idea and wants to communicate something."

Susan Hirschman (Greenwillow Books): "I look for an idea, not necessarily new. Has the author or artist done what he or she wanted to do? There is nothing that cannot be done by someone who cares and has talent. Write what you believe; write for yourself. Do it your own way. Follow your instincts."

Jane Feder (formerly at Harper & Row): "In a story I look for personal expression; I want it to be heartfelt, intense, beautifully written, in simple and direct language. It should have a childlike quality, something that is special. In art, I am fond of round shapes, soft pencil; an expression that is unique, personal, original; an approach I have not seen before; good use of color. I like a large-size portfolio."

Donna Brooks (E. P. Dutton): "Does the story move me in any way? Is it humorous, enjoyable—not necessarily clever or original? Can I react to it? Is it for children, about their world, does it understand their feelings? Could it make a book? Is it well crafted? Does it have freshness?"

Editors' tastes are apparent from the kinds of books they publish. Therefore, look at their books. To make sure that you are looking at recent books that reflect the tastes of the current editor, check the date on the copyright notice. Editors often move from one publishing house to another, and a change in editorial leadership will affect the types of books published.

A Final Word of Advice

If you are both a writer and an illustrator, your chances of being published increase. If your manuscript is accepted, you don't have to wait for the publisher to find the right illustrator. But don't restrict the editor by insisting that your manuscript and pictures be accepted as a package. Unless you have a good reason for illustrating your own manuscript, or want to illustrate only your own stories, it is wise for the beginner to accept an editor's decision to let someone else make the pictures for your words, or for you to make the pictures for someone else's text.

Some editors may ask to see your sketchbook. This will show them how you draw informally, spontaneously, candidly. They may find something in your sketchbook that has been drawn with love and excitement, and suggest that you try something new, something you had not considered.

Perseverence and patience are important. It may take time for an editor to find the right manuscript for you. But once a manuscript is offered to you, don't illustrate it unless it touches or interests you—no matter how difficult it may be to turn the work down.

To get started as an illustrator, you might consider also working in a field other than trade books—for instance, textbooks, various kinds of educational materials, magazines for children or adults, newspapers, or spot illustrations for various publications.

Remember that, as in any career, the right timing is a factor—being the right person for the right job at the right time. That's why showing a wide range of work is an advantage.

And don't get discouraged by rejections. Another publishing house may eventually accept your book idea. But do try to discover why your proposal was rejected: what may be wrong with your manuscript and what can be improved. Turn rejections into an opportunity to learn and to grow.

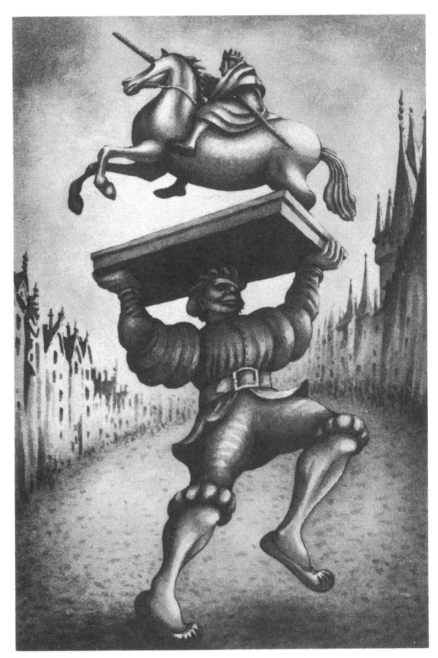

From *The Golem*

Bibliography

Telling the Story

Aiken, Joan. *The Way to Write for Children.* New York: St. Martin's Press, 1983.

Allen, Walter, Editor. *Writers on Writing.* London: Phoenix House.

Aristotle. *Poetics.* Translated by S. H. Butcher. New York: Hill & Wang, 1961.

Brooks, Cleanth, and Warren, Robert Penn. *Fundamentals of Good Writing.* New York: Harcourt Brace Jovanovich, 1950.

Colby, Jean Poindexter. *Writing, Illustrating and Editing Children's Books.* New York: Hastings House, 1967.

Egoff, Sheila, et al., Editors. *Only Connect: Readings on Children's Literature*, 2nd ed. New York: Oxford University Press, 1980.

Gordon, William J. J. *Synectics.* New York: Macmillan, 1961.

Hazard, Paul. *Books, Children and Men*, 5th ed. Boston: Horn Books, 1983.

Huck, Charlotte S. *Children's Literature in the Elementary School*, 3rd rev. ed. New York: Holt, Rinehart & Winston, 1979.

Lanes, Selma G. *Down the Rabbit Hole: Adventures and Misadventures in the Realm of Children's Literature.* New York: Atheneum, 1971.

MacCann, Donnarae, and Richard, Olga. *The Child's First Books.* New York: Wilson, 1973.

Seuling, Barbara. *How to Write a Children's Book and Get It Published.* New York: Charles Scribner's Sons, 1984.

Strunk, William, Jr., and White, E. B. *The Elements of Style*, 3rd ed. New York: Macmillan, 1979.

Sutherland, Zena, et al. *Children and Books*, 6th ed. Glenview, Ill.: Scott, Foresman, 1981.

University of Chicago Press. *A Manual of Style*, 13th ed. Chicago: University of Chicago Press, 1984.

Yolen, Jane. *Writing Books for Children*, rev. ed. Boston: Writer, 1983.

Zinsser, William. *On Writing Well*, 2nd ed. New York: Harper & Row, 1980.

Creating the Pictures

Albers, Josef. *Interaction of Color*, rev. ed. New Haven: Yale University Press, 1975.

Arnheim, Rudolf. *Art and Visual Perception: A Psychology of the Creative Eye*, 2nd rev. ed. Berkeley: University of California Press, 1974.

Bridgman, George B. *Complete Guide to Drawing from Life.* Walnut Creek, Cal.: Weathervane.

Doerner, Max. *The Materials of the Artist*, rev. ed. Translated by Eugen Neuhaus. New York: Harcourt Brace Jovanovich, 1949.

Dürer, Albrecht. *Human Figure.* New York: Dover, 1972.

Eisenstein, Sergei. *The Film Sense.* New York: Harcourt Brace Jovanovich, 1969.

Farris, Edmond J. *Art Students' Anatomy*, 2nd ed. New York: Dover, 1953.

Hale, Robert B. *Drawing Lessons from the Great Masters.* New York: Watson-Guptill Publications, 1964.

Itten, Johannes. *The Art of Color.* New York: Van Nostrand Reinhold, 1973.

Johnson, Charles. *The Language of Painting.* Cambridge: Cambridge University Press, 1949.

Kepes, Gyorgy. *Language of Vision.* Chicago: Paul Theobald, 1945.

Kingman, Lee, Editor. *The Illustrator's Notebook.* Boston: Horn Books, 1978.

Loran, Erle. *Cezanne's Composition*, 3rd ed. Berkeley: University of California Press, 1963.

Muybridge, Eaweard. *Animals in Motion.* New York: Dover, 1957.

Muybridge, Eaweard. *Human Figure in Motion.* New York: Dover, 1955.

Snyder, John. *Commercial Artist's Handbook.* New York: Watson-Guptill Publications, 1973.

Thomas, Brian. *Geometry in Pictorial Composition.* London: Oriel Press.

White, Gwen. *Perspective: A Guide for Artists, Architects, and Designers.* New York: Watson-Guptill Publications, 1968.

Preparing for Reproduction

Craig, James. *Designing with Type: A Basic Course in Typography*, rev. ed. New York: Watson-Guptill Publications, 1980.

Craig, James. *Production for the Graphic Designer.* New York: Watson-Guptill Publications, 1974.

International Paper Co. *Pocket Pal*, 13th ed. New York: International Paper Co., 1983.

Lee, Marshall, Editor. *Bookmaking: The Illustrated Guide to Design, Production, Editing*, rev. ed. New York: R. R. Bowker, 1980.

Stone, Bernard, and Eckstein, Arthur. *Preparing Art for Printing*, rev. ed. New York: Van Nostrand Reinhold, 1983.

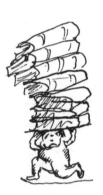

Credits

Grateful acknowledgment is made to the authors and illustrators and to the following publishers and agencies:

To The Blackie Publishing Group, Ltd., Scotland, for permission to reproduce pictures from *The Fools of Chelm* by Isaac Bashevis Singer, pictures by Uri Shulevitz; pictures copyright © 1973 by Uri Shulevitz (p. 164, Figure 41; p. 165, Figure 51; p. 182, Figures 56–57). Double spread from *Sir Ribbeck of Ribbeck of Haveland* by Theodor Fontane, translated by Elizabeth Shub, pictures by Nonny Hogrogian; pictures copyright © 1969 by Nonny Hogrogian (p. 94, Figure 11).

To The Bodley Head, London, for permission to reproduce the picture from *The Juniper Tree and Other Tales from Grimm*, translated by Lore Segal and Randall Jarrell, pictures by Maurice Sendak; pictures copyright © 1973 by Maurice Sendak (p. 124, Figure 7). Picture from *Some Swell Pup* by Maurice Sendak and Matthew Margolis; pictures copyright © 1976 by Maurice Sendak (p. 122, Figure 53). Text and pictures from *Where the Wild Things Are* by Maurice Sendak; copyright © 1963 by Maurice Sendak (p. 17, Figure 3; p. 51, p. 52, Figure 1; p. 169, Figure 8).

To Georges Borchardt, Inc., Literary Agency, for permission to reproduce the picture from *Laughing Latkes* by M. B. Goffstein; copyright © 1980 by M. B. Goffstein (p. 99, Figure 24).

To Jonathan Cape, Ltd., London, for permission to reproduce the picture from *Fables*, written and illustrated by Arnold Lobel; copyright © 1980 by Arnold Lobel (p. 106, Figure 34). Picture from *Mazel and Shlimazel* by Isaac Bashevis Singer, pictures by Margot Zemach; pictures copyright © 1967 by Margot Zemach (p. 101, Figure 27).

To Collins, Publishers, London, for permission to reproduce the box cover illustration from *The Nutshell Library*, written and illustrated by Maurice Sendak, copyright © 1962 by Maurice Sendak (p. 91, Figure 3 left).

To J. M. Dent & Sons, Ltd., London, for permission to reproduce the picture from *Gulliver's Travels* by Jonathan Swift, illustrated by Arthur Rackham (p. 204, Figure 43).

To Andre Deutsch, London, for permission to reproduce pictures from *The Golem* by Isaac Bashevis Singer, pictures by Uri Shulevitz; pictures copyright © 1982 by Uri Shulevitz (p. 151, Figure 52; p. 263).

To Dial Books for Young Readers, for permission to reproduce text from *We Never Get to Do Anything* by Martha Alexander, copyright © 1970 by Martha Alexander (p. 51).

To Dover Publications, New York, for permission to reproduce illustrations from *Art Student's Anatomy* by E. J. Farris (1961), p. 144, Figures 24–25). *Bizarries and Fantasies of Grandville*, introduction and commentary by Stanley Appelbaum (1974), (p. 149, Figure 45; p. 150, Figure 50; p. 154, Figure 4). *A Diderot Pictorial Encyclopedia of Trades and Industry* by Denis Diderot, edited by Charles Coulston Gillispie, 2 vols. (1959), (p. 129, Figure 15; p. 132, Figure 20). *Doré's Illustrations for Rabelais* (1978), (p. 122, Figure 4; p. 128, Figure 13). *Eighteen Hundred Woodcuts by Thomas Bewick and His School*, edited by Blanche Cirker (p. 132, Figure 21). *Graphic Worlds of Peter Bruegel the Elder* by H. Arthur Klein (1963), (p. 171, Figure 15). *Hypocritical Helena* by Wilhelm Busch (1962), (pp. 36–37, Figure 9). *The Rime of the Ancient Mariner* by Samuel Taylor Coleridge, illustrated by Gustave Doré (1970), (p. 131, Figure 19; p. 151, Figure 51).

To E. P. Dutton, Inc., Publishers, for permission to reproduce the illustration by Joseph Low from *The Land of the Taffeta Dawn* by Natalia Belting; illustrations copyright © 1973 by Joseph Low (p. 203, Figure 41).

To Europa Verlag, for permission to reproduce the illustration from *Passionate Journey* ("Mein Studenbuch") by Frans Masereel; copyright © Europa Verlag A.G. Zurich (p. 133, Figure 23).

To Farrar, Straus and Giroux, Inc., for permission to reproduce the picture from *Abel's Island* by William Steig; copyright © 1976 by William Steig (p. 105, Figure 36). Picture from *Amos and Boris* by William Steig; copyright © 1971 by William Steig (p. 100, Figure 26). Text and jacket from *Brookie and Her Lamb* by M. B. Goffstein; copyright © 1967 by M. B. Goffstein (p. 57; p. 96, Figure 16). Text and pictures from *Dawn* by Uri Shulevitz; copyright © 1974 by Uri Shulevitz (p. 60, Figures 4–5; p. 62; pp. 84–88, book pages 5–32; p. 107, Figure 42; p. 253, Figure 32). Jacket and picture from *Elijah the Slave* by Isaac Bashevis Singer, pictures by Antonio Frasconi; pictures copyright © 1970 by Antonio Frasconi (p. 91, Figure 3 right; p. 127, Figure 11). Jacket and double spreads from *The Fool of the World and the Flying*

Ship, retold by Arthur Ransome, pictures by Uri Shulevitz; pictures copyright © 1968 by Uri Shulevitz (p. 95, Figure 14 bottom; p. 97, Figure 19; p. 102, Figure 30). Pictures from *The Fools of Chelm* by Isaac Bashevis Singer, pictures by Uri Shulevitz; pictures copyright © 1973 by Uri Shulevitz (p. 164, Figure 41; p. 165, Figure 51; p. 182, Figures 56–57). Pictures from *The Golem* by Isaac Bashevis Singer, pictures by Uri Shulevitz; pictures copyright © 1982 by Uri Shulevitz (p. 151, Figure 52; p. 263). Jacket from *Gorky Rises* by William Steig; copyright © 1980 by William Steig (p. 95, Figure 14 top). Picture from *The Juniper Tree and Other Tales from Grimm*, translated by Lore Segal and Randall Jarrell, pictures by Maurice Sendak; pictures copyright © 1973 by Maurice Sendak (p. 124, Figure 7). Picture from *Laughing Latkes* by M. B. Goffstein; copyright © 1980 by M. B. Goffstein (p. 99, Figure 24). Picture from *The Little Humpbacked Horse* by Margaret Hodges, pictures by Chris Conover; pictures copyright © 1980 by Chris Conover (p. 112, Figure 52). Picture from *Mazel and Shlimazel* by Isaac Bashevis Singer, pictures by Margot Zemach; pictures copyright © 1967 by Margot Zemach (p. 101, Figure 27). Picture from *My Village Sturbridge* by Gary Bowen and Randy Miller; pictures copyright © 1977 by Gary Bowen (p. 98, Figure 22). Picture from *Naftali the Storyteller* by Isaac Bashevis Singer, pictures by Margot Zemach; pictures copyright © 1976 by Margot Zemach (p. 121, Figure 2). Picture from *Overhead the Sun*, lines from Walt Whitman, pictures by Antonio Frasconi; pictures copyright © 1969 by Antonio Frasconi (p. 105, Figure 37). Text and pictures from *Rain Rain Rivers* by Uri Shulevitz; copyright © 1969 by Uri Shulevitz (p. 14; p. 56, Figure 3; p. 102, Figure 31; p. 157, Figure 10; p. 160, Figure 18; p. 251, Figure 29). Picture from *Sid and Sol* by Arthur Yorinks and Richard Egielski; pictures copyright © 1977 by Richard Egielski (p. 92, Figure 7 left). Pictures from *Soldier and Tsar in the Forest* by Uri Shulevitz; pictures copyright © 1972 by Uri Shulevitz (p. 153, Figure 2; p. 207; p. 249, Figure 24). Picture from *Some Swell Pup* by Maurice Sendak and Matthew Margolis, pictures by Maurice Sendak; pictures copyright © 1976 by Maurice Sendak (p. 112, Figure 53). Text from "Sophie's Picnic" in *Across the Sea* by M. B. Goffstein; copyright © 1968 by M. B. Goffstein (p. 40). Title page from *Toby Lived Here* by Hilma Wolitzer; copyright © 1978 by Hilma Wolitzer (p. 109, Figure 45). Text and pictures from *The Treasure* by Uri Shulevitz; copyright © 1978 by Uri Shulevitz (p. 62, Figure 7; p. 63, text and Figure 8; p. 81; p. 110, Figure 48; p. 254). Picture from *Two Piano Tuners* by M. B. Goffstein; copyright © 1970 by M. B. Goffstein (p. 93, Figure 10 right).

To Greenwillow Books, for permission to reproduce pictures from *Hanukah Money* by Sholem Aleichem, illustrated by Uri Shulevitz;

illustrations copyright © 1978 by Uri Shulevitz (p. 75, Figure 14; p. 78, Figure 23; p. 92, Figure 7 right; p. 156, Figure 9). Pictures from *The Touchstone* by Robert Louis Stevenson, illustrated by Uri Shulevitz; illustrations copyright © 1976 by Uri Shulevitz (p. 154, Figure 3; p. 161, Figure 24; p. 163, Figure 33; p. 163, Figure 35; p. 164, Figure 38).

To Hamish Hamilton, Ltd., Publishers, London, for permission to reproduce the picture from *Abel's Island* by William Steig; copyright © 1976 by William Steig (p. 105, Figure 36). Picture from *Amos and Boris* by William Steig; copyright © 1971 by William Steig (p. 100, Figure 26). Jacket and double spreads from *The Fool of the World and the Flying Ship*, retold by Arthur Ransome, pictures by Uri Shulevitz; pictures copyright © 1968 by Uri Shulevitz (p. 95, Figure 14 bottom; p. 97, Figure 19; p. 102, Figure 30). Picture from *The Grateful Sparrow and Other Tales* by Angela Thirkell, pictures by Ludwig Richter (1935), (p. 203, Figure 42).

To Harper & Row, Publishers, Inc., for permission to reproduce the illustration from *Fables*, written and illustrated by Arnold Lobel; a Caldecott Medal winner; copyright © 1980 by Arnold Lobel (p. 106, Figure 39). Illustration by David Palladini from *The Girl Who Cried Flowers and Other Tales* by Jane Yolen; illustrations copyright © 1974 by David Palladini (p. 104, Figure 34). Text from *Goodnight Moon* by Margaret Wise Brown, illustrated by Clement Hurd; copyright, 1947 by Harper & Row, Publishers, Inc., renewed 1965 by Roberta Brown Rauch and Clement Hurd (p. 55, p. 57). Text and illustrations from *The Happy Day*, written by Ruth Krauss, illustrated by Marc Simont; text copyright © 1949, 1977 Ruth Krauss; pictures copyright © 1949, 1977 by Marc Simont (p. 54, p. 55; p. 57; p. 93, Figure 9). Text from *Mine's the Best*, written and illustrated by Crosby Bonsall; an I CAN READ Book; copyright © 1973 by Crosby Bonsall (p. 56). Illustrations from *The Moon in My Room*, written and illustrated by Uri Shulevitz; copyright © 1963 by Uri Shulevitz (p. 8; p. 108, Figure 43; p. 197, Figure 9). Box cover illustration from *The Nutshell Library*, written and illustrated by Maurice Sendak; copyright © 1962 by Maurice Sendak (p. 91, Figure 3 left). Text and illustrations from *Open House for Butterflies*, written by Ruth Krauss, illustrated by Maurice Sendak; text copyright © 1960 by Ruth Krauss; pictures copyright © 1960 by Maurice Sendak (p. 111, Figures 49–51). Illustration by Donna Diamond from *The Transfigured Hart* by Jane Yolen; copyright © 1975 by Jane Yolen (p. 94, Figure 12). Frontispiece illustration by Geoffrey Hayes from *When the Wind Blew* by Margaret Wise Brown; illustrations copyright © 1977 by Geoffrey Hayes (p. 99, Figure 23). Text and illustrations from *Where the Wild Things Are*, written and illustrated by Maurice Sendak; a Caldecott Medal winner; copyright © 1963 by Maurice Sendak (p. 17, Figure 3; p. 51; p. 52, Figure 1; p. 169, Figure 8).

To the Ezra Jack Keats Foundation, for permission to reproduce text and an illustration from *The Trip*, written and illustrated by Ezra Jack Keats, published by Greenwillow Books (p. 60; p. 61, Figure 6).

Library Association, London, England, for permission to reproduce text from "Three Ways of Writing for Children" by C. S. Lewis, reprinted in *Only Connect*, from the proceedings of the Bournemouth Conference, 1952 (p. 9).

To Macmillan Publishing Company, Inc., for permission to reproduce text and illustrations from *The Magician* by Uri Shulevitz; copyright © 1971 by Uri Shulevitz (p. 83; p. 106, Figure 38; p. 247, Figure 18). Illustration from *My Kind of Verse* by John Smith, illustrated by Uri Shulevitz; illustrations copyright © 1968 Macmillan Publishing Company, Inc. (p. 108, Figure 44). Illustrations from *Oh What a Noise!* by Uri Shulevitz; copyright © 1971 by Uri Shulevitz (p. 64; p. 65; p. 91, Figure 4; p. 156, Figure 8). Photographs from *Push-Pull, Empty-Full* by Tana Hoban; copyright © 1972 by Tana Hoban (p. 123, Figure 6). Illustrations and title page from *Runaway Jonah and Other Tales* by Jan Wahl, illustrated by Uri Shulevitz; illustrations copyright © 1968 by Uri Shulevitz (p. 97, Figure 18; p. 110, Figure 47; p. 119). Double spread from *Sir Ribbeck of Ribbeck of Haveland*, by Theodor Fontane, translated by Elizabeth Shub, illustrated by Nonny Hogrogian; illustrations copyright © 1969 by Nonny Hogrogian (p. 94, Figure 11). Double spread from *What Is Pink?* by Christina Rosetti, illustrated by Jose Aruego; illustrations copyright © 1971 by Jose Aruego (p. 103, Figure 32).

To Samuel L. Nadler, representative for the Estate of Margaret Wise Brown, for permission to reproduce text from *Goodnight Moon* by Margaret Wise Brown, illustrated by Clement Hurd (p. 55, p. 57).

To Oxford University Press, Oxford, England, for permission to reproduce the picture from *Naftali the Storyteller* by Isaac Bashevis Singer, pictures by Margot Zemach; pictures copyright © 1976 by Margot Zemach (p. 121, Figure 2).

To Penguin Young Books, Ltd., England, for permission to reproduce photographs from *Push-Pull, Empty-Full* by Tana Hoban; copyright © 1972 by Tana Hoban (p. 123, Figure 6).

To Charles Scribner's Sons, for permission to reproduce illustrations from *The Lost Kingdom of Karnica* by Richard Kennedy, illustrated by Uri Shulevitz; illustrations copyright © 1979 by Uri Shulevitz (New York: Sierra Club Books, 1979); (p. 264, p. 265). Text and illustrations from *One Monday Morning* by Uri Shulevitz; copyright © 1967 by Uri Shulevitz (New York: Charles Scribner's Sons, 1967); (p. 17, Figure 4; p. 32, Figure 6; p. 96, Figure 15; p. 117, Figure 14; p. 162, Figures 29–30). Illustrations from *The Silkspinners* by Jean Russell Larson, illustrated by Uri Shulevitz; text copyright © 1967 by Jean Russell Larson; illustrations copyright © 1967 by Uri Shulevitz (New York: Charles Scribner's Sons, 1967); (p. 128, Figure 14; p. 135, Figure 26).

To the Sterling Lord Agency, for permission to reproduce illustrations from *Alberic the Wise and Other Journeys* by Norton Juster, illustrated by Domenico Gnoli (p. 97, Figure 17; p. 125, Figure 8; p. 169, Figure 9).

To Frederick Warne and Company, for permission to reproduce the picture from *The Story of a Fierce Bad Rabbit* by Beatrix Potter (p. 93, Figure 10 left). Text and pictures from *The Tale of Peter Rabbit* by Beatrix Potter (p. 16, text and Figure 1; p. 101, Figure 28; p. 105, Figure 35).

To Windmill Books, Inc., for permission to reproduce the illustration from *Boris Bad Enough* by Robert Kraus © 1976; illustrations by Jose Aruego and Ariane Dewey © 1976 (p. 101, Figure 29).

To World's Work Ltd., London, for permission to reproduce text from *Goodnight Moon* by Margaret Wise Brown, illustrated by Clement Hurd; copyright renewed 1965 by Roberta Brown Rauch and Clement Hurd (p. 55, 57). Text from *Mine's the Best*, written and illustrated by Crosby Bonsall, copyright © 1973 by Crosby Bonsall (p. 56).

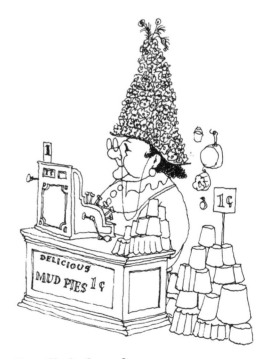

From *Charley Sang a Song*

Index

Aaron Awoke (Marilee Robin Burton), 41
Abel's Island (William Steig), 105, *105*
Acetate, 218–219, 226–227, 252–253
 color preseparation exercise, 226–227
Action, 41, 54, 72
 complete, 30–46
 conclusion of, 43–46
 development of, 33–40
 interest of, 41–43
 objective in, 31–32
 unifying link in, 41
 visible, 53, 84
Actor
 consistency of, 26
 desire of, 33, 36, 44, 53
 as unifying link, 41
 see also Character, Hero
Actor-stage relationship, 19–22, 24, 29, 99, 121
Actual-size dummy, 74–79, 244–245
After the Meal (Uri Shulevitz), 42–43, *42*
Alberic the Wise and Other Journeys (Norton Juster, illustrated by Domenico Gnoli), 96, *97*, 125, *125*, 168, *169*
Albinus, Bernard Siegfried, 144, *144*
Aleichem, Sholem, 156, 183
Alexander, Martha, 51, 221
Alice's Adventures in Wonderland (Lewis Carroll, illustrated by Sir John Tenniel), 149, *149*, 154, *155*, *180*, 181
American Booksellers Association, 258
American Library Association, 258
Amos and Boris (William Steig), 100, 101
Analogies, 53
Animated objects, 150
Art; *see* Drawing, Illustration, Picture
Art director, 67, 117, 208, 212, 217, 220, 223, 259–260
Aruego, Jose, 79, 101, *101*, 103, *103*, 221

Asymmetry vs. symmetry, 99, 106, 145, 178–179, 200

Back matter, 116
Belting, Natalia, 202
Benjamin, Alan, 221
Bewick, Thomas, *132*, 133
Bianco, Margery William, 150
Bierhorst, Jane, 110, *110*
Bilibine, 126, *126*
Binding, 113–115
Bleeds, 102–103
Blue-bristols, 220, 248
Bonsall, Crosby, 51, 56
Book shape, 89, 95–97
Book structure, 113–118
 art and, 117–118
Boris Bad Enough (Robert Kraus, illustrated by Jose Aruego and Ariane Dewey), 101, *101*
Bourges Color Corporation, 219
Bourges Colotones, 219, 223–225
Boutet de Monvel, Louis Maurice, 126, *126*, 139, *139*, *180*, 181, 202, *203*, 205
Bowen, Gary, *98*, 99
Brookie and Her Lamb (M. B. Goffstein), 57, 96, *96*
Brooks, Donna, 262
Brown, Margaret Wise, 45, 55, 57, 99
Bruegel, Peter, the Elder, 171, *171*
Brushes, 194
Bumpō, Kawamuro, *138*, 139
Burns, M. J., 130, *130*
Burton, Marilee Robin, 41
Busch, Wilhelm, 36, *36–37*

CA Color Guide, 215–217
Caldecott, Randolph, 16, *17*, 49, 135, *135*
Cambiaso, Luca, 143, *143*
Camera-ready copy, 209
Carle, Eric, 41
Carroll, Lewis, 130, 149, 154, 181
Cause-and-effect logic, 43
Cel-Vinyl Cartoon Colors, 221
Change, 47–50
 consequences of, 49–50
 stages of, 50
Changes, Changes (Pat Hutchin), 53
Character, 164, 165
 body expression of, 130, 148, 149
 choice of, 53
 consistency of, 55
 see also Actor, Hero

Charley Sang a Song (H. R. Hays and Daniel Hays, illustrated by Uri Shulevitz), 74, *74*, *100*, 101, 127, *127*, 154, *155*
Children's Book Council, 258
Cinderella, 47, 48, 50
Code, visual, 23–24, 27–29, 84, 253
Coleridge, Samuel Taylor, 130
Color
 in *Dawn*, 88, 252–253
 process, 210, 215, 240
 technique, 187, 241; *see also* Color preseparation
Color charts, 215–217, 240, *240*
Color preseparation, 210, 214–241, 250–253
 acetate, 226–227
 Colotone, 224–225
 exercises, 223–239
 flat tint, 232–235
 materials for, 215–223
 multivalue flat, 228–231
 single-value flat, 223–227
 tonal, 236–239
Color study, 215, 228, 236, 240
Color swatch, 223
Colotone preseparation, 224–225
Communication Arts, 215
Composition, 76, 79, 105, 178–185
 dividing picture surface in, 178–179
 geometry in, 180–185
 style and, 200
 see also Design
Conclusion; *see* Ending
Conover, Chris, 112, *112*
Consistency, 22–24, 26, 43, 55, 88, 253
Content, 47–50, 58
 form and, 60, 129–135
 format and, 89–94
 style and, 198–206
Continuity, linear, 54
Continuous-tone copy, 209
Contrast, 121–125, 127, 173
Copy, 209
Copyright page, 116, 117
Costume, 130, 163
Crane, Walter, 93, *93*, 202, *202*
Crosshatching, 187, 189–191, 247
 reproduction of, 211
Cruikshank, George, 150, *150*
Cuteness, 148

Dandelion (Don Freeman), 48–50

Daumier, Honoré, 181, *181*, 196
Dawn (Uri Shulevitz), 48–50, 60, *60*, 62, 69, *69*, 84–87, *84–87*, 106, *107*, 206, 220, 252–253, *252–253*
Deadrick, Lee, 262
Decoration, 104, 120
Dedication page, 116, 117
Depth, 168–173
Design
 content and, 129–131
 jacket, 114
 page, 109–112
 picture, 69, 71
 structure and, 117–118
 see also Composition
Details, 26, 33, 36, 43, 44, 120, 164
 concreteness of, 43, 124–125
 consistency of, 26, 44
 decorative, 104, 120
 readability of, 122–123
 references for, 152–166
 superficial, 140
 whole and, 122–126
Dewey, Ariane, 101, *101*, 221
Diagonals, in composition, 179, 184
Diamond, Donna, 94, *94*
Dickens, Charles, 16, 129, 202
Diderot, Denis, 129, 133
Directness, 53
Doré, Gustave, 122, *122*, 128, *128*, 130, *131*, 133, *133*, 134, 135, 151, *151*, 205, *205*
Double spread, 68, 69, 71, 90, 96, 101, 116, 118, 253
 bleeds and, 102–103
 gutter and, 118
Drawing, 136–151
 animated objects, 150
 depth, 170–177
 with feeling, 151, 187
 figures, 136–149
 geometric form in, 140–144
 hand position for, 195
 objects, 150–151
 style, 198–205
 techniques, 186–197, 200, 246–251
Dummy, 67, 73–83, 260–261
 actual-size, 74–79, 244–245
 in story book, 80–83
 thumbnail, 73
Dürer, Albrecht, 143, *143*, 149, *149*
Dynamic elements; *see* Static vs. dynamic elements

Edges, 99, 101, 106–108
 bleeds and, 102–103

Editor, 67, 74, 259–261
preferences of, 262–263
Egielski, Richard, 92, *92*
Elijah the Slave (Isaac Bashevis Singer, illustrated by Antonio Frasconi), 90, *91*, 127, *127*
Encyclopedia (Denis Diderot), 129, *129*, 132, 133
End papers, 115, 117
Ending, 43–46, 55, 59
change and, 50
happy, 46
Enlargement, 212
Exaggeration, 147, 149, 201
Expression
body, 148, 149, 202–203
facial, 164–165, 202–203, 205
picture space and, 174–177
style and, 198–205

Fables (Arnold Lobel), 106, *106*
Familiar vs. unexpected, 28–29, 43, 44, 57, 58
Fantasy, 127, 128, 149, 154
Feder, Jane, 262
Federated Lithographers-Printers, 215, 217
Figure drawing, 137–149, 201
cuteness in, 148
exaggeration in, 147, 149, 201
expression in, 148
flat vs. round, 137–140
geometric form in, 140–143
movement in, 144–147
Figure-ground relationship, 172–173
Film, 16, 52, 53, 95
Five Chinese Brothers, The, 41
Flat drawing, 137–140
Flat space, 168–169
Flat tint, 209, 232–235
color preseparation exercise, 232–235
Flea, The (Wilhelm Busch), 36, *36–37*, 44
Fontane, Theodor, 94
Fool of the World and the Flying Ship, The (retold by Arthur Ransome, illustrated by Uri Shulevitz), 66, 95, *95*, *96*, *97*, *102*, *103*
Fools of Chelm, The (Isaac Bashevis Singer, illustrated by Uri Shulevitz), 164, *164*, *165*, *182*, *183*
Form
content and, 60, 129–135
of figures, 140–144
Four-color process, 210, 215, 248, 252–253

Frame, 104–106, 125
Francesca, Piero della, 172, *172*
Frasconi, Antonio, 90, *91*, 105, *105*, 127, *127*
Freeman, Don, 48
Frog He Would A-Wooing Go, A (Randolph Caldecott), 135, *135*
Front matter, 68, 116, 117

Geometric understructure
of composition, 180–185
of figures, 140–143
Geometry in Pictorial Composition (Brian Thomas), 181
Ginsburg, Mirra, 221
Girl Who Cried Flowers and Other Tales, The (Jane Yolen, illustrated by David Palladini), 104, *104*
Gnoli, Domenico, 96, *97*, 125, *125*, 168, *169*
Goffstein, M. B., 40, 57, 79, 93, *93*, 96, *96*, 99, *99*
Gold Label Artist Colors, 221
Golem, The (Isaac Bashevis Singer, illustrated by Uri Shulevitz), 151, *151*, 263
Goodnight Moon (Margaret Wise Brown), 45, 55, 57
Gordon, Liz, 262
Gordon, William J. J., 10n
Gorky Rises (William Steig), 95, *95*
Grandville, Sean, 149, *149*, 150, *150*, 154, *154*
Grant, Cary, 154
Grateful Sparrow and Other Tales, The (Angela Thirkell, illustrated by Ludwig Richter), 202, *203*
Gray scale, *216*, 217, 240
Grumbacher Gamma Retouch Grays, 221–222
Gulliver's Travels (Jonathan Swift, illustrated by Arthur Rackham), *204*, 205
Gutter, 116, 118

Half-title page, 116, 117
Halftone reproduction, 209, 211–212, 221, 248, 251
Hand lettering, 109–112
Hanukah Money (Sholem Aleichem, illustrated by Uri Shulevitz), 74, *75*, 76, *76–78*, 79, 92, *92*, 156, *156*, 183–184, *183–185*
Happy Day, The (Ruth Krauss, illustrated by Marc Simont), 54, 55, 57, 93, *93*
Hardcover, 113, 114
Hayes, Geoffrey, 99, *99*

Hays, Daniel, 101, 127, 154
Hays, H. R., 101, 127, 154
Hector Protector (Maurice Sendak), 57
Hero
change and, 48–50
choice of, 53
lively, 53
see also Actor, Character
Hey, Diddle, Diddle (Randolph Caldecott), 16, *17*, 51, 53, 58, 60
Hirschman, Susan, 9, 262
Hoban, Tana, 122, *123*
Hodges, Margaret, 112
Hogrogian, Nonny, 94, *94*
Hopkins, Peter, 122, 125, 170–171
Horn Book, 258
Hue, 241
Hutchin, Pat, 53

Illustration, 120–135
reproduction of, 210–213
techniques, 186–197, 242–254
types of, 130–135
see also Picture
Ink drawing tools, 194, 246
International Reading Association, 258
Invisible elements, 59

Jacket, 114, 117
Jichōsai, 139, *139*
Joan of Arc (Louis Maurice Boutet de Monvel), 126, *126*, *180*, 181
Juniper Tree and Other Tales from Grimm, The (illustrated by Maurice Sendak), *124*, 125
Juster, Norton, 96, 125, 168

Kafka, Franz, 43
Keats, Ezra Jack, 60–61, *61*
Kekulé, Friedrich August, 10
Kennedy, Richard, 154
Keyplate, 217, 222, 223, 251, 252
in color preseparation exercises, 224–241
Kleist, Heinrich von, 205
Kraus, Robert, 44, 101
Krauss, Ruth, 54, 55, 57, 110, 111
Krupat, Cynthia, 109, *109*

Land of the Taffeta Dawn, The (Natalia Belting, illustrated by Joseph Low), 202, *203*
Larson, Jean Russell, 128, 135
Laughing Latkes (M. B. Goffstein), 99, *99*

Leonardo da Vinci, 144, 154
Letterpress, 209
Lewis, C. S., 10
Library edition, 113–115, 118
Light box, 194, 195, 219, 246, 252
Line, 188–189, 248
handwriting of, 109, 133, 202, 205
reproducing, 209, 211, 251
style of, 201, 202, 205, 248, 251
Line copy, 209, 211
Lionni, Leo, 53
Little Humpbacked Horse, The (Margaret Hodges, illustrated by Chris Conover), 112, *112*
Littlest Rabbit, The (Robert Kraus), 44–45
Liveliness, 53, 144–148
Lobel, Arnold, 74, 79, 106, *106*
Loose threads, 55
Lost Kingdom of Karnica, The (Richard Kennedy, illustrated by Uri Shulevitz), 154, *155*, *256*, *257*
Louis Philippe and the Pear (Charles Philipon), 24, *24*
Loves of a Blond, 154
Low, Joseph, 202, *203*
"Lucy" enlarging machine, 79

MacDonald, John D., 33
Magic Trick, The (Uri Shulevitz), 38, *38–39*, 40, 41
Magician, The (Uri Shulevitz), 82–83, 106, *106*, 242–247, *243–247*
Manuscript submission, 259
Margolis, Matthew, 112
Markers, 220–221
Masayoshi, Kitao, *138*, 139
Masereel, Frans, 133, *133*
"Master Humphrey's Clock" (Charles Dickens), 16
Materials; *see* Tools and materials
Mazel and Shlimazel, or the Milk of a Lioness (Isaac Bashevis Singer, illustrated by Margot Zemach), 101, *101*
McElderry, Margaret, 262
Meal, The (Uri Shulevitz), 33, 42
Metamorphosis (Franz Kafka), 43
Michael Kohlhaas (Heinrich von Kleist, illustrated by Jacob Pins), 205, *205*
Miller, Randy, 99

Mine's the Best (Crosby Bonsall), 51, 56
Monet, Claude, 196
Month Brothers, The (Dorothy Nathan, illustrated by Uri Shulevitz), 154, *155*
Mood, 89, 94, 99, 126, 130
  picture space and, 174–177
  style and, 202–205
Moon in My Room, The (Uri Shulevitz), *8, 9, 10,* 108, *108,* 196, *197*
Movement, 144–148, 176, 177
  visual, 71, 72, 84
Muller-Lyer illusion, 92, *92*
Multicolor printing, 210; *see also* Color preseparation, Four-color process
Mushroom in the Rain (Mirra Ginsburg, illustrated by Jose Aruego and Ariane Dewey), 221
My Kind of Verse (compiled by John Smith, illustrated by Uri Shulevitz), 108, *108*
My Village Sturbridge (Gary Bowen, pictures engraved by Randy Miller), *98,* 99

Naftali the Storyteller (Isaac Bashevis Singer, illustrated by Margot Zemach), 121, *121*
Nathan, Dorothy, 154
New York Times Book Review, 258
Nicholas Nickleby (Charles Dickens, illustrated by Phiz) 129, *129,* 202, *203*
Noah's Ark A.B.C. (Walter Crane), *93,· 93*
Nobody Asked Me If I Wanted a Baby Sister (Martha Alexander), 221
Nutshell Library, The (Maurice Sendak), 90, *91*

Objective
  of actor, 44
  of story, 30, 31, 38, 44
Offset lithography, 209, 210
Oh What a Noise! (Uri Shulevitz), *64, 65,* 90, *91,* 156, *156*
One-color printing, 210
One Monday Morning (Uri Shulevitz), 16, *17,* 32, *32,* 41, 51, 53, 58, *70,* 71–74, *72–74,* 96, *96,* 117, *117, 162,* 163
Open House for Butterflies (Ruth Krauss, illustrated by Maurice Sendak), 110, *111*

Ortega y Gasset, José, 41
Outline, 137–140, 199
Overhead the Sun: Lines from Walt Whitman (Antonio Frasconi), 105, *105*
Overlays, 217–219, 222–223, 252–253
  in color preseparation exercises, 224–240

Pace, 24, 25, 55, 85
  in *Dawn,* 84–88
Page design, 89, 91–98, 244
  scale in, 92–94
  shape in, 89, 95–98
  size in, 89, 91
Pagination, 68, 116
Paint
  opaque, 221–222
  watercolor, 187, 220
Palladini, David, 104, *104*
Pantagruel (François Rabelais, illustrated by Gustave Doré), 128, *128*
Pantone Matching System, 215, 223
Paper
  "breathing" of, 108, 187
  coated vs. uncoated, 213
  for finished art, 194, 211, 253
  keyplate, 217
  overlays, 219–220
  sketching, 193–194
Passionate Journey (Frans Masereel), 133, *133*
Pauses, 55
Pencil, 191, 194, 200, 209, 220
Peretz, I. L., 243
Perspective, 171, 172
Philipon, Charles, 24, *24*
Philosophy, of story, 45, 59, 206
Phiz, 129, *129,* 202, *203*
Photographs, 122, *123*
  as references, 152–166
Picnic (Uri Shulevitz), 33, *34–35,* 44
Picture
  book shape and, 95–97
  book structure and, 117–118
  code, 23–24, 27–29, 84, 253
  design, 129–130, 178–185; in *Dawn,* 69, 84–88, 106
  detail in, 122, 124–126
  drawing behind, 136–151, 186–197
  edges, 99, 101–103, 106–108
  frame, 104–106, 125; depth and, 170–173
  portfolio, 259–262
  purpose of, 120–135

readability of, 21–22, 121–128, 139, 172–173
  references for, 152–166
  reproduction of, 210–213, 242–253
  scale, 92–94
  shape, 98–108; in *Dawn,* 69, 84–88, 106
  sketches for, 74–79, 183–185, 196–197, 244
  space; *see* Picture space
  storyboard and, 69–73
  style of, 198–206
  variety, 126–127, 130–133, 260
  words and, 10–11, 60–63, 73, 80–83, 120–121, 244
Picture book, 15–16, 18, 51–63
  action in, 30–46, 53, 54
  characteristics, 51–63
  concept, 15, 16, 60–61
  consistency of, 55
  dummy for, 73–74, 79, 80, 260–261
  length of, 116
  pace of, 54
  pauses in, 55
  philosophy of, 59
  rhyme in, 57–58
  rhythm in, 57, 72
  storyboard for, 67–73
  submission of, 260–261
  words in, 15, 51–54, 56–58, 60–63
Picture collection, 166
Picture sequence, 18–29
  actor-stage relationship in, 19–22, 24, 29
  consistency of, 22–24, 26, 29
  familiar vs. unexpected in, 28–29
  pace of, 24–25
  picture code in, 23–24, 27–29
  progression in, 26–27
  readability of, 21–22
  story vs., 30, 31, 33
Picture space, 125, 127, 128, 167–177
  depth of, 168–172
  expression and, 174–177
  figure-ground relationship and, 172–173
  flat vs. deep, 168–169
  style and, 199, 202
Pinnochio (Carlo Collodi), 149, *149*
Pins, Jacob, 205, *205*
Poetry, 126
Poor Cecco (Margery William Bianco, illustrated by Arthur Rackham), 150, *150*

Portfolio, 259–261
Potter, Beatrix, 16, *16,* 44, 48, 93, *93,* 101, *101,* 104, *105*
Press sheet, 213
Printing, 208–213
  terminology, 209–210
  see also Reproduction
Process colors, 210, 215, 240
Production for the Graphic Designer (James Craig), 209
Production manager, 117, 208, 212, 220, 223
Progression, 26–27, 29, 30, 73; *see also* Unfolding of story
Proofs, 212–213; *see also* Testproofs
Publisher, search for, 258–261
Publisher's Weekly, 258
Push-Pull, Empty-Full, (Tana Hoban), 122, *123*
Puss in Boots, 25, *25*
Pyle, Howard, 204, *205*

Rabelais, François, 128, 133
Rackham, Arthur, 150, *150, 204, 205*
Rain Rain Rivers (Uri Shulevitz), *14,* 56, *56, 102, 103,* 157, *157,* 160, *160, 250, 251, 251*
Readability, 121–128, 139, 187
  design and, 109–112
  details and, 122–126
  figure-ground relationship and, 172–173
  of picture sequence, 21–22
  style and, 198, 206
  varieties of, 126–128
Reader involvement, 41–45, 53, 54, 62
Reduction, 212
Reference material, 152–166
  adapting, 158–165
  collecting, 166
  need for, 152–154
  types of, 156–158
Register marks, 218, 222–223
Registration, 213, 253
Rembrandt van Ryn, 196
Repetition, 51, 53, 57, 72
Reproduction, 208–253
  art for, 210–213
  color preseparation and, 210, 214–241
  printer's role in, 212–213
  quality of, 210–213
  techniques for, 242–253
  terminology for, 209–211
  types of, 209–210
Resoluteness, in technique, 187
Rhyme, 57, 58
Rhythm, 52, 57, 69, 72

Ribtickle Town (Alan Benjamin, illustrated by Ann Schweninger), 221
Richter, Ludwig, 202, *203*
Rime of the Ancient Mariner, The (Samuel Taylor Coleridge, illustrated by Gustave Doré), 130, *131*, 151
Rosetti, Christina, 103
Round drawing, 137–143
Rubens, Peter Paul, 196
Ruby of Kishmoor, The (Howard Pyle), 204, 205
Runaway Jonah and Other Tales (Jan Wahl, illustrated by Uri Shulevitz), 96, *97*, 110, *110*, 119

Saddle stitching, 115
Sample pictures, 261–262
School Library Journal, 258
Schweninger, Ann, 221
Sendak, Maurice, 16, *17*, 49, 51, *52*, 57, 110, *111*, 112, *112*, 124, 125, 168, *169*
Sengai, 56
Sensitivity, in technique, 187
Shape
  book, 89, 95–97
  picture, 98–108; in *Dawn*, 69, 84–88, 106
Sid and Sol (Arthur Yorinks, illustrated by Richard Egielski), 92, *92*
Side stitching, 115, 118
Signatures, 115, 118
Silkspinners, The (Jean Russell Larson, illustrated by Uri Shulevitz), 128, *128*, 135, *135*
Similes, 53
Simont, Marc, 93, *93*
Singer, Isaac Bashevis, 90, 101, 121, 127, 151, 164, 183
Single-value flat color preseparation, 223–227
Sir Ribbeck of Ribbeck of Haveland (Theodor Fontane, illustrated by Nonny Hogrogian), 94, *94*
Size, 89–91
Sketches, 74–79, 144, 183–185, 196–197, 244
  paper for, 193–194
Smith, John, 108
Smyth sewing, 115
Soken, Yamaguchi, 205, *205*
Soldier and Tsar in the Forest (Uri Shulevitz), 58, 153, *153*, 207, 248, *248–249*
Some Swell Pup (Maurice Sendak and Matthew Margolis, illustrated by Maurice Sendak), 112, *112*

Sophie's Picnic (M. B. Goffstein), 40, 41, 43
Sounds, 57, 58
Space; *see* Picture space
Spine, 114
St. Nicholas magazine, 130, *130*
Static vs. dynamic elements, 84–85, 88, 121, 124–125
  in composition, 178–179, 184–185, 200
Steig, William, 95, *95*, 100, 101, 105, *105*
Stevenson, Robert Louis, 44, 154, 164
Story, 30–46
  action and, 30–46
  change and, 47–50
  code of, 55
  details in, 33, 43
  ending of, 43–46, 50, 55, 59
  objective in, 30–32, 36, 38, 44
  philosophy of, 44–46, 59
  specificity of, 33
  unfolding of, 38–43
  unifying link in, 41, 46
Story book, 15, 16, 58, 60–61
  concept, 16, 60–61
  dummy for, 80–83
  length of, 116
Story of a Fierce Bad Rabbit, The (Beatrix Potter), 93, *93*
Storyboard, 67–73, 79, 244
  bird's eye view of, 69–71
  rhythm in, 72
  visual movement in, 71
Studio arrangement, 195
Style, 198–206
  elements of, 199–201
  varieties of, 202–205
Submissions, 259
Suspense, 42
Swift, Jonathan, 205
Swimmy (Leo Lionni), 53
Symmetry vs. asymmetry, 99, 106, 145, 178–179, 200

Tale of Peter Rabbitt, The (Beatrix Potter), 16, *16*, 44, 48, 50, 101, *101*, 105
Technique, 186–197, 242–254
  color, 187, 241; *see also* Color preseparation
  crosshatching, 189–191, 247
  hand position for, 195
  line, 188–189
  pencil, 191, 200
  reproduction and, 242, 246–254
  spontaneity and, 196–197
  wash, 192–193, 200
Tenniel, Sir John, 130, *130*, 149, *149*, 154, *155*, *180*, 181

Test-proofs, 212, 217, 240–241
Text, 116, 117
  dividing, for story book, 80–83
Texture, 97, 105
Theater, 16, 53, 95
Thirkell, Angela, 202
Thomas, Brian, 181
Three-dimensionality, 125, 137, 170–173; *see also* Round drawing
Through the Looking Glass (Lewis Carroll, illustrated by Sir John Tenniel), 130, *130*
Thumbnail dummy, 73, 74
Time, 38, 40, 42, 43, 54
Title page, 116, 117
  examples of, 109, 110, 117
Toby Lived Here (Hilma Wolitzer), 109, *109*
Tom Thumb (illustrated by Gustave Doré), 205, *205*
Tonal color preseparation, 223, 236–239
Tone, 241; *see also* Flat tint, Tonal color preseparation
Tools and materials, 193–195
  brushes, 194
  color preseparation, 215–223
  ink drawing, 194, 247
  paper, 193–194, 211, 217, 219–220
  pencil drawing, 194, 220
Touchstone, The (Robert Louis Stevenson, illustrated by Uri Shulevitz), 44, 45, 154, *154*, 160, *161*, 163, *163*, 164, *164*
Tragical Death of an Apple Pie, The, 41, *41*
Transfigured Hart, The (Jane Yolen, illustrated by Donna Diamond), 94, *94*
Treasure, The (Uri Shulevitz), 62, *62*, 63, *63*, 80–81, 110, *110*, 254
Trim size, 90–94, 104
Trip, The (Ezra Jack Keats), 60–61, *61*
Twelve Dancing Princesses, The (illustrated by Uri Shulevitz), 71, *71*
Two-dimensionality, 168–173; *see also* Flat drawing
Two Piano Tuners (M. B. Goffstein), 93, *93*
Typography, 109–112, 199

Unexpected; *see* Familiar vs. unexpected
Unfolding of story, 38–43, 46, 50

Unifying link, 41, 46

Valéry, Paul, 137
Vellum, 219
Very Hungry Caterpillar, The (Eric Carle), 41, 49
Vicious Cycle, The (Bonnie Bishop), 32, *32–33*
Visible action, 53, 84
Visual code; *see* Code, visual
Visual movement, 71, 72, 84
Visual references, 152–166
Volume, 137–144

Wahl, Jan, 96, 121, 153
Wash technique, 192–193, 200
Watercolor, 187, 220, 251–253
We Never Get to Do Anything (Martha Alexander), 51
Weiss, Ava, 110
What Is Pink? (Christina Rosetti, illustrated by Jose Aruego), 103, *103*
When the Wind Blew (Margaret Wise Brown, illustrated by Geoffrey Hayes), 99, *99*
Where the Wild Things Are (Maurice Sendak), 16, *17*, 48–51, *52*, 53, 56–59, 168, *169*
Wolitzer, Hilma, 109
Wonderful Kite, The (Jan Wahl, illustrated by Uri Shulevitz), *12*, *13*, 121, *121*, 153, *153*
Wong, Jeanyee, 112
Words, 52, 54–58
  images through, 56
  pictures and, 10–11, 60–63, 73, 80–83, 120–121, 244
  repetition of, 57
  simplicity of, 56
  sound of, 57–58

Yolen, Jane, 58, 94, 104
Yorinks, Arthur, 92

Zemach, Margot, 101, *101*, 120, *121*

Edited by Sue Heinemann
Designed by James Craig
Graphic production by Ellen Greene
Text set in 10-point Palatino